ISBN 978-0-282-68380-1
PIBN 10861356

1 MONTH OF
FREE
READING

at
www.ForgottenBooks.com

By purchasing this book you are eligible for one month membership to ForgottenBooks.com, giving you unlimited access to our entire collection of over 1,000,000 titles via our web site and mobile apps.

To claim your free month visit:
www.forgottenbooks.com/free861356

TWENTY-FIVE YEARS' SOLDIERING
IN SOUTH AFRICA

Yours Sincerely
A Colonial Officer

24335

TWENTY-FIVE YEARS'
SOLDIERING
IN SOUTH AFRICA

A Personal Narrative

BY

A COLONIAL OFFICER

LONDON: ANDREW MELROSE
3 YORK STREET, COVENT GARDEN
1909

DT
769
C65

INTRODUCTION

IN putting before my fellow-countrymen a Book on South Africa, I am conscious that some explanation is needed, and something of an apology. I have no great acquaintance with literature, but I know that scores of books have been written about South Africa during the last few years, until I am told the public are pretty nearly sick of the subject. My explanation is, that this book is not about the Boer War, although it is dealt with in one or two chapters in which I relate my experiences as a Captain in Mounted Regiments of Irregulars.

My book is mainly the narrative of twenty-five years of a life crowded with incident, stretching over a period which has seen some of the most momentous happenings in South Africa. I have been more concerned in showing the evolution of a somewhat rough-and-ready corps of Mounted Police into one of the, to my mind, smartest and most efficient regiments in the British Empire. Thus the reader will find that quite half of the book is taken up with my experiences as a young soldier, and the work of the Cape Mounted Riflemen in the various engagements from the date of my joining to the end of the Langberg Campaign.

The experiences of a recruit at the present time are no doubt interesting enough, and the life is still full of adventure —so dear to young men; but the old life of the corps in the days when I joined it has gone for ever, and I am not without hopes that the plain record of that time which I have here set down may have some interest for young fellows, as I am confident it will have for many of my old comrades who shared the experiences with me.

My apology is for the literary form of the book. I have been in many queer positions, and have been prepared for all sorts of things, but in my wildest dreams I never imagined myself an author. I have had no experience in writing anything but regimental orders, and am sorry to say that, even in regard to letter-writing to my friends, I have not exhausted myself with the use of the pen. The following pages have therefore no pretension to literary form. When the book was first suggested to me, during a holiday in England, I thought of nothing more ambitious than to put my crude notes into the hands of a practised writer for the purpose of getting a book made.

When my story was finished, however, I was advised by a literary friend to let it go without getting it rewritten by a literary man. So with all its faults and crudities, the book as it stands is my own. I must add, however, that I owe gratitude to the same literary friend for his careful revision of the proofs.

It only remains for me to add that I hope none of the men,

many of them life-long friends, who find their names mentioned here, will discover any reason for resenting the liberty
I have taken with their personalities. The chief asset which
I have retained from my life in South Africa is the friendship
of some of the most loyal comrades that ever a man was
blessed with.

And now, having made my explanation and apology, I
send my book forth with a little hope, and much fear and
trembling.

A COLONIAL OFFICER.

MANY of the Drawings in this volume are based upon sketches which appeared in *The Graphic* and *Illustrated London News* of the period, and the publisher hereby expresses his sense of the courtesy of the editors of these papers in readily allowing his artist to make use of them.

TABLE OF CONTENTS

——◆——

CHAPTER I.

1879.

CHAPTER II.

CHAPTER III.

CHAPTER IV.

CHAPTER V.

CONTENTS

LIST OF ILLUSTRATIONS

TWENTY-FIVE YEARS' SOLDIERING
IN SOUTH AFRICA

———◆———

CHAPTER I.

I WAS, as it may be expressed, born to the Service. My father was a British officer, my eldest brother had in due course got his commission in the Imperial Army, and I looked forward to following in their footsteps. But my father's death when I had just finished my education at one of our well-known public schools, and domestic circumstances, made my long-cherished idea impossible, and as I had no thoughts that were not connected with soldiering, I turned to the military forces of the Colonies.

All England was then ringing with the news of the Zulu War and the massacre of the 24th Regiment at Isandlwana. Among the fallen officers were two old school-chums of my own, and a great desire to go to Zululand took hold of me. My people, seeing that I was determined to become a soldier somehow, placed no obstacles in my way, and I duly sailed for the Cape.

When I left England, Sir Garnet—now Lord—Wolseley had taken command of the army in Africa, and everybody was expecting great results; but at that time there was no cable to South Africa, and the news of his progress came very slowly.

On my arrival at Durban, Natal, the first news that greeted me was that the Prince Imperial had been killed whilst reconnoitring, and that the battle of Ulundi had been fought, that Cetewayo was captured and the war practically over. This was a great damper on my youthful ardour, but learning that the Cape Colonial forces were engaged somewhere in the Cape Colony, I decided to go to that Colony and see what chance I had of being sent to the front.

I did not waste much time, but went by a coasting steamer to East London, at that period a very primitive port, called Panmure. All the buildings, with the exception of a very few, were built on the west side of the river. It was a great contrast to the same city at the present day, with its splendid breakwater and wharves on the river, with its very fine public buildings and houses. East London is to-day one of the most flourishing towns and ports in South Africa, and the inhabitants of East London and district are the most go-ahead and most manly of our Colonials, as the records of their volunteer regiments will show in every campaign since the Galeka War of '77. As I have soldiered with them in four of my five campaigns, I think I am a fair judge, and I never wish for better comrades in the field, or friends out of it.

After being slung over the side of the ship in a huge basket, and deposited in the hold of an evil-smelling lighter, we were duly towed into the river, and directed to the hotel at

Panmure, where during the evening I was enlightened as to where the war in the Colony was. It was explained to me that an old Basuto chief had shut himself up on a mountain and had defied the Colonial forces for about seven months, that there had been two unsuccessful attacks on the mountain resulting in a fair amount of casualties on the Colonial side, that a new colonel was on his way up to command the Cape Mounted Riflemen, and that all the regiment had been ordered to the front and that it would not be long before it was captured, now that the C.M.R. were going. This news, together with the implicit faith in the C.M.R. evinced by the two fair young ladies of the hotel, who apparently knew every man in the regiment and were most enthusiastic about them, settled me. I determined, if possible, to become a Cape Mounted Rifleman.

The next day saw me in the train, *en route* for King William's Town. This place is situated in a slight hollow, surrounded by blue mountains and the Perie Bush; the Buffalo River running through the town and the white-washed houses and gardens made an effect of beauty that appealed very much to my youthful mind. King William's Town—known to all South Africans as " King "—was at that time the leading town of the Cape Colony; nearly all the principal merchants lived there, and it was the dépôt for all the trading stations in the Native districts surrounding it and the Transkei. Prior to the Galeka and Gaika War of 1877 and 1878 it had also been a garrison town, with one or more Imperial regiments constantly stationed there. On my arrival, I found that the headquarters of the C.M.R. had been re-moved to Butterworth — a place situated about 84 miles distant, in the Transkei—and that there was only a small detachment of the regiment stationed at what was then called the old Police Barracks, about a mile from town, in the direction of Fort Murray. I put up at a boarding-house not far from the station, where I was very much impressed by the kindness and courtesy shown by every one to the stranger. Several people tried to dissuade me from joining the Police, as they called the regiment of Cape Mounted Riflemen. The regiment had been changed in name from the "Frontier Armed and Mounted Police"—abbreviated to F.A.M.P.—to "Cape Mounted Riflemen," by Act of Parliament, Act 9 of 1878. Several members of the force objected to the change, and were tried and imprisoned for mutiny; but up to September '79 there had been no alteration in the condition of the force, and the civilians spoke of them as the Police. The only reasons that my new acquaintance adduced in order to dissuade me from joining, were that it was a very rough life, that the men had to sleep in the veldt, and that they were all harum-scarum young fellows, and they were hardly sufficient to deter any adventurous young fellow from joining. In my case, my mind had been made up at East London by a different version given me by the afore-mentioned young ladies, the scale to my mind being considerably in favour of the harum-scarum young fellows, and not of the sedate youths in an office.

I went the next morning to the Police Barracks, where I met the corporal in charge, who asked me in, and introduced me to a roomful of men, with whom I was immediately at home. These men—about twenty in all—were all time-expired men or men invalided from the front, and waiting the end of the campaign before getting their discharge. They were a mixed lot and, as I subsequently found out, typical of the regiment.

There were a couple of Merchant Service men, one ex-soldier, two or three medical students, and an ex-naval officer, and, with the exception of about four of them, all were public-school men and a good sporting lot. The corporal told me he had no orders about recruiting, and as far as he knew there had been no recruiting under the new Act, but he promised to wire to Butterworth for instructions. In the meantime I was invited to take up my abode with them, and the open-hearted, free manner in which I was treated by them all made me very anxious to become one of them. In due course an official letter arrived to the corporal in charge, giving him authority to "take me on,"—*i.e.*, enlist me,—and I was taken by him up to the Resident Magistrate, Mr. Rose Innes, and there and then I swore to serve Her Majesty, heirs and successors, etc., for the period of five years dating from 14th September 1879. Mine was the first enlistment under the new Act, and I therefore became the first C.M.R. recruit, all the others having joined the F.A.M.P. for three years. However, the extra two years did not seem any obstacle to me, neither did it turn out to be, as I was fortunate enough to obtain my commission in eighteen months, which cancelled my enrolment papers.

Immediately on leaving the Court House I was taken to the C.M.R. contractor, Mr. Ben Ryan, the friend and benefactor of a great many in the regiment, where I duly had my kit handed to me. The uniform was not quite my idea of what a young soldier should have. It consisted of a black corduroy jacket and riding-breeches, ammunition boots and leggings, a peaked cap like a railway porter's, the necessary underclothing, blankets, and so forth. With these, I was a fully equipped Cape Mounted Rifleman as regards uniform.

I remained in King William's Town about a week, when

orders came from headquarters that I was to proceed there in company with two other men as escort and two wagons taking stores. We started the following day at daylight, and the old hands all turned out to see us off with a good hand-shake and a " Good luck, my boy!"—the corporal riding out with us to the first outspan, and giving me useful tips for the road.

He left the regiment soon afterwards, and is now a flourish-ing postmaster in a well-known town in the Transkei. Long may he live and prosper!

CHAPTER II.

FIRST OUTSPAN—WAGON TREKKING—MEET COLONEL BAYLY *EN ROUTE* TO HEADQUARTERS—ARRIVAL AT BUTTERWORTH—INITIATED INTO STABLE AND FATIGUE DUTIES—MOUNTED AND EQUIPPED.

OUR first outspan was on the bank of a small stream. An old-fashioned-looking house stood about 200 yards from us, called "Yellow Woods." It is still in existence, though very much improved. It was here that I learnt my first lesson in veldt life.

The first thing to be done was to get a fire. I was sent off by the senior man to collect dry cow-dung for fuel. As it was a regular outspan site, there was no difficulty in collecting as much as we wanted, and under the able management of the two old hands we soon had a blazing fire. Dried cow-dung makes the very best fuel any one can wish for in the veldt, and throws out a great heat. I then watched the operation of making dry cookies—a simple process when you know how to do it. Mix dough,—the old soldier always carries baking-powder in his kit when trekking with wagons,—tear the dough up into lumps the size of a bun and put them in the ashes scraped to the side of the fire, so that they can be replenished—and there you are ! In a few minutes your patrol-tin filled with water is boiling, and tea or coffee made. The meat is cut into strips or small chunks, and cooked in the same way as the dough, except that you don't put ashes on the top of it, but directly it is set at the bottom, turn it over, and continue the motion till you imagine it is cooked sufficiently, which all depends on the degree of hunger you feel. Your store-box—an old whisky-case—produces plates, knives and forks, as well as a mixture of sardines, jam, cheese, butter, pickles, and tinned beef, commonly known as " Harriet Lane,"— a perpetual reminder of the famous Wainwright murder. The contents of the store-box depend very much on the amount of credit you were entitled to before you went on trek,—the recruits revelling in jam, milk, and sardines; the old stagers in a couple of bottles of Dop,— i.e., Colonial brandy,—plug tobacco, matches, candles, etc. The latter articles a recruit ignores as a rule, till he is taught the full value of a box of matches by getting stranded in the veldt on a wet night without any, when he begins to think soldiering a rotten game.

Breakfast over, I, being the "Rookie," as recruits are called, had the honour of washing up, filling the patrol- tins, and collecting more fuel; whilst the other two sat under the wagon and played a game of twenty-fives—then a very popular game of cards in the regiment, but now almost obsolete. About 4 p.m. the drivers got the oxen in and inspanned—an operation I watched with the liveliest interest. The two spans of bullocks are driven in by the voor-loopers, who are generally small Kaffir boys with very dilapidated shirts as their sole wardrobe, and whose duties are to lead the leading oxen through drifts, or when passing through villages, or meeting other wagons, light the fires for the drivers when outspanned, and then go into the veldt and stay with the oxen whilst they are grazing, till it is time to trek again. The oxen are then brought up to the wagons en masse, with cries of " A now!" the vernacular for "Whoa!"; the drivers then get amongst them with reims and single out the different oxen, throwing the loop of the reim over their horns and calling them by their names. The animal called instantly sticks his head down, comes out of the mob, and falls into line opposite his yoke. The process of inspanning is soon performed. The yoke is placed on the neck of the oxen, and kept there by two wooden pins like tent pegs, only longer, and called "yoke skuys"; they are fastened underneath by a strap made of twisted hide; the oxen move into their places, the long chain is pulled taut, the driver loosens his whip, and they are ready to trek. The whip is a most effective weapon in the hands of an expert, and without it the most experienced driver is helpless. It is a ten-foot bamboo, with a long lash which reaches half-way up the span of bullocks, and is used not only to punish refractory oxen but to direct the team by light flicks if they should happen to get out of the track in any way.

Seating ourselves on the top of the wagon and selecting comfortable spots upon the packages and cases, we are ready. A loud crack of the whip, a yell of "Yaak!" and the whole team of eighteen oxen pull out like one man, and we are off. The driver lets off a few cracks, and brings the lash down heavily on some wretched animal by way of encouragement; the whole team gradually settle down; the little voor-looper throws the loop of the reim with which he has been leading the front oxen over their horns, and steps aside and lets them go on on their own; the driver coils his whip round the stick, and gets up in front of the wagon, and proceeds to utter weird noises only understood by the oxen; and after calling them individually by their names, with queer epithets, he lights his pipe and takes things easy, till, catching sight of a solitary bullock not pulling his fair share, he jumps off the wagon, dragging his whip after him, and immediately the whole span break into a jog-trot.   After administering a half-dozen well directed cuts to the shirker, he climbs on the wagon again, lays his whip down, and the team return to their ordinary breakneck pace of two miles per hour.

It is a marvellous sight to see a well-trained team of oxen with a good driver negotiate an ugly drift, or go down the side of a steep hill, half washed away by the rain, where a man would think twice of going with a buggy and pair of horses. In fact, nothing seems to stop a well-trained team.   Many things have changed in South Africa since those early times, but transport riding—as wagon-travelling is called—is the same to-day as it was then.   The advent of the train has taken a great deal of business from them, and wagons are not nearly as numerous as they were, but there is still a very large percentage of merchants—Kaffir traders—who prefer getting their goods from the port by wagon instead of paying the ruinous rates charged by the railways.   As time is not much object to these traders, the extra time taken by the wagon makes no material difference, and the cost is an important item.

After trekking about four hours, during which time we dozed on the wagon or walked behind it, we arrived at Kei Road, a small wayside hotel, two or three small houses and two shops, and outspanned for the night opposite the railway station.   The oxen are tied up—that is, instead of being let loose to feed, they are simply unyoked and the end of the reim tied on to the trek chain ; they then stand quietly in their places till one by one they drop down, and apparently start thinking deeply of their troubles, only their jaws moving as they chew the cud, coughing and making various other noises all night, not conducive to sleep to the novice lying under the wagon wrapped up in his blankets and trying to emulate the old hands, who are fast asleep.

Before settling down for the night, the tarpaulin or wagon sail is spread over the whole of the wagon and pulled down to the ground on the weather side, a fire lighted on the other side of the wagon, and coffee handed round. The fire is kept alight the whole night by the little voor-looper, who seems automatically to get up from his sleep, put on fresh fuel, and turn in again at regular intervals.

Just as I was getting accustomed to my novel surroundings and dropping off to sleep, I was aroused by footsteps approaching the wagon. A figure appeared by the fire and shouted out, "Who is in charge of these wagons?" In a second the two men, who had been lying like logs, turned over, and one of them answered, "*I* am"; and then, recognising the newcomer, said, "Hullo, sergeant! When did you come down?"

Sergeant Morris, the stranger, stooped down under the wagon, and sat on my blanket and gave us some interesting news. He had just ridden down from Butterworth, and had arrived at the hotel opposite about two hours before. Colonel Bayly was expected by the next morning train from King, with most of his staff, on his way to Butterworth, *en route* for Moirosi Mountain, and we were to await his arrival and take on whatever baggage they had with them on our wagons. The sergeant then told us that he had come down from the front about a fortnight before, that a batch of men were being hurriedly got ready to accompany Colonel Bayly from Butterworth, and that all the other troops were on the march from their various stations to the mountain. He had been present at the second attack on the mountain, which had failed.

The sergeant asked me when I joined, what school I was at, and where I came from. He told me he was a Marlborough boy, asked if I was a cricketer, and appeared very pleased when he heard that I had both my school-caps, cricket and football. When he found out that I had been drilled and could ride, he said he thought there would be no difficulty in the way of my being sent up with the detachment which was being prepared, as he was one of the sergeants returning with them, and he would do what he could for me. After advising us to clean up, and be ready to start by ten o'clock the next morning, in case the colonel wished to see us, he went off to the hotel. My two comrades were soon asleep, but all desire to follow their example was completely banished from my mind. I lay awake the whole night, picturing to myself the stirring deeds I had heard the sergeant calmly relate as if they were an everyday occurrence, till at last daylight came, and the oxen were let loose to graze about at their sweet will.

After morning coffee we went down to the river for a bathe, when I found, to my intense disgust, that my legs were the colour of a nigger's. The others laughed at me, and said it was what I had to expect till my uniform breeches had been thoroughly wet through and dried. The dye had all come out, and my shirt and my lower extremities were as black as the ace of spades. It took me about half an hour's hard work, scrubbing myself with mud and soap, before my skin was restored to its natural colour.

On returning to the wagons, we found Sergeant Morris there, looking very smart and soldierly in a blue cloth uniform jacket and black Bedford-cord breeches, which made me feel more disgusted than ever with the black corduroy uniform I was wearing. To my joy, he told us that the uniform was going to be altered after the campaign was finished, and that meantime we could get decent riding-breeches at headquarters when we arrived.

Shortly after ten o'clock the train steamed into the station, and Colonel Bayly, with two staff officers and about ten non-commissioned officers and some orderlies, got out and walked across to the hotel. As they passed the wagon the colonel stopped and spoke to us. He inquired how long I had been in the regiment, and seemed quite surprised when I told him only ten days. He asked if I could ride and if I knew my drill. I could only say that I thought I did; and he then turned to Mason, the man in charge of the wagon, and gave him instructions about his baggage, and told him to push on to Butterworth.

Colonel Bayly was then a man of about forty years of age, medium height, with fair hair and moustache, rather inclined to stoutness; but a thorough-looking soldier all through. He had been Adjutant of the 9th Regiment, and afterwards commanded the Duke of Edinburgh's Own Volunteer Rifles at Cape Town. He made his name at the battle of Umzinzani, in Galekaland, in the '77 and '78 campaign, when he commanded the column. He had recently been appointed to the command of the Cape Mounted Riflemen, and was then on his way to take over the regiment and to conduct the operations before Moirosi Mountain.

This was my first sight of Colonel Bayly, and the strong impression he made on me then has never been effaced. Unfortunately, ill-health caused his retirement from active service and the regiment at a comparatively early age; but he has never ceased to take the liveliest interest in all things concerning the regiment and the Colonial forces in general. A more popular commanding officer I cannot conceive, and his capacity as a soldier is evident from the fact that he took over the regiment in its transition stage from a Police force, and made it one of the smartest regiments in the field, and out of it, in the British Empire.

Shortly after Colonel Bayly's departure we inspanned and trekked. As the bullocks were in good condition and the roads dry, we got over the ground fairly well; but a good stock of patience is needed when travelling by wagon. Two miles an hour is the average pace, and eighteen to twenty miles a day is counted good going. At that time there were no properly made roads as at present, and this pace was really very good.

We passed through Draaibosch, the scene of the fight between the Gaikas and the 88th Regiment, under Colonel Moore, who gained the Victoria Cross during the engagement. A troop of C.M.R. had been engaged in the same action, and my comrades assured me it was not a very glorious victory for Colonel Moore; for it was touch-and-go with the gallant Connaught Rangers, who were nearly cut off and overwhelmed.

About eight miles from Draaibosch we came to Komgha, then a small frontier village, with very few inhabitants, but now a decent-sized town, with a railway running through it, and the centre of a large and influential farming community. From there we went through the Kei Hills, a very picturesque part of Cape Colony, the road winding in and out of high hills till it reaches the Kei River. At that time there was only a wooden bridge across the river, and the roads were almost impassable; now the railway runs through magnificent cuttings, a perfect triumph of engineering art. The main roads and splendid bridge over the river are kept in perfect order, and trekking by road is vastly different from the time of which I am writing.

After crossing the river we were in the Transkei, the scene of the fighting in '77, and after a long climb we reached Toleni, a small hotel on the top of the hills. From there we trekked over comparatively flat country till we reached Butterworth, which consisted of a post office, Hedding's Store, and two or three small houses. On crossing the river we came to the camp, comprising a few huts and tents, where we found the headquarters of the C.M.R. temporarily established. I was told off to a hut where four other men lived, and my first trek in South Africa was ended, and I was about to learn my first lesson as a rifleman.

I found that my room-mates were clerks in the different offices, two of them being in the Quartermaster's Department, one in the Paymaster's, and the other in the Regimental Orderly Room. Two of them subsequently received commissions in the Cape Infantry Regiment when it was formed in 1882. One of them was killed at Elandslaagte, in Natal, in the Boer War, where he was serving as a captain in the Imperial Light Horse. They all made me very welcome, and I spent my first evening listening to the latest news from the front, and to stories of life in the regiment, and of South Africa as far as they had experienced it. They had then served about three years, and had spent most of that period in the Transkei; they had gone through the Gaika and Galeka campaign, and their accounts of the various engagements and risky patrols which the Police had gone through were exciting to listen to, and made my nerves tingle to share similar experiences; I was quite disappointed when "Lights out" sounded, and we had to turn in.

Before sunrise next morning "Réveillé" sounded, and I was brought back from my dreams to face life in earnest. Up to this time I had been practically under no control since joining, being under a lenient corporal in King, and a private of two years' service in my trek up; now I found what it was to be at headquarters. The "Dress" next sounded. The remainder of my hut companions being on the staff and dismounted, did not budge, but one of them kindly suggested I should turn out, as the "Fall in" would go shortly, and it would not be for the benefit of my health to be late. I accordingly turned out to where there was a scuffled square—i.e., the grass all scraped off for the purposes of parade and drill grounds. The "Fall in," which went shortly after, sounded as only "Jammer" could sound, and I fell in with the rest—some thirty men, most of whom had been left in charge of small out-stations when their troops left for the front, and had now been brought into headquarters to prepare for the front. The roll was called, and my name came at the end of the list. The word was then given by the sergeant, "Break and fall in at stables." I went with the others, and found that the "stables" consisted of two long lines of rope, called picquet ropes, to which were attached some forty horses by the reims of their headstalls.

The picquet ropes were placed about fifty yards at the back of the camp, in the open veldt. The owners of the horses untied them, and fell in line about twenty yards from the ropes, facing the rear of the camp, and, putting the nose-bags containing mealies, which is more or less the standing feed for C.M.R.

horses, on the ground in front of their animals, commenced grooming them.

I stood looking on while the sergeant again called the roll, and the men answered for their horses. They were then told to go on grooming, and the scene became a lively one; some of the horses playfully biting at the men, and others kicking directly they were touched. I was not allowed to take the part of a spectator long. A smart-looking sergeant who was the senior in charge at the station called me, and told me to go to a certain hut and fetch a horse's feed and a curry-comb and brush, and bring a horse which was standing unattended on the picquet line to the ground where the men were, and groom it.

I did so, watching the other men to see how they did it. I slipped the curry-comb on my left hand and began grooming with my right as hard as I could, which drew comments from several old hands who did not believe in unnecessary energy excepting when the N.C.O.'s were passing by. Three sergeants were walking up and down in front of the horses, keeping their eyes on horses and men as they passed, bestowing remarks on any man who in their opinion was not doing justice to his horse :—" What are you flat-ironing about ? " " Put some elbow-grease into it "; " It isn't a wild animal you have got hold of,"—or if the horse showed signs of using his heels, " Get close to it, then it can't kick you." Remarks of this kind were flung about, and, afraid of any of them being directed to me, I groomed away for all I was worth. Fortunately, the horse I was grooming was an old stager who had been in the regiment some time. His owner was on the sick list, and this accounted for him being placed temporarily under my charge. All he seemed to care about was to empty the nose-bag of

mealies before the knock-off time came, and he took not the
slightest notice of my brushing and scraping.   Some mud not
coming off his legs to my satisfaction, I began to scrape it with
the curry-comb, and earned a sharp reproof from one of the
N.C.O.'s, " Now then, youngster, not so much of the comb and
a little more of the brush.   The comb is only used to clean the
brush, and don't forget it."   I didn't.

After the horses had been groomed to the satisfaction of
the senior N.C.O., the feed having been finished some time, the
order was given: "Headstalls off—Let go—Fall in, the horse
guard."   Seeing the man on my right undo his horse's throat-
lash and take the headstall off, I did the same, and the horse
immediately shook his head, twisted round, and went galloping as hard as he could with the majority of them, towards the
place where they were accustomed to graze.

I then saw three men in shirt sleeves and smasher hats,
with greatcoats hanging on their arms, saunter after them,
driving the laggards on as they went, making them go at a
gallop after the others who had reached the feeding-ground.
These, I was told, were the horse guards, whose duty it was
to go out into the veldt with the horses and remain with them
the whole day, bringing them into camp in the evening for
stables—or as many times during the day as horses were
required.   I was told I would soon know all about it, and
would probably be for guard myself that night.

On returning to the hut where I had slept, I found my
companions still in bed, drinking coffee and smoking.   I was
told to help myself.   I got my pannikin—a tin mug with a
handle folding inside which fits in and forms the top of a patrol-
tin—and filled it up from a large tin billy which stood on the
floor of the hut half full of coffee.   There was no milk, but

plenty of sugar, and I enjoyed it after the half-hour's exercise in the early morning air.

About half an hour after, the trumpet again rang out a sharp call, and one of the men remarking, "There goes the fatigue, you had better turn out," I went to the same ground where I had fallen in for roll-call. I found the men already there, all without jackets, and holding brooms and spades. One of them, seeing me without any implement, considerately gave me his spade. I thought it rather kind of him at the time, but when I was told off by the provost-sergeant to go with six other men and dig two latrines, I altered my opinion. The remainder of the men went off to the picquet ropes to sweep them clean, and also clean camp.

In due course the fatigue was over, and I went to my hut and had breakfast; the others were up and dressed, ready to go to their different offices. Breakfast consisted of fried beef, bread-and-butter, with coffee, cooked by the native boy who was the general slave of the mess. The men were not told off into messes, but the occupants of a tent or hut messed together, and provided their own food according to their fancy. A man was entitled to a pound of meat, pound and a quarter of bread, with a ration of coffee, tea, salt, and pepper daily, and one man drew the rations in bulk for his mess every morning. Each man was allowed a canteen account of 30s. per month, so any extra he wished for could be obtained from the regimental canteen. But as a man's canteen account also provided for liquor, his account was often "blocked" in less than a week after it had been opened, leaving him to get through the remainder of the month as best he could—with only his bare rations to live on.

Breakfast over and my companions having departed to

their various duties, I was wondering what would be next, when a corporal put his head inside the hut door and told me I would be required at orderly-room at ten o'clock to see the adjutant, and instructed me to clean up. Ten o'clock saw me standing outside the orderly-room, an old building close to the wagon drift of the river. The place had been a mill and was very much out of repair, but, being the only accommodation available, was temporarily used as orderly-room for the head-quarters, quartermaster's stores, and ordnance. I was marched in, and found myself facing Captain Goldsworthy, who was adjutant to the regiment. He was an Imperial officer seconded from his regiment. Three years afterwards he was made a Major of the Cape Infantry Regiment, and left the C.M.R.

He questioned me as to how long I had been in the Colony and whether I could ride. My replies apparently satisfied him, for he told the orderly sergeant to take me to the quartermaster and draw my equipments. I was taken next door, where I found a party of men breaking open boxes containing saddlery, equipments, and clothing, and I saw my two messmates "up to their eyes in it." One of them volunteered to the sergeant to see me fixed up, and, after telling me to come straight back to camp when I had drawn my kit, the sergeant left.

I waited some time in the store-room, giving a hand to the fatigue party, passing on saddles, etc., to where they were being stacked, when a sudden hush came over the hitherto noisy party. An elderly man came into the room; he was dressed in rather shabby mufti, and had a scraggy grey beard, and stooped slightly. My messmate, who I then found was an issuer of stores, came up to me, saying, "Here, I say, come along," walked me straight up to the new arrival, and, saluting, said, "A recruit, sir, for equipments." Captain Leatherland, the quartermaster of the regiment, as the old gentleman turned out to be, looked hard at me and said, "Where did you get those things from?" I replied that the uniform I was wearing had been issued to me at the contractor's in King William's Town, and was told, "Well, they won't do here. That is an old Police coat you've got on—the new ones are a cut above these old ones." He then sent me to Quartermaster-Sergeant Lock, who, taking down a list of articles I had received at King, told the issuer to make me up a full kit.

The first item that pleased me was a new jacket—a black velvet corduroy the same as the one issued in King, with the difference—to my youthful mind a very big one—that the new coat was ornamented with black braid round the edges and cuffs. It was certainly more fitted for a mounted man, and was a tolerably good fit for one that had not been made to measure. I was then allowed to pick a saddle, and my messmate selected the necessary valise, saddle-bags, and straps, a large mackintosh which proved very serviceable, horse-brushes, shoe-brushes, nose-bag, and razor, the last of which caused a good deal of chaff, and suggestions as to borrowing one of the office kittens made me wish myself outside.

After signing for the long list of articles received, which were entered to my equipment account, I went into another part of the store, and there got my first issue of arms. It consisted of a very ancient Snider carbine with a barrel like a gas-pipe, which had evidently seen a lot of service ; a revolver, an old-fashioned article which threatened more damage to the man behind it than any one in front; a black leather pouch-belt worn round the waist and holding forty-two rounds of Snider ammunition; a black leather gun-sling worn over the right shoulder and used for slinging the carbine when mounted on the line of march, and serving as a badge of duty when dismounted, instead of the cross belt which was issued later. In fact, the whole equipment was a Police one, and it was some two years later before the regiment received a proper military outfit.

With the aid of a couple of the men who were returning to camp, I got my kit up to the hut I had slept in the previous night. To my delight, the sergeant in charge told me I could remain in it, and that he had put me in their mess. This was a great advantage for a start, as I not only had kindred spirits for companions, but as they were on the staff I learnt what was going on in the regiment and our probable movements.

The sergeant told me that I would have a day off to get my traps in order, and that probably some horses would arrive during the day and I would be mounted almost at once. This was good news to me, and I spent the rest of the day soft-soaping my saddle and reins, and trying to work out the new appearance of everything which stamped me recruit. New leather can easily be darkened and made to look well by rubbing the leather with the inside of the skins of bananas, which were easily obtainable, and when once stained will not wash out, so that by the time my saddlery was cleaned and hung up on the rack, it looked quite presentable.

The horses did not arrive that day, but shortly after stables the following morning a civilian rode up with two natives leading six horses, and I was sent down to look at them. The horses all passed the Board, which comprised one sergeant, one corporal, and one 1st class private, and being approved by the adjutant, were ready for disposal. There being three other men besides myself to be mounted, I had the fourth pick, and took a dark chestnut gelding, about 14 hands 3 inches in height—a nice-looking animal, and apparently quiet to handle. It was with great delight that I put my new headstall on the animal, and led him off to the picquet line to be tied up. A group of men soon collected round the horses, and the general verdict seemed to be that although I had fourth pick, my horse was the best of the lot. One of the sergeants came up and took down the description of the animal, colour, age, marks, etc., and then cut a considerable amount of tail off, leaving it cut square exactly one hand above the hock, which is the regulation length a horse is allowed wherewith to knock the flies off. After watering and feeding the four new horses, they were taken out to join the troop, and, after being handed over to the horse guard, were let go, to fraternise with their new chums.

I then had my arms to attend to, and both carbine and revolver badly needed it. They had evidently been soaked in oil at some remote period and put away in store to await contingencies—a solitary recruit like myself to be armed, or a broken carbine to be replaced. The regiment at that period was very badly armed, a Snider carbine and a Colt revolver only being used.

CHAPTER III.

THE Colonial forces, which had hitherto been engaged in the operations at the front, consisted of the three regiments of Cape Yeomanry, some Burgher volunteers and native levies, and two troops of "F.A.M.P." or "C.M.R.," as they were now beginning to be called, and were commanded by Commandant Griffith of the Police, who was now retiring to be succeeded by Colonel Bayly, C.M.R. This force had been unsuccessful in all attempts to subdue the tough old chief Moirosi, who with his five sons and a strong tribe of Baphutis, an offshoot of the powerful Basuto nation, had long defied the Cape Government. After being driven from some of his strongholds, the chief had taken his stand on the celebrated mountain now known as Moirosi's Mountain.

After about a week at headquarters, orders were read out for twenty of us to hold ourselves in readiness to proceed to Moirosi's Mountain. Colonel Bayly and his staff had already left for that place a few days before. This caused a great commotion, and was not altogether pleasant news for many of the men ordered up. These men had already completed their three years' service, and intended taking their discharge when possible; but as the terms of service under which they had joined the F.A.M.P. were for a period of three years, or more if required, there was no help for it, and the sooner Moirosi's Mountain was captured the sooner they would be free men. So, after a lot of grumbling, and a consignment of the powers that be to the lower regions, the majority accepted the inevitable, and the greatest bustle pervaded the camp. Horses had to be re-shod, and new straps, valises, etc., drawn from the store, but within twenty-four hours the detachment was ready to start, and only awaited the arrival of two bullock-wagons which were to accompany it as transport. Imagine my delight when my name was read out amongst the others to "go with the detachment"! The adjutant seemed to be satisfied that if not exactly a trained soldier, I was as good as the rest at my drill, and only required the necessary experience on the veldt to finish my education.

The detachment was to march under the charge of N.C.O.'s, of which there were five, all of them having been at the Mountain in the early part of the campaign. It was with a great feeling of relief that I found my Kei Road friend, Sergeant Morris, was the senior, and would be in charge of the party. Since my arrival at headquarters he had evinced a great interest in my welfare, and I afterwards found out that it was to him I owed the good fortune of being placed in the hut with the four men I have already referred to.

The wagons having arrived, we were ordered to parade in heavy marching order the following morning, and make a start. This meant that practically all the kit we possessed had to be packed in as small a compass as possible and carried on our unfortunate horses. I looked with dismay at my two large red blankets, two extra shirts, half a dozen pairs of socks, slacks,—as any sort of trousers, flannels or others are called,—brushes, and the civilian clothes which I had in the box I had brought from home, and wondered what was to be done. It was soon solved for me by my messmates, who had apparently taken a day off to help to swell the confusion that was going on. With their aid, my packing was soon accomplished. One of them rolled one blanket into an incredibly small space, and fitted it into the valise; another showed me how to pack my saddle-bags, and the amount of kit that was stowed away seemed wonderful to me. Shirts, socks, trousers, brushes, towels, soap, razor, tobacco, matches, blacking, and cleaning gear, all disappeared comfortably into the bags, which are connected by a flat piece of leather, the width of the seat of the saddle, and hang down on either side, being kept in their place by loops attached to the bags, through which the girths are passed. The mackintosh was then rolled and strapped on the top of the valise, which was strapped firmly to the front of the saddle. My saddle was now complete till morning, when my nose-bag with horse-brushes had to be attached to it from one of the Ds on the near side. Everything else I possessed —photos, letters, clothes, etc.—was locked up in my box, of which one of my chums in the quartermaster's store took charge. I did not see that box again for three years, when it reached me at Umtata, on the transfer of headquarters to that place.

A grand smoking concert in the evening, organised at Hedding's Store, in which "local talent" did marvellously, constituted our farewell; but although "shandies" were as freely indulged in as smoking, every man reached quarters somehow, and in great good humour.

Shortly after Réveillé next morning there was a great bustling and hurrying about in camp. The wagons had to be packed with bags of mealies from the store for horses' feed on the line of march. A picquet rope and pegs had to be taken up from the lines and also packed. Next came the rations—flour, tea, coffee, sugar, and tinned corned beef ("Harriet Lane"). Then came the packing of mess-boxes. We were told off in messes of six, and each man made his contribution towards "extras" for the road. Jams, tinned butter, cheese, and chiefly pickles, were purchased from the canteen, each man being allowed full 30s. credit. Eventually the wagons were packed to the satisfaction of the N.C.O.'s, and those who had any appetite went to breakfast, and there was a peaceful hour.

At 9 a.m. "Boot and saddle" sounded. This call is sounded three-quarters of an hour before the "Fall in," and it is not too much time for the unassisted recruit, although it can be easily accomplished in five minutes by an old hand. First of all, the horses are brought from the picquet line to the huts where their respective owners reside. Each one is then rubbed down to knock off any dirt that may have got on the animal since stables. The saddle is then put on and girthed up, and the bridle, headstall, and bits put on over the stable headstall. The reim is carefully put round the horse's neck, and the end put through the ring and pulled till it hangs level, then it is twisted round and round till the spare length is used up and neatly knotted; the knee-band, used for knee-haltering the horse when off-saddled and turned out to graze during the halt, is fastened on the stable headstall below the throat-lash. The horse is then ready. The man then turns his attention to himself, whilst one of the numerous camp hangers-on, in the shape of a Kaffir boy, holds the horse and walks it up and down.

Leggings, boots, and spurs are put on—a hurried wash— then the jacket—the haversack containing your towel, soap, hair-brushes, razor, pipe, tobacco and matches, and very often two packages of cartridges containing twenty spare rounds, is then slung over your left shoulder. (This was before the bandolier was in use.) The black leather belt containing forty-two rounds is buckled round your waist, the buckle to the rear; revolver strap over the right shoulder, gun-sling with carbine suspended by a strap fastened round the small of the butt, and hanging close to your hip, muzzle down-wards; the peaked cap put on, and you are ready for the "Fall in" to sound.

The regimental call, which was the same as the 10th Hussars' at that time, was then sounded. This is termed the "Warning," and takes place five minutes before the "Fall in," and is the signal for the riflemen to mount and move in the direction of the parade-ground. My late messmates, who were all assembled outside the hut, and had in fact not only saddled my horse, but also accoutred me, gave me a hand to mount. This was not such an easy affair as it appears to an onlooker. In the first place, the blanket rolled in the valise with the mackintosh folded on top of it presents an obstacle to getting hold of a lock of the mane; and the saddle-bags and patrol-tin and nose-bag hanging at the back of the saddle look to the beginner as if they left no place for him.

To my eyes my horse did not look the same animal as on previous mornings, when I had mounted him without any difficulty on a stripped saddle, and ridden him about in company with a sergeant. This day he appeared to share my opinion that he had quite enough on his back without my weight in addition; and finding myself something like an overweighted Christmas tree, I did not feel as confident as usual. Anyway, it had to be done. One of my chums holding him tight by the bridle, another on the off side pulling on the stirrup leather to keep the saddle from slipping over with my weight, and another giving me a friendly push up, I managed to land on his back.

Whether it was the unaccustomed weight, or the barrel of my carbine which swung against his flanks and frightened him, I could never make out, but "Frank," as I had christened the animal, who had hitherto been so docile, suddenly appeared to acquire a taste for throwing somersaults. He made a bound forward, my chum let go his head, and before I had the reins firmly in my hands they were jerked out of them, and I found myself deposited on the ground with a bump which made the whole country revolve round me, with the butt of my carbine under my shoulder-blade. Frank having got rid of me, now seemed desirous of getting rid of my kit as well, and galloped into the rest of the men who were riding towards the parade-ground, kicking and jumping for all he was worth. He was almost immediately caught and brought back to where I was standing with my sympathetic friends. They told me he only pig-jumped, and explained what I ought to have done—stretch my legs out, sit back, look up, etc., were some of the many tips. I thought disconsolately, if that was only pig-jumping, what would the buck-jumping be like that I had so often heard them talking about?

After they had rearranged the saddle, which had been jerked nearly on to his neck, and hurried up by a loud voice calling on us to look alive, my chums got me into the saddle again, two of them hanging on to the bridle, and the others walking beside me—I suppose to give me confidence, which I didn't feel. With a kind of crab-like action the horse reached the parade-ground, and was led into position between two men who eased off to let me in, when, apparently thinking he had done enough mischief for one day, Frank stood perfectly still whilst the roll was being called and the troop numbered off.

The paymaster and quartermaster were the only two officers left on the parade-ground to inspect us and see us off; the former made a remark about my dusty appearance, and on Sergeant Morris telling him I had been bucked off, he said I had no business to be sent up if I couldn't ride. I felt very sick at this, but consoled myself with the thought that perhaps the reason he was being left behind was that *he* could not ride. I was not far out. In all the years I have known " Smithfield Jim " I have never seen him astride a horse.

The wagons had started with the usual accompaniment of whip-cracks and cries of " Yaak man ! " etc., and two mounted men falling out to escort them, the remainder of us wheeled into half-sections, the same order as the bullocks, and " Walk march " being given, we started amidst cheers from our comrades, and with all sorts of good wishes and suggestions as to what we should do with the wily Moirosi when we got him. " March at ease " was given, pipes were produced, and we settled in our saddles for a three or four hours' trek.

My horse being as unused to the march as I was myself, could not walk with the old stager he was beside, and was continually jogging at a slow trot to keep up. My hip was very sore, the bump-bump of the butt of my carbine against it didn't improve it, and before an hour was past I was feeling pretty sick of things in general. Sergeant Morris, seeing that I did not look happy, asked me whether I was hurt, and when I said my hip was bothering me, he kindly told me to fall out and wait till the wagons came up, —they were a short distance behind us at the time,—put my carbine on a wagon, and come on with the escort slowly. This I did, and before we reached the camping-ground at midday I had quite regained the confidence the horse had knocked out of me, and had also taught him a lesson that he could not do what he liked with me in future.

As the wagons travelled very slowly, we dismounted several times to let them get well ahead, and then remounted and trotted after them. This did me a lot of good, and I found after three or four attempts I could mount the horse quite easily, and soon got accustomed to the packed saddle —also my horse began to develop a good walk.

On arrival at the camping-ground we rode up to the saddles where the remainder of the men were, who had arrived an hour or more before us, off-saddled our horses, and knee-haltered them. This is done with a knee-band which fits round the horse's leg above the knee, and the reim of the stable headstall passed through the ring of the band and again through the headstall till it is the required length— generally about two feet—and brings the horse's head down to that distance from his knee. The animal is then let go with the others to graze. This makes it very simple to catch them when they are driven in to feed or saddle-up again.

On the arrival of the wagons the mess-boxes were quickly unpacked, and a good meal indulged in. The water having already been boiled in the individual patrol-tins, it did not take many minutes to make tea. Having eaten our fill, we stretched ourselves out by our saddles for a smoke and a sleep, and in a very short space of time every man except those who volunteered to cook the evening meal to be eaten before trekking again, were sound asleep.

About 4 p.m. the word to draw grain for the horses was passed round, and the men shaking themselves together, proceeded to the wagon with their horse-bags, and drew sufficient mealies for the evening feed for the horses.

Plates, knives and forks were then produced from the mess-boxes, and we all gathered round our respective mess fire, on which a large three-legged pot or camp-kettle was already standing, with patrol-tins filled with water all round it. All eyes were centred on the cook, who shortly announced that skoff (dinner) was ready. Each man in turn held out his plate over the pot whilst the cook ladled out his share with a large tin spoon. The stew, which is generally the standing dish for the evening meal, was excellent, and consisted of two or three chunks of mutton or beef, or perhaps both, rice, potatoes, and vegetable cake—the latter an assortment of dried compressed vegetables, cabbage, turnips, etc., which, when well stewed, makes a very good imitation of the real article. This, together with bread-and-butter and coffee, is all that a young Colonial soldier could desire, and when eaten makes him feel charitably disposed to the whole world.

Skoff being finished, each man washes his own utensils, and they are repacked in the mess-box. The order pack up is then given by the N.C.O. in charge, and boxes are stowed on the wagon, the pots slung on the sides and fastened with string, and the bullocks having been brought up, the drivers commence inspanning. The two men detailed for baggage-guard saddle-up, their horses having been caught in the veldt by them some time before, and fed, and the wagons move off on their next stage, while the remainder of the men return to the fires, and sit round them smoking and yarning. Sometimes a mysterious black bottle appears and is handed round, and then disappears again into a haversack.

After the wagons have been gone for about an hour, the troop horses are brought up to the saddles by the horse guard and caught by their respective owners, formed into line, nose-bags fastened on, and the horses fed. In those days "stables" was not observed as strictly as it was later on, and as a rule a man pleased himself whether he groomed his horse on the line of march or not, but in most cases a man brushed his horse down during the time the animal was feeding.

When the sergeant had satisfied himself that the horses had finished their feed, the order to saddle-up was given, and the horses led by their respective owners up to the saddles and saddled-up. This operation, which seemed so simple to my comrades, took me a considerable time. No sooner did I fit the blanket on the horse's back (we carried one blanket under the saddle on the march, besides the one in the valise) and lift my saddle to place it on the blanket, than the wretched horse would turn round, and the blanket slip off, when I had to put the saddle down and start again. Fortunately for me, one of the men, who had saddled his horse and dressed himself almost as quickly as I had folded my blanket, came to my assistance, and the horse, recognising that it was no use playing the fool, stood still and was saddled in time for me to fall in without any uncharitable remarks from the N.C.O.'s.

To my great relief the horse did not indulge in any of the eccentricities he had displayed in the morning, but let me climb up, and walked into the ranks with me as if showing me that he understood his job, if I didn't.

We soon numbered off and marched away in pursuit of the wagons. It was now nearly dark; march at ease having been given, and pipes produced, the files closed up and the singers of the company were called on for a song. Several songs with good old choruses were given; the horses seemed to enjoy the music, and snorted and stepped out gaily. This continued for about two hours, and we had almost caught up the wagons when the halt was called. We were told to dismount and loosen girths—look round our saddlery to see if it was all correct, and nothing galling the horse in any way. After a rest of half an hour, spent in lying on the roadside and yarning, we were told to girth up—tighten the girths, mount, and forward. Songs again enlivened the way, and the mysterious black bottle often made its appearance and was handed back from one to another upon the line, but the only effect it seemed to have was that the choruses got a trifle louder, and the chaffing a little more pointed.

After passing the wagons, we marched steadily on for about two hours, when we were wheeled off the road—"Front form, dismount and off-saddle." This was soon accomplished and the horses led out in front. The new guard fell in and counted over the horses, which were then knee-haltered as in the morning, and let go into the veldt, where they remained till morning.

As a rule when a troop off-saddles for the night on the line of march, the horses are rung—that is, put in a line and then fastened to one another from left to right. The two end horses are then brought together, making a ring, and tied to one another, and the animals remain in that position till untied. But at the time I am writing of this was rarely done except in bad weather, and the old Policeman rarely lost a horse from the troop however dark the night was, even if the animals were turned loose without being knee-haltered.

After letting the horses go, we unpacked our saddles, and unrolling our blankets made our beds down behind our saddles in line; the carbines placed in an upright position inside, the saddles, belts, caps, hung round it, the mackintosh thrown over the top and coming down over the head of the sleeper, making a very comfortable bed. It did not take very long before I was sound asleep, although my left hip was giving me considerable pain. I have a vague sort of recollection of the wagons arriving during the night, but that is all, and I did not wake till daylight.

Next morning shortly after daybreak, I looked around for our two wagons but could see no sign of them. On making inquiries, I was told that they had arrived about midnight, tied the oxen up for a couple of hours, and then trekked on again. I found that a very heavy dew had fallen during the night and the grass was very wet, also my top blanket. Some of the men were standing round a fire watching the water boiling for coffee. I filled my patrol tin from a sluit with running water in it, just below where we had slept, and proceeded to follow their example. In a short time the water was boiling, and with the aid of a tin of cocoa paste, containing milk and sugar among the ingredients, which I carried in my haversack, I succeeded in making a patrol tin full of excellent cocoa.

The sergeant gave the word to pack up, which necessitated rolling the wet blanket up and getting it and then the mackintosh into the valise, then we were ready. The horses, looking rather stiff and wet, were driven up and caught, and we proceeded to saddle up and fall in. I thought I was in for a repetition of the previous morning's performance, as the horse flinched considerably when the saddle was placed on his back, and did not seem to like being girthed up. After getting into my own accoutrements, minus my carbine, which was still on the wagon, I had to be assisted up into the saddle, as my hip was dreadfully sore and stiff; but, contrary to my expectations, Frank took it very calmly, and beyond a plunge which I managed to sit, walked quietly into his place in the ranks. I was then convinced that it was the carbine that had caused the trouble the day before, and decided in my own mind that it should remain where it was on the wagon until I was ordered to take it off.

After about three hours' trekking at a good walk, with a couple of short halts, we came to a nice stream, where we found the wagons already outspanned and the bullocks out in the veldt. We off-saddled, knee-haltered the horses and let them go. Getting out of our belts and coats, and shirt sleeves rolled up, we set about unpacking our blankets and spreading them out for the sun to dry. One man from each mess started the fires, whilst the remainder drew grain for the horses, and got the mess boxes off the wagon and took them up to the fires. After breakfast the horses were brought in and fed, and then turned out into the veldt again, while we spent the time wiping over the steel bit and stirrup irons with oil rags, and cleaning carbines and revolvers. This being finished we were at liberty to bathe, which most of us did, in a splendid stream of water. I then discovered a beautiful bruise on my hip and shoulder, but the bathe did me good, and I was not so stiff after it as I had been in the early morning. I asked and obtained permission to leave my carbine on the wagon till my hip was well, and a load was off my mind for a time.

We remained at the outspan all day; the weather being hot in the daytime, all the trekking was to be done at night. As the duration of the marches depended solely on the state of the roads, the distances covered varied considerably. The owner of the wagons was with them, and being a Colonial and an old Kurveyor, as transport riders were called, he did the trekking independently of the troop, and we as a rule only stayed with the wagons during the day. The usual routine was the wagons leaving about 4 o'clock in the afternoon and trekking till about 10; the drivers would then tie up the bullocks till about 2 or 3 in the morning, when they would inspan and trek on till 8 or 9 a.m. The bullocks were then let go to feed all day till time for the evening trek. By this method we averaged 18 to 20 miles a day.

Men drew grain for their horses, had dinner, and packed the wagons before 4 in the afternoon, fed the horses at 5 p.m., saddled up about 6 p.m., and marched till 10 p.m.; off-saddled and turned the horses knee-haltered into the veldt with a guard, unrolled their blankets and turned in. Next morning, we marched about 5.30 a.m. till we came up to the wagons, which was generally about 8 or 9, and remained with them until they started off again in the afternoon. So all the meals were taken while we were with the wagons except coffee in the early morning, which we carried in our haversacks, our patrol tins being always attached to the saddles. The days were usually spent lying in the shade of the wagons, cleaning gear, talking, washing clothes, etc. Owing to the late Galeka and Gaika Wars, the natives had abandoned the part of the country through which we were marching, and we only occasionally saw a few of them rebuilding huts in the distance. As they evidently distrusted the Ama Police, as we were called, they kept that distance.

CHAPTER IV.

ARRIVE AT QUEENSTOWN—GOOD RECEPTION—SERGEANT COMES TO GRIEF
WITH MY HORSE—ARRIVE AT DORDRECHT—MEET RETURNING YEO-
MANRY—MY IMPRESSIONS OF THEM—HORSE GUARD IN THE VELDT—
MY HORSE GETS LOST—REACH PALMIETFONTEIN—JOINED BY SOME OLD
HANDS—ENTER MOIROSI'S COUNTRY—PRECAUTIONS AGAINST ATTACK
—ARRIVE AT THOMAS'S SHOP—MEET NO. 5 TROOP.

AFTER about a week of marching through a very fine country, well watered, we came to Queenstown, a pretty little up-country town connected with East London and King William's Town, by train. We outspanned on the outskirts of the town over the railway crossing on the Dordrecht Road, and after breakfast and polishing ourselves up we got leave to go into the town.

Queenstown was even then the centre of a large farming community. It is one of the prettiest towns in the Colony, situated at the foot of a range of hills, its white houses surrounded by fine trees and very picturesque gardens. The main street ran straight through the town, with a few smaller streets running parallel to it, connected by smaller ones. Queenstown had the reputation of possessing the prettiest girls to be found in South Africa, and, as far as I can judge, it justifies that reputation still. The Queenstown girl is the most English of all Colonials in her manners, well educated and brought up. They are a most healthy looking lot, some of the finest tennis players coming from that district. Their hospitality is too well known for comment, and if there had been a few more Queenstowns in South Africa in the matter of loyalty it would have been better for the Mother Country. Unhappily, since the Boer War, the word loyalty is one that brings a sneer to the lips of Britishers in South Africa.

At the time of our arrival in Queenstown, great interest was centred in the doings of the troops at Moirosi Mountain, of which a strong contingent of Queenstown volunteers formed part. We were received with open arms, strangers shook hands with us and invited us into their houses or hotels for refreshments, and wished us all kinds of luck and safe return from our expedition. This was my first experience of the great friendship which I found existed between men in private life in the Cape Colony and their " first line of defence," as the C.M.R. were and are. Their intimate knowledge of the individual officers and men of the regiment pointed to the interest evinced by all in the welfare of the corps, and made me feel proud of being a member of it.

As my two chums and myself were leaving Gammer's Hotel we met Sergeant Morris, who instructed us to be in camp not later than 3 p.m., as he had received a telegram from Aliwal North telling him to push on as quickly as the bullocks could travel.

Next morning at daybreak I was awakened by an angry voice telling us to get up and catch our horses. Wondering what had caused the change in the manner of our hitherto strict but genial sergeant, I got up with the others and caught my horse, and then found that there were several missing, amongst them two of the N.C.O.'s horses and Sergeant Morris' pack-horse which carried the N.C.O.'s blankets. Amid dire threats of what would happen when they reached Moirosi Mountain if the horses were not immediately found, the guard saddled up to go in search of them.

One of the N.C.O.'s, anxious about his horse, and seeing me holding mine, came to me and said, "Lend me your moke, youngster, and I will soon find them." He took my horse and put his own saddle and bridle on, and hurriedly mounted, but Frank was "not taking any." He refused to budge, and the sergeant getting annoyed jammed both his spurs home, with a result not altogether expected by him. Frank gave one plunge, got his head down and treated us to a great display of bucking. The sergeant sat him manfully for about three of the awful jerks, and then went flying over the horse's head on to the ground. Frank, whose dormant spirit had evidently been roused by the dig of the spurs, continued the motion in the hope, I suppose, of getting rid of the saddle as well. Finding all attempts at this ineffectual, he raised his head, and raced off as hard as he could across the veldt. It was not till the lost horses had been recovered and driven in by the guard, who had found him on their way, that I succeeded in catching him. When the sergeant picked himself up his language was an education of sorts, and, after abusing the horse till words failed him, he told me I was a cad for not telling him that the brute was a bucker. I reminded him that he himself had told me that the horse only pig-jumped when I met with my downfall. The other N.C.O.'s laughed at this, and he joined in and the incident closed. We were the best of friends afterwards, and had many a laugh over what he termed being let down by a "rookie."

We hurriedly saddled up and made up for lost time by trotting most of the road till we overtook the wagons.

Frank went splendidly with me, and I had a secret feeling of satisfaction that I had regained some of my self-esteem in the way of horsemanship.

After two more days' trekking through rather uninteresting country, chiefly hills, with a good outcrop of boulders, we arrived at Dordrecht, marched through the only street, and camped by a *vlei* in a hollow below the town. Dordrecht at that time was a most desolate-looking place situated under a range of very bleak and high hills. Its population, with the exception of a few English shop and hotel keepers and professional men, consisted of Dutch, the families in the surrounding district being mostly of the same nationality. Relations between the Police and the Dutch had evidently not been very cordial, in this district at any rate, a mutual distrust being manifest. We found a troop of yeomanry in the town, who were on their way to their homes. They had left Moirosi Mountain on the arrival of Colonel Bayly, and seemed very well pleased with themselves on that account. They informed us that all the volunteers and yeomanry had either left or were leaving the mountain, and that only the C.M.R. and about forty men called the Northern Border Guard were remaining, and offered to bet freely that the mountain would not be taken by us. As they had been imbibing pretty freely, and were becoming rather personal in their remarks about the regiment, a row looked imminent, and Sergeant Morris, seeing the state of affairs, ordered us all back to the wagons, and what might have been an ugly row was averted. They rode off shortly afterwards, and seemed to have no semblance of discipline left in them, if they had ever possessed any, riding along just as they pleased. I remember thinking at the time that if they were a specimen of the Colonial troops it was no wonder that Moirosi was still defying the Government.

There were six men told off daily for guard, who used to mount, that is, parade, at 6 p.m.; this gave us two nights in bed, as off-duty is generally termed. At that period the duties were not performed nearly so strictly as subsequently when the regiment became properly reorganised, and the guard used to sleep in their ordinary places. The first relief of two men would mount guard directly the horses were let go, that is, they would go out into the veldt with them and keep a look-out that they did not stray, or any unauthorised person come near them. The time the reliefs would remain out depended on the length of the outspan, which was divided amongst the three reliefs.

On the night in question the reliefs were divided into four hours' duration. I was on first relief with another man, and we went out with the horses, after feeding them, at 6 p.m. and remained out with them till 10 p.m., when my companion went to the saddles to call the second relief. On their arrival they should have counted the horses to see that they were correct, as there were only about twenty-eight, including spare ponies, which the guard were not held responsible for. It was a very clear night and the animals were easily discernible, and the second relief took them over, that is, remained with them whilst my companion and I returned to the camp.

Next morning I found that the wagons had not gone on as usual, and was told by Wilson, the conductor, that his bullocks were lost; they had strayed away on the previous afternoon and the boys had not succeeded in bringing them in. This is a common experience with spans of bullocks whilst trekking, towards the end of the journey. The brutes would crawl along the road at a snail's pace, and an onlooker would imagine that they were absolutely done up, but the moment they are outspanned and out of the yoke, they mouch off, one behind the other, generally in the direction from which they have come, and unless the piccaninny, or voor-looper, as the boy is called, is after them at once, they go wandering on till they get out of sight. I have known the oxen get eight or ten miles from the wagons before they have been discovered and brought back. And I know very few things more annoying to happen on the march than the oxen going astray. It was destined that I should have another experience of the kind that day. When the horses were brought in at 6 a.m. to be fed, we found four absent, my Frank being one of the absentees. The third relief admitted having taken over horses correctly from the second relief at 2 a.m., and the onus was on them. One of the pleasures of the third relief when too good natured to count the animals and accept the other relief's word of "All Correct," is that they pay the penalty of being the scapegoat.

All of the guard were hauled up before Sergeant Morris, who made inquiries from us as to how the horses appeared to be feeding, whether they were giving trouble or not, and in what direction they appeared to want to stray. But it ended, of course, in the fact that the third relief having taken them over as correct at 2 a.m., were therefore responsible for the loss of them. They were denounced as a couple of lazy sweeps, who had been asleep, and would probably get six months and have to pay for the horses. In the meantime, to give us a chance, Sergeant Morris ordered us to saddle up and go in search of them.

The second and third reliefs saddled up together with half

a dozen of the oldest hands, experts at recovering all kinds of stock, and went in search of them, whilst I and the other first relief wandered out into the veldt with the remainder of the horses. At about 8 a.m. the bullocks were visible slowly coming over the hills about three miles away, and on their arrival at the wagons they were kept close by to await the return of the search-party.

The men arrived by twos and threes at intervals during the next two hours, and the last man having turned up reporting no signs of the horses for miles round the town, and no stray animals in the pound in the town itself, I began to feel sick and sorry for myself. Sergeant Morris sent a description of the horses to the Magistrates' Court, gave the order to inspan, as there had already been a trek lost, and told us four unlucky ones to put our saddles and kits on the wagons and "foot slog" beside them, thereby dispensing with a mounted escort. This was much to the delight of the mounted section, who were not sorry to get off the disagreeable duty of keeping pace with the crawling teams of oxen, of the deadly monotony entailed by which duty only those who have experienced it can judge.

Inspanning, we started off walking, and after going some distance we were invited by the owner to jump up. I took up my position at his side, and soon found him very interesting company. His name was Wilson, and he came from Amalinda, a small village not far from East London. He was a Colonial-born man, of Scottish parentage, and had been with wagons since his boyhood. He was very much annoyed at having lost a trek through the oxen straying, and by the way he jumped off the front of the wagon with the huge whip, and sent it coiling round his head and brought the lash down on some unfortunate beast's back, he seemed determined to make them regain the lost time. We certainly got over the ground in a quicker time than I had hitherto seen bullocks travel, and arrived at the outspan place before the mounted men had caught us. It was a short trek, not more than six miles, but it was the middle of the day, and he told me he intended going on late in the afternoon and trekking most of the night.

The mounted men having arrived after dinner, we started off with the wagons just before sundown, and trekked on at a good pace. After dark, the four of us coiled ourselves up in our blankets, picked out soft spots amidst the boxes and sacks of grain, and, assisted by the rocking and jolting of the wagon, went asleep. I never slept better, and only awakened in the middle of the night, when we outspanned for a short while, to go to sleep again and wake with the sun streaming on my face, when we got off the wagon and walked off the stiffness we all more or less experienced from our cramped positions during the night.

It was just on 10 o'clock before we arrived at the outspan, where we found the mounted men impatiently awaiting our arrival. They had been off-saddled for a few hours and were getting hungry; the men's boxes were soon tumbled off, and after a good breakfast we began to be civil to one another. Wilson told me we were quite 30 miles from Dordrecht, and had practically made up for the lost trek. This satisfied the N.C.O.'s., and the world went very well then.

We trekked on in the same regular manner day after day, or rather night after night. The country was similar to Dordrecht district—hills and stones, hardly a tree to be

seen, and, except for an occasional farmhouse stuck under
some prominent little kopje, hardly any sign of life. A few
miserable looking sheep, a span of oxen and some cows,
and two or three horses running loose; a small garden close
to a house with apparently nothing in it; a figure in a
female dress, surmounted by a capje, a bonnet of various
colours, generally white, which might have been a young
girl, or her grandmother, for all an observer could tell,
without actually looking under the overhanging brim of the
thing; two or three tall, gaunt-looking men, or overgrown
boys, with long hair and a general appearance of being
total strangers to the use of soap and water, loafing about,
apparently doing nothing—and you were told you had passed
a Dutch farm.

We met a good many wagons returning empty from the
front, generally passing them during the night. The
mountains of Basutoland were now beginning to show up in
the distance, and we passed Lady Grey some miles lower
down, and were gradually drawing close to Palmietfontein,
a Police station, where No. 4 Troop of the F.A.M.P. had their
headquarters for some years, and where we hoped to hear
some news on our arrival. The N.C.O.'s pointed out a range
of mountains to the front and right as the Drakensberg
Range, and also the direction of Moirosi's Mountain, which
lay behind some of the mountains in sight. All this tended
to liven us up, and make us very anxious to push on and
join our comrades who were already there, but of whose
doings we could get no satisfactory account from the various
wagon-drivers we had passed.

Two or three more treks brought us one morning early
in November to Palmietfontein, where we outspanned the

wagons outside the barracks which we found there. About
a dozen or more men came out to greet us, and we found that
they were details of different troops who had been left behind
sick when they passed through. These men were now fit
again and were to go forward with our detachment. They
were as glad to see us as we were to see them, and the
way they immediately pounced upon the different men
whom they knew, taking their horses from them and off-
saddling, and then taking the animals to the stables for a
feed, gave me my first real insight into the wonderful feeling
of comradeship that existed between the men of the
regiment.

As I had no horse, and was standing rather disconsolately
by the wagon, a cheery voice called out to me, " Won't you
come in and have some skoff ? " and a young Irishman came
up and asked what troop I belonged to. I explained that
I had not yet been posted to a troop, and that I was a recruit.
" Faith," said he, " I wish there were a few more like you ; come
on, me son, we must be chums," and led the way into a room
where there were already about six of my detachment doing
justice to an excellent breakfast of bacon and eggs. I joined
in, my host being most assiduous in his attentions, and
seeming quite concerned when I couldn't eat any more.

After breakfast my new friend took me round the camp,
introduced me to his friends, and showed me the stables,
recreation-room, etc., and then we strolled down to the store.
He told me he belonged to No. 1 Troop, generally called the
Irish Brigade, and that, begad, I must join it directly I got
to the mountain ; that nearly all the troop were Irish, and
" every mother's son of them gentlemen." I afterwards found
out that he was nearly correct in his statement as to the

C.M.R. CAMP, PALMIETFONTEIN, 1880.

nationality of the troop, and that with a few exceptions the officers, N.C.O.'s, and men all hailed from the Emerald Isle and were a splendid lot of fellows. Faulkner, my new friend had the reputation of being one of the best riders and sportsmen in the regiment, and we remained great friends as long as he remained in the corps. Four years later Paddy went as a law agent to East Griqualand, where he died a few years afterwards. There were few more popular men in the regiment than Paddy Faulkner, and I shall never forget his kindness to me when I was an inexperienced lad and needed friendly advice.

After spending some time at the store chatting with the proprietor, who was an ex-Policeman and doing well, we returned to camp, where the afternoon was spent in cleaning our saddlery and equipments. Getting an empty mealie bag from the wagon, I carefully oiled all my gear and put it with the saddlery into the sack, and stowed it carefully away on the wagon, where it would not be thrown about till my arrival at the mountain. Rations issued for four days, ammunition inspected and deficiencies made up, orders issued that ammunition belts were not to be taken off nor arms quitted after leaving the station, began to give an air of reality to the business on which we were embarking, and when I was told that on crossing a stream about five miles from Palmietfontein we would be in the enemy's country, I had all sorts of imaginary visions, and could hardly sleep that night with anticipations of what would happen on the morrow.

We were aroused at daylight next morning, and packing up was proceeded with. One reinforcement packed their belongings on our wagon, which had got considerably lighter on

4

the journey.   The horse rations being nearly finished, had materially altered the weights allotted on commencing the journey, and there was not as much danger of our sticking in the drifts and mountain roads through which we would have to pass as there would have been with full loads. The blankets and saddle-bags of the mounted men were also packed on the wagons, only their mackintoshes being left on their saddles to enable them to move quickly over the country if it should be necessary.   This made a great difference to the appearance of the detachment.   The horses moved more freely, and the men looked much more active and smart in the saddle than formerly.

The wagons were inspanned, and the detachment saddling up at the same time, we all moved off together, two of us dismounted men on each wagon, two N.C.O.'s and the men about 100 yards ahead of the leading wagon, and the remainder the same distance in rear of the second one, keeping clear of the dust and riding on the veldt when possible.   This went on till we reached a stream which divided the two districts.   We were now in the country of the rebels, who were supposed to have fallen back on their last position at Moirosi's Mountain.   The country was of a barren nature, with very strong kopjes standing up in the veldt in all directions, and a very bad road, filled with holes and boulders.   It was marvellous how any vehicle could stand the sudden jolts and shocks that we were treated to, and it got so bad that we were told to get off and walk. This we did, taking our carbines with us.   The road twisted round a hill, then descended into a ravine with the water rushing over the rocks in the drift—generally composed of large stones through which nothing but an African wagon or strong Cape cart could possibly get without smashing up; then up a steep hill, generally straight up the face, no attempts being made at a cutting, at which the bullocks strained every muscle, the drivers swearing and cracking their long whips, stopping at short intervals, sticking stones behind the wheels; then on again, panting bullocks, yelling drivers, and the cracking whips making a scene almost indescribable. Half the detachment on the top of the hill dismounted to watch the progress of the wagons and the surrounding country at the same time; the other half, the other side of the drift, also dismounted and waited till the wagons reached the summit before following up.

Here I may say that it is one of the unwritten rules in the C.M.R. never to march a detachment of men up a hill immediately in the rear of a wagon. The whole weight of the wagon is on the sixteen bullocks pulling on the trek-chain to which are fastened the yokes; and in a bad place going up a steep hill, if the strain should prove too much for the chain, and it were to snap at the dessel-boom to which it is attached, the whole wagon would rush down the hill and crush everything in its course. This rule might well be observed by other corps. I saw some glaring instances of its breach in the late war with the Dutch, when mounted men and infantry often followed close behind wagons in some very dangerous places, where the snapping of a chain would have caused as many casualties as a decent engagement, and have brought home to the officers in command a sense of their utter ignorance of veldt work in South Africa.

We outspanned about four miles after crossing the stream —the wagons, as usual, side by side. The horses were let out to graze more closely knee-haltered than usual; the first relief of two men going out mounted, and the remainder of the guard tying their horses up to the wagons and feeding them, to enable them at any moment to get the horses in quickly should the occasion arise. I also noticed two men climbing to the top of a hill overlooking us, where they remained till they were relieved to get their breakfast. They were videttes keeping a look-out for the safety of the camp. We marched on again from 2 p.m. to 6 p.m., the same order being observed on the march, and outspanned before dark.

We were then on the top of a high range of hills. Stretching across our front, in the distance, looking very high in comparison, we saw the Drakensberg mountains, amongst which was Moirosi Mountain. It was getting dark, and the wagons were now placed about twenty yards apart and abreast of one another, the picquet rope fastened from one to the other, and the horses tied up to it on either side of the rope. The men placed their saddles, half of them on the outer side of one of the wagons, and the other half on the outer flank of the other, whilst the guard and the four of us dismounted men slept on the rear face outside the horses. Fires were lighted behind some rocks, and we soon had dinner, and lay down in our blankets at our various stations with our carbines alongside of us. Shortly afterwards, with the exception of the two sentries who walked up and down the sides outside the men, everything was quiet, except for an occasional snort from a horse or cough from a bullock.

We inspanned and saddled up next morning shortly after daylight, morning coffee being dispensed with, and marched off. We went very slowly, the roads being in a very bad state and gradually getting steeper as we went along, so that it seemed almost impossible to go any farther with a wagon. We consoled ourselves with the knowledge that wagons had gone in the same direction, although there was very little in the shape of tracks to show that they had gone over that way. So the bullocks struggled on, and with the aid of whip-cracks and yelling, which might have been heard miles off, succeeded in doing a very fair trek. While outspanned, the sergeant whom my horse had succeeded in bucking off, called me up and asked me if I would like to ride on to Thomas's shop with him; if so, I could ride his spare pony, which had hitherto been ridden by his Kaffir boy, who led his pack-horse. I, of course, said Yes, and thanked him. He then told me to catch his horse and the pony in the troop, and we would start in half an hour's time. I was highly delighted, and with the aid of the horse-guard easily caught the two animals. The sergeant told me to put his spare saddle and bridle on the pony for myself, and after he had saddled up his troop horse we left the wagons and cantered off to Thomas's shop. We passed through very rugged country, where the mountains seemed to close in on us. I noticed several large caves under the ledges of rock on some of the mountains as we passed These were pointed out to me as the places where Moirosi had taken refuge from time to time, and had been driven out of at the commencement of the campaign. The sergeant was very interesting in his talk, and told me a good many incidents of his career in the regiment. He told me he expected to get the sword shortly—he expected to receive his commission —and as at that period only officers wore swords, a commission was termed "getting the sword." His expectations turned out to be correct, for he was promoted to lieutenant in less than a month from that time.

After about a twelve miles' ride, which I thoroughly enjoyed after the wagon travelling, we arrived at Thomas's shop, so called after the trader who lived at the place. There were several buildings, or rather large huts, which were used as a hospital, in which there were several men in various stages of convalescence, C.M.R. and Yeomanry. There was also a troop of C.M.R., No. 5, the same one that had been knocked about in the second attack on the mountain.

Our horses were taken from us and looked after by men eager to welcome us, and I was asked into a tent where ten or twelve men were, and made to feel at home among them. They were a rough-looking lot; nearly all of them had beards, and their uniforms had only one thing in common, and that was their jackets—all of which had at some remote period been black velvet corduroy of the same pattern that Mr. Ryan had issued to me on my joining, but were now almost white and threadbare; riding breeches of all colours, which had evidently been bought at traders' stores from time to time, were the fashion. The two rings of black braid on the cuffs of their coats showed me that they were all first-class privates—or, to use the C.M.R. term, "They had all got their rings," which meant one shilling a day rise in pay and the first step up the ladder, a man having to become a first-class private before he could be made a corporal. As a man had to wait his turn on the seniority list before he got his ring, and this only as vacancies occurred, he had sometimes to wait three years before his turn came. This made promotion in the regiment very slow, and disheartened not a few, who left the regiment after their three years' engagement as they had joined it, full-blown second-class privates. Promotions went in the troops to which the men belonged, so many first-class men being allowed per troop, and the rapidity of a man's promotion depended greatly on the time he happened to join and on the number of first-class men who were about to take their discharges.

I met a good many of the men who had been wounded at the second attack. They had all recovered and were ready for the next one—everybody being confident that now the regiment had got together, and the new colonel was just the sort, further operations would be of a disastrous nature to old Moirosi and his tribe. Surgeon-Major Hartley was at Thomas's shop when we arrived, and the men were full of admiration of his conduct at the former attack. He received the Victoria Cross for the same action some two years later.

Amongst the veterans I met Heskins, known throughout the regiment as "Snowball," a not very flattering allusion to his personal appearance, which was decidedly tubby. Snowball left the regiment many years ago, and is an old resident in the Transvaal at the present time. He was the "character" of the troop, and no matter what adverse circumstances the men were placed in, Snowball's quaint doings and sayings always brought a smile or a laugh to his down-in-the-mouth companions.

Our wagons arriving the next morning with the detachment, the whole of No. 5 Troop turned out and cheered them. Great excitement prevailed for the time; men met who had not seen each other since they were recruits together three years before, and they walked away in all directions with their chums, swapping experiences and adventures that had happened to them since they last met. Paddy Faulkner soon hunted me up, and we spent the day together visiting different tents and hearing the latest reports from the front, now only fifteen miles from us, till the evening came, when an excellent sing-song round a large bonfire brought a very pleasant day to a close.

CHAPTER V.

THE next morning we left Thomas's shop for our final trek,
hoping to reach the mountain that night. With
" Good-bye, and see you in a day or two " from our friends of
No. 5, who were being held in readiness to go forward at a
moment's notice, we started—the mounted men with drawn
arms, and advance and rear guards. The road, which was very
rocky, wound its way along the side of a range of small
mountains, a spur of the great Drakensberg Range, where the
slightest mistake in handling the bullock teams would have
sent the wagons toppling down the steep sides, which fell
some hundreds of feet. We gradually descended to the level
of the river and crossed the drift of the Buffalo River, where
we outspanned. There was an officer and detachment at this
drift under canvas. The camp was a mixture of bell and
small patrol tents, the latter just large enough to accom-
modate two men with their saddlery at the head, and suitable
only for purposes of sleep. These men were held in readiness

to march at any moment, and were at present fore-laying the drifts and passes leading into Basutoland along the Orange River.   The scenery about here was very grand ; the mountains, varying in shapes and sizes, stood up against the sky in all directions; huge overhanging rocks, that looked as if a touch would send them toppling over and crush everything beneath, including the puny man, who looking up at them felt a very insignificant object indeed.

A sound as of the rumbling of distant thunder occurred at intervals, and I began to think that we were in for a storm, although the sky, or as much as we could see of it, was cloud-less.   Faulkner disillusioned me unpleasantly by coming up and saying, " Do you hear the guns, my boy ? but its little damage they do with all their noise ; they might just as well be shooting peas out of a pea-shooter for all the good they are."   When I remarked that surely they must have some effect on the natives, he retorted, " Effect your grandmother—what do you know about shells—except with eggs in them—you will see the place yourself to-night, and then you will be able to judge what effect it has on the nigger—mighty little, I can tell you ; but the artillery must earn the extra sixpence, I suppose, that's why they keep on blazing away at nothing," an allusion to the well-earned extra sixpence per diem which the artillery troop were allowed above the ordi-nary rate of pay.

We marched again that afternoon, and after a stiff pull out for the open, found ourselves where there had been an attempt at road making, a place called " The Cutting."   The road was hewn out of the side of the mountains, and wound round them for some distance, afterwards following an almost straight line.   On rounding the corner we at last came in sight of the notorious Moirosi Mountain straight ahead of us, standing alone—a giant amongst the surrounding mountains. On our left, at the foot of the hills we were traversing, about 500 feet below us, flowed the Orange River, the boundary between Basutoland proper and the country we were now fighting in, inhabited by the Baphutis, of whom Moirosi was the chief. We had glimpses of the river running in and out the mountains and flowing past the bottom of Moirosi, which rose majestically and, as it seemed, sheer from its bank, dwarfing the other by no means small mountains which surrounded it.

We could distinctly hear the booming of the guns as they were fired; the sound travelling up the valley of the river seemed to lessen the distance. The road being fairly level, though still very rocky and worn in places, the bullocks travelled along very well, and I soon had visible signs that the hitherto easy life I had experienced since joining the regiment was about to undergo a startling change.

We could now see the different camps of tents between us and the foot of the mountain, also troops of horses grazing on the slope between the camps and the river. Between the booming of the guns, which was gradually growing louder, we could hear the sharper report of the carbine, and see an occasional puff of smoke half-way up the mountain, followed by a faint report a considerable time after. I was told that this meant that the niggers were potting at the saddle picquet from the second schanze. Occasional remarks about "Captain Jonas" roused my curiosity, and on inquiry I was told that Captain Jonas was the name given to a "white nigger" (meaning an albino) by the troops; that he was a good shot, and generally supposed to be in charge of the schanzes; and that he made things very warm for any man who exposed

himself or the saddle picquet. From various expressions of
my comrades, I concluded that Captain Jonas would not have
a rosy time of it if he happened to get into their hands.

As we got closer to the encampments we could see several
bodies of men in formation, and by the occasional flash of
the sun on their arms they appeared to be drilling. As we
came closer still we saw that the men were exercising with long
rifles and bayonets, in preparation for the forthcoming attack.
Two horsemen then made their appearance riding in our
direction, clouds of dust rising at every stride of their horses.
On reaching the detachment, which had resumed its position
by the wagons, I saw that one of them was a sergeant-major
and the other a corporal ; they were greeted by the N.C.O.'s, and
they turned their horses and rode back with the detachment.
They had evidently ridden out with orders as to our movements,
for on arriving about half a mile from the camp, and after
passing a small sluit with water in it, the mounted men
hurried off to the left, while we with the wagons went plough-
ing through sand in the direction of the largest of the
encampments, where there were about fifty or sixty other
wagons drawn up. This I found to be the headquarters camp
and artillery, where the foodstuffs for the whole force in the
field were stored under tarpaulins or any other improvised
shelter that could be rigged up.

Our wagons drew up by the others and outspanned, and
crowds of men came round them and asked innumerable
questions from the four of us as to the news from the outside
world. Some of them had not received a letter or seen a
newspaper for months. The men of my detachment came up
to the wagons and took their kits off and went their various
ways to rejoin their respective troops. I, having no troop to

SUMMIT OF MOIROSI'S MOUNTAIN: THE "CROWN."

go to, was making for somebody in authority in the head-quarter lines, when my chum Paddy said I was to go up with him for the night, and I would be fixed up by next day. I went with him, taking my kit with me, up to where Nos. 1 and 3 Troops were encamped in a square, with a small wall outside the tents. I saw Sergeant-Major ——, who told me I could stay there till I got posted to a troop, and asked if I had any preference for a particular troop. I had none, and told him so, but he advised me to think over it and let him know in the morning. I deposited my kit where there were eight others, and being told "skoff" would be ready in an hour after stables, and not having a horse to look after, I went for a look round.

The mountain was a giant among the surrounding ones in a very mountainous country; rising steep from the banks of the Orange River to the height of about 3000 feet, with rocky and precipitous sides, and perfectly inaccessible to man and beast on the back and eastern side. In shape it looked like a square with the edges cornered off, but much broader at the back than in the front; with a flat top where a considerable number of cattle could graze with ease; about a mile from the front to rear and half a mile across. The only way up seemed to be from the front face, which began with a gradual slope and ended on a plateau about 800 feet high from the base, called the "saddle," from its shape. From the plateau upwards were a series of "schanzes"—solid walls loop-holed and covering all the paths. Against these the Colonial forces had made many unsuccessful attacks, which had resulted in heavy losses for the Colonial troops, No. 5 Troop C.M.R. in particular. This troop led the advance from the saddle, and had fifteen men killed or wounded before they had gone fifty yards. Some of the men reached the first schanze but could not get any farther, and had to remain there till night, several casualties occurring, and some very gallant deeds being performed. Sergeant Scott, Artillery Troop, and Private Brown, No. 5 Troop, received the Victoria Cross for their gallant conduct that day; but I shall have more to say of this later on.

It was here that a strong picquet of the besieging force was always stationed, to prevent natives leaving the mountain or reinforcements going up, and it had been the scene of many a skirmish. At the end of the plateau, which was about 400 yards in length and about 80 yards across, the mountain rose almost straight, with paths winding in and out, till it reached the crown, a huge rock which appears to be almost toppling over.

On my right another mountain stood, connected by a ridge with the part of Moirosi's Mountain near the "saddle," and by this ridge or "nek" the men went on their way to the picquet. On this nek, and at the end farthest from Moirosi's Mountain, considerably above us, were stationed No. 2 Troop, and it was not considered an enviable post.

Some little time previously, a troop of the 1st Yeomanry had occupied the position now held by No. 2 Troop C.M.R. The rebels succeeded in surprising the camp, stabbed the sentries, and cut the tent ropes, bringing the tents down on the unfortunate occupants who were asleep. The natives assegaied every man as he was struggling to get out from under the canvas which imprisoned him, and after this wholesale slaughter escaped untouched up the mountain by some paths on the right face only known to themselves. Such a disaster could only have happened through gross negligence on the part of the picquet, which had probably been posted in a

very careless manner; this, at least, was the verdict of the
majority of the other troops who were at the mountain at the
time. It was possibly this disaster, and the fact that other
corps wanted to return to their homes, having had enough of
Moirosi and his ways, that had influenced Colonel Bayly in
asking for the removal of all troops other than C.M.R. With
the exception of about forty men of the Northern Border
Guard from the Dordrecht district, and a few hundred
Fingoes under Alan Maclean, a C.M.R. captain with a great
reputation as a Kaffir fighter, the force at present under
command of Colonel Bayly was composed solely of C.M.R., and
a tough, hardened lot they looked. In all stages of raggedness
in the shape of clothing—more marked in the troops who had
been stationed the farthest away from King William's Town,
and had no opportunity of replenishing their kits even if they
wished to do so—the majority of the men, so far as I could
judge, had completed their term of service, and were waiting
for the present campaign to end before taking their discharges;
but their wardrobes left much to be desired, though their horses
and saddlery were spick and span.

I don't remember ever seeing a regiment so well mounted.
At the time I am writing of each man's horse was his own
property, and looked upon as a valuable asset when the
time came for taking his discharge. The men therefore
looked after them considerably better than they otherwise
would have done. It must be remembered that at this period
"stables" were purely a matter of form, and only consisted of
answering whether your horse was present or not. To these
old stagers of Policemen who formed the greater bulk of men
present in the field, the curb had not as yet been applied in
the matter of parades, and as nobody could teach them more

than they already knew in the shape of fighting natives, and being up to all the dodges of the wily savage, they were left to their own ways to a great extent, and were not troubled by the N.C.O.'s except when necessary. The military spirit of discipline was practically unknown in the corps.

\ Stables were now sounding, and I saw No. 1 Troop on the right side of square, and No. 3 on the left catching their horses and taking them to their positions on the picquet lines inside the square at the back of the tents. I went·as close to the parade as I thought advisable, thinking that there might be some horses without owners requiring grooming, and having learnt if the N.C.O.'s saw any man idle they very soon found him employment, I remained amongst the tents. I was particularly struck with the look of the No. 3 Troop horses— a hard, wiry looking lot of animals with no superfluous fat about them. The men were nearly all unshaven, and some of them quite old looking, with long grey beards; others with all sorts of appendages—long or short as they thought fit. The three officers of No. 3 were also on the parade, looking at the animals with experienced eyes.

They were Colonial men, and splendid specimens of the Police officer, all three over six feet in height and with long beards. One of them was destined in a short time to make a name second to none in the regiment, the man who first set foot on the top of Moirosi Mountain. He was promoted to Captain for this feat, much to the satisfaction of us all. I may add here that Captain —— met his death in the late Boer War in the trenches at Wepener, and died as he had lived, one of the best and bravest men in the regiment, and·greatly missed by every man who had ever served under him or enjoyed his friendship.

I also noticed two officers inspecting No. 1 Troop—a captain and a subaltern—the former a jovial Irishman, the latter a Colonial, who left the regiment less than a year after we captured the mountain. The captain became one of my staunchest friends in the regiment for years, and is now spending his old age in the old country on a well-earned pension.

Stables being over, I returned with Faulkner to the tent where my kit was, and where I was to take up my abode till the time arrived for me to be posted to a troop. Dinner was soon over, and I was interested in the fact that the men in the tent were for picquet that night, and watched their proceedings. They were evidently used to it, and got into their belts, etc., as if they were going out for a short stroll, instead of going on the most dangerous and irksome duty of the expedition. They were forming a part of the saddle picquet, consisting of 1 officer, 3 N.C.O.'s, and 25 men, whose duty it was to march up to the "saddle" at dusk, relieve the old picquet, and remain there for twenty-four hours, till relieved in their turn by another fresh picquet. In fact, the "saddle" was practically the drawbridge of the fortress, and the natives leaving or reinforcing the mountain in any numbers would have to pass over the picquet to do so.

Shortly afterwards the whole picquet paraded by the headquarter camp, and marched off in the direction of the saddle. As they reached the foot of the rock leading up to the saddle, it soon became evident that it was not a picnic they were engaged on. A few puffs of smoke from the schanzes, where the natives were evidently watching our operations, were followed by distant reports which echoed loudly round the mountains, and then by a smart answering volley from the old picquet, who could now be seen lying behind their small shelters on the ridge; then desultory firing on both sides whenever they saw a chance of something to shoot at—but the new picquet kept on their way. They marched in single file along the footpath that led up to the saddle, and on arriving near the summit broke into the double till they reached the entrenchments of the picquet; the firing from the schanzes increased as the new picquet came into range, and was promptly replied to by the men in the entrenchments.

On arrival of the new picquet the old one was seen to leave in the same fashion, the new picquet taking up the firing till the old one was under cover of the hill, when the firing slowed down on both sides till only an occasional shot could be heard.

The old picquet marched down to the headquarters camp and then dispatched to their own quarters, and I saw six or seven of them making for our camp—there were two of No. 1 Troop and four or five of No. 3 Troop. They strolled into their respective tents as if they had been for a walk, and commenced an attack on their dinners which had been kept on the fire for them, no further attention being paid them. To a recruit like myself this seemed quite amazing.

One of the men of No. 1 Troop belonged to the tent in which I was staying, but excepting a careless look he took no notice of me, but proceeded to take off his belts and great-coat and flung them on the ground one by one, accompanied by a succession of oaths, so bad that I began to wonder why the other men did not remonstrate. But nobody seemed in the slightest degree put out by it. I was young and inexperienced, and his oaths fairly staggered me. Faulkner, guessing my thoughts, considerately suggested a stroll by No.

3 Lines, and, glad to get away from such a sulphurous atmosphere, I immediately left with him.

I learned that it was no accidental outbreak, but the normal condition of the man. An Oxford man, he had been intended for the Church, and had now evidently gone to the other extreme. He had a considerable following in No. 1 Troop in a lot of young idiots, who thought it smart to interlard their conversation with oaths and blasphemous remarks. In the two years succeeding I often came across the man. I found no alteration in him: later he became mad, with a form of religious mania, and some three years after our first meeting he died in Grahamstown Lunatic Asylum. It is charitable to suppose that he must have been mad at the time that he cultivated his mania for blasphemy.

The incident I have related had considerable weight in my selection of a troop. Before it occurred, if I had been asked if I wished to go to any particular troop, I should undoubtedly have said No. 1 Troop, that being the troop to which my chum Faulkner belonged; but I had received such a shock from the blasphemer that I would not go back to sleep in the same tent with him, and had a shakedown in a tent in No. 3 Lines, where I received a rough but friendly welcome from men old enough to be my father. That night I decided to join No. 3 Troop, and I never had cause to regret my decision.

The next morning I was duly taken on the strength of No. 3. We were named the Africander Troop by the rest of the regiment, on account of the majority of the men being Colonials. By Colonials I mean men born in South Africa of British extraction, used to the ways of the country and natives from boyhood. Such a class of men exists now in the

Cape Mounted Police, and are the finest breed of men for the work they have to do.

Talking Dutch and Kaffir in most instances, and born horsemen, they make a splendid body of men for the suppression of stock thefts and keeping order in the various native locations in the Cape Colony. In the late war they were invaluable in showing up the Cape rebel—the man of Dutch descent living in the Cape Colony, who, whilst professing loyalty to the British Crown with his lips, was in his heart more bitter and treacherous than his Dutch friends from the neighbouring republics.

I found my new comrades of No. 3 Troop a most interesting lot of men. The N.C.O.'s were with one or two exceptions Colonials, and Policemen of the old type. The horse was the first consideration with these men. Provided a man's horse, saddle, and bridle were in good order—the former kept free from sore back and girth gall, and always ready for duty—the man might go about in any sort of kit that suited his fancy, and nobody checked him. At the time of joining I think I was the only man with a pair of regimental riding breeches in the troop, the majority of the men wearing white Bedford cord pants, bought from time to time at traders' shops or wagons, and fitting wherever they touched; others wore velveteen cord trousers with spurs hanging down their heels. These old veterans had just come down from Natcha's Nek in the Drakensberg Mountains, where they had acquired a considerable amount of money in the shape of loot during the time they were stationed there, and they were now, apparently for the first time for years, enjoying the luxury of living in a bell tent and indulging in their favourite pastime of gambling. They looked upon arms, parades, fatigues, etc., as an attempt to defraud them of their good time, and growled and grumbled at what they termed being made "swaddies" or soldiers of. Picquets they took as a matter of course, or "all the three years," as they expressed it; but horse-guards, in the shape of going out into the veldt all day with the horses, when they could be enjoying themselves at Nap, they strictly barred. They paid willingly any sum from five shillings up to a pound for a substitute to do the day's guard for them, and with the tacit consent of the sergeant-major they always succeeded in finding some less fortunate member than themselves ready to do the guard for a consideration.

Some of these old fellows had served considerably over twenty years, and seeing the changes in the shape of discipline in the regiment imminent, were anxious to get out of it as soon as possible, and were only waiting to fix up old Moirosi to attain their heart's desire. There were also a good sprinkling of men in the troop of about three to six years' service, younger men, mostly Colonial born, who accepted the changes in the regiment gladly, and were rather anxious to get decent kits and start drilling. Quite a number of these men remained on and became very good soldiers.

It soon became evident that our new colonel had some scheme in his head. The fact that the natives had hitherto managed to get supplies on to the mountain made him convinced that there must exist some other path besides those which went up its face, and several reconnoitring parties went out with him to view the sides. To the casual observer the huge precipices and overhanging rocks made the idea of getting to the top except from the front out of the question. A few months before, Sir Garnet Wolseley had sent some engineer officers to examine and report on the state of the mountain, and rumour declared that they had returned declaring Moirosi Mountain impregnable unless aided by very heavy artillery, which might make some impression on the defences. Men were now daily exercised with long rifles and bayonets, so it was clear that we were preparing for a hand-to-hand assault, and opinions as to the superiority of the bayonet over the existing arm of carbine and revolver were freely exchanged. As it was optional which arm a man took, a good many stuck to the carbine and revolver as being more serviceable for climbing and close quarters.

The mortars were now placed nearer the mountain, and an incessant bombardment kept up both on the schanzes and on the top of the mountain. Shells exploded at the back of the Crown, but nobody could see what damage was being inflicted, and the solid rock stood as firm as ever. For three days the guns kept up firing at two minutes' interval, and all night the practice continued. If the firing did not actually inflict many casualties, it kept the enemy on the alert and made sleep impossible for a good many of them.

On the night of the fourth day the regiment was paraded for attack. For two or three days previously scaling ladders had been improvised in the headquarters camp, and it was generally known that an attack was to be made on a flank of the mountain which hitherto had been considered impossible of ascent. Nos. 1 and 3 Troops were told off for the duty, and to lead the way, supported by two other troops. A Native contingent under the Macleans were to threaten the front face supported by more C.M.R., and the attack was to be pushed home if the flanking party made good its footing at the side.

The troops paraded about 10 p.m. on the night of the 19th November 1879, the men clad mostly in dark-coloured guernseys and trousers, and carrying rifles and bayonets, or carbines, as they preferred. Twelve men were told off from each troop, Nos. 1 and 3, to carry the ladders, and so we left camp and moved towards the mountain, making in the direction of the neck below the saddle. We crossed it in single file, led by Lieutenants Sprenger and M'Mullen with No. 3 Troop leading, and made our way along a footpath stretching away to the right flank and upwards towards the summit. After rests and changes of ladder-bearers, we got up to a considerable height. At this point we must have been heard by the natives at the front or on the top of the mountain, for the party was challenged in Dutch. No answer was given, but quietly the order to halt was passed along, and every man stood still or crouched under the shadow of the huge boulders which were all around. Apparently not quite satisfied about some noise they could not understand, the natives commenced rolling stones down. These stones, some of them boulders, came down with a deafening noise, jumping into the air and striking the ground again and again in their descent to the bottom, and making our hearts jump in our throats. Luckily they all passed in front of the men, or clean over the path on which we were stretched. After an interval which seemed interminable, the stone fusillade suddenly ceased. We were told afterwards that the natives thought it was a picquet going to guard some water, and they rolled stones to frighten us. Not hearing any further movement as a result, they took for granted that it was a false alarm, and left their places to get a sleep, which they were badly in want of.

The order was now passed along to go forward, and we continued up the winding pathway with the utmost caution, not talking, and hardly dislodging a stone. The front suddenly stopped, and the word was passed for the ladders. We were then at the foot of a large rock which seemed to tower above us. The ladder was fixed, and up went the officers, the men following in file, till we found ourselves assembled on the top of a large rock, with no room to spare, and what looked like the top of the mountain about eighteen feet above us. The ladders, which were passed up and placed against the side, unfortunately were found short of the top by about four feet. Lieutenant M'Mullen held the ladder, and Lieutenant Sprenger, not to be beaten, mounted up with a carbine in his right hand. On reaching the top of the ladder, he raised his head and looked over the edge. We saw his carbine go up held at arm's length; then a shot rang out, and a body came toppling over, just missed the ladder, and ricochetted off the stone we were standing on, falling a hundred or more feet below us. Lieutenant Sprenger then dragged himself up on to the top, and, bending down, dragged a sergeant up, who in his turn assisted another man up. In the space of a minute twenty of us were standing on the edge of the mountain. Shots were now coming in all directions from the front of the mountain, and the surprise was complete.

The C.M.R. and native levies pressed on the front face, and the rebels, being taken on their flank, broke away to the side of the mountain overlooking the river. We advanced in line across the mountain, being joined by men from the front face, and made a clean sweep of the enemy, shooting at every man we saw. In one hour from Lieutenant Sprenger's first shot the mountain was captured. Only a slight resistance from one cave on the mountain overlooking the river was made, and in this brief time all the Baphutis had been either killed by our men, or dashed to pieces in attempting to escape. Our luck

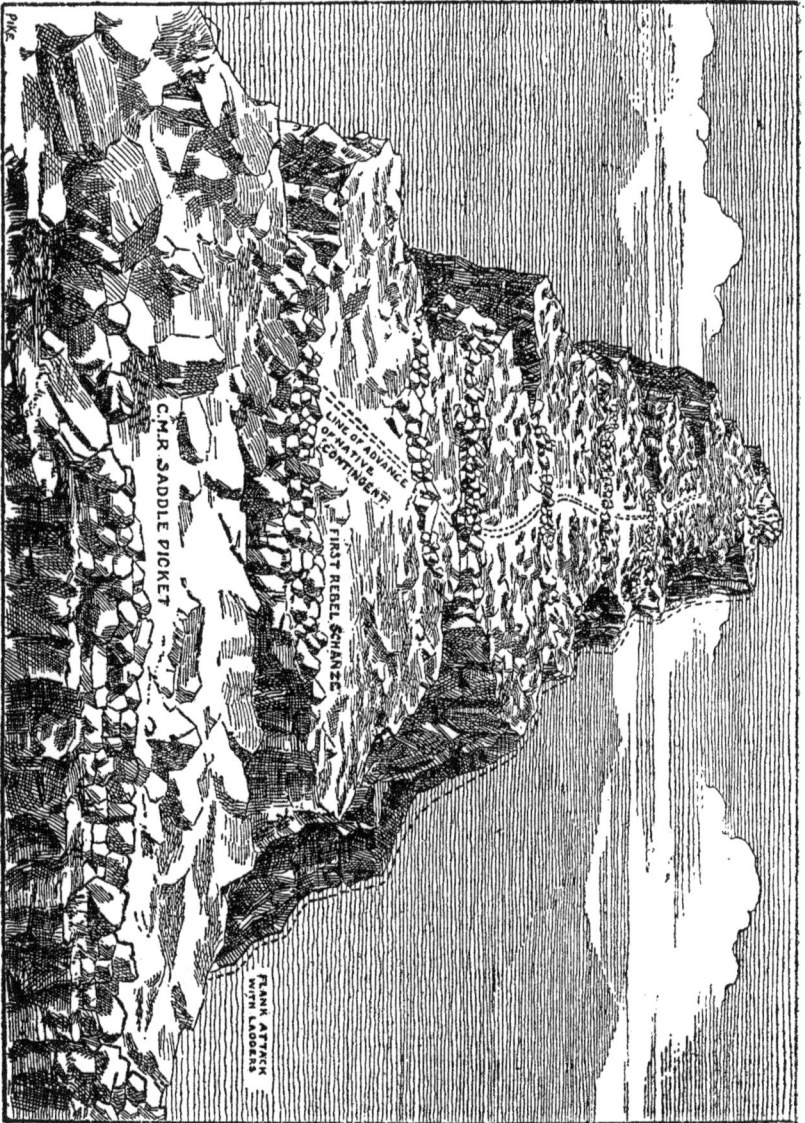

STORMING OF MOIROSI'S MOUNTAIN.

C.M.R. SADDLE PICKET

LINE OF ADVANCE
OF NATIVE
CONTINGENT

FIRST REBEL SCHANZE

FLANK ATTACK
WITH LADDERS

was the happy shot by Lieutenant Sprenger which had killed the sentry, who had probably been asleep.

Moirosi and five of his sons were killed, but his youngest son, Dodo, escaped by jumping over the side. Moirosi himself was shot by Private Whitehead, No. 1 Troop, who had his own cap shot through in doing so. The body was identified by a man named Nevile of the Border Guard who knew Moirosi well, and for this service he was handsomely paid, for he received the two hundred pounds reward which had been offered for Moirosi dead or alive. Whitehead received twenty-five pounds for shooting him—an odd division of profits!

Later examination showed that Moirosi's Mountain was indeed an impregnable fortress which could never have been taken except by a surprise. Behind the huge rock which we called the Crown was built quite a large village of stone huts, all completely under cover, whilst innumerable caves around the inside of the rock, the mouths of which were covered over with dried hides, made them perfectly safe retreats for the natives. Along the top a perfect plateau of green grass gave enough pasture to feed hundreds of sheep, goats, and oxen.

Loud cheering and waving of hats greeted Colonel Bayly as he arrived breathless at the top, after having walked up the front. Too full of emotion for words, he gave the men of the regiment a look which was quite sufficient reward for them, and was remembered by us for years. By this victory he had walked straight into the hearts of the regiment. He also earned the gratitude and praise of the whole of the Cape Colony by the capture of Moirosi's stronghold, which had defied all the efforts of other men for nine months; for he had planned and executed it, with the loss of only three men wounded, in a single night.

Soon dispatch riders were saddled up and off as hard as they could ride for Aliwal North, the nearest telegraph station, and soon the news was dispatched to Cape Town which roused the whole Colony: "Mountain a molehill — Union Jack flying from the Crown." Thus ended a troublesome rebellion which had worried the Government for nine months.

Lieutenant Sprenger was promoted to be captain on the spot, and several promotions were made. For helping to carry the scaling ladders, several of the troopers received small gratuities of money. I was among the fortunate ones.

Strong picquets of natives were left on the mountain, and we returned to camp, down the front, destroying as we passed the several rows of schanzes which covered every path and approach on the front face, and so on to our old picquet ground on the saddle, where we levelled everything in the shape of shelter, and finally returned to camp amid cheers from the artillery troop and details left to guard the camp in our absence. Here we discussed the night's exciting adventures over our breakfasts, but the discussion did not affect our appetites. Wagons which had been outside the camps were allowed in, and bottled beer was retailed at four shillings a bottle, and spirits in proportion. But no one grumbled, and all restraint being thrown off, the men were able to do themselves well, as a great number of them had been unable to spend their cattle money which they had received some months before. My troop especially was in clover, as we had drawn much more than any other troop, each man receiving twenty-five pounds a share, N.C.O.'s three shares, lieutenants five, and a captain seven.

The amount of bottled beer these old stagers put away, over their parties of Nap, was to my inexperienced eyes wonderful to behold. They were generous too, these old veterans, and many a tin of preserved fruit, plum pudding, or potted meat found its way into my tent, with an "It will do for the youngster" as a sort of excuse for their generosity.

For the next week patrols were the order of the day, and every cave along the Orange River was visited where a stray refugee might have hidden. But not a sign of life was visible anywhere, and it was in a cave seven miles away that the unfortunate Dodo, the last of the Moirosi race, was found dying of wounds caused through the tremendous leap for liberty down the side of the mountain. He had broken his thigh in escaping, and how the poor wretch ever reached the distant spot where he was found was a mystery to us, and remains so to me yet.

Colonel Bayly, with the newly created Captain Sprenger and a crowd of smart staff-officers and N.C.O.'s, started off for King William's Town, where the headquarters were to be once more, and the other troops got the route. No. 2 Troop remained at the Buffalo River for some time, No. 4 returned to their old station at Palmietfontein, artillery and head-quarters troop men for King William's Town, whilst the remainder, taking with them pack oxen to carry all their possessions on, were ordered to cross the double range of the Drakensberg Mountains and proceed to Griqualand East, where the process of re-forming the regiment into two wings was to be carried out. The right wing consisted of half the regiment under command of Colonel Bayly with headquarters at King William's Town, and was composed of Nos. 6, 7, 8, 9 Troops and headquarter troop; the left wing, under Colonel

F. Carrington of the 24th Regiment, with headquarters in East Griqualand, consisted of the remainder of the troops, namely, Nos. 1, 2, 3, 4, 5.   The right wing occupied most of the old stations in Cape Colony and Transkei; the left wing, Kokstad and various stations in East Griqualand.

SCENE OF MOIROSI'S DEATH.

CHAPTER VI.

MOUNTED MEN TREK ACROSS THE DRAKENSBERG MOUNTAINS — REMAIN
WITH WAGONS TO TRAVEL BY ROAD—LEAVE WAGONS AND RIDE TO
DORDRECHT — NEWS OF MY LOST HORSE — OVERTAKE WAGONS AT
MACLEAR—ARRIVE AT KOKSTAD—KOKSTAD IN 1879—GRIQUA DANCE
—REJOIN TROOP AT FORT DONALD.

THERE was a scene of great bustle at the foot of Moirosi's
Mountain when the troops paraded for their march.
The pack bullocks, led by Basuto boys from whom the animals
had been hired, were a very novel sight to the uninitiated.
Great unwieldy animals, each with a rein fastened to a ring
through his nose, and easily managed by a small conductor,
they carried large loads, some laden with boxes full of
ammunition, others carrying tents and blankets, cooking
utensils, rations, grain for horses, and every necessary required
for a week's march. The columns start, the men dismount,
leading their troop horses up the sides of the mountains
opposite Moirosi's old stronghold, very cheerful at the prospect
of getting back to civilisation, from which they have so long
been strangers, and making light of the difficulties which lie
in front of them and the large range of mountains covered in
snow through which they will have to pass before descending
the other side, hundreds of miles distant, to East Griqualand.

I was left behind together with some other dismounted
men of the various troops, our orders being to accompany the
convoy of wagons, which carried all the heavy baggage of the

column, office records, etc., and the spare kits of the mounted men—and proceed by road passing close under the mountains of the Drakensberg range, our destination being Kokstad, the then most eastern town of the Cape Colony and not far from the borders of Natal.   Altogether we had to look forward to a journey of, roughly speaking, three hundred miles, travelling at the rate of two miles an hour, and liable to be held up by drifts, swollen rivers, and the hundred and one little incidents that tend to make a long trek with wagons the most undesirable experience of life in South Africa.

The wagons were drawn up together where the remains of the old headquarter camp stood, and we foregathered round them and took stock of one another.   There were about fifty of us all told, and, as on my former trek up the mountain, there was no officer in command.   There were several sergeants, but from that day to this I do not know who was in charge.   The N.C.O.'s and men of different troop kept to their respective wagons, and trekked and outspanned according to the whim of the conductor.

We remained for one night at Moirosi's Mountain after the troops had left, and a disconsolate lot we must have looked. The place was fearfully lonely for a handful of men.   The old mountain, with its dismantled schanzes and general forlorn look, standing straight up against the sky, no living thing to be seen or heard, and occasionally the blood-curdling cry of some Kaffir mongrel which had escaped a bayonet thrust or a bullet, and was wandering around the mountain looking for a master who was not.   The howling of a dog at night is never a cheerful sound, but heard under the conditions I have indicated it is ghostly and depressing.   The whole scene was decidedly jumpy, and we got together unconsciously for mutual support.

Altogether it was the most miserable evening I ever remember spending in the country.

It was a great relief to us all when we started at daybreak next morning on our journey. We made up to No. 1 Troop encamped at the Buffalo River. They had the unenviable duty of remaining in that forsaken part of the country for some months at least, to prevent any rebel natives returning to their old haunts, and to capture any waifs or strays who might be found wandering among the mountains trying to escape across the river into Basutoland.

Moirosi's district remains to this day a deserted country, and the mountain a silent witness to a memorable struggle and a warning to other tribes against the futility of defying the British Government.

We passed Thomas' Shop, and had a look at the wounded men in hospital. They were all doing well, except one who had been shot in the head, and even he eventually recovered and lived to receive a pension. We next got on to Palmietfontein, where No. 4 Troop had already arrived and shaken themselves down into their quarters, and spent the night there. We had now settled down to our journey and were doing very good trekking, and the time passed fairly pleasantly. There were about six horses with us, the owners of which were unable to ride owing to various ailments, so being a light weight I was often asked by these men to ride their horses for a bit. I was very pleased to do so, as it varied the monotony considerably, riding off to farmhouses or Kaffir kraals to buy eggs, vegetables, and so on for the mess.

Shortly after turning off the road on which we had travelled up, to take up our new line of country round the mountains, a sergeant troop clerk, and in charge of our weapons, told me he was going to ride into Dordrecht, and asked me if I would like to go with him.   As I was anxious to find if there was any news of my lost horse, I jumped at the offer, and, having the pick of three horses to ride, I selected one and off we rode.   We arrived at Dordrecht and put up at the hotel kept by an ex-Policeman, and at that time the best one in the place.

I went to the Magistrates' Court, and was told that my horse had been found and put in the pound, but had been handed over to Sergeant ——, who was passing through the town *en route* to King William's Town, where he had gone to receive his commission.   It was the same sergeant who had come up with my detachment and whom Frank had so unceremoniously bucked off *en route*, who had now been promoted to lieutenant.   I received the horse about four months afterwards, when he was brought to Fort Donald by a batch of recruits from King William's Town.

We found Dordrecht full of people.   The men of the Northern Border Guard, who chiefly came from the district, had lately returned from the mountain, and been received with open arms by the inhabitants, and they were having a royal time of it.   We met them everywhere, and heard nothing else from morning till night but how they had taken Moirosi's Mountain, "assisted" of course by the C.M.R.   "Assisted" struck us as pretty cool.

The man who had found Moirosi's body was the hero of the day, and was rapidly approaching the stage when one sees things generally associated with a zoo.   Sergeant —— met many old friends, and was—to use his own expression—"Doing himself proud," and insisted on my joining in.   Altogether we spent a very enjoyable week of it.   At last either funds getting low or a sense of duty made Sergeant —— remember that there was a wagon full of troop office records—equipments, etc.—somewhere on the road between Dordrecht and Kokstad, and that it would be advisable for us to get into touch with it again. So one morning, after good-byes with chums and affecting farewells with some young ladies, we rode off after the wagons.

If you want to find out how quickly the South African trek-ox wagon can get over the ground, do as we did—give it a week's fair start and then try to overtake it. It seemed as if we were never going to catch up to our wagons. After a good day's ride we would arrive at a wayside store to be told that the wagons had passed so many days before, and it was not till we arrived opposite the Calbey, after three days' ride, that we were told that they had passed the evening before, and we would probably catch them up at Maclear. We stayed at Calbey Store that afternoon and night, and there we met for the first time the owner, the redoubtable John Bull. This man was quite a character in his way, and not least in appearance. He had a very large body, and head to match, with stunted legs; and if you saw him seated at a table telling some of his yarns you would have imagined that he was a very big man. To see him quietly slip off his seat and walk round the table at the same height from the ground made one feel inclined to rub one's eyes and look again. The effect was uncanny. This was my first meeting with John Bull, but it was by no means the last—as will be seen later.

There were only about two rooms in the house besides the storeroom, and as the rooms seemed full of four or five off-coloured children, the progeny of John Bull and his native wife, Sergeant —— and myself had to enter the store, after a

6

dinner of sardines and biscuits—the only edible things to be bought in his shop.   Mr. Bull at our invitation joined us, and the hospitality opened his heart and made him produce a bottle of Dop brandy—commonly called "Cape Smoke"—of which he asked us to have a drink, it being Christmas Day. The smell of the stuff was awful, and even Sergeant ——, acclimatised as he was, shied at it and refused.   So Bull made his vrow (wife) make us some coffee; it tasted burnt, but it was better than the awful stuff Mr. Bull kept drinking. Besides having a vile smell its effects were potent, and in a while Mr. Bull was very drunk and very noisy.   Finally, he was dragged out of the store into one of the rooms by his vrow, assisted by two or three native hangers-on; and Sergeant —— and I, pulling all the available blankets we could see out of the shelves, made our beds on the counter and slept till morning.

I often think of my first Christmas in South Africa, and it brings to my mind John Bull and many others like him whom I have met, living out their lives in isolated spots, tied to black women, impossible to shake off, and their descendants; growing up a curse to themselves and every one else—avoided by white men and looked down upon by black.   It makes one think with irony and some anger of the sentimentalists in the old country who prate on platforms and in the newspapers about a united South Africa whilst such a state of things exists.

Next morning we made an early start, and after passing Ugie—then a place with one store, now a decent little village with a railway—we caught the wagons up at Maclear, a small village situated between hills, at the foot of the Drakensberg Mountains.

Since leaving Dordrecht we had travelled at the foot of this magnificent range, which is supposed to stretch right across South Africa. The various mountains rise to various heights, and are all connected. There are several passes or neks over these mountains, the best known and really only wagon road being Barkly Pass, leading into the Barkly East District; the others generally consist of bridle-paths, and are used chiefly by Basutos and speculators or dealers in cattle who cross the mountains into Basutoland, purchase cattle from natives, and drive them back to the various markets. Natal draws its supplies to a great extent from these agencies, who often amass small fortunes in a few years.

The whole range presents a very grand appearance, some of the tops looking like old castles, where they have been worn by time and rain. The slopes afford excellent pasturage and shelter for sheep, goats, and cattle—at that time not very numerous, and at the present time they are all laid out in farms occupied by a good class of farmer, who, after some years of uphill work, become wealthy and prosperous. At the present moment the East Griqualand farmer is the most progressive and flourishing person, and probably the most British, to be found in South Africa.

We found that everything had gone on smoothly during the time we had been absent, and there had been no break-downs. Probably this was due to the fact that the white conductors accompanied their own wagons, and did not leave all their driving to their native drivers—who on arriving at some spot where there is a chance of native beer-drinking are not above breaking a dissel-boom to force a stay. This is a huge pole to which the two hind, or after, oxen are attached, and it can easily be broken by a skilful driver if he wishes to, in the hundreds of holes and bad drifts which occur along the road.

No incident occurred during the rest of the trek of about a hundred and twenty odd miles from Maclear to Kokstad, and at last we arrived at the future headquarters of the left wing C.M.R., then a purely Griqua village with a couple of hotels and five or six stores.

The town had been founded by Adam Kok, a Griqua who had travelled over the mountains from Griqualand West with his following some years previously, and had been given grants of land for farming purposes; Adam Kok settling where the present town, which is called after him, is situated. When the C.M.R. arrived from Moirosi's Mountain the town was composed of three streets,—the principal one, Main Street, containing two hotels. The Post Office is on the site of Adam Kok's house, and a monument to his memory is to be seen at the present time in the garden between two streets.

The Griquas are not as numerous as they were, and as a tribe are fast dying out in East Griqualand. In colour they are quite light, and the girls have long hair, and when young are, generally speaking, quite good-looking. They are supposed to have descended from a mixed Dutch and Hottentot breed; their language is Dutch, but they are equally conversant with English, and can swear with facility in either. Dutch being more impressive in its variety of scum words, they generally use that language for choice.

On arrival with the wagons, we outspanned below the magazine, and walked up to the camp, which was composed of bell tents pitched on a flat piece of ground close to the magazine, and where we found No. 1 Troop had been stationed. We soon heard the account of the march across the mountains to

Kokstad, which had been a very trying one. Not a man had mounted his horse till they arrived on the flats on the East Griqualand side, about fifty miles from Kokstad, to which they had pushed on as fast as possible. On the evening of their arrival there had been a great jollification in the town. This took place at the various Griqua shanties then forming the main street; the men taking liquor with them, treating the Griqua men, and dancing with the girls, a great institution in those days. Imagine a small square-built house with one large room in it, and two or three poky little dens leading off it, all with mud floors hardened with cow-dung, and you have the Griqualand shanty of '79. A wizened-looking object in the shape of an old man is perched up on a table pushed into a corner, playing on an accordion the one and only tune to which they dance, keeping time by stamping and singing the refrain in Dutch—the only words recognisable being, "I love the C.M.R.," etc.

There are half a dozen mad young fellows, and the same number of Griqua girls, hopping round keeping time to the hideous music. The Griqua men and old women sit outside or lean against the wall, drinking and scowling at the merry couples —the young Griqua man watching with jealous eyes his best girl being made violent love to by an amorous C.M.R. private, or some young shop assistant out on the spree, before his face. At last he thinks it time to interfere with the love-making, and gets snubbed by the girl for his pains; then, losing control of himself, he insults the white man, and gets promptly knocked down. A general fight then takes place, which generally terminates the ball.

On this particular night—either through this cause, or through men of different troops clashing at some dance—about midnight there was an alarm of fire in the town, and before it could be put out nearly the whole of the main street of Griqua shanties had been burnt down, and the greatest disorder prevailed all over the place.   Picquets were sent from the different troops, men were all ordered to their respective camps, and three or four troops were made to saddle up on the spot, and were taken by their officers some three miles out of the town across the river, there to wait till morning.   There was an inquiry by the magistrate and the officers, but the origin of the fire and riot was never discovered.

The troops belonging to the right wing—Nos. 6, 7, 8, 9— had been ordered off the next day to Umtata, in the Transkei, and Nos. 3 and 5 had been sent to Fort Donald, a station on the Pondoland border, and the worst station in the regiment, situated about eighteen miles from Kokstad.

These were the news that Paddy Faulkner retailed to me as we sat in his tent discussing breakfast the morning of our arrival.   Further, he informed me that our new colonel was expected shortly, together with an adjutant from the Imperial Service; that my old captain had handed over No. 3 Troop to Lieutenant Mac, and was to become quartermaster of the left wing; that a large batch of recruits were on the march from King William's Town with new officers; that a batch of the 17th Lancers had been transferred to the regiment as drill instructors; that shortly we would all be made to sit up; life wouldn't be worth living; all the old hands would be leaving; finally, that, in Paddy's opinion, the regiment would become a lot of damned soldiers, and he was hanged if he was going to stay a moment after his time expired.   He was surprised when I expressed my satisfaction at the coming changes, and asked why I had come to the country if I wanted to be a Tommy? Why hadn't I enlisted at home and walked about with slaveys, etc.?

However, he soon recovered his good temper, and promised to take me down town in the evening, after he had got through his duties for the day. I had to start with the No. 3 Troop wagons on the following morning, and had nothing to do but clean myself and have a look round the place. I walked up to the magazine, which was built on a small ridge of rocks and commanded a view of the town. It was a new building of brick and stone surrounded by a sod wall with one entrance, at which was a sentry, who—a sign of the times—was sitting on a wall with his carbine leaning up against it. I would have pitied the man found in the same attitude three months later. But the old Police methods had not yet died out, and a regimental sergeant-major was then a thing unknown. The sentry appeared pleased to see me, and informed me that the new magazine was on the site of the one blown up during the Griqua rebellion of eighteen months before.

The rebellion had been a shortlived one. No. 2 Troop went out to the laager at Mount Currie and fairly charged the Griquas out of it, killing a good many, the remainder dispersing and hiding in the surrounding hills. It was during this fight that the magazine blew up, the ammunition boxes flying in all directions and doing a lot of damage amongst the unfortunate women and children who were under the walls, killing one of the daughters of the chief magistrate.

Since then the new magazine had been built, and from it I looked down the town, and saw the long line of street with the ruins of the burnt houses, and the rest of the town with a fine river running below it called the Umzimsulava. Beyond it were blue mountains called the Ingeli, with large forests on the sides; a great treat for the eyes after the stony, barren country we had just come from.

That evening Faulkner and I went down the town and visited the hotel, then, as at present, the only place to go to in Kokstad of an evening, and met a good many of the civilians, most of whom were either in the Civil Service or law agents, and had, with very few exceptions, been members of the regiment at some time or another. One of the hotels was kept by an American negro and another by two other coloured persons; but every one seemed hail-fellow-well-met, and, judging by the amount of liquor every one seemed to imbibe, the business must have been a very thriving one. I did not see very much of the Griquas on that occasion, as they were rather shy of the C.M.R. after the recent disturbance, and kept in their shanties, which it was inadvisable to visit.

The next morning we all parted on crossing the river, the wagons and men of Nos. 6, 7, and 9 going the Umtata road, and those of Nos. 3 and 5 by the old road past Usher's Farm to Fort Donald, which place we succeeded in reaching late that night. The next day I was able to have a good look at the surroundings of my new station.

CHAPTER VII.

FORT DONALD, 1880—OLD HANDS TAKE THEIR DISCHARGES—ARRIVAL OF
RECRUITS—UNDESIRABLES IN THE REGIMENT—COLONEL CARRINGTON
ARRIVES AND |TAKES COMMAND OF LEFT WING C.M.R.—OUR NEW
CAPTAIN—AM SENT TO NATAL ON ESCORT DUTY—IMPRESSIONS OF
NATAL—RETURN TO KOKSTAD—AM PROMOTED CORPORAL—SERGEANT
TRIPPLER COMES TO GRIEF—AM PROMOTED SERGEANT.

FORT DONALD was situated on the Kokstad side of the
Spitzkop, a high hill sloping to a point—hence the name.
The fort was built of sods and in square formation, with a few
huts inside which were used for officers' quarters, office hut,
and storerooms. On a nek stretching towards a large forest
two rows of Kaffir huts had been built. These were made
of wattles plaited together and covered with mud, and
called " wattle and daub huts." Prior to the arrival of the
two troops, the station had been occupied by native levies,
which had now been disbanded and had returned to their
kraals. As can be imagined, the huts were not fit for white
men to go into, and the troop was under canvas whilst the
old huts were being destroyed and new ones rebuilt.

Fort Donald has always had the reputation, and justly,
of being the most undesirable station in the C.M.R. It is
situated in a high part of the country, almost level with the
top of the Ingeli Mountains, which stretch along the valley
between it and Kokstad to the Natal border. The natives
in the district ·are called Xesibes, and their country adjoins

Pondoland, then an independent tribe and a very insolent one. The Pondoland border was about six miles from Fort Donald, and for about eight months in the year the country for about five miles round the Spitzkop was enveloped in a dense fog or mist, and was a very difficult country to find one's way about in. The roads were old sleigh roads, leading towards the bush, where poles for fencing and wood for burning purposes were procured from the sawyers, who were chiefly Griquas who had huts in the bush. These cross tracks made it very difficult to keep in the right road leading from Pondoland through Fort Donald to Kokstad. The fog was so dense, it was impossible to see more than a yard or two in front of your horse's head; and once off the right road, it was next to an impossibility to regain it. Dispatch riders—men told off to carry the post or official letters—were sometimes lost for ten or twelve hours at a time, and were eventually led into the camp by natives whom they had met by chance in their wanderings. This sort of thing was daily happening when we arrived, and we were thought very lucky to have got a fine day for our trek out.

I found that nearly the whole of my troop, No. 3, and a great number of No. 5, were awaiting their discharges from King William's Town to make them free men, and these were expected by every post. These men had ceased to do duty, and simply loafed about the tents, swearing at the delay and weather.

The troops, therefore, being very short-handed, were awaiting the arrival of recruits from King William's Town, and also, it was rumoured, a number of men who had been enlisted for the regiment in Natal,—ex-irregulars from Sekikuni's campaign, who had served there under General Carrington,—

who were expected to arrive with them. In the meantime only horse guard and camp guard were being furnished, and there were no parades.

The rain came down on our first afternoon, accompanied by a heavy mist, which soaked through everything both inside and outside of the tents. It was some days before we saw more than two tents at a time in any one direction. Stables were a farce; the horses, as many of them as the guard could find, were driven in the direction of the camp, which was only to be found by shouting to one another. These were fed and turned loose into a brushwood kraal, a few poles thrown across for a gate, and the animals left to themselves for the night, nobody troubling about the absentees till the next clear day, when men would be told off to go and look for them. They were generally found huddled up against a bush in a hollow not far from the camp.

Shortly after our arrival with the wagons at Fort Donald, the discharges of the time-expired men arrived, and there was a great farewell evening in the canteen, a large wattle and daub oblong hut kept by two civilians, who had also been Policemen. The difficulty experienced by the majority in finding their way home from the end of the camp, where the canteen was situated, to their respective tents in the dense fog and rain, caused a good many to wander wide of the mark and get stranded in the veldt for the night, and it was late in the following day when the whole lot of them rode off on their way to Kokstad as civilians.

We were left with about eighteen men per troop for nearly a month, when over a hundred men came *viâ* Kokstad from Natal. These men were nearly all posted to No. 5 Troop, which was made up to a hundred strong, the balance coming to No. 3. With them came Captain Shervinton, to take the vacant command of my troop. He was the very beau-ideal of a soldier, and had seen service in the Gaika and Galeka War, also in Zululand the previous year. He was a splendid horseman, a good all-round athlete, and a very good drill, and under his command the conditions at Fort Donald altered considerably.

The men who had been recruited in Natal were without exception the biggest lot of blackguards I have ever seen. If they were fair samples of the irregular forces engaged in Sekikuni's war, the officer commanding must have been terribly handicapped. They arrived drunk, more or less, and roamed about the camp, cursing and swearing at every one they met who didn't belong to their particular gang. The guard hut was constantly full of them, but no punishment seemed to deter them from getting drunk again, stealing liquor from the canteen, and fighting amongst themselves day and night. When they could get no liquor, they wandered off and got lost in the fog, till found by natives and brought back to camp. They refused to do duty, and there were not enough men in our troop to cope with them when they broke out of the guardroom. The whole state of the place was sickening to contemplate.

Colonel Carrington had arrived in Kokstad by this time, and, being informed of the state of affairs, did the only thing possible under the circumstances. The men who were charged with an offence were handed their discharges at once, their uniforms taken from them, and they were literally kicked out of camp. Within three months there were only about ten of the whole batch left in the regiment; and the Colony had learned a lesson in recruiting waifs and strays from other

Colonies. For the future, except in rare instances, recruits were brought from England, and the men began to be composed of the class that made the name of the C.M.R. renowned in the British Empire. But this was not done in a day, and it was six months before the left wing began to show signs of what it eventually proved to be—an efficient, highly disciplined regiment.

Some three hundred men having arrived in Kokstad from England, all young English recruits, the necessary number of them were sent out to Fort Donald to make the garrison up to strength. On the arrival of the batch of recruits for my troop, No. 3, I found that my old horse was with them, having been forwarded from King William's Town. I was delighted at once more becoming mounted. My horse looked very fit, and I was told that he had become quite the old trooper, and had been ridden the whole way up country.

A newly promoted lieutenant also joined. So we were now complete—one captain, two subalterns, and one hundred N.C.O.'s and men. Captain Shervinton lost no time in making us as efficient as possible; and considering the awful climate, the incessant wet—not rain, but a soaking mist, which made it impossible to keep anything dry or clean—the progress made was little short of marvellous. Riding school was in all weathers, in the open veldt, with horses slipping all over the place. There were many falls, but the young hands soon began to show signs of improvement, and when the troop marched into Kokstad in June it was no discredit to the headquarter men.

Shortly after the arrival of Captain Shervinton to command my troop I was promoted to first-class private, the wholesale discharge of the old hands in the troop having

created many vacancies; I had also been recommended by
our lieutenant at the time for the rank of corporal, but this
recommendation had been refused on the grounds that I was
too young, and a minute to that effect sent by the acting
adjutant, Kokstad.   I was told by my old friend, Sergeant
——, who had control of the troop office, that Captain
Shervinton had been enraged at the refusal and the reason,
and had told Sergeant —— that he would see the colonel on
the subject the next time he went to Kokstad.

About this time a sergeant in my troop, who was proceeding to England on six months' leave *viâ* Natal, recognised a
deserter from the troop in Durban, and had him arrested.   A
wire had been sent asking for an escort to proceed to Natal
to bring the prisoner back.   Sergeant —— volunteered to
go as the N.C.O., and I was ordered to accompany him; and
glad I was of the opportunity of getting rid of the eternal
mist, and of seeing something of Natal, as, with the exception
of a short stay in Durban, I had not seen the country.

We rode into Kokstad, and from there, proceeding along
the post-cart road *viâ* Richmond, eventually reached Maritzburg, the abbreviated name for Pietermaritzburg.   We stayed
there for a week, and thence went on to Durban, over
very hilly country, but a great contrast to Moirosi's
country.   In Natal everything was green; the fields and
trees looked familiar and more like the old country than
any other place I had as yet seen.   The people of the country
were very hospitable, and the uniform we wore was passport
anywhere.   We had discarded the old velvet corduroy coat
and pants, and the regiment was now clothed in a dark blue
jacket with black braid for bordering, black Bedford cord
riding breeches, well fitting top-boots with regulation cavalry

spurs, and white helmet with brass spike and chain, and a round cavalry forage cap when not wearing the helmet. N.C.O.'s wore silver chevrons on both arms in the left wing, and on the right arm only in the right wing, and their jackets were braided across the front, and looked very smart. I wore a single silver strip above the cuff on my left arm to denote first-class private, and very proud of it I was ; a revolver slung over my right shoulder denoted on duty.

On nearing Durban we came in sight of the sea, and felt the emotions which most Englishmen experience on seeing the sea after a long absence. We passed through Pine Town, where the 6th Enniskillen Dragoons was stationed, a lovely spot, with gardens and luxuriant foliage, wild plantains and bananas growing everywhere, and smart, comfortable-looking villas dotted about the various hills right on to Durban. Durban was then rather a straggling town, built below the hills, and stretching down to the sea—only a few houses were built on the Berea (the hill at the back of the town) where now there are numberless palatial residences.

We put up at the Prince of Wales' Hotel, then quite the largest in Durban, but now one of the smallest, although it has been considerably enlarged since my first visit. We were delayed a week by the authorities before our prisoner was finally handed over to us, and during this time we enjoyed ourselves immensely. We were treated most kindly by the inhabitants, who seemed to have a regard for the old Colony Police as they called us, and we met a number of people who had lived in the Cape, and were never tired of asking after people whom they thought we ought to know.

When our prisoner was handed over to us, we mounted him on a spare pony of Sergeant ——, and started on our return journey to Kokstad. I found that our man had been some years in No. 3 Troop, and was a friend of Sergeant ——; that his time had expired some months before he was ordered up with the troop to Moirosi's Mountain. When he found that he could not get his discharge, he had taken it himself, and had now laid himself open to be tried for desertion in the face of the enemy—a very serious charge even in the old days of Police, but much more so since the regiment had altered to C.M.R. He appeared very cheerful over it, and denied the right of the present authorities to try him, as he had never been a C.M.R. man. Sergeant —— did not contradict him, and let him remain cheerful, and they appeared to pass the time away agreeably talking about their old adventures together.

When within a day's ride from Kokstad, we saw a man coming in our direction, on tramp, with his blankets rolled over his shoulder. As he approached us, I recognised him as one of the undesirable mob that had joined us from Natal. He had been tried by a board of officers, and received three months' hard labour, to be discharged with ignominy for being drunk on duty. He greeted us with " Hullo, sergeant!" and with a grin to me, "Hullo, corporal!" He informed us that he had got his ticket and was off to Natal to get a ship, and that he would stick to the sea in future and not try soldiering again. He also told us that our troop had left Fort Donald, and was now stationed at Kokstad, and that we were having a bad time of it with the blank Lancer-drill instructors and regimental sergeant-major, and that I had been read out in orders, shortly after I left for Natal, as promoted to corporal. After telling me to watch the blank sergeant-major, he continued his journey.

On our arrival in Kokstad we rode up to the main guard at the magazine and handed over our prisoner, and then made inquiries as to the whereabouts of our troop. We were directed to it by a sentry, who was a striking contrast to the last one I had seen at the same place. This man was marching up and down at the regulation pace, his carbine at the support, the brass fittings on his white helmet glittering, and spurs burnished up to the highest degree. I seemed to see visions of trouble ahead for some of our old hands who had remained in the troop, and thought with what pride some of them had remarked to me only six months before, that they had not. blacked their belts for three years, and didn't intend to, and if I started cleaning my boots and belts and they got into trouble for not doing the same, then I should know about it.

We arrived at our camp, which had been pitched on the veldt above the magazine, and about a quarter of a mile away from the depôt troop, who had huts built for them below the magazine; we were out of sight of them, for which we often had cause to be thankful. The troop had left Fort Donald about a fortnight before, and, as we had been informed on the road, had evidently had a bad time of it. The whole troop seemed on the jump, and I was not long in finding out the reason. I was told by our acting sergeant-major that I was a corporal, and to look sharp and get the stripes up before the regimental saw me, or else there would be no need for me to put them up, as I would be made a prisoner by him at once.

Our old sergeant-major had taken his discharge some three months before, and the next senior sergeant was made acting.

7

Sergeant Trippler, so named from his peculiar gait resembling the "tripple," or walk, of a Dutchman, told me that I was in charge of a certain tent, and responsible for the good conduct of the occupants. He would have proceeded to give me my whole routine of duties if I hadn't suggested that my horse wanted off-saddling, when he let me go, telling me to come to his tent afterwards and he would give me the chevrons he had drawn for me out of the quartermaster's store.

I went to the tent which I had been told off to, and a couple of smart good-looking youngsters jumped out, and, taking my horse, off-saddled it, and one of them led it off to the troop, while the other brought my saddle inside, and asked where I intended sleeping. I chose the middle, facing the door, and my saddle was placed there pending my getting the remainder of my kit, which had been placed in troop store on my departure for Natal.

I then went and interviewed Sergeant Trippler, who gave me my kit from the troop store, and two sets of corporal's stripes. He proceeded to impress the various duties of a corporal upon me, and warned me of the pitfalls and traps that awaited me from the staff of the depôt troop, who, as I could gather from him, had been amusing themselves at his expense. There was no doubt that he was in mortal dread of the "regimental," and imagined that he had been appointed to that position for the sole purpose of pulverising No. 3 Troop, and Sergeant Trippler in particular. If any N.C.O. of the troop did anything he thought right, the regimental said it was wrong, and if he did anything wrong he was made a prisoner on the spot. All this was not very reassuring, but I had not known Sergeant Trippler for nine months for nothing. I knew him to be a nagging incompetent sort of man, trying to justify his appointment as sergeant-major in order to have it confirmed; always interfering with the N.C.O.'s in the performance of their duties, giving contradictory orders, and allowing the blame to rest upon the unfortunate man who had listened to him, if they should be wrong, as they invariably were.

In appearance he was not at all the type usually associated with the sergeant-major of a troop. He was very short, with bandy legs, a large head with sandy hair, a high-pitched voice, round shoulders, and when in uniform looked all helmet and top-boots. His incessant nagging manner of addressing the men, such as, "Now then, that 'ere man"—"What are yer doin' of?" was enough to drive any man to an act of insubordination, and I thought it quite probable that the regimental had also taken his measure, and that Trippler's fears for himself might be justified.

There were seven men in the tent besides myself, so we were not crowded. I found that there was one old hand and six of the recruits who had joined us at Fort Donald prior to my leaving for Natal. They were a very nice lot of young fellows, all about my own age, and seemed determined to keep in my good books. During my short stay with them, they never gave me the slightest trouble, and did all in their power to make the tent the show one of the troop.

The old hand laid hands on my cloth and serge jackets and sewed my stripes on for me. It was none too soon, for whilst enjoying what I considered a well-earned rest, the strident voice of Sergeant Trippler was heard at the door of my tent. "Now then, corporal, there ain't so many on yer that yer can sleep in the day! Git down to the depôt and take the orders —which 'as been soundin' for the last 'arf-hour."

I replied that it was the call for orderly sergeant he had heard, and that I was not aware that I was on duty, as I had only returned two hours before from a journey. He informed me that there were only four corporals, two were on guard, and the third one, who was the orderly corporal, he had sent on a message to the quartermaster's store, so I must go, and as soon as possible, and take my notebook, for although I knew it was the Orderly N.C.O.'s call, he knew better, and it was for orders. So I let him have his way, and dressed myself in overalls, jacket, and forage cap, and proceeded towards the depôt troop lines, to face the dreaded regimental.

I remember these incidents vividly, and have written them for the purpose of showing the great change that had taken place in the regiment since I was last in Kokstad, a few months before—also that an N.C.O. who had hitherto been considered smart at his work as a Policeman, was utterly unfit to hold the same position in the regiment that it had now become, and was even a great handicap to his juniors, who, but for his ignorant interference, would have been able to acquire the necessary knowledge in a much easier manner.

On reaching the depôt lines I was struck with the number of new faces, nearly all N.C.O.'s who were bustling about the square; and the squads of men undergoing carbine and foot drill at the hands of instructors, who apparently knew their business, was a revelation to me. I had determined, however, that although I might look young I was not going to be considered a fool, so I inquired of a sergeant I met the whereabouts of the regimental. He replied sharply, "In his hut, the first on the right." So to the hut I went.

I went to the door, which was open, and saw a man lying

on his bed smoking, who catching sight of me shouted out, with a slight Irish accent—

"Hullo—what's your name? What do you want? Come in." I went inside the hut, told him my name, and said I wanted the regimental sergeant-major and had been sent for orders. He got up into a sitting position, swung his legs on to the floor, and looked hard at me, saying—

"You belong to No. 3," with an accent on the "you." "Haven't seen you before. Where have you been?" I told him I had arrived that morning with Sergeant Jack from Natal, and had brought a deserter back with us. He then asked why I was going on duty so soon, and where the orderly corporal was, as he had ordered the call to be sounded for all orderlies half an hour before. He then told me to tell Sergeant Trippler to report himself to him at once, and that I could go back to camp and take it easy for a day, and he would see more of me. He thought I would do, and hoped I would get on. I walked back to my camp as quickly as possible, rather pleased with my first interview with the R.S.M. as he was called by the depôt men, and quite realising the reason of Sergeant Trippler's dislike to him.

The Regimental, or Regimental Sergeant-Major Lowther, to give him his full rank and name, was a man then of about thirty years of age and of splendid physique, about five feet ten in height. He was forty-eight inches round the chest and well built, and perhaps the most powerful man I have come across in my service. He had been a gentleman ranker in the R.H.A. and afterwards in the 17th Lancers, from which regiment he had been transferred to the C.M.R. with eleven others. Six had remained with the right wing, and the remainder came on to the left wing. Lowther, which was his service name,

being the senior corporal, had been promoted regimental
sergeant-major straight off, and the others were drill-sergeants
for the present. With the exception of Lowther, who afterwards got his commission in the regiment, and one other who
succeeded him as regimental sergeant-major, and afterwards
obtained a commission in the B.S.A. Police in Matabeleland
and is now a colonel in that part of South Africa, the others
turned out badly, and were all reduced to the ranks in a very
short time, and took their discharges.

Sergeant Trippler turned green when I informed him that
he was to report himself at once to the regimental, but as I
told him I did not know the reason, he took himself off,
after several inquiries as to what had been said to me, and I
returned to my hut. I did not hear for some time what took
place, and then I was told that he had been well slated for
sending the orderly corporal out of camp when it was his
duty to remain there, and also for putting me on duty. It was
a very humble individual who came to my tent and told me I
would not be required for duty till the following evening,
when I was to be in charge of the camp guard.

That evening, after stables, I spent visiting some of my old
friends in No. 1 Troop, and found, much to my sorrow, that
Paddy Faulkner had taken his discharge and was somewhere
in East Griqualand, that over half the old hands had left and
been replaced by recruits, and that the troop was under orders
for the Basuto border and expected to start shortly. This was
news, as I had heard nothing of the dissatisfaction which was
supposed to exist amongst the Basutos, till that evening. I
returned to our camp and sought out Sergeant Jack, who told
me that an Act had recently been passed in Parliament at Cape
Town, called the Disarmament Act, under which all the natives

in the territories of the Cape Colony were bound to hand in to the Magistrates of their district any firearms in their possession by a certain date, and that it was reported that the Basutos had refused to comply with the Act, and that it looked as if trouble were pending. He also confirmed the news that No. 1 would shortly go to Palmietfontein to reinforce No. 4 Troop, till further developments. This caused some excitement in camp, every man being anxious to go on active service.

The men were being kept incessantly at mounted drills, and the recruits at riding school every morning and dismounted drills during the day, the duties on the N.C.O.'s being very severe. Colonel Carrington was very strict on N.C.O.'s and men, reducing the former to the ranks for anything approaching neglect of duty, and punishing the men severely for slight crimes. Captain Shervinton kept our troop up to the mark in every detail, and was particularly keen on trying to make the N.C.O.'s smart and conversant with their duties, a rather hard task with some of them. All had managed to keep their stripes on their arms up till now, in spite of the eagle eye of the regimental, who never lost an opportunity of showing us up, when any mistakes occurred on the numerous parades.

No. 1 Troop marched away very early one morning for Palmietfontein, and we were left alone on the station, with a captain of the depôt recruits, and an opportunity soon arose, of which the regimental took advantage, to settle Sergeant Trippler's aspirations to the rank of sergeant-major. One morning towards the end of stables, I, as troop orderly corporal, gave the customary order: " Men for riding school file off and saddle up," and the men who had not been dismissed from that drill led their horses away to their tents to saddle them up and dress themselves.

Shortly after the stable parade had been dismissed, when the trumpeter was about to sound the fall-in for the ride, a voice was heard from the direction of the depôt lines, shouting out, " Look alive, No. 3—ride." That was enough for Sergeant Trippler, who immediately came fussing up, with a " Now then, why ain't that 'ere ride ready ? " I replied that it was not time, and he ordered me to fall them in.

Fall in sounded at the usual time, and the men paraded, when it was my duty to call the roll, inspect the men, and report correct or otherwise to the acting sergeant-major, who in his turn inspected the men, and then gave the order for the orderly corporal to march them off. Before I had finished calling the roll, the voice again called out, " Look sharp, No. 3." This put the finishing touch to Sergeant Trippler, who came up to me, saying, " Now then, corporal—why the 'ell don't you march them off ? " I replied that the men had not been in-spected, and that we were before the usual time. He then said, " March 'em off, I tell you—or I'll make you a prisoner." I replied, " Very good, sergeant," and marched the men off. On arrival at the depôt ground, I found we were too early, the depôt men were just falling in ; but as the drill instructors were standing about, I went up to the one who usually drilled our ride and reported No. 3 ride all present, and then returned to our camp, stopping on the way at the hut of an old sergeant who was drinking coffee.

He invited me to join him, and, having some time to spare before my next duty, I stayed talking with him a short while and then went on to camp. As I was nearing my tent, one of my brother corporals came up to me and said, " Give me your gun sling, old chap," meaning the gun sling I wore over my shoulder as a sign I was on duty. I asked him what was the matter, and he replied, "Oh, you are on the peg—I don't know what for," so I gave him my sling and duty roll, and he took over my duties.

I returned to my tent wondering what I had left undone, and with inward misgivings as to the result of my interview at 10 a.m. with Colonel Carrington. Judging by the wholesale reductions that had taken place in other troops, he was not likely to make any exception in my favour.

Orderly room at length sounded with the officers' call, and I saw my captain and one of the subalterns walking towards the building, about 100 yards from our camp, where Colonel Carrington and the adjutant had their offices. I fell in on our parade ground in front of the tents, and a corporal took up his position on my right as escort. I then found that I was not the only representative of No. 3 Troop to interview the colonel, for Acting Sergeant-Major Trippler appeared coming from his tent with a sergeant on his right, and I noticed that he too, like myself, was minus his spurs.

We were both marched off to the orderly room, halted, and stood at ease outside. The regimental sergeant-major, with two or three orderly sergeants, came up—the former looking both escort and prisoners up and down, as if trying to see whether he could not put another charge against us for being improperly dressed. Apparently he detected nothing, for he walked on to the adjutant's office and left us standing for some time the centre of all observers, who were no doubt congratulating themselves on not being in our places.

The regimental returned to the doorway and shouted, in

a very loud voice, "Sergeant Trippler, cap off—escort and prisoner, quick march."

In a few minutes I heard "Right about turn—quick march," and looking towards the door I saw my late fellow-prisoner emerging from the orderly room with his stripes in his hand —they had been cut off by the regimental.

This was not encouraging, but I had no time given me to wonder what we had done.

"Corporal—cap off," made me drop my cap in front of me on the ground, and step behind my escort. "Quick march." On entering the room, "Halt—front form," brought me up in front of a desk at which was seated Colonel Carrington, who looked hard at me and then at the crime sheet in front of him. "Corporal charged with parading a dirty ride," he snapped out; "what have you got to say?" I told him I had obeyed orders when I marched the ride off.

The colonel did not seem to listen to what I said, but dipped his pen in the ink, looked up at my captain who was standing at his side, and said, "What sort of a non-commissioned officer is this?" "The best duty N.C.O. in my troop, sir," answered my captain. Colonel Carrington gave a hard look at me again, and said, "Admonished."

"Right about turn!" was shouted in my ear, and out I went with my stripes intact. I picked up my cap, and was walking away when my captain called to me. I returned and saluted, when he said, "Don't let this morning's business worry you. Keep on in the way you are going, and if any more of these damned old Policemen interfere with you in your duty, come straight to me—I will settle them."

That evening, after stables, regimental orders were read out, and amongst them appeared: No. — Sergeant Trippler

reduced from 2nd class sergeant to 1st class private; No. ——
3rd class Sergeant —— promoted to 2nd class sergeant, vice
Trippler reduced; No. —— Corporal —— promoted to 3rd class
sergeant, vice Sergeant —— promoted; and a 1st class private
was promoted to be corporal in my place.

That evening I spent in the sergeants' mess, where I was
welcomed by Sergeant Jack and the sergeants of the troop,
while my jacket was sent off to the regimental tailor to be
braided and have proper chevrons put on the arms. My brief
career as a corporal had indeed ended—but not in the way I
had expected that morning.

Trippler was shortly afterwards reinstated to the bottom
of the list of 3rd class sergeants and transferred to the depôt
troop, where he was made provost sergeant and the general
utility man of the camp. He was no doubt happier in his
department than as a duty N.C.O., for which he was never
fitted.

The next senior sergeant, having been promoted to sergeant-
major, caused another step up all round, and the troop was
now at its full strength, and by this time in a very fair state
of efficiency. Parades, drills, and musketry filled up all our
days, and our evenings passed at the mess, either at our own
troop mess or at the depôt. On an invitation from the
regimental, Sergeant Jack and myself were constant guests,
and got to know him; and off duty we were the best of
friends.

CHAPTER VIII.

RUMOURS OF TROUBLE IN BASUTOLAND—C.M.R. ORDERED TO BASUTOLAND
—LEAVE KOKSTAD, 1880—PASS THROUGH UMTATA—COLUMN ENTERS
BASUTOLAND, 13TH SEPTEMBER 1880—FIRST SHOT FIRED—RELIEVE
TRADERS AT DIPHERING — OCCUPY MAFETENG — DISARMAMENT ACT—
ARRIVAL OF MR. SPRIGG IN MAFETENG—A PATROL AND ITS RESULT—
DEATH OF LIEUTENANT CLARKE—MR. SPRIGG'S HURRIED DEPARTURE
—FUNERAL PARADE.

RUMOURS of disaffection amongst the Basutos now began to spread abroad, and about the beginning or the middle of July they apparently had some effect on the Government, as orders were suddenly issued for Colonel Carrington to proceed to the disaffected area, taking all available men with him.

Colonel Bayly, with the right wing (which, with the exception of a few details, were left in Umtata), had already left King William's Town *en route* for Maseru, near which place the Basuto chief, Letsea, and his brother Masupha, lived at Morija near Thava Bosigo stronghold.

Colonel Carrington now commenced his long march, which had to be done by road, as railways were then unknown in the territories, as native districts are termed.

The column consisted of Colonel Carrington in command, Captain Shervinton, and two lieutenants with No. 3 Troop, which was made up of about 115 N.C.O.'s and men, and various details, consisting of the staff and about 35 men of Nos. 1 and 2 Troops, under Lieutenant Birbeck and the regimental sergeant-major—a total strength, roughly, of about 150 of all ranks.

Captain Bowers, who was the adjutant, Captain Cecil D'Arcy, V.C., and Lieutenant Carstensen, formerly an officer in the Prussian Artillery, who had gained the Iron Cross at the battle of Gravelotte in the Franco-German War of 1870— were left behind in Kokstad with the staff of drill instructors and about a hundred recruits, who were not yet fit to take the field. No. 5 Troop was also left at Fort Donald, held in readiness to march when required.

The march began in July and lasted through August, the coldest months of the year in East Griqualand. The weather was generally very dry and good for trekking, but bitterly cold for the unfortunates sleeping in their saddles at night, with only two blankets each for their bed and covering.

We marched along the main road leading from Natal to the Colony, which passes through East Griqualand and the Transkeian territories—the country north of the Kei River— and, after passing through Kokstad, continues along the borders of Pondoland till it reaches Umtata—then a small C.M.R. station and the seat of the chief magistrate of the Transkei.

We passed through Mount Ayliff, a magistracy in Xesibe country, about 27 miles from Kokstad, then on to the Baca country, which we entered by crossing the Umzimvubu River; thence to Mount Frere, the seat of the magistracy of that country, where we were snowed in for four days, and had to pitch tents.

From Kokstad to Mount Frere we passed through splendid country, the veldt being good for cattle grazing. Trees, in the form of sugar bush, which made splendid fuel, covered all the hills through which we passed. After leaving Mount Frere the country was very bare, not a tree was to be seen, and the veldt was dried up and forage very scarce. We had to fall back on cow dung for our fires, and this, owing to the snow, was damp and almost useless.

After a delay, caused by the snow, we trekked on to Qumbu, crossing the Tina River into Pondomisi country. Qumbu was the name of the magistracy, of which Mr. Hope was the magistrate. The latter, a fine-looking old gentleman with a long grey beard, rode out to meet our colonel. He was doomed, not long after, to become a victim to his sense of duty, being treacherously murdered by the tribe he governed with efficiency and justice. From Qumbu we marched on to Umtata, at that time consisting of a mission school with a tin cathedral, a small Wesleyan chapel, the C.M.R. camp, and two so-called hotels; these, with a magistrate's court-house, and about half a dozen small houses, composed the "city."

We continued our march the following day, taking with us about 35 N.C.O.'s and men from the camp at Umtata, with two officers—Lieutenants Clarke and Russ. These officers and men belonged to Nos. 6 and 7 Troops of the right wing, and had remained behind when their troops left for Basutoland to join Colonel Bayly at Maseru. They were all old hands, and the officers, who had been promoted six months before, were now attached to the left wing till they could rejoin their own wing.

Lieutenant Clarke was a well-built and particularly smart young officer. Lieutenant Russ had formerly been a sergeant in the 10th Hussars. He, too, was a smart officer, notwithstanding his frequent reminiscences of his former state and his remarks about "when he was in the 10th Prince of Wales' Own," or orderly to the Prince of Wales at Aldershot.

We left the main road on leaving Umtata, and went *viâ* Engcobo, on to the Drakensberg Mountains. We crossed this range by going over Barkly Pass, and here we encountered very heavy snowstorms, which delayed our progress, but at length we reached Barkly, a little village on the tops of the mountains. From there we journeyed on to Palmietfontein, where we were joined by Captain Montague and a portion of his troop, No. 4, and the column proceeded to cross the Orange River into the Orange Free State.

We crossed at a place called Governor's Drift. The column was two days in crossing; the men having to cut away the steep sandy banks on either side of the river, cut down trees, and make a road for the large convoy of wagons that accompanied us. A field cornet, or Dutch district commandant, with three or four men, met Colonel Carrington, with whom they had a discussion. Apparently they objected to armed men entering the Free State, but after a short delay the affair was settled, for we resumed our march.

We then heard that the Basutos had openly refused to disarm, and were threatening the magistrates; and that orders had reached Colonel Carrington to push on to Mafeteng, a magistracy in Basutoland, where Mr. Barkly, with a few white traders and his Royal Basuto Police, were being threatened by Lerothodi, the eldest son of the paramount chief, Letsea.

The column proceeded along in the Free State, the Basuto border being on our right the whole of the march, after crossing the Orange River, till we came to Wepener, a border Dutch town, memorable now for the siege it sustained in the late Boer War. It was here De Wet did his utmost to capture the Colonial division without success.

Without entering the town the column marched to Massayne's farm and encamped. We were then about 300 yards from the Basuto border—a stream dividing us from Basutoland. A number of mounted Basutos were riding about on the other side, all armed with rifles. That night all precautions were taken and picquets posted.

On the morning of the 13th September 1880 the column paraded, and the troops equalised, No. 3 being split up into three troops, which were called A, B, and C Troops, D being composed of No. 4, and E the details of the right wing. Captain Shervinton was second in command, Lieutenant M'Mullen in command of B, Lieutenant Birbeck of C Troop, Captain Montague commanded D, and Lieutenants Clarke and Russ, E Troop.

As soon as the wagons were ready they moved off towards the Drift. The right wing troop were told off as advance and rear guard to the column, and the advance guard trotted down to the Drift and crossed into Basutoland. They immediately extended in skirmishing order and advanced at a walk, straight ahead. The Basutos, who had been watching us since early morning, and were all mounted on their little wiry ponies, stopped the advance guard, and, speaking in English, asked where the men were going to. The advance guard, who had orders not to let them through the line, ordered the Basutos to go back, and rode slowly on at a walk, keeping the natives in front of them, and in some instances pushing their ponies with the butts of their rifles. We could see all this as we were crossing the Drift. My troop, being the leading troop, formed line on crossing, and advanced in close order on the

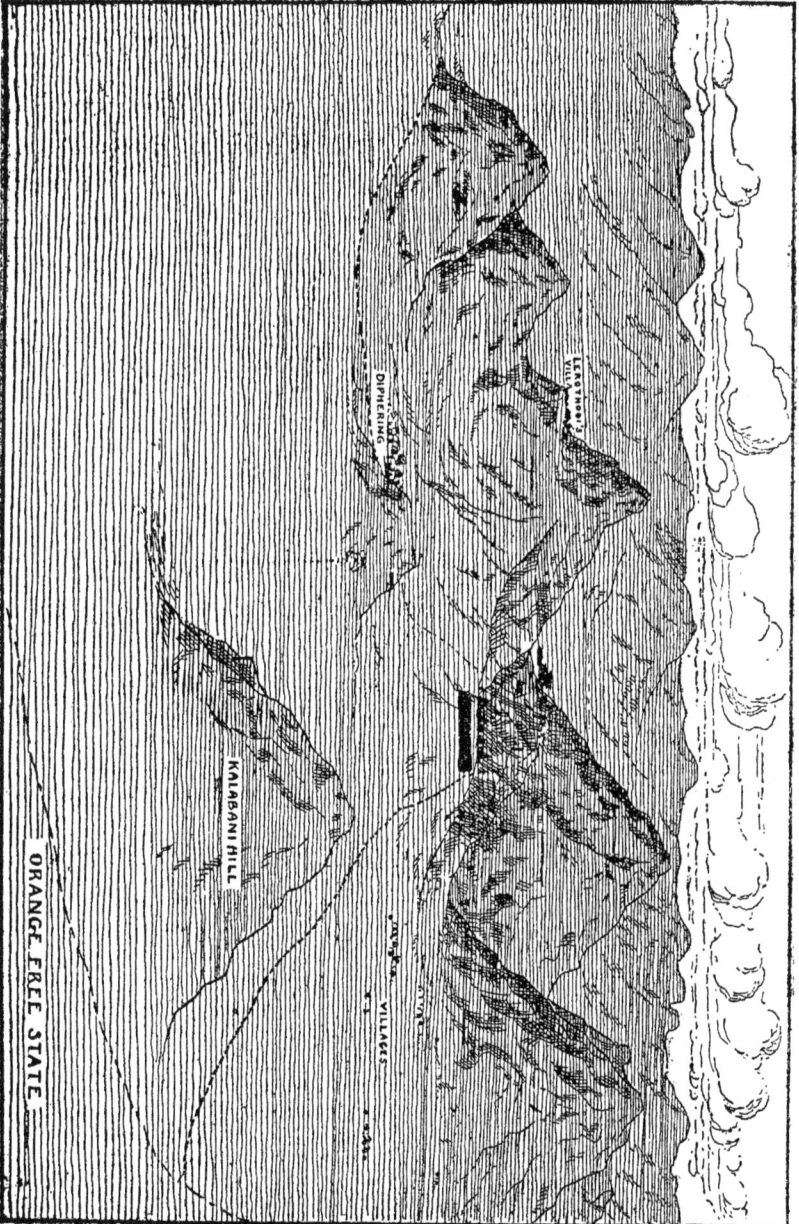

ORANGE FREE STATE

KALABANI HILL

DIPHERING

LEROTHODI'S
VILLAGES

VILLAGES

track of the advanced guard, till we were 100 yards clear of the river, where we were halted to allow the wagons to come up. This they did, forming up four abreast, the remaining three troops formed up in column of fours, one on either flank of the wagons, and the third in line in rear, ready to face about if necessary.

The advance then sounded and we moved off, the wagons keeping together in their formation as closely as possible, and the four troops in position with carbines in their hands, ready to dismount and open fire. The advance guard, about 300 yards in front, seemed to be making their way slowly, the Basutos apparently not trying to break through them. That evening we were told by the advance guard they were very friendly, and had asked the men for tobacco and matches, but as their numbers appeared to be increasing considerably, and the advance guard was very weak, things began to get too exciting to be pleasant. Without any preliminaries they might at any moment charge down on us with their stabbing assegais, which each native carried in addition to a rifle. We had proceeded about 6 miles in this uncomfortable manner, and had almost passed a hill on our left with high ground beyond it, which Colonel Carrington made a detour from the road to avoid—when suddenly a shot rang out in front.

It is generally supposed that the first shot was fired by a Basuto as a signal shot, but not being a believer in such things, I think it probable that some loaded rifle went off accidentally. Anyway it brought great relief. The tension had been getting too great, but now we knew where we were. The advance guard closed in on their centre, whilst the Basutos made for a stony ridge on our left front, and opened fire on us.

8

Captain Shervinton gave the order to extend by half sections, and we galloped straight at the enemy. They did not wait, but galloped along the ridge, and we then got the order to pursue. This was a favourite drill of Colonel Carrington's, and the men of our troop were well trained at it. We galloped after them, dismounting about every 50 yards and firing two or three rounds at them, and then mounting and after them again. On gaining the top of the ridge we could see Mafeteng, about two miles to our right, and the remainder of the column with wagons made straight for it, whilst we kept on driving the Basutos before us.

About a mile to our left, and in a hollow with a high ridge of stones standing up behind it, we saw a large stone building; out of it came ten or twelve white men and opened fire on the retreating Basutos, who turned off more to their right and made for some hills that overlooked this building.

We were then rallied, and trotted down to the building, where we found the white men awaiting us. They cheered as we rode up, and Captain Shervinton spoke to the leader of the party. The building was a large trading station, belonging to Mr. Fraser, a well-known Basutoland trader. It was called Diphering, and was distant from Mafeteng about two miles. Mr. Fraser and the other men, who were mostly his employees, had come to Diphering for safety—from the outlying stores in the country. They were expecting to be attacked any time by the Basutos, and our arrival was most opportune for them. They were all greatly excited, and urged Captain Shervinton to pursue the enemy farther. Captain Shervinton's orders, however, were only to clear the Basutos from the road to Mafeteng; this he had accomplished, and the column had got into Mafeteng without further molestation.

The Basutos were increasing in numbers in front of us, and were keeping up a pretty hot fire, in which two of our men were wounded. One of the excited members of Mr. Fraser's party called out to his friends, "Come on, boys, if the C.M.R. are afraid we will do it ourselves." This was too much for our captain's temper. He rode up to the man, a hulking great Dutchman, and with a blow from his fist knocked him clean out of the saddle, breaking his jaw and arm in the fall.

Captain Shervinton, seeing that the Basutos must be dislodged from the hills in front of Diphering, galloped us to the foot of them and then dismounted us, handing over our horses to the No. 3 of each section. The rest of us stormed the hill in skirmishing order, and drove the Basutos from the top. They retired again to still higher hills, on the top of which we could see some villages, crowded with men. We halted on the top of the hill overlooking Diphering, and it was patent to the youngest soldier that we were being drawn into a trap. Had we pushed any farther, the Basutos would have charged us in their turn and probably cut us to pieces.

Colonel Carrington had evidently seen the state of affairs for, bringing 50 men with him, he rode down to Diphering and came up to our support. After watching the enemy for some time he gave the order to return to Diphering, where the question of the damaged Dutchman was gone into. I think the general verdict was, "Serve him right." A cart and a pair of horses belonging to Mr. Fraser were requisitioned, and the injured man put into it and driven to Wepener, where he was placed in hospital.

Colonel Carrington left Lieutenant Birbeck and ten men to reinforce the party at Diphering, and the rest of us rode along the road to Mafeteng, where we off-saddled and got some food, which we badly needed.   Small patrols had been busy all round Mafeteng since our arrival, burning the villages, capturing goats, pigs, and fowls, and the camp was full of this sort of loot.

Mafeteng was a small village with a magistracy, situated as villages usually are in Basutoland, under overhanging kopjes.   The magistrate's house, a large stone building, with stone kraals for cattle, etc., was at one end of the village, which consisted of one small street of stone houses occupied by the loyal Basutos and their families.   At the other end of the street, which was only about 200 yards long, was Mr. Ashman's store, also a stone building with kraals.   In the centre was the court-house.   At the back of the village was a flat-topped kopje, stretching from Ashman's store to the magistracy, and completely commanding the village.   On the top of this three large schanzes or defences were built, something after the style of the now well-known block-house.

One of these schanzes was on the edge of the plateau above Ashman's store, and built in among the rocks of the kopje, and commanded the approach of the village from the direction of Lerothodi's Kraal.   This schanze was called the Crown.   No. 2 schanze was built at the other edge overlooking the magistracy. It also was a very strong defence, and covered the approaches to the village on the side nearest the Free State border.   The third schanze was built some 300 yards at the back of No. 2 schanze, and covered the approach from the rear.   At the back of this defence a high sloping hill with a ridge from the top to the bottom, and called "the Hog's Back," stood up, the summit being about 400 yards' range from the schanze.

At the back of the Hog's Back ran a range of mountains in the shape of a semicircle which closed us in.   To the front of Mafeteng—the way we had entered the place—was a flat country, quite open, with good veldt stretching down in the direction of Diphering—which we could see from the schanzes—with a large lake or vlei in the hollow. There were also two or three very fine springs of water in the village itself. On this face of the village and by the side of the magistracy the fort was laid out and the tents pitched. The schanzes were manned by one sergeant and ten men, and twenty Basuto Police in the Crown; a corporal and six men with ten Basuto Police to each of Nos. 2 and 3 schanzes. Ammunition was also stowed there in case of emergency. Mr. Barkly, who was the magistrate of Mafeteng at this time, had been having a very anxious time of it for some weeks prior to our arrival; he and his staff of Civil Servants and a few traders being the only white people in Mafeteng.

Lerothodi, the eldest son of the chief Letsea, was the chief of the district. He had flatly refused to surrender his arms, and had expressed his determination to resist the Government if they insisted on carrying out the Disarmament Act. Mr. Barkly with his Police had been powerless to exercise any authority, and could only sit tight and wait the developments, which had now begun by our arrival.

Mr. Sprigg, who was at that time Prime Minister of Cape Colony, must have had little idea of the effect it would have on the natives when he brought in his Bill for the disarming of all the tribes subject to Cape Colony. The Bill was a very necessary one, no doubt, as regards the tribes in the Cape Colony and Transkei, and would have caused little or no trouble had it been carried out at once in those districts, as the Kaffirs had received a severe blow in the 1877 and 1878 campaign. But he seems to have forgotten the fact that it was the Imperial troops which had made that blow decisive; and Mr. Sprigg showed his utter ignorance then, as he often has subsequently, of the inefficiency of the Colonial forces to cope with a sudden outbreak of a strong tribe. The Cape Mounted Riflemen were then—as they are now—ready to take the field at a moment's notice; but what was one regiment against a tribe like the Basutos—a well-armed and mounted race of men, far superior in every way as fighting men and as natives to any tribe in South Africa—Zulus not excepted? True, Mr. Sprigg had three regiments of Cape Mounted Yeomanry of his own creation; but at Moirosi's Mountain they had not proved themselves equal to the ordinary Volunteer either in drill or discipline.

The Volunteer regiments were under strength, and had been neglected since the Galeka War, and the C.M.R., the Colony's only standing corps, were—to the shame of the Government—armed with the obsolete Snider carbine, useless over six hundred yards, and not very accurate at any range.

The Ministry at the Cape also showed a lamentable ignorance of the feeling of the neighbouring States towards Great Britain. The attitude of the Dutch, not only in the Transvaal and Orange Free State but in the Cape Colony itself, was very hostile towards England, as was proved in a few months by the open act of rebellion which ended in that eternal disgrace to the British nation—the peace following the disaster at Majuba Hill.

Colonel Carrington made his headquarters at the magistracy, which was at once put into a state of defence—walls being loopholed, and trenches dug, and everything possible done to ensure the enemy a warm reception should they decide to attack us. The Basutos could be seen riding in large bodies from all directions, and going in the direction of Lerothodi's village, and our videttes, posted all round the village, were constantly exchanging shots. It soon became evident that we were not in for a picnic, but had come to stay.

It had been rumoured that we had only entered Basutoland to relieve the magistrate and the traders, and that we would return to the Free State and go on to Maseru and join the right wing; but, like a good many rumours, or picquet-rope yarns, as they are called, this had no foundation; and apparently the Cape Ministry had imagined that at the sight of two hundred C.M.R. the Basutos would immediately hand in their guns and become submissive to the magistrate.

That evening at sundown the outlying picquet—the main body of the picquet was posted about a hundred yards to the front of the camp in the direction of Diphering—and sentries, consisting of twenty-six men on a relief, were posted at intervals round the sides and front of the camp, the rear being protected by the schanzes, the occupants of which had their own reliefs on the look-out all night.

The duties of the picquet were to fire on any person or thing approaching from the outside, and to challenge anybody approaching from any other direction. An hour before daylight, six mounted men, under two corporals, went out from camp and patrolled from the centre to the flanks—a corporal and three men taking each half. These men went outside the line of sentries, and had to be very careful that they did not lose their direction and get cut off by natives, who, we found, had also put picquets on the hills around to prevent us stealing a march on them in the early morning. In fact, we very soon found that there were not many moves that the Basutos were not up to. In their scouting, and taking advantage of broken country, they could give us points.

As soon as it was daylight, and the whole surrounding country became visible, the entire picquet fell in and marched up to the schanzes, relieving the N.C.O.'s and men already there, and greatly increasing the strength of these defences. The officer returned to camp, and the N.C.O.'s and men remained in the positions the whole of the day and the next night, when they were relieved in their turn by the picquet of the night before.

This strong picquet made the duties come very heavy on the men, as, besides this duty, small patrols were sent out under an officer daily. Mounted videttes posted on prominent positions all day, and the ordinary horse guard had to be found; and keeping in mind that the column was only about 240 all told, it will be seen that there were very few men available for building the fort. This task had been commenced the day after our arrival—officers, N.C.O.'s, and men in their shirt-sleeves, working alike, building a sod wall inside the trenches, and banking it up with earth.

The next three days were occupied in the usual manner, the patrols meeting with more opposition every day in burning the small villages within a radius of about three miles from the camp. Only one casualty occurred—Sergeant Swift of my troop being shot in the leg.

Communication had been maintained with the border up till now, as the Basutos kept well back in their villages near Lerothodi's kraal—probably expecting us to attack in that direction. On the 16th—three days after we had entered the country—an escort under Captain Montague went to

Massaynes Farm and brought out Mr. Sprigg, the Prime Minister, and his Secretary. It was supposed that he had come to interview Colonel Carrington, and see how his blunder could be remedied. I remember that every man was very much disappointed that he had not been attacked *en route*. It was not a charitable wish, but it was perhaps natural.

That evening I was on the outlying picquet, Lieutenant Clarke being in command, and at about nine o'clock an orderly sergeant approached the main body and asked Lieutenant Clarke to spare me for half an hour, as Captain Shervinton wanted me, and that he was to remain till I returned. Lieutenant Clarke having given me permission, I went and found Captain Shervinton at the magistrate's house. He took me into the garden, and told me that he was taking out a patrol the following morning, and wanted me to go with him; that he had arranged for another sergeant of my troop to go to the schanze in my place the following day; that he was going to shift the Basutos out of the hills in front of Diphering, and that probably we would have a stiff fight. Sprigg could see it from Mafeteng, and judge what the Basutos were like. I returned to my picquet, and told Lieutenant Clarke what Captain Shervinton had said. He laughed, and said, "Pretty stiff work—picquet to-night and a tough scrap to-morrow. Turn in, and I will post the sentries."

I have related this to give an idea what sort of man this officer was; it was this sort of comradeship with the N.C.O.'s and men, without any loss of dignity, that made him the most popular officer of the time. Poor Clarke! Little did either of us think that this would be his last night with us.

The next morning, the 17th September,—the date is

engraven on my memory as one of the bad days of the regiment,—we paraded at 7 a.m.—twenty-five men and two sergeants. Captain Shervinton took us down the road towards Diphering, where we could see the Basutos riding along the ridges parallel with us at a distance of about two miles.

We arrived at Diphering, and saw our men and the civilians standing about the place and coming out to meet us. Mr. Douglas Fraser volunteered to come with us as a guide, and he rode with Captain Shervinton at our head. The road from Mafeteng passes in front of the Diphering store, and leads on through the country to Morija, where Letsea, the paramount chief, lived. It was on this road that the column made its first advance from Mafeteng into the country some ten weeks later. The road after leaving Diphering led up a rather steep hill, and then on to a flat through which it went till it reached a nek between two hills into the country beyond. On our arriving at the top of the hill, we left the road and turned into a half-right position, which brought us facing two hills with a very rocky formation, and connected about half-way up by a nek on which we could see a portion of a village, which Mr. Fraser told us was a large one. From half-way up the second hill and stretching away to our right was a long ridge—flat on the top—leading to Lerothodi's village, which we could now see plainly. On the hills and the ridges we saw Basutos on foot getting behind rocks, and others, mounted, riding in different directions. I began to think that Mr. Sprigg would see a fight if his glasses were good enough.

We were then about three miles from Mafeteng, and could see the tents and the trees round the magistracy quite distinctly. We were about eight hundred yards from the ridge when the Basutos opened fire, and the bullets went over us—showing that at any rate they were not armed with obsolete carbines. Captain Shervinton left two men at this place, where they could see Diphering and also any of the enemy who might come up the valley attempting to cut us off. He then ordered me to take ten men and drive the Basutos off the first hills, while he, with the remainder and Mr. Fraser, made for the ridge in between where the village was. We galloped straight for the first hill, and, dismounting at the foot of it, slung the reins over our arms and led our horses up it—firing at any one we could see on the top. There were not many of the enemy to be seen —what there were rode down the other side as we approached the top. We reached the top without any casualty, much to my relief. I would not have known what to do with any wounded man, as I had to push on to support Shervinton, who otherwise would have been between two fires. We mounted and galloped to the other side of the hill overlooking the village, and found our party hotly engaged. I dismounted the men, and we led down on to the ridge, firing as we went at the enemy, who were leaving the village and getting on to the other hill.

We then joined forces and galloped into the village, and began to set fire to it by the simple process of sticking the muzzles of our carbines into the thatch and firing. Very soon we left the place in a blaze, and climbed the second hill. There was not much resistance offered here, the enemy retiring as we advanced till the ridge on the other side was reached, when Captain Shervinton ordered me to remain where I was with ten men and hold the place, while he pursued the natives along the flat in the direction of Lerothodi's village.

My men wanted to burn the huts, but I stopped them, and placed them on videttes on the side of the ridge in the direction from which we had come, and then looked in the direction that the other party were still going and already almost a mile away. My attention was soon recalled to my immediate surroundings by heavy firing in my rear and by bullets knocking up the ground unpleasantly close. My videttes came galloping in and reported a large body of the enemy coming up on the hill we had vacated. I put the horses and men in a couple of stone kraals which stood outside the village and overlooking the ground between us and Diphering, affording us good cover and not exposed to fire from the top of the hill. But the position was not a pleasant one, as the enemy could get into the other side of the village and within a hundred yards of us without coming under fire.

While I was telling the men what points to fire at, a voice called out to me, "Good God, sergeant—look!" I looked in the direction indicated, and saw Captain Shervinton and his party coming towards me as hard as their horses could go, and a mass of Basutos coming out of Lerothodi's village after him. Shervinton and his men galloped past our front, and we opened fire on his pursuers, who scattered and dismounted, and, getting into the rocks, returned our fire with interest.

Captain Shervinton went into a kraal on our left with half his men, and Mr. Fraser got into another one in our rear. We were safe for a time, but in a tight corner. Some Basutos had also got on to the flats between us and Diphering, and had cut off the two videttes from that place. One of them succeeded in reaching us, but the other, a man named Bernard White, was killed and mutilated before our eyes. There was not the very slightest doubt that the enemy meant having the whole patrol, and that we were going to suffer for our last four days of burning huts and looting stock. Shervinton, who had been watching Mafeteng with his field-glasses, now called out that men were saddling up in Mafeteng, and we would soon be relieved.

The Basutos tried to close in on us, and kept up a heavy fire, but we were behind good cover and our men making good shooting; every time the enemy tried to take up fresh positions, we kept them off. Shortly after Shervinton's remark we noticed the Basutos, who were between us and Diphering, galloping back to the ridge to the right and left of us, and we saw a small body of our men coming over the hills from Diphering. They galloped straight up in our direction, and, dismounting to our right, opened fire on the enemy who were on the ridges. A sergeant came across from the party and called out to Shervinton—"Your orders are to retire on Diphering"—and rode back to his party.

Captain Shervinton then gave the order to lead our horses out of the kraals and down the side of the ridge. We did so, and the Basutos, seeing us leave the kraals, came on to the village, within 50 yards. I was ordered, with ten men, to cover the retreat, and, having handed over our horses to some of the men to lead down, with strict injunctions to wait at the bottom for us, we lay down in the rocks on the edge, and kept up a heavy fire on the enemy who had got behind the kraals we had vacated. Our horses were dragged down over the rocks with great difficulty, but eventually got to the flat below us, when Captain Shervinton called out to me to get down as soon as possible. We fired a volley and then got down the side of the hill as fast as we could. The Basutos followed us to the top of the ledge, and made it hot for us, but the party on our right opened fire on them. This probably saved us from destruction, as they were within 20 yards.

We found the men mounted at the foot of the hill and horses pulling in all directions; but we each got our horse and mounted him, and Captain Shervinton gave the order to retire on Fraser's shop. This was at Diphering, and we had to cross the flat about 600 yards and then down a rocky incline for another 400 to the store. The party on our right also mounted, and we started about the same time. Directly we rode out from under cover of the ridge we came under a very heavy fire, but all fortunately high, and over our heads; and at the same time a number of mounted Basutos came charging down from the ridge, to the right and left.

It was simply a mad gallop over rocks and holes as fast as horses could lay legs to the ground. All seemed to be going well, when just before reaching the ledge of rocks overlooking Diphering, down which most of our men were disappearing, I looked across to my left, to where our relief party were galloping about 60 yards from us, and saw two men on the ground and the Basutos coming up to them. I saw one man cutting at them with his sword, and knew it was an officer. The Basutos closing round them I lost sight of him. I could do nothing for him, for it was a tough race for the rocks, and I had my doubts whether I would reach them before the Basutos. I was some distance behind my party, as I was riding a slow horse and one which had stumbled several times with me, but I succeeded in getting over the rocks ahead of the Basutos, who pulled up, and dismounting, commenced firing at us. Then I found that another party of our men, under Lieutenant McMullen, had come out from Mafeteng and had dismounted on a ridge to the right front of Diphering and were firing across at our pursuers. Had it not been for this party the Basutos would have added another ten or twelve of us to their score, as our horses were completely done.

As I rode up to the remainder of our party, I saw Captain Shervinton riding about amongst the men, and asking if any one was missing. I told him I had seen an officer killed, and he said, "Good God, no—has any one seen Mr. Clarke?" One of the corporals of Lieutenant Clarke's party, Corporal Fraser, then reported that Private Magee had been shot and fallen from his horse, and he had seen Lieutenant Clarke pulling up his horse to stop with him. He had called out to him, "For God's sake, sir, don't stop, they are catching us up"—but Clarke pulled up and dismounted, and Fraser saw him surrounded exactly as I had seen. It was an utter impossibility for any force to have saved either of them; before any of us could have pulled up and dismounted, the Basutos would have been on us. And from the start of the retreat from the ridge, every man knew that it was simply a matter of riding, and that a false step of his horse would have finished him.

It was afterwards suggested we might have retired dismounted from the ridge, but if this had been done I do not think a single man would have got away, as the Basutos themselves admitted later that there were four thousand of them out that day. And I state positively that the average of rounds of ammunition per man of Captain Shervinton's patrol, when we mounted and left the ridge, did not exceed two rounds per man, so that line of action was out of the question. If any blame is to be attributed, I think it rests with the man who ordered such a small patrol out in the morning. It was quite evident to the lowest in rank, that the Basutos had been getting more aggressive day after day, and to send twenty-five men out from camp to the distance we went, unsupported, was a simple act of madness. It was only the standing luck of the British army that we were not annihilated.

Colonel Carrington in the meanwhile, having arrived at Diphering with fifty men, advanced up towards the Basutos, who now retired back to the two hills and ridge, the scene of the morning's fight. The bodies of Lieutenant Clarke and Privates Magee and White were recovered and brought down to Diphering, where they were placed in a cart and taken up to Mafeteng. The bodies were all perfectly naked and very much mutilated. The heart of poor Clarke had been cut out, to be afterwards used as a medicine to doctor the fighting men with.

Colonel Carrington marched along the flat, parallel to the ridges, the Basutos keeping along the top, but did not attempt another charge, and after marching to within range of Lerothodi's village, where the Basutos massed in very considerable numbers, he wisely returned to Mafeteng. As we approached Mafeteng, a cart and four, with an escort of our men, started at a gallop for the border. It was the Prime Minister, Mr. Sprigg, who thought it advisable to get out of Basutoland with as little delay as possible. His judgment in this matter at least was quite sound as events proved. The escort on the return journey had a narrow escape of being cut off, and men had to go out to cover them as they came in. That ended a very exciting day, and although the loss of Lieutenant Clarke was felt very much, still it was the fortune of war, and we were congratulated by our friends on returning at all, considering the odds against us in the morning.

Parties of Basutos could be seen moving along the ridge,

the scene of the fight, with led horses, carrying away their dead and wounded, which we subsequently heard were very heavy. That night all tents were struck and we all slept at our station in the trenches, but the Basutos did not disturb us. Next morning, every man, except those on duty in the schanzes, attended funeral parade, and our three comrades were buried about 200 yards from the fort on the right of the road to Wepener, the first of a good many afterwards buried there.

CHAPTER IX.

BASUTOS SURROUND MAFETENG—CARSTENSEN'S PATROL—R.S.M. MEETS
WITH MISHAP—BASUTOS ATTACK MAFETENG—HEAVY FIGHTING—BARE-
BACKED CHARGE ON BASUTOS — DEFEAT OF ENEMY — LOSS OF OUR
STOCK—REDUCED TO EAT HORSE-FLESH AND MEALIES.

THE Basutos began to think it was time to put a stop to
our patrols and communication with the border.   During
the day a large number of them could be seen riding along
the ridge from Lerothodi's village, and round the back of
Diphering on to the Kalabani Hill, which commanded the road
from Mafeteng to Wepener, where they took up their positions
in such numbers as finally to put an end to any patrolling in
that direction.   They also began to show up in numbers on
our left between us and the Free State Border, and our
videttes in the front, and also No. 3 schanze, exchanged
shots with some of the enemy who appeared on the top of the
Hog's Back, and were firing down into the village.   The walls
of the fort were now practically finished, and the men slept
inside that night, with of course the exception of the
picquets.

The following day, some Basutos rode into a village about
1000 yards from the end of Mafeteng where the Crown
schanze was, and a patrol of twenty-five men, under Lieutenant
Carstensen, were sent to drive them out and destroy the
walls.   Our miserable carbines were non-effective at that
range, but the Basutos had a number of Martini-Henry rifles

and Wesley Richard sporting rifles that could reach us easily, and they were annoying the schanze from that position.

We watched the patrol go out from the fort, and had a troop ready saddled up to go to their assistance if necessary.

The patrol trotted down the street, formed up on the flat, and, extending in half-sections, galloped up the incline to the village, the Basutos opening fire as the patrol advanced. Our men rode on, and as they neared the village we could see a horse and man fall, the horse going on with the remainder. We could see the Basutos riding away to the next hills, no doubt with the intention of drawing our men on, but Lieutenant Carstensen had his orders, and while the men were pulling down walls, and burning the wood parts of the huts, we saw two of the men ride back with a led horse to where the man had fallen, and after laying him across the saddle come slowly back towards Mafeteng. We were all anxiously watching the proceedings of the Basutos and the patrol, expecting to see the enemy charge our men when they found that they were not pursued, but they contented themselves with firing at long range—our men not returning a shot. As the two men approached us with the led horse and man lying across it, a third man from the patrol with a message to the Colonel from Lieutenant Carstensen passed them and rode up to where we had collected at the bottom end of the fort. Amongst us and unnoticed by the man who had ridden up, were Colonel Carrington, the magistrate, and two or three other officers.

The messenger, a Cockney of the veriest type, and quite an original member of my troop, no doubt wishing to break the news to us as gently as possible, called out, with a broad grin, " Hooray chaps, 'ere's the —— regimental gone and

broke his —— neck!" His surprise can be imagined when
he saw the colonel standing close by, but if he felt any
shock he didn't show it. Bringing his carbine to the carry
as a salute, he said, "Mr. Carstensen's compliments, sir, and
the 'uts is all destroyed, and can he come back, as the enemy
is a-massing and looks like coming on?"

The colonel said, "Tell Mr. Carstensen to retire slowly,"
and then turned on his heel with a smile, no doubt thinking
of his regimental sergeant-major.

It was the regimental sergeant-major who had met with
the mishap, but when he had been carried into a room set
apart in the magistrate's house for a hospital it was found
that he was alive, though unconscious. Two days later he
regained his senses, when he told us that during the gallop
up to the village his horse put his foot into an ant-bear
hole and came down on his head and rolled over him,
stunning him. Lowther laughed as heartily as any of us,
when he heard how the Cockney had announced his demise.

The patrol returned at a walk and reached camp without
any loss, much to the relief of a good many of us. It proved
to be the last patrol for a considerable time. That evening,
and during the night, we had several alarms, some of the
enemy riding up in the dark and firing at the picquets; but
while this kept us on the alert and occasioned loss of our
sleep, nothing happened to cause us to anticipate an attack in
force.

While we were sitting round the sergeants' mess fire at
breakfast the following morning, our native servant boys, who
had accompanied us from Kokstad, became very much excited,
and one of them, running up to Sergeant Cruttwell and
catching him by the arm, pointed in the direction of

Lerothodi's village, and said, "Look, Boss—mosuto." We all stared in the direction, and gradually made out an unending stream of horsemen coming round the side of the mountain below the village. The Basuto Police had evidently seen them too, for three shots went off in quick succession from the Crown schanze.

The alarm rang out from the different troops' trumpeters, tents were struck, men took their positions, and the horses were brought up at a gallop from where they had been feeding close by, and rushed into the high stone kraal between the fort and the magistrate's house, when the gate was blocked up with wood to prevent a stampede. We then saw the enemy emerging from behind a hill about a mile away, spreading out as they came till they faced the front of the whole village and coming straight at us, shouting and waving guns and battleaxes. The Crown schanze met them with a heavy fire, and brought down a good many men and horses. In the fort we let them charge up to about 400 yards, when we put a volley into the thick of them and commenced independent firing. The smoke got so dense, it was impossible to see what was going on, and when the Cease Fire sounded all round, I half expected to see the enemy at the walls. But as the smoke lifted we could see them galloping back out of range, dragging their dead and wounded with them. It was only the commencement; the heavy firing from all three schanzes, and from Ashman's store, indicated that they had not all retired, and bullets flying over the fort showed that they were all round us.

About three hundred Basutos had succeeded in galloping right under the Crown schanze and about thirty yards from Ashman's store. There they dismounted, and took cover under a sod wall which surrounded Ashman's garden. Their horses were soon shot by the men in the schanze, and they were left dismounted, and at the mercy of the men in that position, for they could neither advance nor retire. A large number of Basutos came over the hills from the back, and kept up a heavy fire on the schanzes; but, with the exception of wounding Corporal Brownlow, who was in charge of No. 3 schanze, and killing two Basuto Policemen in the same place, they did no further damage. Several thousands were on the flat between Lerothodi's village and the fort, but after the first attempt at rushing us, they contented themselves with firing at the fort from long range, and we could not return their fire. A large number had also got into the ruined villages opposite the left face of the fort, which the right-wing troop held, and at a distance of four hundred yards were keeping up a heavy fire—the bullets that came over the wall passing over our heads, who were on the lower side. From the heavy firing which we could hear from Diphering, and the mass of the enemy on the hill at the back of the store, we could tell that they were having a very hot time of it.

As the day wore on it became evident that something had to be done to clear the Basutos out from behind the wall at the end of the village, and Colonel Carrington ordered Captain Shervinton to take some men and drive them out. The latter called for thirty volunteers, and instantly got many more than were wanted. So, telling off the first thirty, and calling myself and Sergeant Cruttwell, we got our horses out of the kraal, put the bridles on, and mounted them barebacked, taking revolvers only. We rode past the magistrate's house towards the end of the village, and then circled out in the veldt to our left till we cleared the end of the wall.

The Basutos saw us coming on their flank, and stood up to fire at us, when the schanzes poured in a heavy fire upon them, and they turned and ran in the direction of Lerothodi's village, throwing their guns and blankets away. Captain Shervinton wheeled us into line, and we charged and rode right through them, firing our revolvers at them point-blank. We pursued them a short distance, and then were rallied and galloped back to the village, the schanze and fort opening fire as we cleared the front. Very few of the three hundred got away. Three or four of our horses were hit, and the men fell off; but the Basutos were anxious to get away, and, having thrown away their arms, could do no damage. We returned to the fort, having attained the object for which we were sent, and cleared the enemy out of the village.

Towards sundown the enemy withdrew from the vicinity of Mafeteng and took up positions all round us at a distance of two miles, and reoccupied the deserted villages which we had driven them out of in the early part of our occupation. We were now fairly besieged. It was estimated that 10,000 Basutos took part in this the first attack on Mafeteng, and it was extremely fortunate for us that they deferred the attack till the fort was completed and the ground around it cleared—otherwise, our losses would have been very severe, and I doubt whether we would have succeeded in beating them off. As matters now stood, the enemy had lost very heavily in their first wild rush, both while advancing and while galloping out of range.

It was not till the Basutos retired, and we were able to settle down to ordinary routine again, that we heard, much to our disgust, that all the cattle, goats, etc., that we had succeeded in capturing from the enemy had been recaptured by them in the morning, in addition to which they had taken all our wagon oxen; and, with the exception of a few sheep and fowls, we were without meat. We collected the guns that the Basutos had thrown away in their flight; others were picked up in the veldt in different parts where men had been shot, and their friends had only succeeded in dragging them away, without troubling about the arms. The Basutos had a peculiar method of their own in moving their dead and badly wounded out of action. They carried a reim of rawhide with a hook attached to one end and by another to the saddle. Basutos generally wore corduroy trousers, with a striped blanket or rug slung over their shoulders, and straw hats of their own manufacture with broad brims and very small high crowns, fastened on with a chin-strap. The hook was generally attached to the man's waistbelt or trousers, and he was bumped along the ground at the end of the reim till out of range. If he was not quite dead when he was hooked on, he had every chance of expiring by the time his kind friend had finally unhooked him.

We found their guns mostly of modern pattern, only a few old muzzle-loaders being among them. The loyal Basutos who were in the village made a fine haul of saddles and bridles which were on the Basuto ponies lying about in all directions, but mostly at the wall where they had come under the fire of the Crown schanze.

The Basuto pony is without exception the best of its kind in Africa. Standing anything from twelve to fourteen hands in height, they are very strongly built, with short, thick legs, broad quarters, and strong shoulders. They will carry a Basuto all day, up and down mountains, as surefooted as a goat; they will scramble over rocks and down the sides of mountains where a man would hesitate to walk. A Basuto never dismounts, and a sight worth seeing is a Basuto pony twelve hands high—a miniature cart-horse in build—trotting down a rocky footpath with a hulking great Basuto weighing seventeen stone jogging about on his back, keeping his seat entirely by balance, and not attempting to guide the little beast, who takes his own way, turning and twisting down the path, jumping boulders and stepping over stones. He seems never to tire or make a mistake in his footing.

On going to the hospital to see how Corporal Brownlow of my troop was getting on, I found him sitting up with his arm in a sling, and very cheerful. He explained to me that, seeing a Basuto crawling up a good deal in advance of the others towards his schanze, and only about fifty yards distant, he stood up on some ammunition boxes and leant on the top of the wall to get a shot at the native from that position—where he could see better than through a loophole. The native saw him, levelled his rifle, and they both fired together. Brownlow felt a jerk in his arm, and his carbine fell out of his hand. The bullet had struck the carbine on the side of the breech-block, entered his hand between his finger and thumb, and come out above the wrist—a very narrow escape for his head, and not a bad shot for the native. Brownlow had gone one better with his shot: his bullet struck the Basuto fairly on the forehead, and tore half the back of his head off, as a Snider bullet is apt to do; Brownlow had an enemy's rifle, which one of the Basuto Police had managed to get for him during a lull in the firing. It was a sporting rifle in good order, and had probably cost the late owner a couple of good ponies.

About a week after, we managed to get communication with the border by means of a heliograph, manufactured by Captain Shervinton and two sergeants—late of the Lancers—who were signallers. We heard briefly that troops had been called out in the Colony and were marching to our relief. Our commissariat by this time began to give out, in the matter of ordinary rations, and we had to fall back on our horses. The first victim belonged to a sergeant and was an old trooper, but now, being weak and unfit for work, he was shot and handed over to the butcher, to be issued out as rations—1½ lb. per man per diem. Some curry powder and rice bought from the store helped the old horse along, and we soon got used to it, and found it not bad eating.

We began to get news by helio of the column which was being organised for our relief. Several regiments had arrived on the border, and were encamped at our old starting-point, Massayne's Farm.

One night Captain Montague, with a Basuto Policeman, managed to evade our besiegers and reached the Free State, where he joined the column at the border. He carried dispatches from Colonel Carrington to the officer commanding the troops, who had just arrived—Brigadier-General Clarke, an Imperial officer recently appointed Commandant-General to the Colonial Forces. The dispatches were understood to contain suggested route for the column to take, also the strength and probable tactics of the enemy.

The Basutos in the meantime were not idle. Diphering appearing to annoy them during their frequent journeys from Lerothodi's village to the Kalabani Hill, and probably attracted by the prospective loot to be obtained there, they streamed out of their chief's village one morning, and, keeping along the ridge to the scene of our recent fight, came down on the flats, and took up positions all round Diphering, and then tried to rush it. At the same time a large force appearing on our left and rear faces drove in our picquets and commenced keeping us employed.

The firing was very heavy at Diphering, and the Basutos appeared to be getting close to the buildings, which consisted of a solid stone house, well loopholed and with bastions of sand-bags at the corners which were held by our men and the volunteers—Fraser's men, now enlisted and drawing pay. About twelve yards on the side of this building was a large wood and iron store, lined with brick and containing all the articles usually required by the natives. This store was nearest to Mafeteng, and we could see the roof from our fort. There were bastions at the corner of this store, and it was hoped it would be sufficiently strong to resist attack. Suddenly we saw smoke rising from the buildings. It was clear that the Basutos had succeeded in getting one of the buildings at least, and it seemed that our comrades were doomed men. The firing, however, still continued as briskly as ever, and we knew that so far they were safe in the stone building. We then saw Basutos coming from the direction of the store in single file, and carrying all kinds of articles, and from the frequent flashes caused by the sun we could see that they had a good few looking-glasses amongst the loot, which they were doubtless taking for the womenkind.

Occasionally we could see a man fall, who evidently had not kept in the line, and had been picked off by one of our men in the house. After coming up the valley a short distance, they circled round the hill at the back of Diphering and disappeared with the loot.

After the store had burnt out, the enemy, apparently satisfied with their success, returned to their villages, and from the long line of ponies which we could see carrying killed or wounded men, we knew that they had paid very dearly for the goods they had taken.

There was no means of communicating with the detachment at Diphering, and we were all very anxious to know what had happened. It was not till night, when a native in the employment of Mr. Fraser was brought in by the picquet, that we learnt that the wood and iron store had been looted and burnt; that the garrison had only two of our men slightly wounded, one in the hand and the other in the head, both bullets having entered a loophole; and that the defenders were running short of ammunition.

The next morning sixty of us saddled up; six pack-horses, with a box of ammunition on either side of each horse, were led by six men, and we moved off on the Diphering road. The Basutos showed up on the hills above Diphering. Thirty men went to the right and faced the hills opposite Diphering, whilst the remainder of us, under Captain Shervinton, rode in the direction between Kalabani Hill and the side of Diphering, both parties covering the road leading down to the house. The Basutos showed up strongly in all directions, and we opened a heavy fire on them, to keep them from getting into position on the hill above the store. Then the six men with pack-horses, and three corporals whipping up, made a dash down the road to the house. They reached it in safety; the ammunition boxes were tumbled off, and the men on their way back before the Basutos realised what had happened. Then they tried to get round our rear and cut us off from Mafeteng; but we extended in half-sections and retired at a gallop, dismounting and firing in our rear every fifty yards till we got back safely within range of the fort. The other party retiring in the same way on their face of the fort, we rode into camp without having met a single casualty, amid cheers from our comrades and with a great deal of satisfaction to ourselves at outwitting the wily Basuto. Colonel Carrington was very much pleased with the performance and the steadiness displayed by the two troops when retiring on the camp in the face of tremendous odds.

We now had a signal station on the Hog's Back above No. 3 schanze, and videttes were posted along the top to protect the signallers. The camp on the border could be plainly seen from that position, and the signallers reported that it was growing larger day by day as fresh troops were arriving. The remaining left-wing troops, Nos. 1, 2, and 5, were with the relieving force, and also the artillery troop C.M.R.

We were by this time on very short rations, our only food consisting of horse-meat and mealies. We managed, however, to get a little Kaffir corn from the loyal Basutos, which when boiled with mealies and salt kept us from feeling very hungry. Tobacco had for some weeks been a minus luxury, and, after having smoked dried tea-leaves mixed with Kaffir snuff for a little while, most of us gave up the pipe till better days arrived.

The Basutos could be seen every morning marching in some semblance of a formation, from Lerothodi's village, round the back of Diphering towards the border, and returning every evening. They must have numbered close on 20,000 mounted men, besides the men on foot, who still remained in their positions round Mafeteng, and it looked as if our relief column would have their work cut out to get to us. We knew that in the event of the column being driven back, the Basutos would probably turn their attention to us, and we might not be so fortunate as heretofore in keeping them off, as the loyal natives had informed us that Lerothodi had been reinforced by his brothers and their followers—that practically the whole of the fighting force of Basutoland was concentrated round us, though our men did not know of it. We non-commissioned officers knew that we had not much ammunition left, and that another day like the first attack would about finish it. So, taking one thing with another, our lot and prospects were not very enviable.

CHAPTER X.

COMMUNICATIONS BY HELIO. WITH BORDER—RELIEF COLUMN MASSING ON
BORDER—COLUMN UNDER GENERAL CLARKE MARCH TO OUR RELIEF—
HEAVY FIRING — FIRST SIGHT OF RELIEF COLUMN — MAFETENG RE-
LIEVED — LOSS OF YEOMANRY AT KALABANI — WE RECEIVE FRESH
REMOUNTS—ATTACK ON LEROTHODI'S VILLAGE—CHARGE ON DONGA
—VILLAGE CAPTURED AND BURNT—RETURN TO MAFETENG.

AT last we got news by heliograph that the column was
ready and would shortly march in. One morning the
signallers sent a message from the Hog's Back that the camp
on the border had been struck; the continuous stream of
Basutos from their villages to the border, from early morning,
all tended to show that the big fight was about to come off—
which would decide our fate.

It was about 9 a.m. when we heard the first shot in the
report of a 7-pounder gun, and knew that our men had
crossed the border. We next heard very heavy firing as of
volleys from massed troops—then desultory firing—and at
last our signallers could see the skirmishers of the column
nearing the Kalabani Hill. Colonel Carrington gave the
order to saddle up every available man, and we were not long
in doing so and falling in dismounted, in front of the fort.
We waited anxiously for further orders; the Basutos in
the villages on our right could be seen saddling up their
ponies, and riding in our direction. A troop of us was sent
along the village to Ashman's store, where they dismounted

and waited in the event of the enemy trying a flank movement on the village. The Basutos also halted and remained
out of range, watching our movements.

During the time occupied by us in these preparations, the
firing had been very heavy—both big guns and rifle fire; and
we could see streams of Basutos going in the direction of
Lerothodi's village, carrying dead and wounded men as we
judged by the slow movement and the exclamations of the
Basuto Police, who, with the exception of the men in the
schanzes, were saddled up and waiting with the magistrate
close by us. Suddenly there was a lull in the firing, and
men looked at one another with anxious faces, and remarks
such as, "Basutos rushed them," "They are retreating," were
exchanged. Then sudden volleys echoed out, and we saw
the Basutos galloping back towards Diphering—apparently
beaten—and finally, to our great relief, we saw a troop of
white helmets coming over the ridge, this side of Kalabani,
and in line with Diphering.

The Basutos on our flank evidently knew what was the
matter, for they made off towards the hills, which the whole
Basuto army seemed to be making for. A large number of
them were galloping between Diphering and us pursued by
C.M.R., when Carrington shouted, "Stand to your horses—
mount—gallop," and away we went as fast as our weak
horses could carry us, to cut them off.

Seeing us coming, the Basutos turned to their left and
made for the hill in front of Diphering.

Then we had them.

Dismounting, we poured volley after volley at them at
from 300 to 400 yards' range. The men from Diphering
turned out and gave it them on their left as they went

LEROTHODI'S STRONGHOLD.

up the hill, and the men pursuing them dismounted and got them in the rear. The bottom and slope of that hill was dotted about with men and horses either killed or badly wounded (a snider bullet does not leave much chance for recovery when it strikes). We were mounted and marched back out of range, satisfied that we had in some measure repaid the enemy for our enforced six weeks' diet of horse meat and mealies.

We now saw the whole of the relief party forming a laager with their wagons on the flat above Diphering, and between the Kalabani and Mafeteng, and also wagons being drawn on to our camp, and we knew that our visions of fresh meat, tea, coffee, tobacco, and all kinds of luxuries were about to be realised. Colonel Carrington rode up to the column to interview the general—and we to the fort to off-saddle—and let our horses have a run for the first time for weeks.

As I went towards the wagons, on the look-out for old friends, I came across a ghastly sight. Two wagons, which had contained fresh meat for us, were piled up with dead bodies of men—who by their uniforms were of the Cape Yeomanry regiments. They were lying in all positions, just as they had been hurriedly picked up and thrown on the first wagon which came along and which happened to contain the meat intended for us. It was a gruesome sight to look at. They had all been either battleaxed or assegaied, and were covered with gashes or stabs—in some cases half their heads were nearly cut off—and the jolting of the wagons caused these half-severed heads to open and shut as they moved along, and made most of us half-starved creatures very sick.

We then heard the story of the march to our relief. It seems that all went well at the start, the Basutos being kept

10

well away from the column, which marched in the same formation as we had entered the country—with wagons massed in the centre flanked by infantry, with mounted men outside them skirmishing. The relief force being nearly 3000 strong, had plenty of men to resist a sudden charge, and the 7-pounder guns appear to have made the enemy rather cautious in approaching the main body too closely. The column had got as far as the Kalabani with only a few casualties, when the general sent a troop of the 1st Yeomanry to occupy the crest of the hill at the back of the Kalabani whilst the column went past. This troop cantered away up the hill, but through the ignorance of the officer in command, who did not send advance scouts to the crest, as is usual before taking a body of men there, they went up in troop formation and actually dismounted before reaching the crest of the hill, and went forward on foot.

This was just what the Basutos had been waiting for. Like a whirlwind they charged round the Kalabani Hill and right into the unfortunate men, who had no time to rally, and cut them down to a man; the Basutos were back over the brow of the hill before a shot from the column could be fired at them. The officers who had not dismounted bolted at the first sight of the Basutos, and saved themselves, leaving the whole of their troop, to the number of 50 men, to be cut up, with the exception of a sergeant-major who got away, and three or four men who were picked up badly stabbed, but eventually recovered.

The Basutos then tried the same tactics on the front of the column; a troop of C.M.R. was in line in advance, with 300 infantry of the Duke of Edinburgh's Own Volunteer Rifles, Cape Town regular Volunteers, and well drilled, in their rear. On the Basutos showing up in front as if they meant to charge, the D.E.O.V.R., who were dressed in Service kit of corduroy of a sandy colour, lay down four deep with fixed bayonets. The C.M.R. troop retired, wheeled round the infantry, and formed up in their rear, remaining mounted The column had halted while the killed and wounded yeomen were being recovered, and the Basutos, thinking they had a chance of repeating their success on the C.M.R. troop, charged wildly down on them, swinging their battleaxes and shouting. The C.M.R. did not move. When the Basutos got within 100 yards of the infantry, who were lying down and had evidently not been seen by the oncoming Basutos, the command rang out, "D.E.O.V.R. prepare for cavalry!" and to the astonishment of the Basutos the men rose, two ranks kneeling and two standing, and fired volleys straight into the enemy, who dropped in all directions and broke away to the right and left, where they encountered similar fire from both flanks. Those were the volleys we heard in Mafeteng, and they decided the day.

The C.M.R. pursued and cleared the front, chasing the enemy into the trap Colonel Carrington had prepared for them. Had it not been for the bad management of the officer in command of the troop of Yeomanry, Mafeteng would have been relieved with very few casualties. There were not more than 70 casualties all told.

The Cape Yeomanry consisted of three regiments, and were recruited from three different parts of the Cape Colony. They were clothed in very gaudy uniforms resembling that worn by an Imperial Lancer Regiment. The first regiment wore a blue tunic with white front, the second blue tunic with a red front, and the third blue tunic with a yellow front. These uniforms they wore in the field, and were doubtless intended to draw the young Colonial into their ranks. The bait was successful in peace time, but when the war broke out, great difficulty had been experienced in getting the men to turn out, and a great many of them sent paid substitutes in their place.

Consequently, what little drill and discipline the Yeomanry had managed to acquire in peace time was entirely lost through the number of substitutes who joined the different regiments. I cannot recall a single instance during the campaign in which they justified their existence, and they were a source of danger to the remainder of the column whenever they accompanied it on the several expeditions that subsequently went out from the main camp. The Basutos held them in the greatest contempt, and never missed an opportunity of charging them when occasion arose. They were mostly employed in garrison work in Mafeteng, and on convoy duty to and from the border, when they always had a good body of infantry to fall back on. It was the organisation that was to blame and not the men, who were English Colonials and Dutch Colonials. The two races have never succeeded in working together, and in my humble opinion they never will, whatever biassed or ignorant politicians say to the contrary.

A fatigue party of our men pitched tents in the garden of the magistracy and laid the bodies of the victims of the fight in them, till they could be identified and sewn up in their blankets, and a guard was placed over the tents.

Owing to our meat being rendered unfit, we had another day of horse meat, but the fresh vegetables and other luxuries we obtained made it one of the most palatable dishes we had indulged in for some time.

The remainder of the C.M.R., who had arrived with the column, marched over to Mafeteng, and we had a happy reunion with old friends and exchanged experiences. The picquets were lessened in number, and our tents allowed to remain standing for the night to sleep in; and last, and not by any means the least of the changes, we were allowed to take our belts and boots off, which had hitherto been disallowed under a heavy punishment.

The relief column under Brigadier - General Mansfield Clarke, consisted of three troops of left wing C.M.R., and Nos. 7 and 9 of the right wing; three regiments of Cape Yeomanry and Kimberley Horse composing the mounted force; the D.E.O.V.R., the P.A.V.G. or Prince Alfred's Volunteer Guard from Port Elizabeth, 1st City Volunteers from Grahamstown, Kaffrarian Rifles from East London, the infantry force with medical staff of C.M.R., and Cape Town medical staff corporal, with three guns of C.M.R. artillery troop. Major Cochrane of the 32nd Regiment was the brigadier's staff officer.

This force, with the exception of the C.M.R. who joined Colonel Carrington in Mafeteng, had taken up a strong position on the high ground between Kalabani Hill and Diphering, and the scene was now a busy one—wagons going to and from the border with supplies, ammunition, etc., which was stored in great quantities in Mafeteng, the base of operations.

The Basutos fell back on the line of hills to the left and front of Diphering, and reached to Lerothodi's village; and excepting an occasional exchange of shots between our

picquets and the enemy, nothing of any moment occurred.
The unfortunate men of the 1st Yeomanry were buried at
the spot where we had buried our men, with military
honours and an impressive service, all the staff and representatives from each corps attending, and an enclosure was
fenced in to prevent horses and cattle from disturbing the
graves.

Remounts were brought in from the Free State, and all
the horses of the late Mafeteng garrison were sent into the
Free State to be turned loose on a farm, to recover if possible
from their trying time of semi-starvation. We were all soon
occupied in selecting our remounts and breaking them into
their places in the ranks, and as they were all Free State
horses and broken to the saddle, this was an easy task; in a
short time they were as much at home in the ranks as their
riders.

About a week after the relief the general decided that
it was time to impress on the Basutos that the order of things
had changed, and that it was their turn to be worried.

A column consisting of about a thousand men, mounted
and infantry, and two guns, under command of Colonel
Carrington, was ordered out to Lerothodi's village, where we
were certain to meet a strong resistance, and from where the
brigadier who was to accompany the column could get a good
view of the surrounding country. Up to this time the hills
and ridge above Diphering had been the limit of our vision
of the future scene of our operations. The Mafeteng garrison
was to form part of the column.

One of the regiments of Yeomanry coming from the main
camp took our place during our absences from Mafeteng, and
we marched over and joined the column, who were ready to

proceed. The C.M.R. were told off for the advance guard, and, knowing the country, we started off, very well pleased with ourselves in getting out of Mafeteng once more, and on fresh horses were quite ready for anything that might turn up. The contrast of being all together, with a strong support to fall back upon if necessary, was very great compared to our small patrols of thirty men and no support, as had hitherto been the case.

We started off in the direction of Diphering, and after passing that place, A Troop, to which I belonged, with Lieutenant M'Mullen in command, were extended, and we galloped up the rise on to the flats, where on the occasion of our last visit we had been chased back so ignominiously with the loss of our three comrades.

Dismounting on the top, we waited till the main body of the column—consisting of the infantry, the "Duke's," as the D.E.O.V.R. are called for short, and the P.A.V.G.—arrived, when we went forward over the flat at a gallop towards the ridge where we had been surrounded on the former occasion. This was now occupied in force by the Basutos, and large numbers of the enemy were to be seen along the whole of the position to Lerothodi's village. The enemy opened a heavy fire on us, and the whole C.M.R. were ordered forward to take the ridge. With a cheer we went over the ground at a great pace, and, dismounting at the foot of the ridge, handing over our horses to be held by the Nos. 3 of each section, we went up the front in skirmishing order, running through one another by alternate troops, firing as we went. The Basutos galloped back along the top of the ridge to Lerothodi's village, and we halted till our horses were brought up, and the remainder of the column followed.

We were now formed up on the top of the ridge, with our front facing Lerothodi's village; we could see Mafeteng to our right across the intervening flat and valley. The main camp being on our right rear at about the same distance, figures could be seen quite distinctly moving about at both places. From the top of the ridge where the column was, all the country could be seen for some miles around, except in the direction of Lerothodi's village, which had high hills on either side and mountains at the back of it. Narrow defiles passing between the mountains seemed the only route by which any entry could be made into that part of the country. Looking in any other direction, one could only see a succession of hills and mountains with valleys and small open spaces where lands were cultivated and innumerable villages dotted about, generally built under rocky kopjes or ridges with flat tops similar in formation to the one we were on. Altogether it looked an impossible country for a small force to operate in with any prospect of success, as the facilities for concealing large bodies of men, and the shelter afforded on any one of the numberless defensive positions that showed up in all directions, made the task of preparing anything like a plan of attack almost an impossible one for the commanding officer of an attacking force. We could see Lerothodi's village from Mafeteng, and had more or less formed an idea of the surroundings of the place; but all ideas fall flat when confronted with the reality.

The ridge we occupied was about 300 or 400 yards across, and strong flanking parties had to be kept on both sides. About 600 yards to our front rose a plateau, with almost perpendicular sides, which stretched away to the nek where the village was situated. The sides of this plateau were very rocky and steep, and on the top schanzes had been built commanding the approaches. At the foot of this hill was a large village built at the end of the ridge we were occupying. The Basutos occupied this plateau in large numbers, and parties of them were seen riding on to the ridges on our left flank, where they dismounted and opened fire on the flanking party. We were slowly approaching the plateau, the C.M.R. skirmishing in front, and halting on each ridge to allow the infantry to come up with the ambulance wagons and guns. The guns now unlimbered and opened fire on the schanzes, and we were ordered to gallop into the village at the foot of the plateau, leave our horses, and storm the hill.

This we succeeded in doing, and the enemy fell back on to the nek, where from behind walls in front of the chief village, they kept up a heavy fire in our direction. We lay amongst the rocks at the top, whilst the remainder of the column came up to the village below us, and preparations were made for the attack.

The Basutos from the ridges on our left rear were being reinforced in large numbers, and were driving our flanking party back to better cover; seeing which, Colonel Carrington sent some infantry in that direction to take up a position and keep the enemy back. They succeeded in doing this, but the column were worried considerably, as bullets were frequently coming from the rear and left as well as from the front. It soon became apparent that things were not going to happen as Colonel Carrington wished. Suddenly, to our right front and to the back of the hills at the side of Lerothodi's village, about four thousand mounted Basutos came galloping into the valley to the right of the column, and got between us and Mafeteng. Almost before the 7-

pounders could fire on them, they had ridden into a large donga or sluit that ran for some hundreds of yards parallel with the ridge the column were on, and emerging from the other end, raced for the side of the ridge, and finally cut off our retreat. They had played the same tactics with Carrington's force of a thousand men that they had found effective with the thirty under Shervinton. A large number of them remained in the donga on our right and opened fire on the column; so we now got it from all sides.

From the bottom of the plateau the country sloped gradually down to the donga where the enemy had taken up their position. It was about 600 yards from where the column were halted, and it was evident that they had to be cleared out of that position before we could do anything in the way of attacking the village. Colonel Carrington decided to do so. The Duke's were ordered down to the side of the ridge facing the donga. My troop was ordered down from the edge of the plateau from where we had been taking cover and watching operations. Captain Shervinton took us off the ridge, and we joined the Duke's, extending as we advanced in the direction of the donga, when, a cross-fire coming on our left, we were halted. Lieutenant M'Mullen with A Troop changed front, and we advanced in the direction from which the firing was coming, and found a few Basutos had crept out of the donga and were trying to get on our flank. We soon drove them out and back on to the donga, but not without some casualties, amongst the wounded being Lieutenant M'Mullen, who was hit on the tip of his nose and through his cheek. He was taken to the rear swearing horribly.

The command of the troop devolved on me as senior sergeant; so I ordered them back to our original line. The order then came from Colonel Carrington that the donga was to be taken at the point of the bayonet, by alternate rushes. The Duke's, with fixed bayonets, in extended order, made the first rush of about 100 yards, and then lay down and fired at the donga. Then we advanced, also extended, and on reaching the Duke's doubled forward for the same distance, and opened fire till the Duke's passed through us. As we neared the donga we could see the Basutos trying to make their way up to the end of the ravine; but they were evidently jammed, and could not get up the sides with their ponies— they had to get out one end or the other, or else leave their animals and try to escape at the back on foot. They kept up a very ill-directed fire at us as we neared them, the bullets going over us. Notwithstanding the bad firing, there were several casualties. The ground—old mealie lands—was very heavy going, and several men tripping on the ground during the rushes, fell, and it seemed to the onlookers as if we were having a bad time of it. As it was described to me afterwards by a chum, they couldn't see us for dust, and thought half of us were knocked over. The final 100 yards we rushed together, and came on to the struggling mob, firing as quickly as we could load, till none remained in the donga except killed and wounded, the others swarming up the side and running for shelter in the hills beyond. We got a number of their ponies and guns, and mounting the former we chased the enemy right out of the valley, when we were brought back by the rally to our former position.

·As we were coming back we heard heavy firing and loud cheering from the plateau above; presently we saw smoke rising in the nek where Lerothodi's village was, and we found that it had been captured by C.M.R. and P.A.V.G. General

Clarke, who was up with Colonel Carrington on the plateau watching our advance, had seen the Basutos bolting from the donga, and called out, "Now it's your turn. Five pounds to the man who fires the first hut in the village." That was enough. The men, who were heartily sick of lying still and being shot at without replying, jumped up from their cover, and, cheering as they went, rushed straight into the village. The Basutos, seeing their men getting shot down in the donga, turned and ran into the surrounding hills, and left the village at the mercy of our men, who burnt the whole place to the ground and knocked down the walls. A man of my troop, No. 3, named Kirk got the reward given by the general—having set fire to the first hut by sticking the barrel of his carbine into the thatch and firing it off. After destroying the villages round about, the column commenced the march back to camp; but no sooner had we commenced to move than the Basutos came swarming after us, taking up the positions we had vacated. The C.M.R. were dismounted, and we held the edge of the plateau till the remainder of the column had retired out of range, and then we retired by alternate troops.

The Basutos followed us at a distance to the flat overlooking Diphering, when a shell from the main camp reminding them that they were coming too close, they dispersed and rode back to their hills. General Clarke was highly pleased with the conduct of the column, and issued very flattering orders through Colonel Carrington about the behaviour of the C.M.R. during the day's fight.

We left the main camp and marched on to Mafeteng, the Yeomanry returning to their own quarters at the main camp.

CHAPTER XI.

GENERAL CLARKE LEAVES FOR CAPE COLONY — OUTBREAK OF THE PON-
DOMISI — MURDER OF MAGISTRATE — ATTACK ON MAQUAISBERG —
BASUTO TACTICS — MAJOR GRANT'S COLUMN SURROUNDED — SECOND
ENGAGEMENT AT LEROTHODI'S VILLAGE — RETREAT OF COLUMN — 1ST
CITY VOLUNTEERS CUT OFF — C.M.R. COVER RETREAT.

THE commandant-general was now recalled to the Cape Colony, where a serious outbreak had occurred among the Pondomisi—a tribe inhabiting the country beyond Umtata, by whom Mr. Hope, mentioned in a former chapter, magistrate of Qumbu, had been murdered with two of his clerks, Messrs. Warren and Henman.

Colonel Carrington took command of the forces during the absence of the commandant-general, and preparations were made for another expedition—this time to a mountain called Maquaisberg, situated at the back of the mountains at the rear of Mafeteng. It was reported that Lerothodi the chief had taken up his abode in the villages round the foot and on the side of this mountain, and that we would meet with much opposition in the event of attempting to drive him out of the locality, as the position was a very strong one.

The column was about sixteen hundred strong, and paraded at Mafeteng at 2 a.m.—the troops from the main camp marching over and joining us at that place. We marched out in the dark and in strictest silence, the C.M.R. leading the way along a road leading up the valley between the hills to the right of Lerothodi's village. On arriving in line with the village, Major Grant, with 500 men, composed of two troops of C.M.R. and P.A.V.G., 1st City Volunteers, and some Yeomanry, left us and went off to the left to occupy the village, which had been deserted since the last attack. The remainder of the column under Colonel Carrington moved on, and, circling slightly to our right as we marched over rocky and rising ground, we reached a position on a plateau in front of Maquaisberg at daylight.

Our march through the darkness had been uninterrupted, much to our surprise, for a great noise had been occasioned by Major Grant's column turning off the road, and also by the mule drivers with their teams drawing the 7-pounder guns. Since the last engagement at Lerothodi's village, the hills through which we had marched had been constantly occupied by large numbers of the enemy during the daytime, and it appeared hardly credible that they should retire to such a distance away during the night that they had not heard us. To some of the old hands the quietness seemed ominous; a general feeling among the men was that we would return and find Mafeteng taken during some of our wild-goose expeditions, and there were other cheerful suggestions of a like nature. The valleys around us, and the top of the mountain in front of us, were covered with a light mist, which after clearing away disclosed to view a perfect panorama of plains, valleys, and hills, with mountains in the background—a view which proved more than ever the utter futility of the attempt to conquer such a country with the small force at the disposal of the Cape Government.

Shortly after the mist had cleared off, some shots were fired at the advance guard, who were approaching a village near the foot of Maquaisberg; the guns were brought to the front and on the ridges to our left, but they had only the effect of sending thirty or forty mounted Basutos scampering to the nearest cover—showing that it was not a case of surprise, as the men would hardly have been saddled up if it were. A score or so of Basutos appeared on the top of Maquaisberg, and a few more rode from round the side, and dismounting, from behind the rocks commenced firing at us. The column had now been massed on the plateau with the usual flanking parties out, and the men were dismounted and taking things easy, sitting about on the wet grass, watching the mountain and looking at the surrounding hills and ridges with suspicion. To us there seemed something uncanny about the business. If the mountain in front of us was strongly occupied, then it was unusual for the Basutos to show themselves as they had done, apparently challenging us to come on.

After a short rest, the Kimberley Rifles who were with us galloped away to a village on the left of the mountain, and after a few shots, the smoke from the burning village showed that there had not been much opposition there.

Three troops of the C.M.R. were now ordered forward on foot to attack the mountain. Leaving our horses in the square by the guns, we marched through the village at the foot of the mountain, which looked as if it had recently been occupied, and then extending we commenced the ascent. The mountain did not appear to differ in any degree from the many others to be seen in Basutoland;—standing alone, it rose out of the valleys and ridges and towered up some 2000 feet above the plateau, with rather sloping sides and shelves of overhanging rock; huge rocks jutting out of the sides, and giving sufficient cover for twenty men, were studded about the face at various intervals. A good few shots came from the top and sides as we clambered up, and some stones came rattling down, but nobody was hit, and we went on without firing—as we could see nothing to fire at. About a hundred yards from the top we were halted, and advanced alternately—in case of a surprise; but the firing had ceased, and nothing stopped us. On reaching the top we could see a long flat in front of us, and a few Basutos disappearing down the other side after emptying their rifles at us. There was no need to take precautions—the summit was deserted. So we all sat down on the rocks and swore at the way we had been done by the wily natives, and wondered what mischief they were up to, and where. Colonel Carrington came up and had a good look round the country; the view was certainly a good one, but not sufficient to make up for the energy expended in getting there on an empty stomach. We remained on the top for a considerable time—eating our breakfasts and enjoying a smoke in peace.

The picnic was not to last, however. We had been idly watching a few Basutos riding about the ridges in the rear of our column and in the direction of the column under Major Grant, who apparently had as little opposition as ourselves, judging by the few shots heard occasionally from that direction. Thinking that they were a few men told off by their chief to watch our movements, we took no further notice of them, when suddenly the boom of the 7-pounder gun was heard in the distance, echoing up the valleys and making it difficult to locate the direction the sound came from. Following on the report of the gun came incessant rolls of musketry rumbling along. Every man of us jumped to his feet and looked in the direction whence the sound appeared to come, but everything looked quiet, and the Basutos who had been riding about had disappeared.

Colonel Carrington hurried down the mountain and ordered us to follow. The pace at which we went down the side of the mountain was considerably quicker than our pace in going up. On nearing the remainder of the column, who were all on the alert and waiting for Colonel Carrington to join them, we saw two horsemen riding towards us at a furious pace, pursued by a party of Basutos, who, seeing that they could not overtake the men, dismounted and opened fire on them, the bullets striking in amongst the column; but a shell from one of the guns dispersed them. The two men turned out to be a couple of Yeomanry with an appeal for assistance from Major Grant, who had suddenly found himself attacked—driven out of the village with a heavy loss of men—and in a precarious position. One of our guns, with the C.M.R. who had remained on the plateau with the column, and the Kimberley Horse, were ordered off with all speed back the way we had come; the remainder followed on more slowly with the other guns, prepared at any moment for an attack, as Basutos were now appearing on our rear, where shortly before we had not seen a living thing,—a disturbing fact, again demonstrating the natural advantages of the country for concealing a defensive force. These men increased in numbers every minute, and it looked as if they meant charging us—for a moment, as if they had out-generalled us, and got our column in three separate parties for the purpose of attacking each in detail. We faced about, dismounted, and fired into them, with an effect made visible by the numbers of ponies running about loose, and the 7-pounder put two or three shells right in their midst. They dispersed round our flanks, and made off in the

11

direction of Lerothodi's village. We mounted and trotted back along the road after our advance party, and rounding the hill came in view of the whole scene of operations. Major Grant and his column were at the end of the plateau in front of the village which they were holding, and in the ruins of the village below, on the ridge—the same positions which we had held in the previous attack on the village, before storming the donga. The Basutos were occupying the village and the donga in force, and were on the ridges on the left flank and rear. Grant was no doubt in a critical position.

Upon our arrival on their flank, the Basutos between us and the besieged column retired to our right in the direction of the hill overlooking Lerothodi's village, followed by shells from our two guns. We then galloped across the intervening space, and, leaving our horses at the foot, we clambered up on to the edge of the plateau and re-inforced the C.M.R. who were holding it. A strong body of our troops had been sent out from the main camp to the assistance of Major Grant when they saw the position he was in. This force had driven away the Basutos who had cut off his line of retreat, and were now halted to cover the retirement if necessary.

Colonel Carrington ordered Major Grant's column, who were running short of ammunition, to retire from where they were, along the ridge in the direction of Diphering. They did so, and halted in a square formation, with the ambulances and guns out of rifle range, and waited orders. Colonel Carrington led the C.M.R. forward along the plateau towards the village, and under cover of the fire of the rest of the column we succeeded in reaching the ledge of rocks at the mouth of the village, and opened a heavy fire on the enemy at short range. The remainder of the column was then retired along the ridge below the plateau to join the column under Major Grant.

We still remained under cover in the ledge of rocks, and were attracting the attention of the entire body of the Basutos, and we could judge for ourselves what Colonel Carrington's move meant for us. He had sent the whole column—with the exception of 300 of us—clean out of action, knowing that had he attempted to retire the whole column from the position, the Basutos would have been on the top of them, and the loss of life would have been very heavy. The Basutos having met with success in the early part of the day, when they charged a picquet of 1st City Volunteers, consisting of 25 men and an officer, and succeeded in cutting them up, probably would not hesitate to charge the column if they got them all at a disadvantage, perhaps with serious results. It now remained to be seen how he would succeed in bringing 300 of us out from within 100 yards of the enemy's position to the protection of the guns on the ridge, 1200 yards away.

The order was given to retire by alternate troops. There being four troops of us, two were to form one line. Colonel Carrington himself took one line. Captain Shervinton, with my troop and a right-wing troop, took the other. The first line turned about and went slowly to the rear, where they took what cover the ground afforded, and faced about and lay down and waited for us. We had kept up an increasing fire on the walls of the village in front of us, behind which we knew the Basutos were in force. We now ceased firing, turned about, and doubled in extended order back to the first line, when we were made to break into quick time and walk slowly away. The enemy were not long in grasping the

situation, and before we reached the supporting line of skirmishers they rushed out of the village into the position we had
vacated and opened fire on us—our other line keeping them
in check till we took up our position again to allow No. 1 line
to go through us.   This went on till we reached the end of the
plateau, and the Basutos were still in the rocks by the village,
evidently not caring about facing our fire on the flat.   But
now came the trying time of our retreat.   We had to get from
the plateau on to the ridge below, and then retire along the
flat to the column.

It meant that one line would have to remain on the top
while the other descended and retired to 100 yards to
enable them to command the edge and fire over our heads, as
we retired, at the Basutos, who we knew would rush to the
position directly we vacated it.   No. 1 line with the colonel
went down first, and doubled back in order to take up a
position from which to cover us.   The Basutos, guessing what
was happening, began to rush along the flat towards us, and
got within sixty yards, notwithstanding our fire, which must
have inflicted heavy loss among them.

When Colonel Carrington had taken up his position on the
ridge below us, we were ordered to fire a volley in the direction of the enemy, leave the position, and get down on the
ridge as quickly as possible.   The manner in which we got
down the side of the hill can best be described in the words
of the bluejacket, who when asked how he got on at Majuba
Hill, replied, "It took us six mortal hours to climb
the bloomin' 'ill, and I touched three times comin' down."
We must have come down in a similar manner; but quick as
we were, the Basutos were on the edge of the plateau before
we reached the bottom, and had it not been for the supporting

party under the colonel, who opened a heavy fire over our heads at the enemy, we must have suffered severely in the way of casualties.

We doubled back in line and lay down in the rear of the line of skirmishers, and opened fire on the Basutos who had followed us.

The enemy not attempting to close on us, we again retired —this time in line and firing independently: a man would drop on to his knee, fire a shot, then get up and double back till he rejoined the line, the whole of which was moving slowly to the rear; by this means we kept up a heavy fire on them, at the same time getting nearer to the column.

At 600 yards we were ordered to cease fire—our wretched carbines were useless at anything beyond that distance—and, still extended, we marched back to the column. Any attempt at undue haste was promptly checked, and more than once the line was halted and made to face about in the direction of the enemy, by way of making the men moderate their pace. The Basutos redoubled their firing when ours had ceased, and the bullets that had hitherto been going over our heads and striking the ground in front of us when we were retiring, began now to cause some casualties among us. It was a trying time for the men under a hail of bullets and not able to fire a shot in return, but they were as steady as if on drill-parade, and the three 7-pounders now coming into action and bursting shells very accurately over the enemy's position, soon brought their fire to an end, and we rejoined the colomn, which had been watching our retreat with great anxiety and received us with ringing cheers.

The whole column now broke up: the C.M.R., with the ambulances, which were full of killed and wounded men, returned to Mafeteng, the remainder to the main camp, by Diphering. The Basutos contented themselves with following as far as the ridge below Lerothodi's village, but did not molest us farther.

The 1st City Volunteers were the principal sufferers in the day's fight, about fifteen of them being killed outright, and ten badly wounded. Captain Sampson, their commanding officer, had a very narrow escape. A Basuto rode up to him and fired a gun point-blank at his chest; but it was a muzzle-loading weapon, and evidently the bullet had not been rammed home, for although it struck him full on the chest and burnt his coat, the bullet only bruised him severely and did not penetrate. The C.M.R. had lost Sergeant Sherratt, a very promising sergeant, killed, and six or seven wounded, but we considered ourselves fortunate in getting off so lightly.

It now became manifest that it was useless for a column to attempt any further operations in the direction of the last two engagements, the country being so mountainous and treacherous that an invading force could not do more than burn a few kraals or drive the enemy out of their positions, without achieving permanent results. The Basutos let themselves be driven out of their positions, but only to take up others in the vicinity, and on our retiring to our base of operations they invariably followed us up, re-occupying the positions and generally harassing us pretty severely the whole return journey. The last engagement clearly showed the risk incurred by an isolated force left at any one position, of being surrounded and suffering heavy losses.

This was evidently the opinion that Colonel Carrington entertained—for no more expeditions were made to that part of the country till the campaign was finished.

CHAPTER XII.

WAGON CAPTURED BY BASUTOS — EX-C.M.R. KILLED — COLUMN LEAVES
MAFETENG FOR KOLAH MOUNTAIN—FRENCH MISSIONARIES AND THEIR
WORK—LAAGER FORMED AT NIGHT—MARCH ON KOLAH MOUNTAIN—
COLUMN HEAVILY ATTACKED ON ALL SIDES—RETURN TO CAMPING
GROUND—A PANIC—"ALL'S WELL"—RETURN OF COLUMN TO MAFE-
TENG—GENERAL ADVANCE INTO THE COUNTRY—SEVERE FIGHTING—
CAMP PITCHED—ATTACK BY BASUTOS ON THE HORSE-GUARD—NIGHT
ATTACK ON OUR CAMP—THE BAND PLAYS—PATROL MEETS WITH
SEVERE FIGHTING—KIDDY KILLED.

A SIGNAL station had now been established in the Free
State, close to the Basuto border, between Massayne's
Farm and Wepener, and Captain Waring, of No. 1 Troop
C.M.R., was stationed in Wepener as signalling officer and in
command of the base in that place. A range of high hills
formed the border between the Free State and Basutoland,
and situated under these hills and in Basutoland was a mission
station, the missionaries of which were French, who not only
looked after the spiritual welfare of the natives, but their
bodies as well. The mission was being turned into a hospital
where the wounded Basutos were treated. This led to a great
number of the fighting men also frequenting that part of the
country, and the convoys, which since the relief of Mafeteng
had hitherto come from the border unmolested and with a
small escort, were now being attacked. One wagon coming
out alone had been captured and driven away by the Basutos,
the white man in charge being killed, and his body left on the

veldt.   A party of us went out and brought the body in.   It
proved to be a man named Ditchbourne, a former member of
the F.A.M.P., who had been in No. 3 Troop with me at
Moirosi's Mountain, and subsequently took his discharge from
Fort Donald.   He had been stabbed to death and mutilated.
The men from the signal station on the border had informed
us of the capture, and also that the wagon had been driven
towards the mission station.

Colonel Carrington determined to visit that part of the
country.   A strong column, consisting of C.M.R., two regiments of Yeomanry, D.E.O.V.R., P.A.V.G., Kimberley Horse,
and three guns, with wagons and ambulances, and six days'
supplies, started from the main camp one morning and moved
off in the direction of the border part of the Kalabani Hill.
The Basutos streamed out of the positions by Lerothodi's
village and marched parallel with us on the different ridges
and hills, keeping in touch with our flanking parties and
exchanging shots with them.   It soon became obvious to us all
that we were in for six days' hard work.

As Colonel Carrington was not taking any risks of being
rushed, we marched in square formation—wagons massed and
abreast, with the infantry on all sides of them, and the guns at
the corners of the threatened sides—C.M.R. forming advance
and rear guards, the Yeomanry on both flanks.   This was
our first experience of being on an expedition with the
Yeomanry, and we watched their flanking parties with interest
and with rather selfish feelings, wondering whether in the
event of the Basutos making a charge on them, they would be
able to form quickly enough to repel the attack, or whether
they would retire on the wagons without giving us a chance
of falling back.   As we were some considerable distance in

advance of the column, we should have had a very uncomfortable time, to say the least of it, if the Basutos succeeded in driving in our flank.

The country in front of us was more open than any other part we had yet seen : the mealie lands could be seen stretching along for miles, and it was evident that the Basutos had not been neglecting their food supplies in that direction. We were marching parallel with the border, which was on our left flank and about 2 miles off—and were nearing Hermon mission station, as the place was called, when some shots came from that direction. Our videttes and advanced skirmishers returned the fire, when we saw a white flag hoisted in front of a stone building in the centre of the station, and a group of white people on the verandah. The column was halted, and Captain Shervinton with a sergeant and six men cantered up to the house.

The Basutos in our front and on our right flank were still keeping their distance, and looking on at our proceedings.

The French missionaries complained that our men had fired on the mission. Captain Shervinton demanded the reason why armed men had been seen riding out of the mission station, and why the place should not be burned down ? The missionaries claimed their right to act as they pleased, as they were French; but on being told to pack up, preparatory to being sent over the border, and their station destroyed, they altered their tone, and pleaded for consideration on account of the humane work they were carrying on with the wounded. The upshot was that an arrangement was made by which the Basuto chiefs were to be told by the mission people that no armed men were to be seen within a mile of the mission, and we in our turn would not interfere with the station or with their work with the natives.

The column was halted here for the night, horses off-saddled, and we formed camp, with strong picquets all around. The Basutos, apparently satisfied that we were not going to burn the mission station, began to move on in large bodies to our front in the direction of the Kolah Mountain, which we found was to be the objective of the patrol. The next day the column moved on in the direction of the Kolah Mountain, the Basutos taking up positions on every available ridge and hill in front of us, and trying to draw us away from the main body of the column and the guns. But on taking any position we halted, and allowed the guns to come up before advancing.

Reaching a plateau on rising ground, with a fine vlei or small lake below it, and the Basutos assuming a very threatening attitude all round us, Colonel Carrington halted the column, and formed a laager with the horses and cattle inside, and the troops told off to their various positions outside. The mounted men were sent out in various directions to drive the enemy off and burn villages in the vicinity. This work occupied the remainder of the day, and the Basutos did not offer serious opposition to the destruction of the villages except in the front, where they seemed determined to prevent any further advance.

The mounted men were then recalled to the laager with the exception of the picquets, who remained out some distance on each face of the laager till evening, when they returned to the camp, and infantry picquets were posted for the night in the usual way. We had a good opportunity for inspecting the Kolah Mountain, which was about four miles to our front, and was situated on the left of a range of high hills stretching away to our right as far as we could see. Villages could be seen dotted about the slopes of these hills, and it was very evident that the district was thickly populated. Towards evening the numerous fires on every hill, and the horses we could see in the distance off-saddled and grazing, showed us that we had the major portion of the Basuto army from the Mafeteng district around us, and watching our next move.

The position we were on was an ideal one for a camp, as the enemy would have to cross some hundreds of yards of flat ground before reaching us, and a fine moon put all idea of a surprise out of the question. The remainder of the column, not on duty, settled down for the night, and after being served with a good meal and fresh ammunition, we were soon sound asleep in our saddles outside the laager, and lulled by the sound of the picquets—" Number ——. All's well."

Réveillé sounded shortly after daybreak. We fed our horses, and picquets were sent out, and the infantry picquets dismissed. We were all ordered to cook breakfasts and take a day's food in our haversacks. Colonel Carrington had apparently given up the idea of attacking the Kolah Mountain, as otherwise we should have started before daylight. This was his usual custom when any position had to be captured; but that he intended having a closer view of the stronghold was soon indicated by orders to inspan the wagons and the men to saddle up; further precautions were then taken to ensure the safety of the main column. Three troops of C.M.R. were sent out—one to the front as advance guard, and the other two on either flank, with a troop of 2nd Yeomanry covering the rear. The remainder of the mounted men rode close to the infantry on all flanks of the wagon—so that they could easily face outwards and dismount and form a complete square in the event of an attempted rush by the enemy. We marched off in the direction of the Kolah—the advance troop extending in line with scouts well out to the front.

The Basutos could be seen in all directions taking up positions covering our line of advance, and there was no more rushing of the positions and waiting for the column to come up as on the previous day. On the enemy opening fire, the advance guard dismounted and returned it, the scouts coming back to the troop, and we marched steadily on foot to the positions. The two guns on the front face of the column did the necessary work—clearing the enemy away from our front as we advanced. Our objective was a plateau on slightly rising ground to our front, with ridges of stones in front of it, which when gained would have given a strong defensive position, and enabled us to shell the village on the mountain in front and right of us.

The Basutos around us had not shown up in nearly such large numbers as the previous day, and kept retiring without much opposition as we slowly advanced; but we were beginning to know the tactics of the enemy, and knew them to be more dangerous when only a few were visible than when they massed and seemed about to rush us. Seeing a fairly good position slightly to our right, Colonel Carrington changed the direction of the column, and we made for the ridge, and the wagons were drawn up under it. We were not a minute too soon.

The three C.M.R. troops galloped in and, dismounting, were soon in position among the rocks, the remainder of the column taking up their different positions, when a black bull appeared on the plateau we had originally intended to occupy. It was evidently a signal, for instantly in all directions thousands of mounted Basutos rode out of cover and charged straight on to us.

The troop of Yeomanry on the rear flank had taken things too easily, and had not formed up, and seeing the Basutos charging straight for them, they rode as hard as they could for the rear of the column. The Basutos cut some of them off and killed them instantly; the remainder came in almost mixed up with the Basutos, who were checked by a troop of C.M.R. and some of the Duke's Infantry, who, fortunately for the column, were in position in the rocks. The latter sent a volley into the enemy at point-blank range, a Basuto and his horse falling dead within six feet of where I was standing with a group of our men. The enemy broke all round us, but could not get into the square, and the three guns opening on them with case shot, aided by the heavy fire of the whole of the column, the Basutos turned about and rode for cover behind the hills they had charged from.

The withdrawal of the enemy gave us time to collect ourselves and enabled us to form a more compact square, in the improbable event of another rush. As they had failed to break us when the column was partly in a state of confusion, they could hardly hope to succeed when we were prepared. Our guns shelled the villages at the foot of the Kolah, and the positions which the enemy was supposed to occupy, but the Basutos were plainly saving their ammunition as much as possible, and were playing a waiting game, hoping to cut off any detached parties that might be sent out; but they were doomed to disappointment. It would have been sheer madness to have attempted an assault on the mountain, or even to burn the villages, as the country on all sides of us was swarming with mounted men, ready to overwhelm any part of the column that might be sent away any distance from the protection of the field guns. One of our guns was making particularly good practice whenever any party of the enemy appeared within range. A shell would burst in their midst, and the stampede of the horses in all directions and men running on foot, showed that it had found its mark. And after a time there were no movements made by the enemy that the guns could take advantage of.

Captain Bremner, who had commanded the troop of Yeomanry, had been killed, together with some of his men, and we had with some difficulty recovered the bodies and placed them in a wagon. After this had been done and the wounded made as comfortable as possible in the ambulances, Colonel Carrington made preparations to retire from the awkward position we had got into; knowing that the first move made to the rear would mean the sudden appearance of the enemy in all directions, and an attempt on their part to inflict as much damage as possible on the column before we reached the comparative safety of the open country, our front face—which would become the rear when we had started on our backward move—was reinforced. The two guns kept with them, and a heavy fire was directed on the hills in front, the shells breaking at the back of them, where it was supposed that the enemy was waiting under cover. One by one the wagons were moved out and turned round towards the rear, and formed up to the right of the ridge held by my troop of C.M.R. and some infantry, the whole of the Yeomanry being moved back with them and remaining on their right flank. When everything was ready the order was given to march, and we moved off on our return journey out into the open country. The rear guard waited till we were clear of the ridge of rocks, when they entered and occupied them, remaining until we had reached some distance from them and were well on the flat. We then halted on the flat, and closing on the wagons waited for our rear guard to make good their retreat.

The guns with two troops left the ridge, and kept up a heavy fire to their front on the enemy, who were now appearing on the hills. They had evidently found out that the guns had gone, and were preparing for a rush, as they suddenly appeared on the right of the ridge as well, and no doubt thinking that they had the small party on the ridge at their mercy, commenced riding towards them. The C.M.R. were not to be caught, however, for, jumping up from the rocks, they ran to their horses which were being held in the rear, mounted them, and were off at a gallop to rejoin the party with the guns before the Basutos realised what had happened. Clearing the front as they galloped, the C.M.R. rode round the flanks of the other troops who were dismounted and formed up in their rear, and when the Basutos reached the ridge they were met by a volley of musketry from the men and shells from the guns, that made them wheel round and scatter in all directions. The rear guard then continued their retreat, and joined the remainder of us without the loss of a man.

The column marched back to the ground we had occupied the night before and had left that morning. The wagons were laagered up, and the horses let loose to graze with a mounted guard. A strong picquet of Yeomanry with one 7-pounder gun occupied a stony kopje on the plateau which commanded the water and the valley between us and the hills which the enemy were on. We were able to take our belts off and make ourselves fairly comfortable, as we had received notice that we would remain there the remainder of the day and night. Cooking was soon indulged in, and some of us made shelters with our patrol tents between our line of saddles and the wagons, and had the luxury of a sleep.

The enemy kept at a respectful distance the remainder of the day, and after the horses and cattle had been brought into the laager and tied up, the former to the picquet ropes fixed across the laager, and the latter to their trek chains, fresh picquets were posted, and the column lay down in their different positions about twenty yards distant from and encircling the laager.

The night was a beautiful one. A full clear moon made every object round quite visible as in the daylight. We could see the sentries of our picquets quite 200 yards away, standing motionless in the veldt, with nothing to break the stillness but occasional " All's well," and we all anticipated a good night's rest, free from alarms. What was the cause of the extraordinary thing that happened to us that night I have never been able to find out, and often in after years, when talking over events of the campaign with old comrades, the conversation has come round to the question, "What the devil happened to us that night at the Kolah?" and the invariable answer is, " Give it up." I can only relate my own experience of what actually occurred, and leave the explanation to the reader.

About one o'clock in the morning every man of the column, as if moved by a sudden impulse, jumped up from where he had been sleeping and rushed in a frenzied manner back to the wagons. Men trampled on others as they passed, who in their turn jumped up, swinging their carbines or any sort of weapon they grasped in their hands—some with nothing at all—ran in amongst the bullocks, which they fell over, and continued the way amongst the horses, till they were brought up by other men in the same excited state who had run in from the other side of the laager. How it would have ended in another few minutes can be imagined, but suddenly a cry from the sentries in the distance rang out, " Number ——. All's well." Men looked at one another, and then at their hands, and what they held in them, and then silently went back to their places where they had been sleeping, for their arms. When I realised where I was, and what had happened, I found myself standing in my riding breeches, shirt-sleeves, and socks, with my amunition belt held by the strap, and swinging the buckle in all directions, with a lump on my head where I had fallen over a saddle head first against the wheel of a wagon; and my chum, a sergeant of No. 9 troop, rubbing his shins and using most violent language to some man who had brought him down by ducking between his legs. Order was at length restored, and the men all fallen in at their posts. Inquiries were made at which face the alarm had come from in the first instance; but nobody seemed to know anything whatever about the cause of the panic or the reason why we had all made such fools of ourselves. It was finally classed among the causeless panics, which sometimes seize men after a heavy engagement, when the sound of the guns still ringing in their heads during sleep causes a complete loss of nerve when suddenly awakened. The men who were on picquet and saw the whole occurrence, said there was' an utter absence of noise about the whole proceeding that made it look very uncanny to the onlookers. They could not imagine what had happened when they saw the mass of men struggling in the moonlight making their way to the wagons.

12

Réveillé sounding at daylight, we were soon packed up and on our march towards Mafeteng. The Basutos did not cause much trouble, and, with the exception of a few shots exchanged between the rear guard and themselves, they did not attempt to oppose our return, and on the column reaching the flats by the Kalabani Hill, the enemy left us, and riding round to the far side of Diphering they returned to their quarters in the direction of Lerothodi's village.

It was now becoming obvious that the whole of the Colonial forces in Basutoland were insufficient to inflict a severe defeat on the Basutos, and that hitherto we had only just managed to hold our own in the engagements we had fought with them. The Colonial Government had already begun to raise a force of Burghers, and we were informed that a large reinforcement would shortly arrive. Colonel Carrington in the meantime was determined not to keep us idle, and recognising that our previous engagements had not tended to bring the Basutos any nearer to submission to the Government, he decided to extend the operations farther into the country. The 2nd Regiment of Yeomanry marched into Mafeteng and relieved the C.M.R., and some details of other regiments were also sent there, making up the garrison to sufficient strength, and Colonel Southey of the 2nd Yeomanry was left in command.

The whole of the main column camp was then struck, the tents, rations, and forage for horses all being packed on the different wagons allotted to each regiment or unit. These, with ammunition wagons and ambulances, made a very large convoy, which the infantry had to guard on the march. The whole force commenced the forward march about the beginning of December, and moved off along the road past Diphering, which leads into the heart of Basutoland and in the direction of Morija, Letsea's great place, and of Masupha, Lerothodi's father and uncle.

The Basutos had ridden out in very strong numbers from Lerothodi's village, and had massed on the hills above Diphering watching our movements. When the advanced scouts of Basuto Police and C.M.R. reached the ridge on the far side of the enemy, they opened fire. The wagons of the column were all drawn up in the hollow by Diphering, and the infantry remaining with them, the whole of the mounted troops, with two guns, moved on to the ridge. On the right of the road, which led over a nek where we had fought the day when Lieutenant Clarke was killed, and on the left of the road was high ground with a flat top.

On these hills to the right and along the high ground to the left the Basutos were in great numbers, and the guns coming into action, we commenced shelling the tops of the hills and the nek in front of us. The mounted men were extended and advanced in the direction of the nek, the guns following.

On arriving within 500 yards of the nek the column halted, and the guns re-opened fire on the hills to our right front, and the Yeomanry were ordered forward to take the position. They went forward at a gallop, and dismounting at the foot climbed the hills in good style, the Basutos riding down the opposite face into the valley below. The C.M.R. were then ordered to take the position on the left of the road, whilst the Kimberley Horse occupied the nek under the hills the Yeomanry were in possession of. Leaving one troop of the C.M.R. to follow on with the guns, we charged straight at the position, the Basutos retiring down the steep slope into the valley below; they crossed this, and took up positions in a long range of broken hills on the opposite side and parallel to the position we were on. From the nek the road continued down the side of the hill into the valley close under the position we occupied for about two miles, and then wound away to the right under a series of kopjes of white stone formation; they were called the white kopjes; they formed a very strong position, and were the extreme left, facing us, of the range the Basutos had now occupied.

The wagons with the remainder of the column now came on from Diphering and reached the nek. The Yeomanry came down from the hills to the right of the road, leaving a small picquet on top to keep a look-out on the flank, and took up their position on the flats on the left of the road, with orders to keep on the top and march parallel with the column when we descended into the valley. The C.M.R. were then sent on ahead into the valley, and on arriving there we advanced in troops towards the opposite side, and halted when about 1200 yards from the line of hills which formed the enemy's position.

The wagons came down the hill into the valley, and forming up four abreast went on in the direction of the road parallel to the two positions, and near to the one occupied by the Yeomanry. The C.M.R. then changed direction and marched on the right flank of the column. At the point where the road turned in the direction of the enemy's position, the column wheeled to the right facing the enemy, advanced about 200 yards, and then halted, and the wagons were outspanned and pulled by the men into a square formation, the wagons of the different corps being placed on the face allotted to the regiments.

The C.M.R. had the front face directly opposite the enemy's position, the D.E.O.V.R. had the left face, the P.A.V.G., 1st City and Kimberley Horse the rear face, and the two regiments of Yeomanry the right face looking up the valley towards Lerothodi's village. The horses were off-saddled and let loose to graze between the column and the hill, on which a strong picquet, composed of a troop or company of every regiment, had relieved the Yeomanry.

Picquet lines were laid down for the horses, and trek chains for the oxen, inside the square of tents which were pitched immediately inside the wagons, and about three feet high, and it must have appeared to the Basutos as if we had come to stay. Bastions were built for the guns at each corner, with a large space at either side of them to allow the horses and cattle to be driven in, and shortly after midday the camp was completed and looked capable of defying all attempts to take it.

Situated about 400 yards to the left front of the C.M.R. face, and about 1000 yards from the nearest white kopje, was a small ridge of stones, from which the ground sloped down to the bottom of the range of hills occupied by the enemy. In this ridge of rocks a picquet of twelve men had been placed, where they could see any movements of the enemy should they approach from the direction of the white kopjes; but after a few shots from the enemy as they took up the position, they were left unmolested.

I was sergeant in charge of the horse guard of the C.M.R. on that day, having a corporal and twelve privates on guard. The horses were feeding in the direction of the hill on which the picquet was posted, and the guard, which was a mounted one, were posted at intervals between the enemy's position and the horses. We were dismounted and holding our horses' bridles, smoking and passing the time, which always appears much longer than usual when employed on this tedious duty, when about 3 or 4 o'clock in the afternoon the rain, which had been threatening for some time, came down in torrents. It developed into a hailstorm, and the horses, after moving uneasily about for some time, bolted in the direction of the hills and ridges occupied by the enemy. Mounting our horses, we galloped round them and succeeded in stopping them, but the animals would not face the hail, but stood with their tails towards it and their heads down.

I had no idea where we were, and could not see 20 yards from me, when I heard some shots to my right. The hail suddenly stopped, and I saw the camp about 300 hundred yards away to my right, and about 200 yards behind me a crowd of Basutos coming up the valley in our direction as hard as they could. I shouted to the corporal and two men to drive the horses, and the remainder of us faced about and fired from our horses' backs at the oncoming Basutos. The picquet on the stony ridge were firing into them as they passed, and the men were running out to the front of the camp. The horses, alarmed by our fire, turned and galloped off towards the right of the camp, several of the Basutos trying to turn them. The rest of us galloped after the horses to prevent the enemy from turning them, and an exciting time ensued. The men from camp were firing at the Basutos behind us and checked them, and we rode at the few who had got on the flank of the horses nearest the camp, and were trying to head them off. The corporal and the men with him were shouting and striking the horses on the other side. When the Basutos saw that the attempt had failed, and their companions were in full flight, they turned their ponies and rode straight past us, cutting at us as they passed with their battle-axes, we turning our horses and firing our carbines, pistol fashion, at them. Three or four of them fell, and we got their ponies. The whole of the position of the Basutos was crowded with men watching the attempt at capturing our horses, and I am confident that had the bail-storm lasted another two minutes they would have succeeded in getting the whole lot of them. As it was, we brought them all into camp, with the loss of one man of my guard wounded, and five horses, which were subsequently destroyed.

At dusk the mounted picquets returned to camp, and out-lying picquets on foot were posted on each face of the camp. The night being very dark, they were not posted so far out as usual, so that in the event of alarm they could regain the face of the square easily. About 9 p.m., when the column was settling down for the night, a volley was fired straight into the front of the camp, and the picquets fell back on the square, and the whole column stood to arms. Another volley came from the same direction, and we knew that the enemy had crept up to the ledge of rocks about 400 yards away, where a mounted picquet had been posted during the day. One of the 7-pounders opened fire, and we fired from our face of the square in the same direction, but the shots from the enemy still came from the same place, and the bullets, singing over the laager or striking the side of the wagon above the men's heads, made us keep pretty close to the walls. After the first volley it became apparent to us that the enemy did not mean to try an attack on us. Natives, as a rule, do not attack at night, not liking to face an unseen foe, but they evidently intended to annoy us and keep us awake. It was useless for a party of us to attempt a sortie, as we should probably lose touch with one another in the dark, and might get mistaken for the enemy by the men in the laager. So, after an hour of desultory firing at one another, Colonel Carrington sent a message to the commanding officer of the Dukes asking him to let the band play; and soon above the sound of the firing could be heard the inspiriting sound of a march, played by the Duke's band which accompanied their regiment. Our men ceased firing, and whether the Basutos thought that we were coming out to attack them, or, as the old adage goes, " Music hath charms," etc., they ceased firing at us, and the picquets, going out to their original positions again, the column settled down for the night, and we were not further disturbed. On the mounted picquet going out to the ridge on the following morning, they found ample evidence that the Basutos had been in that position the night before: three or four dead ponies being found lying there, and marks of blood amongst the stones.

Some two days afterwards a strong patrol went away to the right of the camp to reconnoitre the enemy's position, and see if there was any possible way round the defence in that direction; but the Basutos turned out in large numbers, and after some hours' fighting over a small position, we succeeded in driving them back for a mile, and then returned to camp. There were several casualties during the day, amongst them being young Kiddy of No. 7 Troop C.M.R., who was killed, much to the regret of all of us who knew him. The column returned to camp in the evening, the Basutos reoccupying their old positions in front of us.

CHAPTER XIII.

CHANGE CAMP TO BOLEKA RIDGE—ENEMY SHELLED—BURGHERS ARRIVE
IN MAFETENG—BURGHERS VISIT COLUMN—ATTACK MADE ON BASUTOS
BY TWO COLUMNS—BEHAVIOUR OF BURGHERS WITH OUR COLUMN—
ENEMY IN LARGE NUMBERS — COLUMNS RETIRE ON CAMP — AM
WOUNDED—SENT TO HOSPITAL—CHRISTMAS IN HOSPITAL, ALIWAL
NORTH—ARTILLERY PASS THROUGH *EN ROUTE* TO FRONT—C.M.R. RE-
ARMED WITH MARTINI-HENRY CARBINES.

COLONEL CARRINGTON now decided to change camp, and after packing up tents, etc., on the wagons, the process of in-spanning the oxen and saddling up the horses was gone through, and the column was ready to start.

All the mounted men were drawn up facing the enemy, who were watching the proceedings. The wagons moved off in the direction of the hill in the rear, which had been occupied by a strong picquet of our men the whole time that the camp had been pitched, and drew up at the extreme end of the position. The mounted men were then moved away to the left, which brought us between the wagons and the white kopjes, the end of the enemy's position. The road, as before mentioned, led close under the kopjes, through a pass, and the Basutos were massing along the ridges of the hills, evidently expecting us to march in that direction.

To the left of the picquet hill where the wagons had been halted was a large plain about two miles across, and reaching to a chain of hills called the Boleka Ridge, by far the highest of the ranges we had come across. They stretched from the Kolah Mountain on the right to opposite the white kopjes on their left, the road to Morija passing between the two and round the left of the Boleka Ridge. Some parts of the range were much higher than others, and there were several passes through which the Basutos rode, over some of the smaller hills, villages being built on the sides of the hills and in the passes.

The column moved round the picquet hill away to the left, leaving the white kopjes to our rear and the Boleka Ridge on our right, into the open, and in the direction of the border, and proceeded to a position about four miles distant. Directly the wagons moved off from under cover of the picquet hill the mounted men followed; the Yeomanry took up position as rear guard to the column, and the C.M.R. galloping across, formed up on the right flank, the Kimberley Horse going on as advance guard.

The Basutos streamed down from the positions they had occupied, and raced across the flats to the Boleka Ridge, and, keeping on the flat, rode parallel with us. The column was halted occasionally to enable the 7-pounders to send some shells into them when an opportunity occurred. We inclined towards the range as we marched, till we reached a position opposite a village, where there was a plentiful supply of water. Here we formed laager and pitched camp. The Basutos contented themselves with taking up position along the ridge, and did not interfere with the march of the column during the day.

We were all very much relieved at the change of camps, the last position having been an almost untenable one, and the duties entailed by the picquet and guards, which were of extra strength to ensure the safety of the column, extremely hard on the men. The new position was infinitely better in every way; it was on rising ground, with flat country on three sides of it, the Boleka Ridge distant about 1600 yards from the front face. The laager was also spread out in larger dimensions than the last, and men and animals were not so cramped for room. There was not so much danger for the convoys of wagons which were constantly going to and from the border with provisions, grain, etc., as there was no position the enemy could take up en route from which to harass them. Columns were sent out nearly every day from the camp, who attacked and burned villages to the left and right along the foot of the ridge; but the attempts on our part to take a position on the ridge and hold it proved abortive, and always ended in the column having to return to the camp, hard pressed, with the enemy on their heels.

Shortly after the change of camps, we heard that reinforcements in the shape of 1600 Burghers had arrived at Mafeteng, and that their camp had been pitched near the site of the old main camp, but nearer to the Kalabani; that they were nearly all Dutchmen, the exceptions being a few Colonials and Englishmen who had joined as substitutes for some farmers who preferred paying for other men to do the fighting for them, instead of going themselves. Sums of from £50 to £100, and sometimes more, had been paid to these substitutes, who in a great many instances deserted on the march up and joined some other corps, after having had their sprees out with the money they had dishonestly got.

The Sunday after their arrival, some two or three hundred of these Burghers rode across from their camp to where we were. Their "leaders" or officers went to pay their respects to the officer commanding the column, and the remainder, sitting on their horses or dismounted outside the camp, were immediately surrounded by an inquiring and critical crowd. The Burghers looked well enough, and were typical Dutchmen in their appearance, tall bearded men in smasher hats, cord coats, and mostly wearing trousers, with one spur upside down, the correct fashion with the "Dopper." They were all well armed with the best rifles of that day — chiefly Westley Richards and Winchester repeaters—and their bodies were hung about with crossed bandoliers or leather breastplates, with cartridges sticking out of leather holders. They professed a great interest in the position occupied by the enemy, but did not appear very enthusiastic when some of the men suggested they had better ride over and have a closer look at the Basutos. On their leaders leaving the colonel's tent and rejoining them, they all clustered round and listened to what they had to say, and rode off to their own camp without any attempt at military formation.

A day or two afterwards two columns left the camp, consisting of both regiments of Yeomanry. The Duke's, with one 7-pounder gun, under the command of Colonel Brabant of the 1st Yeomanry, went away to the left of the camp in the direction of the Boleka Ridge, and the other column under Colonel Carrington, four large troops of C.M.R., the P.A.V.G., Kimberley Horse, and 100 of the newly joined Burghers, who had come over from their camp early in the morning, and one gun, moved out to the right of the camp in the direction of the white kopjes and of our late camp. Ammunition wagons and ambulances accompanied each column. The Burghers led the way, the C.M.R. advanced in columns of troops behind them, while the infantry with gun and Kimberley Horse followed with the wagons.

The Basutos were to be seen in great numbers to our front coming to meet us from the ridge on our left, and the kopjes in front. A number now appeared on the picquet hill to our right front, and the Burghers were sent forward to drive them off the position. They rode up as far as they could, the Basutos firing at them as they advanced; then they dismounted and got amongst the rocks and commenced firing at the Basutos on top, but made no attempt to go forward and drive the enemy off. A large body of Basutos could now be seen galloping towards the position and reinforcing their own men, whilst another large body approached from our left, evidently with the intention of cutting the Burghers off. Colonel Carrington, seeing that things looked critical for the Burghers unless they drove the Basutos from the top of the hill, ordered three troops of C.M.R. to go and take the position. We went away at a gallop, a number of Basutos riding for the same position from the other side. We dismounted and went up the hill, passing the Burghers who were lying behind stones in a helpless manner, and calling out to them to come along. We gained the top of the position, drove back the Basutos from the ruins of a village where our picquets were formerly stationed, and took up our position there. Our horses were brought up and placed under cover of a ledge of rocks below the village. The Basutos did not retire any distance, but remained at the edge of the hill opposite to the side we had come up, and kept up a heavy fire on us.

We could see that Colonel Carrington, who was on the flat about 800 yards away in a small square, had been attacked by a very large number of the enemy, and had great difficulty in keeping them off. At last, finding the fire too hot for them, the enemy retired out of range, and the column slowly made their way towards our position. The Burghers had come farther up the hill, and were huddled up amongst the horses, and behind stones on the edge of the hill, and would not come up to the firing line. Several sergeants were sent by our adjutant, Captain Bowers, to try to persuade them to come up and assist, as our men were barely holding our own, and the Basutos seemed to be increasing in numbers and might at any minute try to rush us. I was one of the sergeants sent, and with my chum, a sergeant of No. 9 Troop, we went to a group of Burghers who were getting under the wall of an old cattle kraal close to where our horses were being held, and told them to go up to the top of the hill to the C.M.R. Not one of them would move, and they pretended not to understand us. We began to lose our tempers, and used some strong and contemptuous language. At last, when I asked if there was an Englishman amongst the crowd, a voice called out, " I am. What do you want me to do ? " A man appeared from behind the wall and said, " I am an old Naval Brigade man—here's my medal," showing us a Zulu War medal. " Don't mix me up with this —— set of curs. Where shall I go ? " We took him back with us, and he was the only man amongst the whole of the Burghers' force that day who stood in the firing line with the C.M.R. on the hill, and in the subsequent retreat.

Colonel Carrington had in the meantime approached to within 500 yards of us, where he halted and sent Captain Durrant, his galloper, across to us with orders to retire from the hill and fall back on the square. The Burghers understood that order at least, and, dragging their horses down the hill, they cleared off to the square, leaving us to get away in the best manner we could. Our horses were first sent down to the foot of the hill, and then came our turn. There was no room for any extended order movement, and we had to retire in groups, one covering the other as best we could as we went down the hill to where our horses were standing. Directly we left the cover of the village we fell back to the ledge where the Burghers had distinguished themselves, and here we found that the Basutos had immediately taken up the position we had evacuated. We kept them in check for some time, to enable half our men to get to a position lower down in order to cover the retreat of the remainder, and then left the ledge and got away as quickly as possible to our left, to give our supports a clear front to fire at the enemy, who followed firing on us at short range. We crawled down the best way we could, and I was in the act of turning round after firing, when I felt a severe blow on my shoulder as if some one had struck me with the butt of the carbine. Down I went head over heels over a stone, and the first knowledge I had of what had happened was finding myself being half carried and half dragged between my chum and one of the privates towards the square on the flat, with bullets kicking up the dust all around us. I was then told I had been fool enough to stop a bullet, and was put into the ambulance with a half-dozen other men who had tried a like experiment with some damage to themselves.

Colonel Brabant's column had met with similar opposition, and he retired back to the main camp and then on to the relief of Colonel Carrington, who had signalled saying that he was hard pressed and wanted assistance. The C.M.R. managed to regain the square with the small loss of three, one being shot dead.

The Basutos were keeping up a very heavy fire on our

column, and a good many casualties occurred before Colonel Brabant's column came up and covered our retirement.   The ambulance wagons were not the safest spot in the column; several bullets had passed through the tent or cover of it, and one coming through the thick plank at the side went through a man who had already been shot and killed him on the spot. He simply gave a kick and lay still, his head resting on my leg.   His name was Von Plaster, and he belonged to the 3rd Yeomanry.   I met his mother in Aliwal North shortly afterwards when I was in hospital, and spent rather a bad quarter of an hour with her answering questions about his death.   It certainly was rather hard luck after being hit once to get a final one in the ambulance, but it was his day out and there was no getting away from it.

An incident occurred during the retirement of the C.M.R. which is a sample of the callousness often provoked by frequent contact with death.   Private Murphy, of No. 4 Troop, was a very popular man in the regiment.   He had been a medical student before joining, and was on the medical staff of the regiment for a considerable time, but, owing to his failing for drink, had been reduced from corporal to the ranks. He was known as "Spud" Murphy, or "Spud," as soldiers generally call potatoes, our Irish friends calling them murphies. Murphy was in the skirmishing line, and the order being given to cease fire and march at ease, the men as usual pulled their pipes out of their pockets and commenced to smoke. Although out of range for the wretched weapons the Colonial Government had deemed good enough for our men, the distance was by no means too great for the enemy, who generally, after we had ceased firing, redoubled their efforts to bring us down.   Next to Murphy in the line was the Cockney

friend who had been premature in announcing the death of
the regimental on a former occasion. The bullets were
striking the ground among the men, when one suddenly
struck poor Murphy on the back of his head, the bullet
coming out of his mouth and causing the pipe which he
was smoking to fall forward as he fell. The Cockney looked
at Murphy, and then picked up the pipe, and, looking at it,
turned to the man on the other side, and remarked with
a sigh, "Well, that's put Spud's pipe out, anyway;—give us a
hand to carry 'un 'ome for the last time." They brought him
to the wagon, deposited him underneath, and strolled off to
rejoin their troop. Yet the Cockney was not lacking in
heart.

My wound, though not dangerous, was very painful; the
bullet had broken my left shoulder-blade, and it was some
weeks before I could use my arm at all. That night I spent
in a hospital tent in camp, and the following morning was
packed off with some dozen other unfortunates for Mafeteng,
there to be overhauled, and reported upon as unfit or otherwise
for further service.

We remained in Mafeteng three or four days, during
which Colonel Carrington paid us a visit in the hospital; he
appeared pleased when he was told I was only temporarily
disabled and would be fit for service again, and spoke very
kindly to me. We were then attached to a convoy of wagons,
and moved on to the Border, and thence proceeded to Wepener,
where the English church had been converted into a temporary
hospital. Here we were treated with every kindness by the
English community in the town. We remained till the advent
of more wounded and sick from the column necessitated the
removal of the patients who were fit to travel in the ambulance

down to Aliwal North, the front town on the Cape Colony side of the Orange River. I went with the party, and arrived in the hospital at Aliwal North on Christmas Eve.

The hospital was in a large house on the bank of the Orange River, the first one to the left after crossing the bridge. The rooms, which were large, had been turned into wards with eight to ten beds in each. The officers' ward was directly opposite the one I was located in, and I saw Captain H. of the C.M.R. for the first time since I had left Fort Donald. He was the senior lieutenant of No. 5 Troop then, and had come up with his troop in the relief column; he had been wounded in the relief of Mohalie's Hook, and had been in Aliwal North since the event. He had recently been promoted to captain, and was almost convalescent, and enjoying himself with many visitors of both sexes who were constantly calling. My old lieutenant, who had been hit in the jaw, was also in the officers' ward, and he came to my bed and greeted me, with his hands full of cigars, tobacco, and cigarettes, which he insisted on putting in the locker beside my bed. It was against the rules, but the orderly of my ward being a C.M.R. they remained there for the use of the ward in general.

There were five other C.M.R. in the ward, one of the Kimberley Horse, and a bandsman of the P.A.G., a splendid clarionet player, who whiled away many an hour playing. With the exception of one of our men who had been shot in the thigh during the relief of Mohalie's Hook, and was in rather a critical state, the bullet being still in his leg, the rest of us were well on the road to recovery. Our appetites were good, and were able to indulge in the luxuries that were provided for us on a very large scale by the ladies of the town. English papers and books of every description were sent to the hospital by various people, who vied with one another who could do most in the way of cheering us up.

The news of the column was brought to us directly it arrived, and we were kept posted as to the movements, casualties, and so on. We were told that Colonel Carrington had shifted the whole column back to Mafeteng for Christmas week; races and sports were to be held during the period of inaction; wagons laden with Christmas presents from almost every town in the Colony had gone forward to Mafeteng to be distributed to the various regiments they had been consigned to by friends and relatives. The C.M.R. had not been forgotten by our old friends from King and Queen's Town, and, as I was subsequently told in letters received from my chums at the front, the presents not only consisted of plum-puddings, tobacco, etc., but knitted socks, caps and mufflers and gloves had been sent for the C.M.R. from other towns besides the two already mentioned.

Christmas Day was a great event in the hospital. A magnificent dinner had been provided by the townspeople, and after church the hospital was packed with visitors, who passed through the wards distributing cigarettes and tobacco, and watching the preparations being made for the dinner. I was confined to my bed that day; the jolting of the wagon on the journey down had caused my shoulder to become very much inflamed and caused me rather more pain than usual, so I did not enjoy the scene as I would have done a month later on. But I was rather amused at some of the sympathetic looks of the young ladies who were conducted through the wards by the doctors, and the " Poor young fellow—isn't he young too ? " from a good-looking lady who evidently thought I was asleep, caused me to open my eyes and laugh, when she stepped back under cover of her mother, blushing very prettily.

Shortly after Christmas the Cape Field Artillery marched through the town on their way to the front. They had been newly formed from the old C.M.R. Artillery Troop, and they looked an uncommonly smart lot of men as they passed us. In addition to 7-pounder guns, they had four 75-pounder howitzers, a very heavy gun and pulled by oxen; these were to be used for the defence of camps and shelling the enemy's positions. The C.F.A., as the artillery were called to distinguish them from the C.M.R., were commanded by Captain Giles, late of the Royal Artillery, with three lieutenants, the senior of whom I recognised as my friend Gipsy, the corporal at Butterworth, who had got his commission on the reorganisation of the corps. A long line of wagons followed them, and they halted and outspanned across the bridge on the Free State side. Several of the N.C.O.'s and men visited us during the day, and we learned to our satisfaction that some of the wagons contained new carbines for the C.M.R.—Martini-Henry's of the pattern used by the imperial troops at the time; also that there were several hundreds of swords in the wagons for the regiment. About five hundred swords had been sent to the column two months previously, and the officer commanding had them issued to the 2nd Regiment of Yeomanry which had been left behind at Mafeteng for garrison work, and had ample time at their disposal to undergo instruction. Sergeant Glover of my troop, an old 5th Dragoon Guardsman, and a very fine soldier, had been detailed as instructor to the 2nd Yeomanry, and had remained behind with them; on the various visits of our men to Mafeteng on convoy duty, Glover had been subjected to much good-natured chaff about his budding cavalry regiment ; he was advised to give the job up and rejoin his troop and see some decent fighting, but he was confident of being able to do something with his unpromising material, and always replied : " Wait till we come out, and you will see something that will astonish the lot of you." As will be related later on, they did see something, but not in the way poor Glover meant.

CHAPTER XIV.

1881.

AM INVALIDED TO KING WILLIAM'S TOWN — PASS RELIEFS ON ROAD —
ARRIVAL AT KING WILLIAM'S TOWN—C.M.R. BARRACKS—NEWS FROM
THE FRONT—BURGHERS DISTINGUISH THEMSELVES IN THEIR CAMP—
COLONEL CARRINGTON GOES ON A WOOD PATROL—BURGHERS CHARGED
BY BASUTOS—HEAVY LOSSES—SWORD CHARGE BY YEOMANRY—CAR-
RINGTON'S DISPATCH—C.M.R. LOSE THEIR HORSES.

DURING January the principal medical officer, Surgeon-
Major Hartley, V.C., who, it will be remembered, gained
the cross at Moirosi's Mountain, inspected the hospital.
Patients and all men sufficiently well to be moved, and whom
he did not consider fit for return to the front at once, were
ordered down to King William's Town, the headquarters for
both wings of the C.M.R. I was amongst the number, and,
being the senior sergeant (I had recently been promoted to
second-class sergeant), I was placed in charge of the convoy,
consisting of two ambulances with mules and a wagon for the
medical staff which accompanied us.

We had passed several detachments of men on their way
to the front, reliefs for the different volunteer corps, who had
been only called out for six months in the first instance, and
whose time was approaching for their return to their homes.
This was another serious handicap for the commandant-
general. By the time he succeeded in getting the different
corps into something like a disciplined force, and the men

accustomed to the hardships of active service, it was time for them to return; and the same anxiety and trouble had to be gone through again in handling raw, untrained troops in the face of a determined enemy, quick in detecting the slightest confusion on our side, and taking advantage of it. The commandant-general had now returned to Basutoland, and the troops had left their Christmas quarters and had again advanced to the former position at the Boleka Ridge. The 2nd Yeomanry had been relieved by the 3rd Yeomanry under Colonel Minto, and had now accompanied the column, and were expected to give a good account of themselves with their swords should an opportunity occur. A series of engagements occurred which ended in our forces successfully assaulting and occupying the ridge which the enemy had held since our first advances from Mafeteng; the main camp was now moved to that place.

King William's Town at the time of our arrival was the scene of great activity, as all Colonial towns are during war. No matter how far distant the scene of operations may be, there is always some business going on in connection with supplies for the front,—forage being brought in from the country districts in large quantities, or troops of horses brought in by various dealers for remounts for C.M.R. and volunteers. The old Police barracks was a thing of the past, and the C.M.R. now occupied the old Cape Corps barracks situated in the Reserve, the other end of the town from the old Police camp, and next to the fine barracks formerly built for the Imperial troops, which were now taken over by the Colonial Government, and used as offices and stores for the Colonial Defence Department.

There were about six hundred recruits for both wings of

the regiment being trained and drilled as quickly as possible, that they might be sent to the front. They were a fine lot of young fellows, all English recruits, and were arriving in batches from home monthly. They were armed with swords, Martini-Henry carbines, and revolvers, a contrast to the miserable weapons with which we were sent to face the enemy; and the instructors were hard at work from early morning till evening, teaching the young recruit to ride and use his weapons. Some of them had only been in the country about three months, and were already passed as fit for the front to join the "squadrons," as the troops were now called, the almost last relic of the old Police disappearing with the new title.

In those days it took a month or six weeks to travel the distance between King William's Town and Basutoland, provided there were no breakdown of wagons; and the use of weapons on the march was reckoned to increase the efficiency of the recruit by the time he arrived at the scene of operations.

Some of the youngsters who could ride before joining, and were quicker than others in picking up the sword exercise and manual and firing with the carbine, were quickly put through their facings, and sent on to finish their education in the way of sleeping out in their saddles. If they could not cook, they starved till they were able to, and in a very short space of time they were as much at ease in the ranks under any condition as the old article, and hard to recognise as the youth who had left school and home some four months before. Active service in a well-disciplined regiment is the best and quickest method of drawing out the best in a man.

Major Grant was in King William's Town as officer commanding lines of communication at base, and also in command of the garrison. The paymaster and his staff were also there, and I had an opportunity of renewing my former friendship with his clerks, who were now third-class sergeants, and appeared very glad to see me. As I was now convalescent, I could visit any part of the barracks and surroundings, and I used to watch the recruits going through their sword drill till I became, as far as theory went, quite an expert. As I regained the use of my shoulder, I used to practise half an hour every morning, till I was pronounced efficient and duly qualified as an instructor.

During this time we were well posted up in news from the column, from both official and private sources, my chum in No. 9 writing frequently and giving me all the behind-the-scenes part of the programme. The column had succeeded in gaining possession of the Boleka Ridge and establishing itself on the other side, only to be confronted by a still stronger position than anything encountered previously. This was the Tantjesberg range of mountains, very high and precipitous in parts, all the accessible positions being strongly fortified by the enemy in anticipation of the capture by the troops of the Boleka Ridge. There had been incessant skirmishing, but nothing of any importance till the general decided to bring the Burghers out to the column and give them a chance of distinguishing themselves. They had hitherto remained in their camp between Diphering and Kalabani, and had not been engaged with the enemy since the time they left us to bear the brunt of the retreat from the Picquet Hill on 13th December. They had been indulging in several imaginary encounters, and had repulsed several "attacks" on their camp at night by the "Basutos." This fierce foe invariably turned out to be a stray horse or bullock which had strayed in an unlucky moment into view of an excited sentry, who invariably fired in any direction and ran to the camp as hard as he could, yelling in Dutch that the Basutos were on them. This was the signal for every man to let off his rifle indiscriminately in any direction—generally through the top of the tent, as the riddled tents showed. After wasting some thousands of rounds in this amazing "defence," they would report next day that they had been attacked by the whole Basuto army, but had driven them off, killing thousands.

As it was an impossibility for any number of the enemy to be within miles of them without the column, or Mafeteng, or Diphering garrison seeing them, and the only sign of slaughter generally being a disabled transport mule or ox, their report was not taken very seriously, but I suppose the general thought that if Government ammunition was to be wasted, it might as well be at least fired in the direction of the Basutos, for he ordered them out to the column camp to form part of a force detailed for a wood patrol. This meant taking empty wagons with the column for the purpose of bringing back wood from the various huts of the villages which we intended to be destroyed, and often resulted in the wagons returning with dead and wounded men instead. Colonel Carrington's wood patrols were a well-known institution during the war, and one was always certain of an average good fight whether the wood was obtained or otherwise.

On this occasion Colonel Carrington, who was in command, had a strong column with him, C.M.R., 2nd Yeomanry, who took the field with their swords on for the first time, and a strong body of infantry and the 7-pounders and the

Burghers. The column went in the direction of Tweefontein, to the right of the camp, the left of the column facing the Tantjesberg, the country being a series of ridges with villages at the back of them. The column had proceeded about two miles, the Basutos appearing on the ridges to the front, when Colonel Carrington told the Burgher commandant to take his men and drive them off the ridge. The Burghers went off at a gallop, and after a few shots the Basutos retired on to the next ridge. The Burghers followed, firing and shouting at the easy way they were driving all before them, and doubtless thinking they were showing the "Rooineks," or Englishmen, the way to treat the Basutos. The Basutos still retired before them, and the Burghers still followed, but not so keen as at the first ridge, some of them suddenly realising that they had gone farther than they were intended to go, which was the case. Colonel Carrington, who was with the column marching slowly on in the Burghers' tracks, now saw what would happen, and closing the wagons up he formed a square round them and waited events, the only thing he could do under the circumstances.

In the front of the square, about 500 yards away, was a troop of C.M.R., 35 men with 3 officers, Captains Shervinton and D'Arcy, V.C., and Lieut. Cruttwell, who were acting as support. Seeing the Burghers galloping on without orders, they had halted and kept their distance in front of column. What Colonel Carrington anticipated happened. The Burghers in the act of riding at the third ridge, some of them having already halted, were suddenly charged by mounted Basutos from the front and sides. The Burghers didn't wait to fire, but turned and rode as hard as their horses could gallop straight back for the column. The Basutos on their wiry little ponies, and swinging their battle-axes, rode after them, gradually catching them up and battle-axing them as they rode past them. Captain Shervinton, seeing the mass coming straight on to the front of the camp, and knowing that if he retired the Burghers and Basutos would come on the column all mixed up, and would probably break the square and cause a disaster, decided to face the rush. He called out, "Dismounted Service dismount," and the men were off their horses, which they handed over to the No. 3 of their section, and were fallen into line ten paces in front of them, when the mob appeared a hundred yards off. The officers and men shouted to the demoralised Burghers to clear the front, and by waving made them understand to some extent; but it was too critical, and the men opened fire straight to their front, firing as quickly as possible and from the hip as the Basutos got closer; the enemy fell in great numbers, and, swerving to the right and left as they got close, rode past the flanks of the little party, cutting at the flank men as they did so.

The check given to the centre of the Basutos by the C.M.R. broke them, and they galloped to the right and left of the column, where they met with a heavy fire. The infantry let the Burghers through and reformed, but the Basutos had broken and retired to the flanks, from where they returned to the front and opened fire on the column.

In order to clear the ground in front, and recover the bodies of the Burghers who had been killed and stripped, Colonel Carrington ordered the 2nd Yeomanry to charge. They formed up, drew swords, and rode towards the enemy. Captain Ellis of the 3rd Yeomanry, and Sergeant Glover, C.M.R., their instructor, who expected so much of them, rode in front of them, but although they had passed their sword drill, it was evident before they had gone 100 yards that they had not imbibed the necessary amount of dash and pluck required for the particular service they were ordered on. Although "Charge" was shouted by their leader, it did not seem to evoke the usual enthusiastic response; perhaps the attitude of the enemy, who seemed inclined to meet them half way, decided them, but the sad fact remained that out of the whole number who started away from the column to charge the enemy, only four succeeded in getting within touch of them. Captain Ellis fell from his horse, struck by a bullet on the ear which stunned him; Regimental Sergeant-Major Hooper's, an ex-C.M.R. man, horse stumbled and he was immediately battle-axed; another man was wounded, but got away.

Sergeant Glover, who had asked permission to join in the charge, rode alone through them, and was seen on the ridge the other side of the enemy. He looked for a moment in the direction of the column, and then sent his horse at the thickest part of the Basutos. The whole column was watching, as nothing could be seen except the occasional flash of sword or battle-axe, when suddenly Glover appeared in the intervening space of ground between the Basutos and the column, alone, and not pursued by the enemy. He was cutting to the right and left of his horse in the air in terrific fashion, and only stopped when he pulled up in front of Colonel Carrington and his staff, and looked vacantly round him. He was covered in blood from his shoulder to the heels of his boots, but on being lifted off his horse and examined, it was found that he had not a single scratch on his body, the blood being all from the enemy.

He mounted and rode straight back to where his troop

No. 3 was standing, and fell into his place silently. His comrades tried to cheer him up with chaff and praise, but he took no notice of them, and remained quiet till the column returned to the camp, after the recovery of the bodies of the Burghers, and the dispersal of the enemy by the 7-pounders.

Glover was sent into Mafeteng the following morning, and found to be suffering from camp fever (now called enteric). He was sent on to Wepener, where he remained. Some days after his admission into hospital at that place, the padre, Father Stenson, took him a sword which had been sent, subscribed and bought by the colonel, N.C.O.'s and men of the 2nd Yeomanry, and handed it to Glover with their kind message. Glover took the sword, looked at it, and returned it to the padre. "Take it back with Sergeant Glover's compliments, Father," he said, "and say I would not be seen dead in the same ditch with any one of them!" Nothing more could be got out of him, and he died about a week after the event. Glover was much regretted by the whole regiment, who deeply sympathised with him in the shock he must have sustained when he realised how badly he had been left by the mob he had taken such a pride in teaching to handle a sword.

Colonel Carrington had the swords promptly taken away from the Yeomanry, and they were issued to the C.M.R., but the Basutos never laid themselves open to a sword charge again, and to this day they talk of the man who rode alone through them, cutting them down right and left as he rode, as too wonderful to be understood by any ordinary mortal.

During the time the column was in a square at Tweefontein, and parties were sent out recovering the killed

and wounded men, the Basutos kept up a heavy fire and
several more casualties occurred. Surgeon-Lieut. M'Crae of
the 1st Yeomanry greatly distinguished himself by attending the wounded under this fire and saving many lives.
While he was performing this duty, he was himself shot in
the chest, but plugging up his wound himself, he continued
his work till he collapsed. He received the Victoria Cross
for this day's action, and became a surgeon-major in the
C.M.R., where he became very popular with us all, till the
day of his death, fourteen years later.

Colonel Carrington in his despatches to Government
summed up the cause of the heavy casualty list in a very few
words—"Burghers bolted." The curt despatch caused a lot
of bitter feeling in the Colony amongst the supporters of the
Dutch, and it must have been a sad blow for Messrs. Sprigg
and Company, sitting in Parliament, to have the conduct of
their trusted Burghers treated in such a contemptuous manner
by a soldier, who of course did not understand the method of
handling such a body of warriors as Dutch Burghers. It was
an awkward position, however, and the best way out of the
difficulty was to let them go home if they wished. As a great
number of them had already started without leave, the
remainder were allowed to go as they felt inclined, and the
Burgher forces melted away in a very short space of time,
their departure bringing a sense of relief to the whole column.

There is no doubt that the feeling of the Dutch in the
Cape Colony at this period was greatly in favour of their
countrymen in the Transvaal. Only a few months before,
they had openly defied Great Britain, and asserted their independence. By treachery they had caused several British
garrisons in the Transvaal to capitulate, and the wholesale

butchery of Colonel Anstruther's column at Bronker's Spruit. For this, in my opinion, the Dutch ought never to have been pardoned. From behind safe cover, and at previously marked-out ranges, they opened fire on a British regiment on their march to Pretoria, while the men were marching along at ease, with bands playing in front, and their women and children sitting upon the wagons, and mercilessly shot them down in cold blood, till what was left of them surrendered. It was a glorious victory indeed for the Boers, of a character quite in keeping with their record. And then, after the crowning disgrace of Majuba Hill, the British Government made a disgraceful peace and gave the Transvaal its independence, a piece of sentimentality on the part of the Government in power which was to cost a later generation dear. They had the opportunity of smashing once and for all this hybrid race of unwashed farmers, and instead they condoned the murders that had been perpetrated on British soldiers, and the insult to the British flag, and withdrew, leaving all Britishers who had elected to make their homes in South Africa at the mercy of a race of men of whom it is simple truth to say that they don't know the meaning of the words "truth" and "honour." And perhaps it was as well for the Burghers that they left Basutoland before the news of Majuba reached the column, for they might have been handled by the British section of the column with even less ceremony than they had been by the Basutos.

The enemy were now showing more activity than usual, attacking the convoys very frequently on their journeys to the border, and threatening the picquets on outpost duty from the main camp. One morning, when the horses were let out of the laager inside the camp to graze, and were being driven by the mounted guard to the ground where they were in the habit of feeding, a large body of the enemy appeared from the back of a hill, on the left of the camp, where they had been awaiting their opportunity, and charged down between the camp and the horses. In spite of the efforts of the guard, and the fire of the men from camp, who were promptly turned out, they succeeded in driving the whole of the C.M.R. horses over the hill and amongst their own people, the whole affair lasting only three or four minutes.

The Basutos must have been waiting for this opportunity for some time, but the horses had hitherto been feeding on the other side of the camp, where they were not easy to get at. The Yeomanry horses had been feeding for days where our horses were captured, and the enemy never made the slightest attempt to capture them; but seeing the C.M.R. horses change their feeding-ground on the day before, they laid their plans, and successfully carried them out. It now meant that if any fighting was to be done the column would have to go on foot, as although the Yeomanry had improved considerably as regards their discipline, and had regained some of their lost confidence, they were hardly to be relied on to keep off a sudden rush of the enemy, and might endanger the safety of the column by retreating à la Burgher. So the next expedition was made by the infantry with guns, C.M.R. dismounted, and was in the direction of the nek to the right of the Tantjesberg Range, and in the direction of Hell's Poort, a vicious looking pass between two ranges of mountains where the Dutch commando had met with disaster in the Dutch and Basuto War about thirty years before. The howitzers were taken out for the first time, drawn by spans of bullocks, and escorted by C.M.R.

14

The column moved towards the nek in a square, the Duke's infantry on the left face, the C.M.R. on the front and right, with Kimberley Horse and P.A.V.G. on rear face, a troop of C.M.R. in skirmishing order a short distance in front, as this was to be a reconnaissance. Not much fighting was expected, and the C.F.A. commenced shelling the range with the huge unwieldy guns from the left-hand corner of the square. After three or four rounds, the wheels began to sink in the soft ground, and the men could not move the trail of the gun; the bullocks were attached to it, but it still stuck, and the C.M.R. and the C.F.A. got out drag-ropes. During the confusion the Basutos took it into their heads to charge, and before the men were in readiness were almost on the guns. The infantry formed round with fixed bayonets and poured in a heavy fire, and the C.M.R. fired into them from the front, but they rushed up on their ponies so quickly and determinedly that they fell actually on the bayonets of the infantry and in front of the gun before they were driven off. Some of the C.F.A. got under the gun to avoid being cut down. The gun was eventually shifted, and the column retired to camp.

It was the last time these guns were attempted as field guns; they were only used for defensive purposes afterwards; also the risk of going out without reliable scouting was brought home to the mind of the general. The result was that all expeditions for a time ceased till fresh horses had been purchased in the Free State and the C.M.R. remounted.

CHAPTER XV.

WHILST these events were occurring in Basutoland, the people of the Colony were beginning to get impatient with the Government for having created a war and then displaying inability to carry it on to a successful issue. The whole system of the Colonial Defence Department had been found to be absolutely rotten. Men without the slightest knowledge of military matters were at the head of affairs, and refused to recognise any suggestions made by men who knew what they were about. Mr. Spriggs' pet scheme of three regiments of Yeomanry, backed up by his Burgher force, to put the whole Colony in a perfect state of defence, turned out to be one of the many blunders he has inflicted on the long-suffering people of the Colony. It was a dismal failure, and a distinct waste of public money to keep up such a force as the Yeomanry during peace time, only to discover its uselessness when war broke out. A corps recruited in Cape Town, and composed chiefly of Cape boys dressed in yellow corduroys, were more useful to the country than three regiments put together when in the field. Seeing that there were no indications of the Basutos getting tired of fighting, or of any signal success being likely to be attained by the Colonial forces, the Ministry thought they would try the effect of representations to the paramount chief, Letsea. They urged him to stop Lerothodi from the very objectionable course he was pursuing. They assured Letsea that they knew he was guiltless of rebellion against the Cape Government, and that it was his son Lerothodi who had defied them, against Letsea's wishes, but that even then it was not too late for Lerothodi to be forgiven. He had only to desist from knocking the Colonial forces about. Finally, they suggested an armistice to enable the wise men of the Cape Government to go to Maseru and talk things over with their friend Letsea.

While these negotiations were proceeding, another wood patrol took place, with the usual engagement; the Basutos trying their charging tactics once more, only to be driven off with loss. They then took to the mountain, and fired long shots at the square as it was retiring towards the camp, inflicting a good many casualties; amongst the wounded was our colonel, who, whilst riding with his staff in the centre of the square, was hit in the side, the bullet travelling round towards his back, inflicting a dangerous wound. Colonel Carrington was now put out of action for the first time since the commencement of the campaign. Captain Shervinton, the senior as well as the most efficient officer we had, who had been promoted to local major, took command of the C.M.R. in the field.

Shortly after hearing the news, while I was in my room in the barracks in King William's Town, an orderly came to me, and said Major Grant wished to see me. It was Sunday morning, and I was in flannels; but the orderly said I was to go just as I was. So, putting on a blazer and cap, I went across to the headquarter offices, above which were the officers' quarters. I saw Major Grant standing at the office door watching me coming, and wondered what had happened. As I reached him and saluted, the major held out his hand, saying, " I heartily congratulate you on having received your commission—have just received a wire from Cape Town," and he handed me the telegram, announcing that the regimental sergeant, another sergeant, and I had been promoted lieutenants from the 24th March, a week ago. Major Grant then took me upstairs to his room, and told me to take possession and to make myself at home till I arranged quarters for myself; then, saying he would see me next day, he went off to his house in the town, leaving me to try to realise the change that had come over my position in the regiment.

As it was near dinner-time, I thought I would go to the sergeants' mess and have my farewell meal' there, not intending to let my late brother non-coms. know of my promotion till they saw it in orders. But the orderly-room clerk had seen the telegram, and had lost no time in circulating the news round the camp. As I neared the messroom I saw it had leaked out, and, strolling in as usual, I was met by one of my old Butterworth chums, who stepped up and gave me my first salute, and wished me every luck. Soon I was shaking hands all round, and my health was being drunk with noisy, if not musical, honours. After dinner I left to take up my new quarters, and ceased to be a number and a sergeant.

Such is the system in the C.M.R.; all promotions are made to the commissioned rank from the ranks. A man may be a sergeant one day, with all his particular friends and companions in the ranks, but the moment he is promoted to lieutenant he is treated as if he had been an officer for years, and the greatest respect is shown him by all ranks. The discipline of the regiment is unique in that respect. It is only on one of his chums getting promoted to the same rank that he can renew his former friendship and intimacy; and although the officers and men rub shoulders in a football scrum, and down one another in a most unceremonious manner, or meet in the cricket field, or compete one against another at race meetings, the moment the sport is finished the respect due to the badge on the shoulder is shown to the officer in every detail.

On reporting myself to Major Grant next morning, I was introduced to my brother officers who happened to be in King William's Town at the time. Major Grant, the paymaster, and one lieutenant, were the only duty officers at headquarters; but our late adjutant, who had given up the duties and had taken command of one of the squadrons, was down on sick leave, and Captain H—— of No. 5 Troop, who had recently been granted leave of absence to visit Europe to recover from his wound, was passing through on his way to East London. Major Grant informed me that I would not be wanted for duty for two or three days, and that I would have time to arrange my quarters and procure the necessary uniform and equipments. The two skippers and myself went down the town, where I became a member of the club, that privilege being granted to all officers of the regiment, and was introduced to all the leading lights of the town. I had met them on previous occasions and had been welcomed to their houses as a non-com., but now I was admitted into their private lives, behind the scenes as it were, and the foundation of friendships was laid which lasted for many years.

I next visited the contractor, the universal benefactor of the regiment, Mr. Ben Ryan, and acquainted him with my promotion, and left myself in his hands. He was delighted, and proceeded to supply me with the necessary equipment of a full-fledged subaltern, cross belts, sword, and helmet being dispatched at once to my quarters; an invitation given and promptly accepted for dinner that evening, finished my shopping for the day. My horse had been left behind at the column amongst the captured ones, so I had to provide myself with two chargers, and as batches of horses were constantly being brought to barracks for recruits, I succeeded in picking out two that took my fancy. I had to perform the duties of acting adjutant, the other subaltern having taken a batch of recruits up to the front, whence, after handing them over to the column, he was to return to his duties at headquarters.

I now had my first experience of Colonial home life. Hitherto my life had been confined to camps and small villages up country, and although I had only been in the regiment eighteen months from the time of my enlistment till I received my commission, I had seen more of the country in that time than a great number who had been years in the country, having already been as far as Basutoland on one side, and Natal on the other. But I had never had an opportunity of meeting civilians such as I now had the good fortune to be associated with, and the kindness and hospitality shown by my new acquaintances made a great impression on me at the time, an impression which has never been effaced, during many years of intimate friendship with the majority of the good people of King William's Town. Dinners, dances, picnics, and riding parties seemed part of the day's work to me at that period of my service, my soldiering duties being very light and finished by 1 o'clock. I spent one of the best months of my life in King William's Town at that period.

When I was declared fit for duty, I was ordered by the officer commanding to accompany Captain B———, who had also been declared fit, back to Basutoland, taking with us some sixty recruits for the right and left wings who had been pronounced competent to join the squadrons in the field. About four days before starting, Major Grant called me into the office and introduced me to a stranger, a brother officer just from home, who would accompany us on the march up to join the regiment, and asked me to show him round and help him in procuring the necessary camp equipments, servant, and so on. We went off together, and soon became the best of friends. The friendship begun that day increased as we got to know each other. Soon we were known as the two biggest chums in the regiment; we were, and are to this day, that rare thing to be met with nowadays—real Pals.

We marched away from King one morning on our long march after sad farewells, and our sadness actually lasted till we got out of sight of King; but the fact of being on the *march*, and the sense of responsibility, soon banish thoughts other than of the business in hand; and the feel of the reins, of the sword scabbard swinging against the spur, of a good horse between your legs, the sight of a line of fresh smiling faces, all looking as keen as you feel yourself, and a sense of adventure in the air make it a pleasure to be alive. I could not help contrasting the present march with my former one over the same ground. Then I was sitting on a wagon, crawling along the road dressed in a corduroy velvet uniform with a peak cap, everything looking very strange and wonderful to me, about to make a start in the corps: now I was riding as an officer in a swagger patrol jacket of blue cloth, cross belt with field glasses, the former with silver ornaments (lion's head), whistle and chain with badge of regiment in centre, making a very handsome set-off to the uniform; a sword, white helmet with brass chain and spike; blue doeskin riding breeches with well-fitting top boots; mounted on a good horse with cavalry saddle and equipments, and journeying over a road I knew back to my old comrades at the front,—what more could a youngster want? I at any rate was perfectly satisfied with my lot at that particular period.

Captain B——, who was in command of our party, was a thorough good sportsman of the old school, very fond of horses and a good horseman. He was most careful to impress on us the necessity of watching the men to see that they did not lounge in their saddles, as it was calculated to give the horses sore backs. He seemed rather inclined to treat the newly joined sub as if he was incapable of taking care of himself, and required more looking after than the recruits; but he was soon disabused of that idea, and to his surprise the new arrival soon showed that he knew more about mounted work than Captain B—— had ever learnt or was ever likely to learn at his age.

The march up was a most agreeable one. We passed through Queenstown, Dordrecht, and Aliwal North; at the last place I renewed my former friendships and was made very welcome at several houses where I called, and received

general congratulations on my promotion. Here we met
Colonel Bayly of the right wing C.M.R., who had been in Cape
Town for an interview with the members of the Government
about affairs in Basutoland; he was now returning to Maseru,
where he had been since the outbreak of the war. He rode
through the town with us; he recognised and was particularly
kind to me, although I had not seen him since the C.M.R. had
been divided into wings. He was very interested in our
doings during the war, and asked many questions about the
right wing men who had been with us throughout, and
appeared very much pleased when mention was made of any
one of them.

It was not strange that Colonel Bayly was the most
popular officer of his day ; he made a point of knowing every
man in his regiment, the peculiarities of the man, what school
he had been educated at, and his qualifications as a sportsman.
The right wing cricket and football teams were about the
best in the Colony, all the members having been good public
school boys; and the keenest sportsman of the lot was the
colonel.

After leaving Aliwal we passed through the Free State to
Wepener, where we found Colonel Carrington in hospital, but
we were not allowed to see him, as the bullet had not yet been
extracted and his condition was very serious.

The news of the armistice had just been received at
Wepener, and I was ordered to carry dispatches from the
column to Maseru. Captain B—— with the remainder of the
detachment went on to the Border to join a convoy proceeding
to the main camp. Selecting an old soldier, who had been a
trumpeter and bandsman in the 6th Dragoons, from the detachment to accompany me as my orderly, I started from Wepener

on my ride to Maseru, and soon became aware of the fact that my orderly was something of a character. He was rather fond of liquor, and had managed to coax a bottle out of one of the hotel proprietors, which was against orders, and had stowed away what remained of it in one of his wallets. He also carried a cornet in his haversack, with which he had beguiled away the time on the line of march on one or two occasions. He was without doubt a first-class musician, and could sound anything at a gallop as easily as sitting still.

I was soon to be made aware of this accomplishment, for, shortly after leaving the town, as I was getting along the wagon road at a good canter, I heard an increase of pace from behind; a field call sounded in my ear, and turning I saw my orderly checking his horse beside me with the cornet in his hand. On my inquiring what the devil he meant, he replied, "That's fours right, sir," and on my damning "fours right" and him too, he would reply, "Beg pardon, sir, thought you would like to know," and reined back to his distance. He would remain quiet for a time, but after a pull at his bottle his trumpeter instincts were too much for him, and he would repeat the operation, much to my annoyance. After some strong language directed against himself he would fall back, with an injured innocent look on his full-moon face, which at any other time I would have enjoyed looking at. But as the road to Maseru ran very close to the Border, I had been advised before leaving Wepener to avoid as much as possible being seen by the Basutos, as they were hardly likely to know anything about an armistice; or, if they did, it would not prevent them trying to put an end to my journey by the expedient of a bullet. In short, I was too anxious to enjoy the clowning of my orderly.

After riding for about three hours we came to a small trading station at Lowe River, only a few hundred yards distant from the Border. I rode up to the door of the shop, and a white man came out and in a very nervous manner asked me round to the back of the house. He explained that there were some Basutos in his shop, but that they had not their guns with them, and that if I stayed in his private room he would see that refreshments were brought to us, while my man was left in charge of the horses in the stable.

Having given detailed instructions to my orderly, who had finished his liquor without seeming very much the worse for it, and impressing on him the necessity of feeding the horses at once and keeping himself quiet, I went into the trader's private room at the back of the store. Looking through a small window into the shop, I saw eight Basutos in their blankets and trousers, talking very loudly and drinking vile Cape brandy, and the sight did not tend to make me any more comfortable.

The trader came into the room where I was, and produced some cold meat, bread and butter out of a cupboard, and a knife and fork, and invited me to help myself, as he had to get back to the shop. He informed me that the Basutos living across the Border were constantly at his place getting liquor, and he was making plenty of money out of them whilst the liquor lasted, and that they behaved very civilly to white men whom they happened to meet, but he did not know how they would treat a C.M.R. if they saw one, and thought it advisable to keep them in the shop, where they could not see us when we rode off. He refused to take payment for the food and forage, so I told him I would saddle up and start off when the horses had finished their forage and my man had something to eat.

He then pointed out the direction our road lay to the back of the stables, said "Good-bye," and returned to the shop.

I finished my meal and went round to the stables, and told my orderly, who was now looking rather sorry for himself and penitent, to saddle up, and watched him perform the operation. I then told him to go to the room and get some food, and to look sharp, and we would proceed. I waited in the stable with the horses for some time, when I fancied I heard the sound of a cornet; going to the door, I met the trader, who said, "That man of yours has come into the shop, and is drinking brandy and playing to the niggers. God knows what will happen!" I shouted to him to bring the horses out, and made for the shop as quickly as possible, where, to my horror, I found this quondam bandsman sitting on the counter, his back against some blankets, helmet at the back of his head, blowing his cornet for all he was worth, while the natives were dancing in front of him, all drunk, and shouting at the top of their voices.

I made a dart at the culprit, and catching him by the collar of his coat pulled him on to the floor, and fairly kicked him out of the door before his friends realised what had happened; I shouted to him in not exactly official language to get on the horse, which he, in a dazed sort of manner, did. Then I mounted my horse and chased him away from the shop, pursued by the drunken mob of Basutos, who, irate at their chum being unceremoniously taken from them, showed their dissatisfaction by picking up stones and shying them at me as hard as they could. But, thanks to the potent "Cape Smoke" or brandy, they didn't succeed in hitting me, and congratulating myself that they had not their spears or guns with them, we quickly got away from them. I then halted to give my friend the ex-dragoon time to recover himself, and a bit of my mind at the same time; and before we proceeded had thoroughly impressed upon him that punishment in the army was a mere bagatelle to what he must expect in the C.M.R., and that he would probably be shot on our arrival at Maseru. It was a very dejected specimen of an orderly who followed me tamely the rest of the day's journey.

We reached a farmhouse built under a high hill called Mabula, on the top of which was a signal-station connecting Maseru with the station on the Border, and to which C.M.R. used to ride over from Maseru in the early morning and return in the evening. They had already left for their camp on my arrival. The farmer, who was a Boer, had been in the habit of supplying the garrison at Maseru with vegetables and forage, and had evidently made a good thing out of his connection with the regiment, for he received me with an unusually friendly welcome. He took me inside his house at once, and presented me to his vrow and numerous offspring of all sizes, from grown-up sons and daughters to a baby in arms; after the round of touching one another's hands, which does duty for a handshake with these peculiar people, had been gone through, one of the sons was despatched to look after my orderly and the horses. Much to my relief, my man was stowed away in an outbuilding which he shared with the grown-up sons, and I did not see him till the following morning. After the evening meal had been discussed, the old farmer and I strolled round and had a look at the horses, and whiled away the time smoking until he suggested it was time for bed. The house, as far as I could see, contained only one room, with a curtain hung across the end of it; behind this a large wooden bed had been visible at such times as one of the numerous members of the family pushed the curtain aside in going to and fro.

On the floor of the part of the room in which we had been eating several beds were now made down, and by the dim light I could see that they were occupied by the girls and the younger boys of the family. Pointing to where a couple of blankets had been laid down over some sheep-skins, a little apart from the rest, my host intimated that was my bed, and picking up the candle off the table he closed the door and locked it; he retired behind the curtain to where his spouse was evidently awaiting him. Seeing no help for it, I got out of my boots and patrol jacket, got under one of the blankets, and went to sleep as soon as I possibly could, amidst the titterings and whisperings of my stable companions, who apparently were accustomed to that sort of thing. To me, not used to it, the situation was rather awkward, to say the least of it.

At daylight next morning I was awakened by the door being opened and the family flitting out. Seizing the opportunity, I got into my boots and coat and outside as quickly as possible into the fresh air, much to my relief, and watched the horses being fed. Coffee was brought to me by one of the boys, when we saddled up. My host pressed me to stay for breakfast, but being rather young in those days, I could not face the family again, and after thanking him for his hospitality we proceeded on our way to Maseru, which place we arrived at in about two hours' fair riding.

On crossing a river on the Border between the Free State and Basutoland, which we did by means of a pont, I found myself on a flat-topped ridge, at the end of which, about half a mile from the river, were the fort and camp of the right wing C.M.R. The magistracy was situated across a small valley to the right front of the fort, amidst a fine plantation of trees, and was overlooked by high hills at the back of it, very similar to the situation of Mafeteng. To the front, about two miles distant from the fort, was a range of mountains, flat-topped, called the Berea. A large gully running from the top to the bottom in the front of the mountain made a considerable gap, and was called the Lancers' Leap. It was the spot where a squadron of the 12th Lancers were driven over by the Basutos, some thirty years before; horses and men all being killed and piled in a heap at the bottom.

I reported myself to Major B——, who was in command of the garrison during the absence of Colonel Bayly, who was expected to return that day, and was introduced by him to my brother officers of the right wing, whom I had hitherto only known by repute. They made me heartily welcome, and did all in their power to make my short stay with them as enjoyable as possible.

I was shown round the place, and the positions were pointed out to me where the Basutos had made their attack in their one and only attempt to capture the magistracy and fort, early in the campaign, the result of which had been a heavy loss to the enemy, and one private in the C.M.R. killed and several wounded.

There had already been meetings between the representative of the Colonial Government and of the Basuto chiefs, and as my despatches were concerned with negotiations which were still pending, my arrival was anxiously waited for by the Commissioner Colonel S——, a fine old German, who had been a member of the famous legion which had landed at the Cape in the early days, and now representing Government in the pitso,

MASERU MAGISTRACY, FROM CAMP, 1881.

or meeting, which was to decide the question of submission or continuation of the war.

The garrison had been keeping themselves in form for some months with football, hockey, and various other games, and there was an excellent football match in the afternoon, Officers and N.C.O.'s *v.* the Men. As an onlooker I was very much interested in the game, when, to my surprise, I saw both teams suddenly stop playing and rush off in the direction of the drift. Shortly after I heard great cheering, and saw the crowd returning, dragging a cart from which they had out-spanned the horses; in the cart was seated Colonel Bayly, whose smiling face announced the pleasure he felt at the great reception acccorded him by his officers and men.

After dragging him up to his tent amid cheers, to which Colonel Bayly responded in a spirited speech, they returned to the football ground and resumed the match; and some very good football was witnessed,—not a matter for surprise when one learns, as I was told by the major, who was also looking on, that the players represented almost every public school in England.

Colonel Bayly was very kind to me, and seeing I was anxious to rejoin the column, allowed me to depart the next morning. I reached Wepener the same evening, having been directed by a nearer road, and reported my arrival to Captain W——, C.M.R., who was in command of the signalling station, Wepener, and all details in connection with the column. He and his wife lived in a comfortable house in the town, and I remained to dinner and spent a pleasant evening with them, the first of very many happy visits which I have spent in the various houses of this hospitable couple, whose kindness to the subalterns of the regiment is proverbial. Captain W—— told

15

me that there would be a convoy going out to the column on the second day from then, and advised me to stay and accompany it, as it was not considered safe for one or two persons to ride through the country, an officer of the Yeomanry having been killed a short time before when endeavouring to overtake the convoy which had started an hour before he reached the border.

The next morning I went to the hospital and saw Colonel Carrington. He was looking very ill, and suffering great pain from his wound; and his temper, which was generally very bad, had not improved under the present conditions. He asked me when I had arrived, and what I was doing there. I informed him that I had arrived from Maseru the evening before, and that I was returning to the column with the convoy the following day.

He snapped out, "Damn the convoy—I don't want my officers travelling by convoys—get to your regiment!" I took the hint and my leave at the same time; and, telling my orderly to saddle up our horses, lost no time in getting out of Wepener, and crossing the border at Massayne's Farm, rode straight for Mafeteng, which I reached in time for lunch.

I lunched with an infantry corps called Dymes' Rifles, a recently raised regiment which had seen no service. The officers appeared a very decent lot of fellows, and were rather bitter at having to remain at Mafeteng; but as their men were rather a raw-looking set, I thought perhaps there was good reason why they should remain, unless the Basutos had altered their tactics during my absence.

I rode on in the afternoon past Diphering, and the scenes of some fights; saw a picquet of some C.M.R. on the white kopjes as I passed close to them, and arrived at the main camp in front of Tantjesberg at sundown, very much pleased at having rejoined my comrades after an absence of six months. The C.M.R. tents were pitched on the front face of the camp, and faced the Tantjesberg range—a most formidable looking line of mountains, with huge rocks standing up on the skyline, looking like fortresses in the distance; and I no longer was surprised that the column had only advanced such a short distance during my absence.

I was met by Major Shervinton and a group of officers as I rode up to the embrasure where a howitzer was pointing out with a threatening and business-like air. Dismounting, and handing my horse to my orderly, I was warmly greeted by my commanding officer and my comrades, some of whom I had known as non-commissioned officers. We adjourned to a large marquee tent, which I was informed was the C.O.'s mess, and I was invited by him to join it.

My tent had already been pitched in the officers' lines, and occupied by my companion of the march up, and we now shared it between us. I was greatly disappointed that he had not been asked to join the C.O.'s mess; but he had joined the regiment direct as a lieutenant, an innovation much resented by officers, N.C.O.'s, and men, as it had always been considered a standing rule that all commissions must be given from the ranks; and this was the first occasion on which a young man had been brought into the regiment as an officer, without having been previously connected with the Colonial forces in some capacity or other. It was the precedent that was objected to, not the man; every one who had met him admitted that he was likely to become an acquisition to the regiment, and had no fault to find with him personally. But it was generally resolved to see how he shaped before inviting him as a permanent member to any one of the several messes then existing in the camp.   So on my arrival I found that he had been living by himself, and getting his food cooked by his "batman," or soldier servant.

I found that during my absence from the column my captain had handed the troop to another officer, and had taken over the duties of adjutant from Captain B——, who had taken command of another troop.   After Colonel Carrington had been wounded, Shervinton took command of the C.M.R., and the regimental Sergeant-Major Lowther, who had received his commission on the same date as myself, had been appointed acting adjutant in his place.   On receiving his commission he had changed his name from Lowther, which had been an assumed one when he enlisted in the army, and was now Lieutenant G——. He was very good at his drill, and made an excellent adjutant.

On joining my mess at lunch, I found it consisted of Major Shervinton, Captain C——, who was the new skipper of No. 3 Troop, to which, to my delight, I found myself still belonging, a captain of a Right Wing Troop, three subalterns of the C.F. Artillery, of whom my friend Gipsy was the senior, and who during the absence of the major on sick leave was in command of the battery, and my brother subaltern of No. 3 Troop, who had been an N.C.O. with me some months before, but had received his commission shortly after the relief of Mafeteng and—seven in all, splendid fellows and good comrades, as I subsequently found out.   The general opinion seemed to be there would not be much more fighting, as not only was the Cape Government anxious to finish the campaign, but the Basutos were having trouble amongst themselves.   Some of Lerothodi's younger brothers were not in favour of his taking the whole conduct of the affairs of the nation on himself, as he had practically done since the outbreak of the war. Lerothodi at that time represented the more uncivilised party of the Basutos, having lived all his life in Basutoland, and knowing only the language and traditions of the Basutos. His younger brothers had been educated at the French mission schools in Basutoland and Cape Colony, and two of them had been to school in France, and their ideas were more ambitious with regard to the position of the native with the white people of the Colony. Although these young men were keen on the war, and on obtaining what they thought they were entitled to, still they held their father Letsea, the paramount chief, in greater reverence than their elder brother, and were more inclined to listen to their father, who was anxious for peace, and had been opposed to the war from the commencement. But since Lerothodi had taken the initiative and opposed the troops, the paramount chief had no other course to pursue than acquiesce until the time should arrive for negotiations. These were now pending, the Minister for Native Affairs being just then at Maseru, and in communication with Letsea. In the meantime an armistice had been arranged, but no precautions had been in any way relaxed as regards the safety of the camp. Mounted picquets and cattle guards were out all day, and the necessary picquets and guards at night, just as if the armistice did not exist; every one knew that the accidental discharge of a rifle on picquet might bring on an immediate action, so we were well prepared for any emergency that might arise.

I went on evening stable parade with my skipper, and saw the old familiar faces of the N.C.O. and men I had been associated with, but I was very much struck by the number of men I missed, the troop bring only about half the strength it had been before my departure. When I inquired what had become of them, I was told, to my surprise, that with the exception of about a dozen who had been wounded or invalided the remainder had deserted. For some time the men had been dissatisfied, chiefly on account of the smallness of the pay they had been receiving: old accounts from Kokstad had cropped up against a good many of them, which had been deducted from their pay, without any opportunity given of questioning the correctness of the accounts. Some of the men had not drawn any pay at all during the whole of the campaign. This and the fact that Volunteers, who had been recruited for the war, were drawing 5s. per diem clear pay, horses and equipments being free issue, and the rations supplied by Government, accounted for the state of affairs.

With the C.M.R. the free rations commenced from the day the first shot was fired, all the food and grain on the march from Kokstad to Basutoland being supplied by the contractors, on account of which the men had sometimes as much as 3s. per diem deducted from their pay. There were also the C.M.R. equipment debts, for which £2 per month was stopped from every man in the regiment till his horse and equipments had been paid for; there was also his clothing to be included; for although the Government gave each member of the regiment a bounty of £10 towards his horse, the balance was usually another £15, which had to be paid by the man.

Then again the cost of living varied very much. Troops stationed away from towns were supplied by contractors; the contracts for the supply of food for men as laid down by scale of rations, and of feed for the horses, were tendered for by the various merchants; the successful merchant generally

getting the contract for one year's supply. The contract for
rations at Fort Donald and Kokstad was something like 4s.
per diem for man and horse; add his equipment debts on to
this, and the wretched second-class private on 5s. per diem
was signing in debt at the end of every month. This had
accumulated until, in spite of drawing free rations in the
field, the man was left with nothing to draw when his accounts
were made up, owing to the back stoppages coming in
against him.

This had not been noticed much by the men during the
time the fighting was going on, but since the armistice had
been declared, men had time to look into their accounts; and
when the pay-lists showed very small balances, sometimes
none, the men began to get dissatisfied. The Free State was
close at hand, from which a man could not be brought back
if he were caught; several whilst on convoy escort had taken
advantage of the halt on the border to take leave on their
own account, with their horses, saddles and bridles, leaving
their arms and belts behind them; and in every case had
succeeded in getting clear away.

The men who had deserted were composed of the rougher
element in the regiment, and no doubt had been influenced
by tales they had heard from the Kimberley Horse, of money
to be made on the diamond fields, which made them deter-
mine to try their luck at mining. The majority of the
regiment, however, were of a better class of men, and thought
twice before bringing disgrace on their people at home; they
preferred sticking to their work, with its drawbacks as regards
money, to incurring the risk of being captured and brought
back to be tried for desertion, with its inevitable punishment.

The men were not allowed to be idle during the armistice;

in addition to the ordinary pickets and guards, parades were held every day, and troops of men in front of our lines were to be seen from early morning to afternoon learning the sword exercise in its different stages; officers, N.C.O.'s, and men all alike having to go through it from the commencement. The recruits who had passed their drill at King William's Town had another course, to prevent them from crowing over the old hands. Drills over, football was taken up, and there was keen competition amongst the officers of the various corps to procure the best Basuto ponies for polo; at the time of my arrival some very good matches had already been played between regiments.

As time went on and the armistice continued, relations between the troops and the Basutos became more amicable, and although no native was allowed inside our picquets, we used to meet on mutual ground between the enemies' positions and our picquets, the Basutos bringing ponies, tobacco, and vegetables for sale. A very good pony could be bought for £10 or less.

Shortly after my arrival, Major Shervinton, accompanied by half a dozen officers, myself among the number, went out to meet some Basuto chiefs who had ridden close up to our picquets and expressed a desire to meet some of the white chiefs. We found two of Letsea's sons amongst them. We all dismounted and exchanged compliments. Mama Letsea, one of the sons, who had been educated in France, and who spoke English fluently, was introduced to me by Major Shervinton, who mentioned that I had just returned after being wounded. Mama held out his hand, and asked me if I had quite recovered. On being assured that I was perfectly fit, he said, "I am so glad to hear it. I should never have forgiven myself if anything had happened to injure a young gentleman like yourself"; and began asking several questions as to the different engagements we had both figured in, and as to the hardships in Mafeteng; whether it was true that we had eaten our horses. On being answered that it was a fact, he exclaimed, "I was told so by my men, but I hardly believed it. By Jove! it puts me in mind of the French at the siege of Genoa."

I thought to myself if these were the men the Basutos had as chiefs, it was no wonder the Government had taken on a hopeless contract when they determined to disarm them.

We spent an interesting hour with our friends the enemy, and returned, after mutual good wishes, and appointments to meet again at a future date. I saw a great deal of Mama during the remainder of our stay in Basutoland, and found him a very interesting personage. He was quite a young man, good-looking, and a thorough gentleman in his manners. Although he has on one or two occasions given trouble to the British Resident in Basutoland in later years, I consider that, on the whole, his conduct towards the Imperial authorities has been that of a loyal, intelligent man, and he has aided them greatly in their administration of this easily excited, warlike tribe of natives.

Negotiations between members of the ministry and the Basuto chiefs had been carried on at Maseru, and had ended, as far as we could gather, in a patched-up peace; one of the ministers, Mr. Sauer, who was secretary for native affairs, paid the column a flying visit. He was rather a conspicuous figure, wearing a tall white hat, which called forth remarks from the men hardly suitable to the dignity of this self-important individual as he walked about the camp. We were told that the Basutos had been heavily fined, and on the payment of the indemnity in cattle the troops would evacuate the country.

It evidently took the Basutos a considerable time to select the class of animal suitable for the occasion, the cattle round about in the district being in too good condition for such a fate as payment of a fine; but, after several weeks had elapsed, several thousands of ancient, scraggy animals in the shape of oxen were driven to the vicinity of the camp by the Basutos, and duly handed over to the Colonial Government representative, and the dispersal of the forces commenced.

The Volunteers and Yeomanry took their departure for their various centres, there to be paid off, and to return to their respective vocations. The C.F.A. and the C.M.R. returned to Mafeteng, where we awaited final orders as to the evacuation of the country, which in due course arrived for all except No. 2 Troop, which was ordered to remain at Mohalie's Hoek for a short period. The Artillery and the remainder of the C.M.R. were ordered down to different parts of the Cape Colony; the Artillery to King William's Town; my troop, No. 3, to Ibeka, in the Transkei; the right wing troops to rejoin their wing, and the remainder of the left wing troops were to proceed to Umtata for redistribution. My friend and tent chum had been posted to No. 2 Troop, and had to remain behind. We parted with mutual regrets, and plans for a future meeting if possible.

Skilled stonemasons had been selected from some of the Volunteers, and had for some months past been busily engaged in cutting out a huge monolith from solid rock, to be erected at the graveyard in Mafeteng as a memento of the dead, by their comrades; and before we marched away we had the satisfaction of seeing the splendid stone erected in its place, where it still remains a lasting memorial to our gallant comrades, and of humiliation to the Cape Government that such a fine country as Basutoland should have been lost through their short-sighted policy in engaging in a war when not in a position to carry it out to a successful end.

Shortly after the war Basutoland was handed over to the Imperial Government, a British Resident Commissioner was appointed, with sub-commissioners and inspectors as magistrates, and a Police Force of Basutos, with European officers, was formed, and stationed at various centres throughout the country. With the exception of occasional quarrels among the chiefs, which have been amicably settled by the paramount chief, Lerothodi, who succeeded on the death of his father, Letsea, or by the British Resident, the Basutos have given no trouble to the authorities up to the present; but I am not confident that this pleasant state of affairs will be permanent.

Should the scheme which is on foot in South Africa for the federation or unification of the different states ever come into effect, and the Basutos be handed over by the Imperial Government to the Dutch—which federation of the different Colonies will mean, the Cape Colony being already under a Dutch ministry, or Bond, the strings being pulled by Mr. Botha from Pretoria,—Natal, the only country loyal to the Crown, will have either to join or go to the wall.

Then there will be the biggest native war yet fought in South Africa. The Basutos will fight rather than live under Colonial control. For years past they have been known to possess arms and ammunition, and when the truth comes out they will probably be found to have a number of the missing guns which the Boers mysteriously disposed of when the war went against them, and which have never been accounted for. This awkward fact will make the annexation of Basutoland by force of arms a harder task than most people, even in South Africa, imagine.

CHAPTER XVI.

1881-1884.

MY TROOP STATIONED AT IBEKA—VELDTMAN, THE FINGO CHIEF—A VISIT—
LEAVE FOR UMTATA—CIVIL SERVANTS—BISHOP CALLAWAY—CAPE
INFANTRY FORMED—GENERAL GORDON VISITS UMTATA—STATIONED AT
QUMBU—ARRIVAL OF CAPE INFANTRY—C.M.R. MASSED AT STOCKWE'S
BASIN — EVICTING SQUATTERS — COLONEL CARRINGTON RETURNS —
CRICKET TOUR TO EAST GRIQUALAND—AMALGAMATION OF BOTH WINGS
OF C.M.R.—CARRINGTON TAKES COMMAND OF B.B. POLICE.

THE C.F.A. marched out of Basutoland in advance of the remainder of the C.M.R. on their return to King William's Town. No. 2 Troop also left for Mohalie's Hoek, where they remained for nearly six months. The remainder of the troops finally left the country about the middle of August, a year from the time we had left Kokstad. Captain C—— was in command of the troops on the return journey. Major Shervinton, with some of the staff, had gone on some days previously to Umtata, to which place the left wing head-quarters had been transferred from King William's Town under the command of Major Grant, during the absence of Colonel Carrington, invalided to England. We were received with rejoicings at every town we came to *en route*, my circle of friends and acquaintances rapidly increasing. The men of the troops all being well-seasoned and used to roughing it, gave us no trouble whatever on the march, and the officers had nothing to do except enjoy themselves, which they did, spending two or three days at each town, and catching up to the men on the march.

In due course we reached Ibeka, a most dreary-looking spot, situated about four miles from the old headquarters at Butterworth, a place now deserted, except by the magistrate and a few traders. Ibeka at that time consisted of a sod-walled fort and ditch, with huts built in rows inside, and two Kaffir trading stores about 400 yards from one another, and a few native huts on the surrounding hills, occupied by natives who had returned to the district after being driven out during the Galeka War of 1878. The veldt was very long, and there was not a single head of cattle to be seen in any direction; and the prospect was not a very lively one for us about to be stationed in the district.

About three miles from Ibeka were a tribe of natives called Fingoes. This tribe has the reputation of always having been loyal to the Government, and is therefore the most hated by all other tribes in the Colony. They are mostly " school natives," that is, mission stations have been built extensively among them, and they have become more or less " civilised," a very doubtful blessing to natives. A school Kaffir is generally at the bottom of all the mischief that goes on amongst the different tribes; knowing how far to go without danger to himself, he backs out of the trouble which he has stirred up, and leaves his less civilised brother to bear the brunt when it. comes to being interviewed by the magistrate.

The Fingo headman was called Veldtman; he was a superior man for a native, and had rendered good service to the Government during the war in the Transkei, which made him rather a privileged person with the officials in his district. Shortly after our arrival at Ibeka, Veldtman paid us an official visit in state, riding up to the camp, preceded by his drum and fife band, consisting of about 30 boys and young men dressed in a uniform of white with red braid, and forage caps on the side of their heads; the big drummer flourished his drumstick in the orthodox manner, evidently acquired after long study of the drummer of an infantry regiment during the period of the occupation of the country by the Imperial troops. The whole "turnout" was distinctly smart, and the one tune which seemed to be the extent of their repertoire was easily recognisable when the drummers gave the fifers an opportunity of making it heard.

Veldtman, a big heavily built man, attired in the full dress uniform of a naval officer, with the cocked hat jauntily stuck on the side of his head, dismounted from his horse, and, followed by his leading men and their followers, walked up to where we were standing, and welcomed us to the country. Captain C——, who had known him during the Transkein War, asked him in to our mess tent, where he was duly refreshed. The band, which was surrounded by our men, keeping up the one tune, drowned all attempts at conversation, till Veldtman ordered them to stop. After a short conversation, during which he gave us an invitation to his house, Veldtman took his departure in the same style in which he arrived, evidently well pleased with his reception.

Our camp pitched on a flat piece of ground about 300 yards below the fort, and consisting of tents and picquet lines for the horses, was the most desolate-looking camp I was ever in. The water supply consisted of a very meagre spring at the top of a sluit and was not at all suitable for a station, but we had to make the best of it, and it is wonderful what a change can be made by a body of C.M.R. when thrown on their own resources. In a couple of months from the time of our arrival a fine bathing-place had been dug out, and a large square of ground scuffled off for cricket and sports ground. Cricket matches were soon in full swing with the traders of the district and adjacent villages.

Shortly after Veldtman's visit, about 300 C.M.R. from King William's Town arrived, mostly recruits *en route* for Umtata. Out of this number we received about 60, which made up the troop to its original strength of 100; and our time was fully occupied the next few months in making the troop efficient. I discovered some very good cricketers amongst the new arrivals, and made the start of the cricket team, which more than held its own against all comers in the Transkei for several years.

Some months afterwards I got a letter from head-quarters asking me to bring a cricket team to Umtata to take part in a tournament to be played there. I took No. 3 Troop team up, and although we did not win, we made a very good impression, and some of the men were selected for the regimental team and transferred to the Depôt Troop or No. 5 Troop.

As No. 3 Troop were to be relieved in the course of a couple of months and were to proceed to headquarters, I remained behind when the balance of the team returned to Ibeka, and very pleased I was at the change. Umtata had grown considerably since the last time I had visited the place. New buildings and stores had sprung up in a very short time, and as the natives had all settled down peaceably in the surrounding districts, business was in a flourishing condition. The C.M.R. camp consisted of huts built outside the old fort, and the men were very comfortable. We also had excellent

CHIEF MAGISTRATE'S HOUSE, UMTATA.

officers' quarters in huts; the old right wing canteen had been renovated and turned into an officers' mess, and we were in clover after our late campaigning experiences.

Major Grant was our commanding officer. Major Shervinton had given up the local rank he had held in the field and was now captain and adjutant, in which capacity he kept us subaltern officers very much up to the mark both in our military and social duties. The remainder of the officers consisted of paymaster, quartermaster, captain, and two subalterns of No. 1 Troop, and two subalterns of No. 5, to which troop I was attached till the arrival of my own from Ibeka.

Umtata was the principal town in Tembuland, and was, and is at the present day, the seat of the Chief Magistrate of the Native Territories. The Umtata which runs on the side and the back of the town is the boundary between Western Pondoland and Tembuland on one side, and East Griqualand on the other; it furnishes the water supply for the town, and as usual with Colonial rivers is low in winter and high in summer, and, before the bridge which now spans it was built, was often impassable for days at a time. The other rivers between the Colony and Umtata being in the same condition, the post-carts carrying the mails and passengers were often delayed a week or more. For a mule or a horse to be drowned, the cart capsized in a drift, and the passengers treated to a good ducking, when on the way from Kei Road to Umtata, was rather the rule than the exception in those days. The railway now extends as far as Butterworth from Kei Road, the rivers are all bridged along the main road as far as Natal, and travelling is at the present time, if not any more comfortable than formerly, safer for human life and more expeditious in point of time.

16

The Chief Magistrate was Major Elliott, C.M.G., now Sir Henry Elliott, a retired British officer, a splendid specimen of the thorough English gentleman, who ruled his large staff of civil servants and the thousands of natives under his control with a kindness and firmness which won for him the universal esteem of all classes. The Great White Queen herself could not have been treated with more veneration by the native tribes than "the Major," as he was called throughout the whole country. He has now retired from the Colonial Service on a well-earned pension and is living in Natal, where I trust he may live to enjoy many more years of the happiness he deserves.

There was also a Resident Magistrate and a large staff of civil servants, all of whom were good sportsmen; cricket matches were a weekly institution. Riding parties were a great feature at that period of the town's existence, and picnics to the waterfalls, a picturesque spot about three miles from the town.

Umtata also boasted of a cathedral with a bishop and a staff of clergy of very good class, and the relations between the mission and the camp people were always of a friendly nature. It almost compensated one for the long dusty march from camp to cathedral, every Sunday church parade, to see the venerable Bishop Callaway enthroned in his high-backed seat, with his white hair and beard and kindly looking old face as he sat throughout the service listening intently. At the conclusion, when he stood up and in a weak but clear voice gave us the benediction, I for one always got an uncomfortable feeling about my throat. Nor was I the only one impressed, as the various noises around me proclaimed as if the congregation had been seized with violent colds in their heads.

St. John's Pro-Cath-edral Umtata

PIKE

About this period Brigadier-General Clarke gave up the command of the Colonial forces, and was succeeded by General Gordon, then known in the army as Chinese Gordon. The new appointment brought about another change in the regiment. The two wings were temporarily amalgamated, for a reason I could never make out, and Colonel Bayly, with his headquarters and about 300 men, arrived at Umtata from King William's Town. Government acquired a large portion of the Umtata commonage in a good position, known as Calverly's bend, the river running round three sides of it, and less than a mile from the centre of the town. A barracks and stables were soon in course of erection; the troops in the meantime being under canvas at the old camp.

A regiment of infantry was now being raised by the Cape Government, and called the Cape Infantry. It was to be composed of army reservists, with headquarters at King William's Town, pending the arrival of all the drafts of men from England. The regiment was to take up its headquarters at Kokstad in East Griqualand, with detachments at the various magistracies, a scheme of General Gordon's to ensure the safety of the magistrates in the districts from a repetition of the Hope murders at Qumbu.

About this time, General Gordon, who had been visiting Basutoland and interviewing the Basuto chiefs (whose opinions of the settlement of that country were not at all in accord with those of some of the Cape ministry), was on his way to visit the Transkei and East Griqualand. He rode into Umtata, one morning, accompanied by his staff officer and secretary. The C.M.R. were drawn up in line for his inspection, and the general, who was attired in mufti, rode down the ranks 'and looked steadily at every man as he passed, this being the first occasion on which he had met the regiment. He intimated to Colonel Bayly, who accompanied him, that he wished to speak to the men, and we were promptly formed into close column. The general then addressed us, and after an allusion to the late Basuto War, complimented the regiment on the splendid work done by them during the campaign. He expressed a hope that if ever we were required by him for similar service, we would stand by him to a man, and finished by saying, "Men, look to your sergeants,—sergeants, look to your officers,—officers, look to your colonel,—and the whole of you look to me as your father." He then turned to Colonel Bayly and complimented him on the appearance of the regiment, and requested that the men might have the rest of the day to themselves.

We were then dismissed, no more drills or parades for the day were given out, and the camp was given over to pleasure. Later on in the evening we heard sounds of strong language and a tramping of feet passing our mess room, *en route* to the fort; some youth had strayed down the town, imbibed too much, and become a trifle riotous, and was being assisted to the guard tent by the picquet, shouting at the top of his voice, "Let me down, you ——. I will tell Father Gordon about this." "I will tell Father Gordon" remained a familiar saying in the C.M.R. for many years.

My relief, in the person of my old chum in Basutoland, having arrived from Palmietfontein, where he had been stationed on leaving Basutoland, I was ordered to Engcobo, there to take command of 50 N.C.O.'s and men and return with them to Umtata, from which place we were sent on to Qumbu, in East Griqualand—37 miles from Umtata, on the main road to Kokstad. I remained at that place till relieved by a company of Cape Infantry six months later.

Qumbu at that time consisted of the magistracy and one store. The court-house had been destroyed by the natives during the rebellion after the murder of Mr. Hope, the former magistrate, and was now being held in a Kaffir hut, the magistrate and his clerk being also housed in huts. The store owned by Mr. Peter McGlashan, an old soldier, was not destroyed by the natives. Mr. McGlashan was made a prisoner, and sent, in company with Mr. Davis, whose life had been saved as before mentioned by the chief, to· a mission station at Shawbury, about five miles distant from Qumbu, where they remained till relieved by a column from Umtata.

Out-station work in those days was very tedious for the officers in command; the usual routine of troop work, and keeping the men up to the mark, varied by cricket or paper chases was the only means of passing the time, which hangs very heavily on the hands of the solitary subaltern, who has nobody to associate with except a chance visitor. The Cape Infantry passed through Qumbu on the march to Kokstad, and a very fine regiment they looked, clothed in their red uniforms, every man in it wearing one or two medals, mostly for Indian campaigning.

They were commanded by Colonel Cherry from an imperial regiment, but the remainder of the officers were men who had served in Colonial corps, a good sprinkling of Yeomanry officers having been gazetted to the regiment when Mr. Sprigg's pet creation were disbanded. A company of them relieved my detachment, to my intense satisfaction, and I was ordered to march as quickly as transport would allow to Stockwe's Basin situated on the border of the Queenstown district, there to join the regiment which was being concentrated on that place, for some reason unknown to any one except Government.

I marched my detachment to Umtata, where I was met by the C.M.R. band and played through the streets to the camp. The band had been newly formed and already had reached a fair stage of efficiency, the bandsmen being all musicians from the ranks, with a few boys from a training-ship, who had been sent out from home as trumpeters, under the control of Bandmaster Jammer. The band was fast becoming one of the institutions of Umtata, and did much to enliven the cricket matches and sports meetings which were frequently held at the rising city.

After a week's trekking I reached Southeyville, where I found my old troop, No. 3, stationed. We marched on together and arrived at Stockwe's Basin, at which place Colonel Bayly with some 400 men had already arrived. We went into camp there and awaited orders. Stockwe's Basin, as the place where the camp was pitched was named, was in conquered territory, or country from which a chief named " Stockwe Charley " had been driven when he rebelled against the Government, some three years previously.

The country had been confiscated and was now being cut up into farms to be sold. Seeing the country unoccupied, a large number of Dutch squatters from the Barkly district had calmly trekked over Barkly Pass and taken up their abode on the parts that appeared suitable for farms, and had erected dwelling-houses of a primitive description in different parts of the country, which they occupied with their wives and children. They were practically defying the

Government to turn them out, no doubt thinking that as their relatives in the Transvaal had been too many for the Imperial Government — in their ignorance they honestly believed this to have been the case—they could do the same with the Colonial Government, and take whatever land they wished in the Colony.

This was the state of affairs when the C.M.R. were concentrated at Stockwe's Basin awaiting orders, which, when they arrived, were very simple—to send the Dutch back to where they had trekked from. Parties of men were sent out under officers, and notice given to the squatters to move within a certain date. No notice being taken of the warning, men were sent to the hovels in which the Dutch lived, and, after putting everything in the shape of furniture and household effects outside on the the veldt, pulled the dwellings down. We received plenty of threatening language from the squatters, but, to our disappointment, no resistance, and finally the would-be land-grabbers trekked to their wagons and returned to the districts from which they had come.

The C.M.R. were moved on to T'Somo Valley, and camped there for a few months till the farms were sold and the purchasers in occupation. The site where the C.M.R. camp was pitched is now the flourishing town of Cala, the centre of a prosperous farming community. The evictions of the squatters having been successfully carried out, the regiment was again divided into wings, and the troops left T'Somo Valley for their respective stations. My detachment, composed mostly of right wing men, I handed over to an officer of that wing and returned to Umtata, and was once more posted to headquarters.

Colonel Carrington returned from England and resumed

command of the left wing, and patrols were instituted weekly to the surrounding country.   One officer and twenty-five men would leave Umtata on a six days' patrol, carrying rations and blankets on their saddles, and patrol through the native kraals, sleeping on the veldt, generally marching about twenty-five miles a day, visiting one of the several magistracies in an adjacent district, and then returning to camp.

These patrols had an excellent effect both on the natives and on the C.M.R.   The former got used to the sight of the Quakamba, as all natives call the C.M.R., and the men got accustomed to veldting it, sleeping out in all kinds of weather, lighting fires to cook with in rain, and learning the art of packing and saddling up their horses quickly.

The new barracks had been completed and occupied, and the long stretch of level ground between the barracks and the bend of the river daily presented a lively scene to the onlooker. Tent-pegging and lemon-cutting were greatly encouraged amongst all ranks, and the men soon became proficient in both these interesting tests of skill; competition between squadrons was very keen, and resulted in some very good exhibitions of riding, and skill with the weapons used.

I had been elected captain of the left wing cricket club for some time past, and hearing from Colonel Carrington one evening at mess that he was leaving on a tour of inspection of the different stations of the regiment in East Griqualand, the band being included in the tour, I ventured to suggest that a cricket team might go with the party and play a round of matches.   As the Cape Infantry had established a record against civilian clubs in East Griqualand, and had also come out victorious against the troops and club at Maritzburg, in Natal, I was anxious to try conclusions with them.

The colonel seemed doubtful, but on my assuring him I thought we had a chance of winning, and at any rate would not disgrace ourselves, he promised to wire to the officer commanding the Infantry, and find out if a match would be acceptable; Colonel Cherry wired back that his men only averaged five feet eight inches, but they could beat the C.M.R. at cricket any day, so the colonel told me to bring the team along. We had a most enjoyable tour through East Griqualand, playing the different squadron teams as we passed their stations, and finally meeting the Cape Infantry and Kokstad. We managed to win both matches, and were equally fortunate in our match against the civilians of East Griqualand.

General Gordon had by this time given up the command of the Colonial forces. It was supposed that his views of the treatment of natives did not coincide with those of the Cape Ministry, and I think it more than likely that this was the case. I cannot conceive any man with the record that General Gordon already possessed allowing himself to be dictated to, or have his actions criticised by the class of individuals of whom the Cape Ministry was composed, mostly office-seekers for the emoluments attached to the positions, working for their own personal advancement, and not for the interests of the country they represented.

On General Gordon's departure from South Africa, Colonel Bayly was made the Senior Officer Colonial forces; and as the natives had apparently settled down peacefully at their kraals, and the hut taxes were paid in to the magistrates at the various districts without trouble, the Government turned their attention to other matters. The farmers had been complaining of the want of police protection for the prevention of stock-thieving, which was pretty rife in the Colony, and the Cape Police, formed some two years previously, were not sufficient in numbers to control the large area assigned to them; so the Government decided to increase the strength of the Police at the expense of the C.M.R., and retrenchment was the order of the day for the regiment. Men who were out of regimental equipment debt were offered free discharges, not all time-expired men were allowed to re-enrol, and bad characters were discharged. Officers of three years' standing were retrenched with gratuities, and the regiment was finally brought down to 750 strong, from about 1200. Some of the N.C.O.'s and men joined the now augmented Cape Police, and a great number of them followed Colonel Carrington, who had been appointed to the command of the Bechuanaland Border Police. The two wings of the C.M.R. were again amalgamated for the last time, and Colonel Bayly took command of the regiment, with the additional title of Senior Officer Colonial Forces.

There being only one staff now required for the regiment, Colonel Bayly naturally preferred keeping the adjutant of the late right wing. This necessitated Captain Shervinton's retirement, with several others, and the regiment thus lost, in my opinion, the smartest all-round man it ever possessed, both as a soldier and an athlete. He left us amidst general regrets and went to Madagascar, where he became Commander-in-Chief of the Hova Army, in which capacity he successfully fought off the French till peace was proclaimed. He has now joined the majority, but his name is still spoken of in the Colony with respect and admiration when any special feat of horsemanship or a successful break at billiards is the topic of conversation amongst old inhabitants.

The Cape Field Artillery was also disbanded at this period,

the officers all leaving the Colonial Service in disgust, and obtaining appointments in other colonies where soldiers are more appreciated than they are by the Cape officials.

Colonel Bayly left Umtata with the headquarters of the regiment and the band for King William's Town, much to the dismay of the tradespeople of Umtata and the delight of the men and the people of King William's Town. Major Grant was left in command of Umtata with No. 5 Troop, Lieutenant Tim and myself being the subalterns, and the barracks assumed a very deserted appearance, owing to the departures of men discharged and the removal of headquarters.

CHAPTER XVII.

1885–1892.

NATIVE TROUBLES—PONDOS *V.* XESIBES—GAGO, THE XESIBE HEADMAN—
FIGHT AT SUGAR BUSH—C.M.R.'S EXPEDITION TO N'TOLA'S KRAAL—
COLONEL BAYLY RETIRES FROM COMMAND OF COLONIAL FORCES—
MAJOR GRANT PROMOTED COLONEL—SURRENDER OF UMHLANGASO TO
C.M.R.—SIR HENRY LOCH VISITS PONDOLAND—GOVERNOR'S ESCORT—
UMFUNDISWENI MISSION STATION—CHANGE OF OFFICERS AT UMTATA.

I WAS not left to enjoy the comforts of town life very long. For some time past a tribe of natives called Xesibes, who occupied a tract of country in the Mount Ayliff district in East Griqualand, on the border of the country of an independent tribe called Pondos, had been suffering from losses of cattle, which they had attributed to the Pondos, and had made reprisals into Pondoland, which had ended in kraals being destroyed on either side of the border and several men being killed. The C.M.R. stationed at Fort Donald and Mount Ayliff now received orders to patrol the Pondoland border and stop any aggressive move being made by either side.

I was sent to Mount Ayliff with a reinforcement of men from Umtata, and found myself transferred to A Squadron, whose headquarters were at Kokstad, with the right troop at Fort Donald and the left troop at Mount Ayliff. I took command of the latter, having a junior acting subaltern with me and a company of Cape Infantry under a captain who commanded the station. We had some months of very hard work to perform, outstations composed of a corporal and three men being placed at intervals along the Pondoland border, from the Umzimvubu on the one side and as far as Fort Donald on the other. These stations had to be constantly visited, and patrols kept up from Mount Ayliff and Fort Donald along the border daily.

There was an old Xesibe headman who owned a kraal close to the Pondo border, about five miles from Mount Ayliff, and was very bitter against the Pondos. This old fellow, named Gaga, had managed to kill his enemy, a Pondo headman who lived on the opposite hill. Gaga had cut off his enemy's head and boiled it down, and finally made a drinking cup of the skull. He was in the habit of drinking Kaffir beer out of it, and shouting across the valley to his late enemy's relations that he was doing so, and inviting them to come across and try and get his own head, of which, if they could manage to do it, they were at perfect liberty to make the same use as he was making of their late chief's. This did not tend to make matters any more peaceful, and long firing was engaged in by both parties day and night, without much damage being inflicted by either party. C.M.R. at the various outstations had orders to prevent the Xesibes from being the aggressors as far as practicable, whilst negotiations were being carried on between the Chief Magistrate of East Griqualand and the Pondo chief Umquikela.

Riding to the border one morning with an orderly to visit the stations, I heard shots being exchanged from the vicinity of Gaga's kraal; as I neared that place the firing seemed to increase, and I could see some Pondos on the opposite hills on the border, and see the smoke and hear the distant report of their guns as they fired in the direction of Gaga's kraal. I cantered up to the kraal and dismounted at the hut which was being used as temporary quarters by the C.M.R. detachment, but could see no sign of the men. The firing still continued from some rocks below the kraal, where there was also a small bush of wood, so I walked towards the place and surprised my men lying down behind some Xesibes, among whom was old Gaga, instructing them how to put up the sights on their rifles in firing at the Pondos on the opposite hill, and highly pleased with their occupation until they caught sight of me. I let them off with a wigging, and sent them back to their hut. Old Gaga was mightily pleased with himself, and kept patting his head, intimating that that was what the Pondos wanted, but they would not get it as long as he could help it.

Shortly after this the Xesibes made a raid in force, and drove the Pondos back on to the mission station at "Umfundisweni," burning all the huts and kraals *en route*, and killing a great many Pondos. The C.M.R. were on the border all the day, but we did not cross it, and waited till the victorious Xesibes returned with their spoils of war in the shape of cattle.

One night I was awakened by the orderly sergeant, who told me that a man had ridden in saying that the Pondos were massing on the border about twelve miles from camp, in the direction of Rhode, a mission station on the road to Mount Frere. I gave orders for fifty N.C.O.'s and men to saddle up at once, and went with them in that direction, accompanied by the magistrate. We arrived opposite a store at the Sugar Bush, kept by two Europeans, and found the ridges on the Xesibe side of the border occupied by the Xesibes, and a large force of Pondos extended for about two miles to our front crossing the border and firing at the Xesibes in Colonial territory. I took up a position on a ridge about 800 yards from the front of the store, and, dismounting the men, awaited developments.

The Xesibes retired as the Pondos advanced, leaving their kraals and belongings to be burnt by the advancing natives. The Pondos far outnumbered the Xesibes as far as I could judge, and the latter began to run towards the hills at the back, where the Inciswa Mountains formed the background. Those who were retreating in our direction halted when they reached us and squatted down in our rear, but to our right and left they continued the retreat; the Pondos firing at them as they followed, and burning the huts as they reached them, and bullets began to come in our direction.

The magistrate being with my patrol, I could only act by his authority. I represented to him that I could not leave the ridge I was on, and that the Pondos had already burnt huts in Colonial territory, and it would endanger my patrol if I let them get much closer. He was equally anxious to avoid any hasty action on the part of the Government; but seeing that the Pondos appeared to ignore our presence, he at last consented to my opening fire if they approached 100 yards closer to us. As I was well aware that after the first shot was fired by our men the whole conduct of the affair would devolve on me, I extended my men along the ridge, and waited for the Pondos to advance to the indicated distance, which was about 600 yards range.

The Pondos in front evidently saw our movement, for they at once halted and sent men out to inform the others who were pursuing the Xesibes on our right and left, and the majority of them returned to the main body in front of us, which soon began to assume very large proportions. A large number on our left, however, were apparently too excited to listen to the main body, and followed the Xesibes into a valley on our left; the Xesibes in our rear immediately took advantage of this, and, charging down on the flank of the party of Pondos, succeeded in killing nearly a hundred of them before they could get back to the main body.

Encouraged by this success, the Xesibes began reassembling from all parts of the district, and it was with some difficulty that the magistrate, with his Native Police, managed to restrain them from attacking the Pondos, who were being largely reinforced, and must have numbered five or six thousand men, burning to avenge the loss they had sustained.

After a consultation with the magistrate I sent two men back to Mount Ayliff with a note to the officer commanding the infantry there, informing him of the state of affairs, and asking him to send out the remainder of the C.M.R. as soon as possible, intending on their arrival to send an order to the Pondos to retire to their own side of the border, and to enforce it in the event of their refusing to obey.

The magistrate now sent a Policeman to the Pondos, telling them to retire to their own country; but it was not till they caught sight of the C.M.R. trotting along the road from Mount Ayliff towards my position that they made any movement, and turned back and slowly returned to their side of the border.

On the arrival of my brother subaltern with about forty men we advanced to the border, and took up a position there till the Pondos had finally dispersed to their kraals and the Xesibes had also broken up and there was no immediate prospect of a resumption of hostilities. I then returned with the C.M.R. to Mount Ayliff, where I found the Cape Infantry under arms awaiting our return, very much exaggerated reports having reached them through native sources during the day, to the effect that we had been heavily engaged and had lost a number of men. These reports even reached Kokstad and caused great excitement, which only the Magistrate's and my dispatches managed to allay.

After some months of unsatisfactory negotiations between the Chief Magistrate and the paramount chief of the Pondos, a meeting was at length decided upon between the representatives of the Government and the Pondo chiefs, to be held in Pondoland. The regiment was again massed at Fort Donald. Colonel Bayly and staff arrived from King William's Town, and a regiment of native levies was also formed about three thousand strong, and officered by magistrates and men who understood the native language and customs. The levies went forward and occupied a large hill, covered with bush and rocks, and the C.M.R. took up a position at N'tola's kraal, where the meeting was arranged to take place.

The chief with his councillors and a large following of men came to the meeting, which lasted three days, innumerable cattle being slaughtered for the occasion. A settlement of the Pondo and Xesibe question was at last arrived at, and professions of goodwill made by the Pondos towards the Government. The chiefs were treated to an exhibition of firing by our Maxim gun squads, a few shells from our 7-pounders were burst on an adjacent hill for their edification and future guidance, and the meeting broke up. The native levies were disbanded and the C.M.R. returned to their various stations.

The Cape Infantry, having completed the term of service for which they had enrolled, were disbanded. A number of the

17

men who wished to remain in the Colonial Service were transferred to the C.M.R., and formed a dismounted branch of the regiment stationed at Port St. John's. Two captains and four lieutenants were also transferred to the regiment, an injustice which delayed promotion for a considerable period, and caused great discontent among senior lieutenants and non-commissioned officers who were expecting promotion. One of the captains took over the dismounted troop with two of the subalterns, as was expected, but the other captain took command of one of the squadrons, and this was an injustice to the senior lieutenant of the regiment. They had no qualifications that any one could see. One of them happened to be a brother of the Prime Minister, and the other was an ex-Cape Yeomanry man from the Imperial Service. They are both out of the Service now.

My squadron was now relieved from the Pondo Border and stationed in Kokstad and Matatiele, where the men were employed patrolling the newly populated farming districts and preventing stock thefts by the natives from the Drakensberg Mountains. Shortly afterwards I was transferred to Cala township, built near the scene of the old camp at T'Somo Valley from which we had evicted the squatters some years previously. This district contained a great number of the poor class of Dutch farmers, generally with large families, and apparently nothing to feed them on. Their only habitation was a small stone building containing one room partitioned off for a bedroom; their stock, a few cows, a span of bullocks, and a small flock of sheep and goats. Some of these so-called farmers being too poor to buy a branding iron to mark their stock with, contented themselves with clipping a hole in the ears of their sheep in various fashions, which they designated

" private ear-marks." As the sheep change hands constantly, the marks get added to or cut out until it is quite impossible to identify the ownership of the animal, and very tall swearing in the Magistrate's court results. One farmer will claim some of his neighbour's sheep and swear to the ear-marks being his own make; his neighbour brings all his friends and relatives to swear that the sheep was born on the farm. The biggest liar generally wins the case, and goes up in the estimation of his admirers forthwith, earning the greatest praise that one Dutchman can get from another, " Man, but he's slim," meaning smart; but, used in the sense generally applied to Dutchmen, it means that he is too big a liar to be bowled out, and worthy of emulation.

After a considerable period spent at this uncongenial work, I was ordered to Umtata, and rejoined my old squadron E, late No. 3, and the change to garrison life was much appreciated. About this time Colonel Bayly, who had been under the doctors' hands for some time, suffering from an internal complaint, decided to relinquish the command of the regiment, and amidst universal regret retired from the Service. He settled down at East London and quite recovered his health, and is now a member of the Upper House in Parliament, one of the most popular and respected men in South Africa. Major Grant assumed temporary command of the regiment, pending decision of Government as to Colonel Bayly's successor.

Internal troubles now took place in Eastern Pondoland. The old chief Umqikela had died about a year after the N'tola's Kraal meeting, and had been succeeded by his son Sigcau, a headstrong young fellow, who, immediately after assuming the chieftainship, quarrelled with his uncle Umhlangaso, the late chief's principal adviser. Umhlangaso resented this treatment, and, retiring to his part of the country near the border, defied Sigcau, and refused to attend the Great Place, as the chief's kraal was called. Consequently Sigcau began assembling his fighting men in order to punish his uncle, who, in his turn, collected all his followers with the intention of resisting the chief's army. The C.M.R. were again on the alert on the border to prevent any disturbance taking place near Government territory. I was sent with a detachment of twenty-five men to reinforce the men at Fort Donald, and spent a wretched couple of months at that most desolate station. At the end of that time Sigcau made up his mind to attack Umhlangaso, and after severe fighting, not all in his favour, he succeeded in driving his uncle with his followers over the border close to Natal, where we were waiting for them. We disarmed and made prisoners of them as they crossed the border, and finally we returned with Umhlangaso and some 600 of his followers to Fort Donald, where they were detained till the paramount chief allowed them to re-enter the country, under his own conditions. Umhlangaso was sent by the Government down Colony, where a grant of land was given him. He was afterwards allowed to return to Pondoland when the country was annexed to the Cape Colony some four years afterwards.

After the arrest of Umhlangaso I returned with my detachment to Umtata. Sir Henry Loch, who had recently been appointed Governor of Cape Colony, arrived in Umtata in the course of a visiting tour through the native territories. He was met outside the town by a field officer escort of C.M.R., and, mounting a horse, rode with us through the streets, which had been highly decorated in his honour, to a house which had been hired for the occasion. Umtata was the scene of great gaiety for three days, everybody being very much impressed by the Governor's charming personality.

Sir Henry Loch held several meetings with the native chiefs of the Umtata district, and a march past of about 10,000 Tembus was organised by the magistrates in his honour. It was a sight well worth seeing, the mass of natives, under the leadership of their headman and chiefs, keeping time by stamping on the ground as they passed by with uplifted sticks and chanting their native songs in praise of their chiefs and of the Governor, and winding up the ceremony with cheers for the Queen. It seemed to impress Sir Henry and his staff very favourably as a proof of the administrative powers of the Chief Magistrate and his subordinates, and of the influence possessed over the natives.

The Governor, who was returning to Cape Town *viâ* Durban in Natal, had decided to travel through Pondoland, and a meeting had been arranged between himself and the Pondo chief Sigcau at Palmerton in Eastern Pondoland. A strong escort of C.M.R. accompanied him, Major Grant in command. We passed through Western Pondoland to Port St. John's, which is without doubt the most picturesque spot in South Africa. Magnificent forests with tropical foliage through which the road passes, hills and valleys with bush and rushing streams of water with which that part of Pondoland abounds, and the magnificent Umzimvubu River which divides Eastern from Western Pondoland and in which splendid fishing is to be obtained, make Fort St. John's a place to remember for a lifetime.

On leaving St. John's we crossed the river by the pontoon, not without difficulty, the river being some three or four hundred yards wide at the crossing. We were then in

Eastern Pondoland, and proceeded on our journey to Palmerton, where we arrived without mishap,—a rather unusual occurrence where the travelling is over only partially made roads.

The Governor and his staff were made welcome at the mission station, and we pitched our camp of patrol tents in the vicinity. We found 60 C.M.R. awaiting our arrival at Palmerton, they having travelled from Mount Ayliff in order that a good show of force might be present at the meeting in the event of Sigcau becoming insolent, a not unlikely contingency, especially if he had been indulging in too much Kaffir beer. The Governor did not seem the kind of person to stand much nonsense from any native, so we looked forward to a somewhat lively meeting should the chief arrive in his usual state of semi-intoxication.

The next morning messengers arrived saying that the chief was coming during the day. Towards midday, Sigcau, with an immense following of thousands of mounted men, came from the direction of the Great Place, and proceeded to show off before the Governor by riding round Palmerton several times, gradually lessening the distance, till eventually he halted in front of the mission station and dismounted, his followers doing the same. He walked slowly up to the house where the Governor was standing watching the proceedings and was introduced by Mr. Stanford, the Chief Magistrate of East Griqualand. Apparently Sigcau was not in a mood for the meeting, for, after waiting a short while on the verandah, he returned to his horse, and mounting it rode off in the same manner in which he had arrived, circling about the mission station, followed by his mob of followers, till he finally went off in the direction of the Great Place.

We were then told that a meeting had been arranged for

the next day, and that the Governor was very angry at Sigcau's demeanour, and that if he attempted any nonsense we should probably get orders to arrest him and rush him out of the country before any organised resistance could be offered. The magistrates and missionaries who were present at Palmerton expected great results from the meeting between the High Commissioner and Sigcau, and were very much concerned at the aspect of affairs; they were afraid that the Governor was acting in too high-handed a manner with such a powerful independent chief, and they prophesied all kinds of disaster to us all should any attempt be made to teach Sigcau the lesson he required.

In my opinion the magistrates were themselves largely to blame for the arrogant manner in which they had allowed the Pondo chiefs to treat any representative of Government with whom they had had dealings hitherto. On several occasions I had visited the Great Place in company with the Chief Magistrate or with the special commissioner to interview the former chief Umqikela, and, after his death, Sigcau, and on no single occasion do I remember being able to accomplish our mission under three or four days. We were generally kept hanging about talking to one of the native secretaries, whilst the chief remained in his hut talking to some of the many hangers-on, low-caste white men, who plied him with liquor to keep him in a state in which it was impossible to obtain any reply of a satisfactory nature, and we could only return to Palmerton to sleep, in the hope of finding him in a reasonable frame of mind on the following day. This treatment of Government officials not having been severely dealt with at the commencement, had now become a matter of course, and I was dubious whether Sigcau would return at all to meet the High Commissioner.

But I was mistaken. Either the personality of Sir Henry Loch had made an impression on Sigcau, or the principal missionary, Mr. Peter Hargreaves, had more influence over him than he was generally credited with. Whatever the reason was, Sigcau arrived the following morning with a large following, quite sober and amenable to the severe lecture he received from the High Commissioner, who rated him for the manner in which he ruled the country, and gave him sound advice as to the conduct of the country for the future.

We had been saddled up with the wagons and carts packed ready for any emergency during the day, but the meeting passed off in a very satisfactory manner, and at its conclusion we started away from Palmerton for the border, Sigcau and his men accompanying the Governor for some miles, when they left us with expressions of goodwill and loud shouting.

The whole of the responsibility of the trekking practically devolved on me as the senior subaltern of the escort, the major in command contenting himself with riding with the Governor, and it was against my inclinations that the troop of men from Mount Ayliff joined in the escort on leaving Palmerton. I should have preferred them to return quietly with their own officer to Mount Ayliff, but the major ruled otherwise, so they came along with us, and it was in a perfect cloud of dust that we trotted along keeping pace with the carts to the out-span where we were to halt for two hours for lunch.

On arriving at the selected spot we off-saddled, and let the horses run, the troop horses being kept apart from the animals used for the transport of the Governor's party, which were generally fed at the carts by the contractors. When we were ready to proceed the call for "Horses in" was sounded, but to my disgust I saw the whole of the troop horses which the guard were driving in turn round suddenly, and, headed by six or seven of the Mount Ayliff Troop, charge wildly across the veldt towards the range of hills in the direction of Mount Ayliff, the guard being powerless to stop them. Major Grant's face was a study, but I did not linger to look at him; catching sight of one of my own horses feeding with the cart-horses, I ran to him, and, slipping the reim into his mouth, jumped on to his back and was after the bolting horses as hard as the horse could go. After galloping up and down hills, over rocks and sluits, I at last managed to head the brutes, and, with the help of a few raw Pondos, who assisted me by shying stones at the horses, I turned them and drove them back to the out-span as fast as possible, arriving there as the Governor's conveyances were nearly in-spanned. The men caught their horses and saddled up in record time, and we were formed up in time to give the usual salute as the Governor took his seat in his cart.

Major Grant was most profuse in his compliments, and told me that I had saved his reputation; but I was feeling too sore to appreciate compliments. I told him if he had taken my advice about the Mount Ayliff Troop it would not have happened, and advised him to send them off across country to Mount Ayliff before anything more occurred; which he did, and we proceeded with our original escort. Not having had so much bare-backed exercise for a good many years, I could hardly sit in my saddle, and was very pleased when the Governor told Major Grant that we could take a short cut to the mission station where he intended staying for the night, whilst the carts kept to the road some four miles farther round.

We remained at Umfundisweni that night, and experienced

the hospitality of that grand old missionary the Reverend John Peter Hargreaves of Umfundisweni, who had been about thirty years amongst the Pondos and knew them thoroughly. It was largely through his instrumentality that the Pondos, some years later, accepted Colonial Government without bloodshed; the younger generation being much in favour of resisting the occupation of the country by the C.M.R.

There is a native church and school at Umfundisweni, and the mission covers a large area of land with huts occupied by Christian natives, other tribes besides Pondos being represented. There is rather an amusing tale told of Sir Henry Loch's visit to this mission. On his arrival, Mr. Hargreaves, wishing to show him the native in his civilised state, escorted him round some of the huts, taking with him an old headman to act as guide. Several small children were playing about, and Sir Henry, pointing to one, asked what he was; the old headman with delight said, "Pondo." On being asked about others he answered with less pleasure, "Fingo" or "Tembu"; but when the governor, catching sight of a small half-caste child, laughingly asked what that was, the old headman looked severely at Sir Henry, and, spitting on the ground to emphasise his contempt, said, "Missionaries."

The next day we left Umfundisweni, and on our arrival at Fort Donald our pleasant duties as escort to Sir Henry Loch ceased, a small travelling escort of G Squadron accompanying him to the borders of Natal, while we remained the day at Fort Donald for a much-needed rest. Major Grant handed over the command of the escort to myself, and returned to Umtata by post-cart, to which place we returned by easy stages some six days later, without having had a single man or horse disabled on the long journey, a very creditable performance considering the bad state of the roads and absence of grain for the horses.

Colonel Grant shortly afterwards left Umtata for King William's Town, and his place was taken by the newly promoted Major Waring, who had been my old skipper on the Pondo border a few years before, and was one of my dearest friends in the country. My old friend "Tim," who had gone in for gunnery, had been appointed to the command of the artillery troop, and was at that time in King William's Town going through a course preparatory to his being sent home to pass the necessary examinations, which he eventually did with great credit to himself and the regiment, and returned a fully qualified captain of artillery.

CHAPTER XVIII.

1892–1893.

CECIL RHODES, PREMIER — FOOT - AND - MOUTH DISEASE — AN ENGLISH CHRISTMAS DAY — EAST GRIQUALAND FARMERS — AM ORDERED TO KING WILLIAM'S TOWN AS ASSISTANT ADJUTANT — MATABELE AND CHARTERED COMPANY — ORDERED TO MATABELELAND — TRAIN JOURNEY — ARRIVE AT VRYBURG — THIRSTY HORSES — RESULT — MARCH TO MAFEKING — OLD FACES — ARRIVAL OF IMPERIAL CONTINGENTS — VISIT OF SIR HENRY LOCH — GREY'S COLUMN LEAVES MAFEKING — REMARKS ON TREKKING — ARRIVE AT PALACHWI — LUNCH WITH "KING" KHAMA.

THE two succeeding years passed very uneventfully as far as the natives were concerned in the Transkei, but they were marked by great changes as regarded the administrators of the country. A better and more progressive class of man was now being sent to Parliament to represent the white people of the Colony; and with a new premier, in the person of Mr. Cecil Rhodes, the old imperial ideas had to a certain extent been revived, while the old system of pandering to the Dutch by renegade Britishers, under the control of the Bond, for the time ceased to exist. The word Majuba was not so freely bandied about by young Dutch farmers as had been the case whenever a few of this ignorant class happened to be in the majority at a race meeting or public function in the country parts of the Colony.

But although the natives were quiet and not giving us more than the usual amount of patrol work, something always crops up to prevent the C.M.R. officer or private from living too luxurious a life. Thus in this case foot-and-mouth disease broke out in Basutoland and the northern countries, and a cordon of C.M.R. was drawn along the borders. I was sent with a detachment of thirty men to the Drakensberg Mountains, in the Matatiele district, in order to guard the passes leading from Basutoland into East Griqualand.

We arrived at Matatiele in a snowstorm on a Christmas Eve, and spent Christmas Day in the village consulting the Magistrate as to the passes he wished occupied. The men were treated by the genial host of the Matatiele Hotel, who was an ex-sergeant of the regiment, to a splendid Christmas dinner, and I spent a typical English Christmas Day with my old friend the Magistrate, whom I had known many years. I mention this day because snow fell, and snow on Christmas Day, which in that part of the world is really Midsummer Day, made the day unique in my experience. The men simply revelled in it, and were like a pack of schoolboys, snowballing every individual they met, and generally enjoying themselves. People in that district still remember Christmas Day in 1892, and the succeeding weeks of snow and ice. We had particularly good cause to remember the time, as we spent it in the snow, our only covering being our small patrol tents, of which every man carries a half, rolled on his saddle, and which when joined to another half makes a shelter for two men with their saddles and equipments. It is a very tight fit, but better than nothing.

My time for the next six months was mostly spent riding along the foot of the mountains to the different stations of three men and a corporal at the foot of each pass, and in visiting the farmers' houses in the vicinity, where I always found a hearty welcome and a bed if I elected to stay the night. The farmers of East Griqualand are generally of a good class of English gentleman-farmer, with some real good sportsmen among them. The district has of late years become a very prosperous one, and the farmers form a wealthy and influential community.

When the foot-and-mouth disease died out I was ordered to proceed to King William's Town, having been transferred to headquarters as assistant-adjutant. Leaving my detachment to return to Umtata under charge of a sergeant, I started on my three hundred miles' ride to King William's Town, with my kit on a led pack horse, and my polo ponies in charge of a native servant. I spent an enjoyable two days at Umtata *en route*, and then proceeded to headquarters, where I once more settled down comfortably in the officers' quarters in the barracks at King William's Town.

My duties at headquarters not being of a very arduous nature—consisting chiefly of supervising the drill instructors in their training of recruits—I had plenty of spare time at my disposal to enter into sports and gaieties, for which King William's Town is justly noted, and the time passed very pleasantly.

About this time frequent allusions were being made by some of the papers to a tribe of natives called the Matabele, living in a country situated north of Bechuanaland, and on the borders of Mashonaland, a country which had been acquired by the Chartered Company some two or three years previously, but nothing of a serious nature was apprehended.

One evening, whilst at a dance, my attention was directed by my partner to a C.M.R. sergeant, who, in uniform with a cross belt, was standing in the doorway evidently searching in the crowd of dancers for somebody. On catching sight of me he crossed the ballroom, and with a salute informed me that the colonel wished to see me at once. Making apologies to my partner, I left the ballroom, took a cab to barracks, and went to the colonel's quarters. He appeared very much excited, and greeted me with "Look at this," handing me a telegram, on which was written: "Select one officer and thirty-five picked men to act as scouts for column proceeding to Matabeleland, without delay." The wire was from the Military Secretary, Cape Town. I handed him back the wire and waited. The colonel said, "You are the officer to go— how about the men? Can you get them in time?" As there were none but recruits available in King, I suggested that he should wire to my old squadron at Umtata for volunteers, and guaranteed him the number of men, and that they would be up to time. He agreed to my plan; and as nothing further could be done till next morning, I returned to the dance, determined to have a farewell night of enjoyment.

At the door of the hall I met a brother-officer, who inquired what was up; when I told him, he ejaculated, "Lucky devil," and the news was soon spread round the room. I was inundated with inquiries as to what part of the globe I was off to now. Nobody seemed to know anything about the Matabeles. The Commissioner of Cape Police, who was much interested, took me into the card-room and told me all about the country and the kind of native living there. He had been in that part of the country shooting years before, and was full of conversation, and it was some time before I could get back to the dance-room and my fair partner.

Colonel Grant sent a telegram in the morning to Umtata calling for volunteers, and within an hour received reply:

"Whole squadron volunteered—how many shall I send?"
As there was a squadron of C.M.R. at Komgha, only about
forty miles from King William's Town, Colonel Grant decided
to give them an opportunity of furnishing ten men, and wired
to Umtata for twenty-five from my old squadron. By lunch-
time we received a reply that the N.C.O.'s and men had
started. So keen were the men that they actually arrived in
King William's Town before the men from Komgha.

King William's Town was in a great state of excitement
the morning we left barracks for the railway station. As my
detachment marched through the streets, headed by our band,
we were greeted by thousands of our civilian friends who had
left their businesses to see the last of us. The train that was
to convey us north as far as possible consisted of a very
powerful engine with three large bogey trucks, two being for
the horses and equipments, and the other for the men and kits.
We soon had our horses off-saddled and entrained and the men
told off to their seats, and everything ready for the start.
The platform was crowded with the youth and beauty of King
saying good-bye to their friends of the detachment, the band
adding to the enlivenment of the proceedings. After the
colonel had shaken hands with me and wished me good luck,
we steamed out of the station to the strains of "Auld Lang
Syne," and amid cheers from a thousand well-wishers began
our long journey.

It soon became apparent that we were not travelling at the
ordinary South African train rate. In less than half the time
it usually took to accomplish the distance, we steamed into
Queenstown. We found the station decorated with bunting of
all descriptions, and literally packed with people, a long table
placed on the platform covered with refreshments of all kinds,

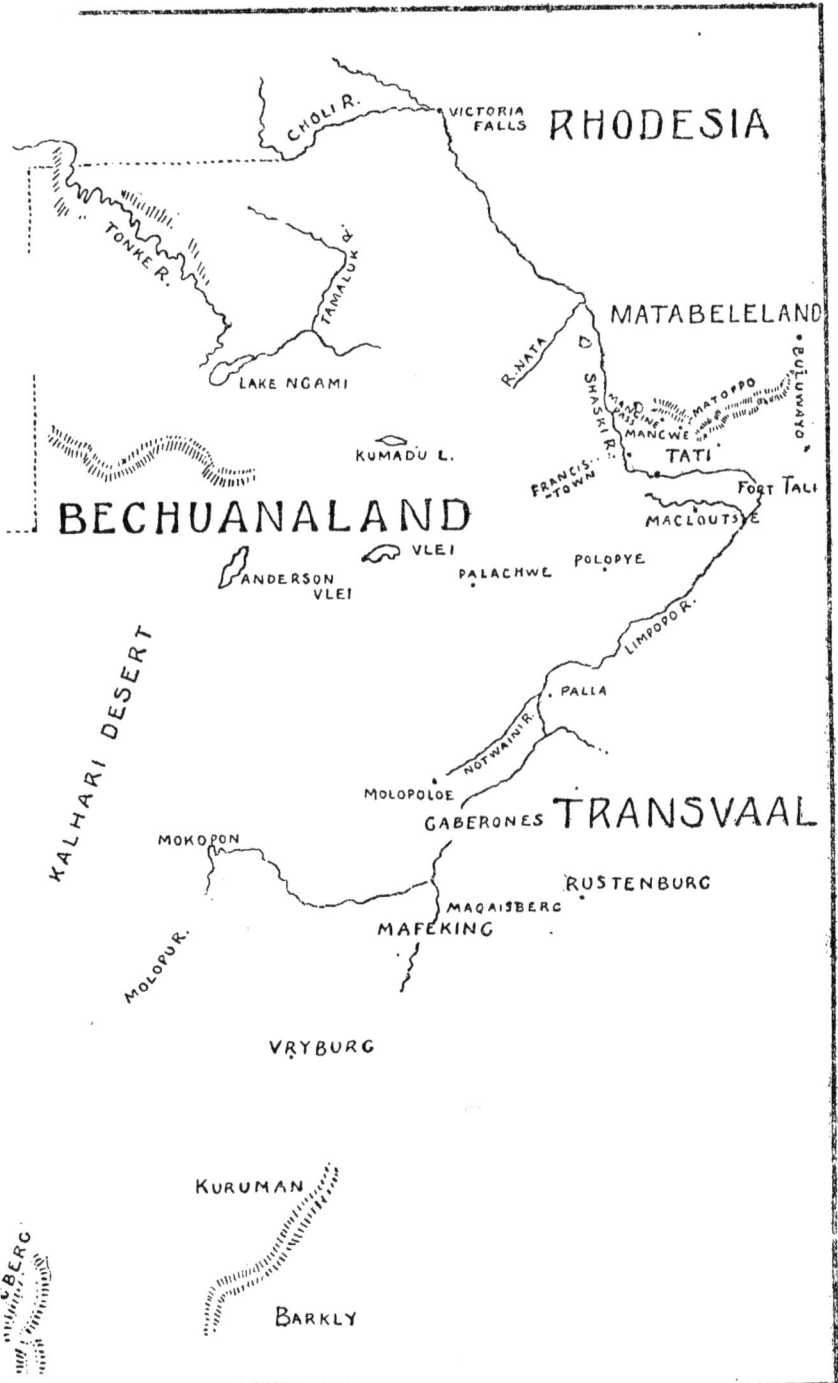

SKETCH MAP.

and a regular army of the young ladies of Queenstown waiting to minister to the wants of the detachment. The mayor of the town came to my carriage and requested me to allow the men to leave their carriage and partake of the hospitality which had been provided, and I was in the act of giving the order when a railway official, who had been travelling on the engine with the driver, came forward and stated that we could not remain longer than two minutes, orders imperative. I expressed my regret to the mayor and thanked him for his hearty reception, and asked him to convey our thanks to the town and regret that the men could not dismount. After a moment's expression of disappointment, the young ladies of Queenstown grasped the situation, and a unique sight was witnessed. Seizing everything that had been spread on the tables, these young ladies, assisted by their male friends, immediately began handing them through the carriage windows to the men inside. Fowls, hams, joints of meat, and varieties of pastry disappeared inside the carriages, followed by bottles of beer, cigars, and cigarettes, in quantities that would have served for a regiment instead of thirty-five men. Amidst cheers and waving of handkerchiefs we steamed out of the station in a very friendly frame of mind with our generous and resourceful hosts.

My compartment, which I shared with my two senior sergeants, owing to want of room in other compartments, presented a wonderful appearance. Every imaginable kind of food was thrown on to the seats, and baskets of fruit and liquors of all descriptions were piled on the floor, till there was hardly room to move; in fact, the supply of cigars and tobacco that had been given us lasted for some weeks, notwithstanding the fact that we gave boxes of both away to men of

18

the Bechuanaland Border Police when we arrived at the railway terminus at Vryburg.

I was so much impressed by the excessive kindness of the Queenstown people that I sent a long telegram at the first halt to the mayor of that place, again thanking him and the inhabitants for their extreme kindness to myself and men, assuring him that the esteem in which the C.M.R. had always held the inhabitants of Queenstown would continue as long as the regiment existed, and hoping at some future date to thank him personally for the compliment paid to my detachment.

The inspector, who since leaving Queenstown had stayed in the guard's van, at my request now joined me in our compartment. He expressed his regret that our stay at Queenstown had been so brief, but explained that the train had to catch a connection farther up the line, after which we would have a clear run to Vryburg, and would probably travel much faster.

Taking advantage of a halt for the engine to take in water, we watered our horses and lightened the carriage of half the provisions which had been thrust on us. There was plenty of bottled beer, but knowing every individual man of the detachment since his enlistment, I knew they could be trusted not to go to excess, and my confidence was justified. I never had cause to check a single man of the detachment for a breach of discipline, from the time of our departure from King William's Town till we rejoined the regiment nine months later. Yet I do not think I was ever considered very lenient in any matters where discipline was concerned, especially on active service. I have mentioned the incident to show the type of man the regiment was at that time composed of. Once trusted by an officer they would undergo any hardship rather than betray that trust, and to my mind that is the kind of feeling that makes a regiment.

We evidently caught the connection, for after leaving the Stormberg the train rattled along at an increased rate, and evening coming on, we made preparations for sleeping and fixed the bunks up. In the middle of the night I suddenly found myself on the floor of the compartment, and on struggling to my feet saw the inspector standing up holding on to the strap by the window and peering anxiously into the darkness outside. In reply to my question as to what had happened, he replied, " Nothing—we are going round a curve "; and in answer to another query, he said he did not know whether it was very safe, but we were an experiment; Government had issued orders to see what time the journey could be completed in, in the event of reinforcements being required to be sent up. I thanked him for the information, and tried to settle down again, but it was no use : the carriages were rocking from side to side, and it seemed impossible that we could continue at the rate we were travelling, and I heartily wished that some of the members of the Government were included in the experiment. Nothing happened; fortunately, the horses were all packed closely together, and there was not much danger of one of them being thrown, and we steamed into Vryburg in thirty-five hours from the time we entrained, a distance a passenger train at that time usually took two and a half days to accomplish.

I marched the detachment up to the camp of the Bechuanaland Border Police, situated on a hill above the town, where I found a sub-inspector in command of a few men, who told me that I was the first to arrive, **and he did** not expect the detachments from the Imperial regiments to arrive till the next day. I then learnt that there was a mounted infantry company of the Black Watch, and another of the West Riding Regiment to join the expedition, which was being mobilised at Mafeking, about 100 miles from Vryburg, whither I received orders to proceed as soon as rations and transport had been obtained. There were also about 150 horses in a kraal at the back of the fort, which it was intended that I should take on to Mafeking with me.

I was not very favourably impressed with Vryburg; the stores were nearly all owned by Jews, and the inhabitants mostly Dutch; but there was a great deal of activity in the vicinity of the railway station, goods and stores being loaded up on wagons as fast as they arrived by train and forwarded on to Mafeking. The next morning I paraded my detachment at camp for our march, and rode up to the kraal where the horses were kept, intending to tie them up in batches of fours or sixes by their head-stalls, and have them driven slowly along the road by half a dozen men. But no sooner did one of the B.B. policemen take down the wooden bars from the gate than the animals, catching sight of the opening, made a rush, and before they could be checked they had broken away in all directions, mostly making straight for the town, where there was a vlei of water. Others disappeared over the hills in the surrounding low bushes, and were soon out of sight. I then discovered that the wretched animals had been confined for three days in the kraal without a drop of water. I spent fully five minutes in letting the sub-inspector know my opinion of him, and of the low trick he had played on me; finally telling him that as I had not taken over a single horse, he would get no receipt, and therefore had better do what he could towards recovering them. I said I would pick up as many as I could on my way through the village, and take them on with me, and that he would be held responsible for the rest.

I sent a N.C.O. with six men to collect what animals they could from the vlei, and marched the remainder of my men along the road taken by our wagons, which had left camp some hours before. By the time we reached the first outspan the men had collected about 100 of the animals, who, having had their fill of water, were easily driven along the road, and by the evening when we had encamped for the night the remainder had been recovered by the men of the Police, and handed over to me. I had them all caught and tied in a ring, and after checking them with the list, and finding them correct, sent back a receipt to the humbled sub-inspector, who had sent me some very piteous appeals by different men during the day.

The horses were a very good lot and were intended as mounts for the Imperial troops on their arrival at Mafeking, to which place they would have to march on foot, where they were to be equipped. My detachment horses needed rest after their shaking up on the railway journey; so, on resuming our trek, I let the men pick horses from the remounts and ride them, driving their own along with the troop. This varied the monotony of the march considerably; the new horses feeling the sword bump against their ribs for the first time, invariably treated us to an exhibition of buck-jumping, but only on rare occasions did they manage to unseat a rider. I saw great possibilities in the near future when they would come into possession of the Tommies. Mounted infantry at that time might be said to be in its infancy, and it was not to be expected that a company picked out of a regiment would prove very expert horsemen. My expectations were realised, as will be seen later on in this narrative.

The country between Vryburg and Mafeking is very uninteresting, being of a flat nature, with a sandy soil and not much vegetation in the shape of bush; the veldt is not unlike the Karroo in appearance, the only water obtainable being from springs or vleis which were on private property. We passed several stores on the road owned by German Jews, who relied on Dutch farmers for support. Judging by the size of the stores and large amount of stock kept on hand, I should say that they found it a fairly profitable occupation.

We reached Mafeking and marched to the camp of the Bechuanaland Border Police, where tents had been pitched for our accommodation. I was met by the acting adjutant, who had been a C.M.R. private, who pointed out the various staff officers to me, and volunteered the information that Major Grey was to command the column on the march up to Matabeleland, a distance of about 500 miles, and also that the High Commissioner, Sir Henry Loch, was expected in Mafeking shortly. As to news from Matabeleland, there were only vague rumours to the effect that the Matabeles had fired on a Police patrol, hence the reason for the Imperial Government sending up troops to assist the Chartered Company's forces.

After seeing the horses we had brought from Vryburg with us handed over to a guard of the B.B.P., and obtaining a receipt for same from the adjutant, I saw that my men were comfortably installed in their tents with their kits, and warning them that they must make themselves acquainted with the standing orders of the camp, and strictly conform to them, I proceeded to the hotel in the town, about half a mile from camp, where I took up my quarters pending the arrival of the remainder of the troops composing the column.

On returning to the camp in the afternoon to inspect the troop horses on the stable parade, I was informed by one of the sergeants that an old gentleman who had been spending most of the day in the C.M.R. lines, and appeared very much delighted at having seen some men of the regiment, was waiting my arrival in the sergeants' tent. I went to the tent, and recognised in the visitor Major Boyes of the old Cape Mounted Rifles, or Cape Corps, as they were called some forty years before.

I had seen him often in King William's Town, where he was a well-known figure at the club. He appeared delighted at seeing me, and informed me that he was on a visit to his son, who was Resident Magistrate of Mafeking; he insisted on my returning with him, which I did, after showing him the men and horses. He was keenly interested in the changes, and it was very clear that the old gentleman had not forgotten his young soldiering days.

I was made very welcome by the Magistrate, Mr. George Boyes, whom I had known for a considerable time, he having been on the Chief Magistrate's staff at Umtata, and by his mother, who with the Major had taken up her temporary abode with their son. I spent a most enjoyable evening with the dear old couple, who were very keen to hear the latest from King. Before leaving for my hotel that evening I had accepted all challenges made by the younger member of the family to play the shining lights of Mafeking at tennis with teams from my men, subject to the exigences of the service.

Major Grey having arrived when I visited the camp next morning, I reported myself to him, and was informed that there were a number of volunteers who had been recruited in the Cape Colony on the way up to Mafeking, and on their arrival my troop would be made up to 100 strong, the Black Watch and West Riding contingents made up in the same manner, and that I had been promoted to captain from that date. During the interval there was nothing to do, except make my men clean up their equipments and prepare for the march. Major Grey inspected my detachment, and complimented me on their appearance, and hoped that we would assist him as much as possible in the future.

That afternoon, taking one of the sergeants for my partner, and two of the privates who were used to playing together, we went to the tennis courts and played the four champions of the town, and managed to beat them after some very close games. They accepted their defeat with good grace, and entertained us most hospitably.

On the arrival of the regulars and the volunteers, the business of mounting and equipping them was quickly gone through. My time was much occupied in getting the addition to my men put into shape, but I took very good care not to mix them. I kept the C.M.R. intact as a right troop, with the exception of four privates, whom I made non-commissioned officers and posted to the left troop, which consisted of 60 odd volunteers mostly from Port Elizabeth, with a lieutenant who was a sergeant in the C.M.R., and lent to the B.B.P. for the occasion. This man proved to be a good officer, and his commission was confirmed when he rejoined the regiment at the end of the campaign. Before we had been on the march a week the left troop had become quite useful and efficient.

Being mostly good horsemen they proved very good material, and working with trained men were much easier than some of the other troops turned out to be.

There was a captain with the Black Watch; a captain and two subalterns with the West Riding; a subaltern of the 20th Hussars attached to the Black Watch troop; and a captain from the 3rd Dragoon Guards as adjutant; myself and subaltern in my troop. All the troops, with the exception of the C.M.R., were clothed in the B.B. Police uniform, my men retaining the C.M.R. Service kit, but adopting the B.B.P. smasher hat instead of our helmets, as being more uniform in the veldt. Major Grey of the 6th Dragoons was in command of the column, and an ex-Imperial officer was transport officer.

Sir Henry Loch, having arrived from Cape Town, inspected the column the day before we commenced our march, and recognising me, congratulated me on my promotion, and invited me to lunch in company with Major Grey and the Secretary of Native Affairs, who had accompanied the Governor from Cape Town. The Governor's aide-de-camp, Captain John Ponsonby, of the Guards, who proved to be one of the best of companions on the long march, obtained permission from His Excellency and joined the column as staff officer to Major Grey, and the expedition was complete.

The following morning the column commenced the march from Mafeking. Some amusement was afforded at the start by the men of the West Riding Regiment, who, having had no training whatever in mounted work, had experienced a difficulty in packing their saddles and saddling up correctly. When it came to mounting, at least half of the men were thrown by their horses, and it was after some delay, and a great deal of assistance rendered by the C.M.R., that the column got under way.

The country from Vryburg to Mafeking was of a very open nature, but two or three miles beyond Mafeking we began to enter into bush country—not bush in the sense as applied in the Cape Colony, where it means country covered by large forests of trees with thick undergrowth. In Bechuanaland, bush means country with small thorn trees, rarely exceeding 10 or 12 feet in height, with occasional trees thrown in, dotted about at intervals, which get thicker as one advances into the country. By riding round the bushes a horseman can always make his way through the country, and this cannot be done in the Cape Colony. The roads were simply clear spaces through this bush, and, like the rest of the soil, composed of sand, and very heavy in places for wagon transport. Our rate of progress was necessarily slow, the drivers not being able to make the free use of the whip as they could in the open country, owing to the lash catching in the surrounding bushes. The oxen seemed to grasp the situation, and acted accordingly, crawling along at a much slower pace, if possible, than I had hitherto seen the most miserable teams travel at.

Water was only obtainable at certain distances. The treks were very long and tiring for men and horses, owing to the innumerable halts; and I soon perceived that in the officers of the column I had struck a collection of novices, in the methods of trekking at least. On reaching the out-span, the horses, instead of being knee-haltered and let run to roll and graze, were immediately tied up, whilst the numbers on their hoofs were checked to ascertain that they were all correct. I objected strongly to my horses being treated in that manner, and sent them out to graze with a guard. It was at least an hour before the other horses were let go after being off-saddled. The captain of one of the other troops came up to me, remarking, " I say, old chap, have got a bally conundrum. Told to knee-halter my horses. What the devil am I to do?" I turned out my men to instruct the other troops in the art of knee-haltering their horses with the reims of their head-stalls. The incident caused me some amusement, and made me think that Major Grey had a " conundrum " in how to convert typical infantry " Tommies " into serviceable mounted men between Mafeking and Matabeleland.

The march for the first week from Mafeking was the worst of its kind I have ever experienced. I had been accustomed to everything working like clockwork to the trumpet-calls, and to every officer, N.C.O., and man knowing exactly what duty he had to perform. But here nobody seemed to know what to do next, and orders, issued and countermanded as soon as issued, only added to the general confusion.

The hours that should have been spent trekking were wasted in packing up the wagons and saddling up the poor horses in the morning; men seemed unable to recognise their horses; or horses being insecurely tied up to the picquet-lines got loose, and, the guards not watching them, strayed into the surrounding bush to feed, which necessitated some of my men having to search for them and drive them in. When at last every man had succeeded in saddling up a horse, the odds were against its being the animal originally told off to the man who had saddled it up; then came the " Fall-in," when the Irish adjutant had full opportunity of storming at them in his endeavour to arrange them in some semblance of formation of column of troops.

The post of bringing up the rear and seeing that no stragglers fell out, generally fell to my lot, with the C.M.R., the left troop going on with the remainder. The wagons, having got such a short start, were overtaken in a short space of time, and then the men were dismounted and made to lead their horses at the back of the wagons till they arrived at the outspan—a most demoralising method of trekking for both men and horses.

The extra work caused through our riding about the country collecting stray horses, and the long hours under the saddle, began to tell on the C.M.R. horses, and I was very much concerned as to their arriving at the front in anything like a serviceable condition. I suggested to Major Grey that the whole of the saddlery of the expedition, with the exception of C.M.R., should be packed on the troop wagons and the men marched in their troops on foot, all the horses being left in the charge of my men to be driven from one camp to another, and that the hours for the wagons to trek should be altered to the proper time. The system worked in the following way:—

Réveillé would sound at 4 a.m., the men immediately packing their blankets on the wagons, which would be immediately inspanned, and trek. Shortly after their departure the men would parade in their troops, and march on with occasional halts to the next outspan. After they had left the camping ground—generally about two hours—I would give the order to the C.M.R. to turn out and pack up. This did not take very long, and when the men were saddled up and ready to start, the horses of the other troops were loosened from the formation in which they had been tied up during the night, the reims fastened round their necks, and with half a dozen mounted men riding in front to prevent them galloping, the horses were driven along the road at a slow trot till the next camping ground was reached, when the other troops would catch their horses and feed them, after which they would be turned out to graze in the open spaces by the outspan. The column would remain at the outspan all the day till about 4 p.m., when a feed for the horses being taken off the wagons, the latter would inspan and commence the evening trek. Horses would then be brought in and caught and fed by the troops, who would leave them in the care of my men, and march off after the wagons to the place where it was intended to halt for the night. Just before dusk, my men would saddle up, and we would collect the horses from where they were feeding, and drive them along the road till we arrived at the sleeping-place, when the horses would be caught and " rung " by troops—that is, horses tied to one another in a line, the two ends being then brought towards one another in a circle, till they met, when they were fastened together, thus forming a circle or ring. This is by far the best method of securing a troop of horses during the night; it does away with the impedimenta of picquet ropes and pegs and is more secure.

The change was made, and it effected a great difference in the horses. They quickly began to get back into proper condition; also the men had much longer rests and proper meal hours, and the whole day in which to cook or wash themselves, and their clothes if they wished, and a more workmanlike looking and contented column was the outcome of the alteration.

Tommy also, now that the trouble of saddling up and having to lead his horse for four hours at a stretch was done away with, became more interested in his " long-faced chum," and was generally to be seen waiting our arrival at the camp with a cup of coffee in one hand for a C.M.R., and a nose-bag in the other containing a feed for his horse, and apparently anxious to see how his animal had fared since the previous night.

We passed through a village called Gaberones, where we found a troop of the Bechuanaland Border Police stationed. The village consisted of the camp and two stores, and there was a large "Staadt" or native village close to the camp. The Bechuanas are different from the Cape Colony natives; they are more akin to the Basutos, the languages being very much the same, but they are not such a well-made race as the latter, being a scraggy, emaciated lot in comparison.

The country about this part is very thick with bush, and it was dangerous for individual men to get off the beaten tracks. Any such unfortunate would probably wander about the bush for days, till he eventually died of thirst, unless rescued by the natives.

Water was scarce, and every morning and evening fatigue parties of men off duty had to dig for water in the bed of the dried-up rivers, as we outspanned at them. In addition to digging holes for drinking water for the column, long trenches had to be dug along the bed of the river till sufficient water had been obtained to water all the horses and the cattle belonging to the wagons; but as there were plenty of men available for the work, it was soon performed after the column reached the outspan ground. We shortly afterwards came upon running streams and rivers, and spent a most enjoyable day at the Crocodile River, the country being more open at this point.

It was here that I saw the small red locust for the first

time, as they do not frequent the lower parts of South Africa. These insects have no wings, and are called " voetgangers " or foot-marchers. They were in myriads, trying to cross the Crocodile River and tumbling into the river in thousands, others crossing over the backs of the others and in their turn falling into the water. How did they cross? On what? It was a very fine sight, the fish rising and snapping them off in hundreds, but the never-ceasing mass of locusts struggle on till they eventually reach the opposite bank.

The men had a good day's sport fishing, and the sportsmen of the party managed to shoot a few dozens of guinea fowl, which were in great quantities, and gave the whole column a very agreeable change of diet for a couple of days.

We passed through Palla, another village with trading stations, and on to Palachwi or Palapye, the capital of Bechuanaland, and the residence of the Paramount Chief Khama, who, with his son Sekomi, paid us a visit and was invited to lunch by Major Grey, the invitation being extended to the other officers to meet " His Majesty." It was rather amusing to me to witness the excitement the event caused among my brother officers, the majority of whom had seen very few natives before they joined the expedition. To lunch with a " King " was an honour they were nervous about, and they were rather offended when I advised them to keep well out of " His Majesty's " range, as his domestic and company manners were not of the politest sort. For me, I preferred the company of my subaltern at lunch to that of dusky royalty.

CHAPTER XIX.

MR. RHODES JOINS COLUMN—IMPRESSIONS OF RHODES—A WET MARCH—
FLOODED RIVER—RHODES LEAVES WITH ESCORT FOR BULUWAYO—
ARRIVE AT TATI, MATABELELAND—CASUAL TREKKING IN ENEMY'S
COUNTRY — COLUMN ARRIVES AT KHAME RIVER — C.M.R. ORDERED
FORWARD — MEET COLONEL GOOLD-ADAMS AT BULUWAYO — KING'S
KRAAL, BULUWAYO—MARCH TO INYATI—MEET CHARTERED COMPANY'S
TROOPS—DISSATISFACTION OF TROOPS—C.M.R. REMAINS AT INYATI—
EXCITING PATROLS—A DEFIANT HEADMAN—RETURN TO BULUWAYO.

THE next day, after the column had left Palachwi, Major
Grey and myself met Mr. Rhodes, who had just arrived,
and accompanied him through the Staadt on our way to
rejoin the column. There must have been, roughly speaking, some 6000 huts in the Staadt. They were spread over an
extensive area, with a large open square near Khama's huts,
on one side of which were built a telegraph office and two
or three large stores. The huts were fenced off with grass
matting; very narrow passages left between them served as
paths to the different parts of the Staadt. Through these
paths we rode in file till we reached the open country, and
my chief recollection is of the horrible smells that assailed
our nostrils before we got to the outside of this, the most
insanitary portion of the globe I have ever visited.

This was my first meeting with Mr. Rhodes. Although
his photograph had appeared before the general public during
his term of office as Prime Minister, and his features were
familiar to every one in South Africa, he had not up to the

GROUP OF C.M.R. N.C.O.'S, WITH "A COLONIAL OFFICER" IN THE CENTRE.

present travelled round the native districts of the Cape Colony, and was personally unknown to all living in that part of the Colony. There was nothing in his general get-up to suggest the extraordinary personality of the man, nor even to make me recognise him as the Honourable Cecil John Rhodes, whose photographs were familiar enough. His appearance suggested the proprietor of an up-country trading-station. A smasher hat, shabby grey coat, grey flannel shirt, a very dirty pair of white flannel trousers, and leather boots, made up his attire; and on studying his face I came to the conclusion that the photos had rather flattered him. He was a tall, powerfully-built man, his massive head with its rugged face suggesting a resolute character. His voice was a very peculiar one when heard for the first time, alternating between a bass and a falsetto, and not at all in keeping with his appearance.

He chatted to me very affably during our ride, asking me leading questions about the C.M.R., and the conditions of the Colony from my point of view. On our arrival at the outspan Mr. Rhodes had his tent pitched beside Major Grey's, and I told off one of my men as orderly to him, to look after his wants during his stay with us, until we reached Matabeleland.

We heard from Mr. Rhodes that Colonel Goold-Adams, commanding the B.B.P., was on the border of Tati awaiting our arrival, and, with the Chartered Company's troops under Major Forbes, had already got to Buluwayo after much fighting. There was not much detail in the news that had been wired from Mashonaland, and we were all anxious to push on as fast as possible.

The wet season had begun to show signs of coming on, and the rivers might at any time become in flood, but we managed

19

to get over the ground till nearing Matabeleland, when we were almost caught napping. It had been raining rather heavily all day, and culminated that evening in a heavy thunderstorm. I had pushed on ahead of the column with the horses until the darkness became too thick for us to see the horses with any degree of certainty, when I halted them, on what I judged to be a sandy flat, and made my men catch them and tie them together in groups. We took the shelter we could get under the bushes at the edge of the sand, and waited for the storm to spend itself. I had an idea that we must have halted in the bed of a dry river, which must have been a pretty broad one, and I did not feel comfortable. Taking a sergeant with me, I walked straight across to a bank, and climbing it, found a large open space easily discernible in the light caused by the vivid flashes of lightning. We returned to the horses, and before we reached them saw a stream of water slowly trickling down the centre, which had not been there five minutes before. I shouted out to my men to stand to the horses, and lead them through. It was not a moment too soon. Before we had got the last of the horses up the opposite bank, on to the flat, the water had risen up to our ankles.

Telling my sergeant-major to have the horses "rung" and the men to off-saddle, I rode back across the river, where I met three or four wagons, Mr. Rhodes' wagon being the first. I told the drivers, who wanted to halt, to drive straight through as quickly as possible, and managed to cross about six of the wagons as they arrived; but the sound of rushing water some distance up the river made me order the rest to stay where they were, and I turned and followed the other wagons across, the water reaching up to my saddle-flaps; it was with great difficulty that the last wagon managed to get out. The river now came down in earnest, and within an hour was running very high. In the morning I found that we were completely cut off from the remainder of the column; Major Grey, Mr. Rhodes, and the C.M.R. were on one side of the river, and the horses and the remainder of the men were on the other side. Fortunately, we had the grain for our horses on the leading wagons, and also my men's rations, so we were all right, and I gave the order to pitch tents, and we made ourselves comfortable.

Mr. Rhodes, taking with him Major Grey and an escort of twelve C.M.R. N.C.O.'s and men, left the column with the intention of getting to Buluwayo as soon as possible, and seeing how events were shaping at that place, which was in possession of the Chartered Company's forces, with Dr. Jameson as civil adviser.

As soon as the river became passable, which was not until about a week later, the remainder of the troops crossed, and the column resumed its journey, arriving in due course at Tati, on the border, and in Matabeleland. The village con- sisted of a large store and a small mining camp, the ground having been granted to two brothers by Lobengula, the Mata- bele chief; it was then called the Tati Concession, but is now named Francistown, and has fair mining prospects.

We left Captain Lindsell, who had been acting as trans- port officer to our column, at Tati as Magistrate, and pushed on to the Mangwe Pass. We were now getting near the hilly part of the country and in the vicinity of the Matoppo Hills, where a large body of the Matabeles were supposed to be in position under Gambo, Lobengula's principal fighting chief. We had been warned at Tati that we were

likely to encounter opposition during our passage of the
Mangwe Pass, but we continued our march in the same
casual manner in which it had hitherto been conducted—the
troops marching along as infantry, whilst the horses were
left entirely in my charge, to be driven along from camp
to camp at whatever time I chose.

The country in Matabeleland was a striking contrast to
that of Bechuanaland. In place of the thick scrubby bush
with its limited range of surrounding country, there were now
fine open flats, interspersed with small woods and glades, and
hills with large overhanging rocks surmounted by trees and
bush. The scenery was most delightful after the weary trek
through Bechuanaland.

At night no precautions were taken for the safety of the
column—no attempt being made to form a laager. The
Imperial officer in command preferred to risk disaster rather
than display his ignorance by asking advice from others as
to how to construct one. This called forth indignant protests
from the adjutant and several others, but the only replies
vouchsafed were, "We did not do this in Egypt," or "We
did not do that on the Nile." We all wondered what they
did do in that wonderful country that was likely to be of the
least use in any other part of the world, but we agreed that
the use of common sense had not been acquired there, at
any rate in this particular case.

On my arrival with the horses at the foot of Mangwe
Pass, however, I found that the wagons had been formed up
in a primitive attempt at a laager, a sub-inspector of the
B.B.P., whom we found in camp there, with a troop of the
corps, having been requisitioned by the O.C. to instruct him
in the methods of constructing one. There was no room for

the horses, but as they were a secondary consideration with this wonderful infantry expedition, it did not trouble the embryo general in the least.

The B.B.P. at this post having confirmed the rumour that "Gambo" was in the Matoppos, I insisted that the different troops should take over their horses, and declined to act as horse guard any longer. The adjutant backing me up, the saddles were unpacked from the wagons, and the column became mounted once more, and proceeded on its march up Mangwe Pass. If the slightest opposition from an enemy had been encountered, the result would have been most disastrous to the column, for no attempt had been made to occupy any of the surrounding hills, to cover the long convoy of wagons as they toiled up the Pass. The whole column straggled along, dragging their horses with them, till they finally reached the top, without having seen a sign of the Matabeles. From the top of the Pass the country is very open to the Khame River, where we eventually arrived, and Major Grey, returning from Buluwayo, took command of the column, and camp was formed on the ground above the river.

This camp was the farthest point north that the Imperial troops and the volunteers of the column went into Matabeleland, and is about 20 miles south of Buluwayo. On the second day of our stay in camp, a dispatch arrived for Major Grey, ordering him to send on the C.M.R. at once to Buluwayo, and it was not long before I had my men in saddle, and had taken my last look at the camp.

We arrived at Buluwayo the next morning, where I met Colonel Goold-Adams of the Royal Scots, who was then commanding the B.B.P. and the Imperial troops in the field. He received me in a very kindly manner, and informed me that Mr. Rhodes had gone on in the direction of the column under Major Forbes, who was retreating from the Shangani River, after losing a troop killed under Major Wilson of the Chartered Company's forces—the inevitable result of sending small parties of men ahead of the column without supports, and without knowing the strength of the opposing force.

Mr. Rhodes had taken my men on with him to Inyati to meet the column, and had left orders for me to push on as quickly as possible to that place with the remainder of the C.M.R. After giving orders to my men to be ready to march that evening, I walked from the colonel's tent up to Lobengula's kraal, which I found had been completely destroyed by him before clearing out of Buluwayo. The huts had been built in a circle, with a large open space in the centre for drill purposes for his own particular regiment. On a ridge at the back of the huts there was a square stone building, evidently used as a magazine, which had been blown up. Some of the huts were still smouldering. A small silver elephant was picked up amongst the ruins shortly afterwards by some men who were searching around for curios.

There were two stores below the king's kraal, in one of which two traders, Fairburn and Usher, had been kept prisoners, but otherwise left unmolested by the king, till the arrival of the Chartered Company's forces, when they found themselves free. I had known Usher in East Griqualand some years before, his father and mother being well-known dispensers of hospitality at their farm just outside Kokstad. There was also a house in which Mr. Colenbrander lived, who, together with his sporting wife, were the only married people in the country at that time.

As I had orders to push on, I decided to leave my wagon containing our rations and kits behind in charge of a corporal and three men, until it had been settled which part of the country we were to operate in. I paraded the remainder of my detachment in marching order, taking two days' rations with us in our wallets. Colonel Goold-Adams inspected the men before marching, and expressed to me his satisfaction at their appearance and wished me luck.

Leaving Buluwayo, we took the Inyati road, and after a three hours' trek off-saddled for the night. Continuing our journey the next morning, I met several men riding to Buluwayo. One of them happened to be Colenbrander, who told me he had been with Major Forbes' patrol, and had left them on the other side of Inyati. He confirmed the report that Wilson's party had been cut up and that the column had been attacked several times on the return journey, and informed me that Mr. Rhodes with his escort of C.M.R. had joined the column.

We reached Inyati that afternoon, and met the column straggling into the place, which had been a mission station, with two large houses 200 yards apart. These buildings had been partially destroyed, about three rooms remaining with the roof on, which were utilised as a hospital. The men of the column presented a dejected appearance as they came up; with the exception of the B.B.P. who had accompanied the column, they were volunteers of the Chartered Company, and had been promised farms on the settlement of the country. They were quite out of hand, and were clamouring to see Mr. Rhodes, cursing their leaders, and saying they had not beaten the Matabeles, and that the promises of farms would not hold good in an unconquered country. Mr. Rhodes told them all he would see them at Buluwayo, and not before, and eventually they moved off as they pleased in the direction of that place.

Mr. Rhodes, who appeared to be greatly distressed at the condition of affairs, asked me if I would remain at Inyati with my men, as it was his intention to return to Buluwayo, where he would interview the men of the Chartered Company; he added that a number of the B.B.P. would also remain at Inyati and that I would find them a good lot of officers and men. I informed him that I would remain wherever I was ordered. Mr. Rhodes then asked me whether, in the event of the Chartered Company's raising a Police force for Matabeleland, my men would join it as a nucleus for that force. I told him that was a matter for the Cape Government to decide; I did not know whether the men would be willing to forego their service in the C.M.R. and join a new force. He reminded me that he was the Premier of the Cape Colony, and could arrange it, and asked me to ascertain the feelings of the men on the subject.

I paraded the detachment and put the proposition to the men. They were not very keen on accepting the proposal; several of them spoke of the behaviour of the Chartered Company's men, who had evidently a grievance against the authorities, and asked what guarantee they would receive against similar treatment. Eventually, after they had consulted one another, they told me they would join the Chartered Company provided I did, and not unless.

I returned to Mr. Rhodes and told him what the men had said, adding that, for my own part, I would not leave my regiment for a new force where back service would not count; but I told him that if he got the consent of the Colonial

Government and of the officer commanding the C.M.R., I was willing to remain in the country with my men until the Police force had been thoroughly organised and in working order, but nothing more. Mr. Rhodes seemed disappointed that his offer had not been jumped at, but thanked me, and said he would arrange the matter with the Government and let me know. He then called Dr. Jameson, who was passing at the time, and introduced me, and told him that the C.M.R. would remain at Inyati, and that we were to be placed on the loot list, meaning that we were to receive our share of the money realised by the sale of captured cattle, in common with the B.B.P. and Company's forces.

I met several old friends from the Colony amongst the officers of the expedition, Gipsy of the C.M.R. Artillery being one of them. He had been a Magistrate in Mashonaland, and was now about to be appointed in the same capacity at Buluwayo. He had altered very much in appearance since he had left the regiment, and was full of fever. The majority of the Company's forces seemed to be suffering from this malady, and it accounted for the listless air of the whole column.

At last the Chartered Company's forces took their departure for Buluwayo, and we were left the task of settling the country round the Inyati district. Matabeleland had been inhabited by two classes of natives, called Matabeles and Makalakas; the latter were the original occupiers of the country, but were conquered by the Matabeles, an offshoot of the Zulu tribe, to whom they had become practically slaves, and whom they held in great fear. Our object now was to allay these fears and impress on the Makalakas that the former conditions had ceased to exist, that the Matabeles and themselves were equal, and all subject to the Chartered Company, and that any attempt made by Matabeles to revert to the former state of affairs would be severely dealt with. I took up my position in Inyati in the ruins of a dwelling-house with an enclosure, told off my men to their different positions in the event of an attack, and proceeded to clear the bush for a considerable distance. The buildings about 200 yards from us in the direction of the river were occupied by the B.B.P., commanded by a captain and three subalterns and an Artillery officer, with several machine-guns. The bush was also cleared from the vicinity, and within twenty-four hours the place presented a formidable appearance, with its bastions and guns pointing in all directions, and sheltered trenches for the men.

I had sent a message to Buluwayo to have one wagon with kit forwarded, but through an oversight it was not complied with, and we were stranded at Inyati without a change of raiment or toilet necessaries. This caused us much discomfort. Soap, for example, was unobtainable after the first few days, the one and only piece in the possession of our mess being lost by one of the members whilst bathing, amidst universal expressions of disgust.

We patrolled the district for miles around, collecting cattle with very little opposition, and driving them into Inyati, which soon presented an animated aspect; thousands of head of cattle were driven through by natives, impressed for the occasion, *en route* for Buluwayo, at which place they were handed over to the stock-agent of the Company, to be disposed of to speculators, who were doing a big business. We surprised a large village called Jin-Jin one morning, and the natives, on hearing our approach, left their cattle, amounting to several thousand head. These we annexed, and had them driven off to Inyati for transmission to Buluwayo. The rainy season had now fairly set in, and we were wading about in mud, generally wet through. My men mostly discarded their breeches and boots when not on mounted duty, and were to be seen in ragged shirts with the cape of their mackintoshes strapped round their waists, and bare legs. They called themselves the Inyati Highlanders, but they were all in good condition and gave the medical department no trouble, in spite of the hardship they endured sleeping without cover in all weathers, and a not too plentiful supply of food.

Shortly after my return to Inyati, some natives reported that the Matabele Impis had recrossed the Shangani River and were raiding the Makalakas, driving off the cattle and killing the natives. Saddling up thirty of my men and taking the natives who had brought in the report with us, we proceeded in the direction the Matabeles were supposed to be in. We started in the evening, and rode along a track through the Mapani bush, a species of thorn trees difficult to ride through. The track was very narrow and only allowed the patrol to ride in half-sections. About midnight we came to more open country with large hills covered with bushes and stones, amongst which we could see a number of fires. These fires, our guides explained, meant Makalakas hiding in the hills from the Matabele Impis. It seemed a peculiar method of showing their fear, but it was too dark to attempt to leave the track to investigate, so I continued, with occasional halts, till daylight, when I discovered that the guides, with the exception of one whom I had kept guarded with me, had disappeared, and the Shangani River was to be seen with its fringe of black trees running through the valley below us.

The guide, who appeared to be in a terrified state of mind, stated in reply to questions that we had arrived where the Matabeles had been raiding the cattle; that he lived some distance back on the way to Inyati, and that we had passed his kraal in the night. He begged me to allow him to return home. I asked him if there was any other way back to Inyati than the track we had come by, and he pointed round to the right of the range of hills which we had discovered at daylight in our rear and through which we had ridden during the night, and said we could get back to Inyati by going round the hills.

Telling him that if he attempted to leave the patrol he would be shot, I selected an open space with a large ant-heap in the centre, and offsaddled the horses and let them graze close by, placing the saddles round the ant-heap as a rally point in the event of a surprise.

There were no signs of any cattle having been driven about the spot, nor of any natives. We gave the horses a much-needed rest of two hours, and then saddled up and resumed our march, keeping the hills on our right and leaving the river on our left rear. The ground was very boggy, the horses sinking up to their fetlocks at every step. This soon began to tell on the animals, and necessitated the men dismounting and leading them for a considerable distance till we reached higher and firmer ground. Finding that we had reached the side of the hills, and that the country between us and Inyati was comparatively open, so that we need have no fear of a surprise party of Matabeles appearing on the scene, we offsaddled at a stream and gave the horses a good rest, and, with the exception of the sentries, indulged in a sleep.

Resuming our journey, we came across a large village

which we had not previously visited during the patrols from Inyati, and I was surprised at the unconcern evinced by the natives at our sudden appearance. There were a number of men lying about the outside of the huts, and, with the exception of one or two, who came towards us as we halted, they remained in the same position as when we first appeared.

I sent a man who could speak the language—which was the same as that spoken in the Cape Colony—to tell the chief, or headman, of the village to muster all the people in front of the kraal. He quickly did this, and I dismounted my men, and, taking six of them with me, went and interviewed the headman, whom I found to be a Matabele. In reply to my questions, he stated that he had not been fighting and had not seen any of the white troops, but had been told by other natives that the King Lobengula had run away, and that the white men had taken possession of the country; also that his cattle had been taken away by the chief's men some time before. His followers were mixed Matabeles and Makalakas, and hearing their language spoken by our men, they began to be less reserved and were anxious to hear the news.

I enlightened them as to the change in their country, and impressed the fact on the headman that the Makalakas were no longer slaves, but equal as regards rights with the Matabeles, and that the headman must go to Inyati and give an account of himself and his cattle. I had considerable doubts in my own mind of the truth of the headman's statement as to his not having taken part in the fighting, and I told the natives to sit down and stay where they were, and, taking my six men with me, I proceeded to search the different huts in the village for any arms that might be concealed there.

We found no guns but plenty of assegais and shields, and

about forty war dresses of black ostrich feathers, consisting of a head-dress not unlike a Highlander's full-dress bonnet, and a waist-covering of ostrich feathers. Passing through an enclosure between two huts, I saw what appeared to be a bundle of blankets lying in a corner. I walked towards it and stirred it up with my foot. It felt soft, and, pulling the blanket off, I discovered a young native girl huddled up under the blanket quite nude, who commenced moaning directly I touched her and appeared unable to move. I then found that the poor girl had been unmercifully beaten with a sjambok (a whip of raw hide) and was cut all over her body, her breast being nearly cut in two. I demanded from the headman who had done it, and he coolly replied that he had. The girl was his slave and had run away to another kraal. He had sent after her and beaten her. The headman seemed to take a pride in what he had done, and his bearing being too insolent towards me, I determined to teach him a lesson.

I told my men to bring him along to the front of the kraal where the remainder of the natives were sitting. On again being questioned, through an interpreter, he repeated in an insolent manner that he was a Matabele, and the girl was his slave, and that he would do what he liked with her. I ordered him to be tied up to the gate of a cattle kraal, and, procuring a good thick sjambok from one of the huts, told one of the men to flog him till he was tired. After a good many cuts the native hung loose by his wrists, and I ordered him to be cut down, where he lay as if he were dead. I then ordered four of the native men who had been looking on to carry the girl into Inyati to the doctor, and told the onlookers that if such a case occurred again the culprit would be shot and not treated so lightly as the headman had been. After packing up the

assegais and shields and head-dresses into bundles, I told off
several natives to carry them and to accompany the patrol
back to Inyati, and then went to have a look at the headman.
I found he had recovered his senses, and on my approach he
crawled towards me and tried to kiss my boots. Having
warned him to be careful in future and to come to Inyati as
soon as he could travel, we mounted and continued our march
to Inyati.

A heavy storm came on towards evening, and it was late
at night before we reached Inyati, very wet and hungry. To
my astonishment, I found the whole garrison on the alert, and
I was greeted with great surprise but much satisfaction by the
officers of the B.B.P., who informed me that a report had
arrived the night before saying that my patrol had been surrounded and cut off, and a dispatch had been sent on to
Buluwayo to that effect. I was eagerly questioned as to what
had happened, and was scarcely credited when I stated that
we had seen no signs of the Matabeles. A dispatch was
immediately sent to Buluwayo acquainting Colonel Goold-
Adams of the safe return of my patrol.

Some natives arrived from the vicinity of the Shangani
River the next day, and reported that three Matabele Impis
had been across the river; that the patrols had passed through
an Impi during the night, and that the fires we had seen on
the hills were Matabele watch-fires, and the only reason we
had not been attacked was that we were taken for Queen's
soldiers. The clatter of our scabbards against the horses' sides
as we were marching associated us in the minds of the
Matabeles with the soldiers who had formed part of the envoy
sent by Queen Victoria to Lobengula about a year before, who
had worn their full-dress uniforms with swords for the edifica-

tion of the chief. The natives knew that the Company's forces did not wear swords, and had concluded that we were on a different mission. Whether there was any truth in their reports, of which we heard several from various sources, or not, I was never able to ascertain, but the fact of the guides disappearing from my patrol about the spot where the fires were seen gives ground for believing that we did have a narrow escape. If we had been attacked from the bushes on the right and left of the track which we travelled for some miles, I believe that we would have shared the fate of Wilson's party; as I have no doubt that if the truth were ever told that would be revealed as the manner in which that patrol was destroyed, and not in the manner represented at Drury Lane, which was the one that gained general credence.

My dispatch to Buluwayo arrived too late to prevent the former one from being sent on to Government, and a full account appeared in the Colonial papers, headed, "Disaster to the C.M.R." It caused considerable commotion amongst our numerous friends in the country, and, for some reason unknown, was uncontradicted for some days.

Some few days afterwards, the headman whom I had punished whilst on the patrol arrived at Inyati. Excepting for a few scars, he had recovered from the effects of the flogging, and seemed quite pleased to see me. His insolent bearing had vanished, and he was anxious to afford us any information he possessed. He confessed that three of his men had been in one of the Matabele regiments with the king, but that they had left the king with others, and returned to his kraal when Buluwayo was abandoned. He could tell us nothing about the subsequent movements of the chief and his small following. We gave him some cows for milk for his children, and he departed in a happy frame of mind. On a subsequent visit to his kraal we found everything satisfactory, and his people working on their lands quite contentedly. The idea of the Makalakas being slaves to the Matabeles was exploded, and both tribes were now on the best of terms with one another.

From the day Mr. Rhodes left Inyati I had received no communication from any one in authority, and affairs began to get very monotonous, when one morning Major Brown, a Royal Artillery officer, arrived with a strong force of the B.B.P., and told me that I was to return to Buluwayo with my men, and that all Imperial troops had been recalled to their regiments.

We had nothing to pack, and were soon on the return march to Buluwayo, where I was told that the Colonial Government had refused to allow us to stay any longer than required, and that we were to return to the regiment. The detachment of the West Riding Regiment had already left, and the detachment of the Black Watch were waiting my arrival to pay off my left troop, which had been attached to them on my departure from Khame River before marching southwards.

We found our kits in safe custody of the men I had left in charge, and experienced great pleasure in being able to shave, and in discarding our rags for decent clothing.

Dr. Jameson asked for my men to remain to guard these stores till the B.B.P. could arrive and relieve them. I consented to this, and, taking my sergeant-major and clerk with me, I proceeded to Mangwe, where I found my left troop had been paid off and departed on their return to the Colony, and I remained awaiting the arrival of my detachment.

20

CHAPTER XX.

1894.

AFTER a delay of about two weeks, which I spent riding
about the country accompanying the patrols who were
collecting cattle from the surrounding country, my men
arrived, bringing me orders to proceed to Maclontsie in
Bechuanaland, the headquarters of the B.B. Police, at which
place I was to make arrangements for rations and transport for the remainder of the journey down country to the
rail-head.

Before leaving Mangwe, I was to hand over our troop
horses to the Chartered Company, as they were not in a
fit condition to carry the men on the long march, the
Company guaranteeing full compensation for the animals
on our rejoining the C.M.R.

This I was glad to do, as I had already lost two of the
number through horse - sickness, and was afraid that the
remainder were all more or less infected with the disease,
which was very prevalent at that time in Matabeleland.
Taking two wagons with us, containing our saddlery and

six days' rations, we commenced our march on foot. We left the road by which we had entered the country on our right, and proceeded towards the Samokwe River, on the road leading to Maclontsie, by which road the volunteers and remainder of the West Riding Regiment had travelled about three days before.

On the second day of our march, as we got near the Samokwe River, we came across a white man in a dazed condition, wandering about the veldt. He was recognised by my men as being one of the West Riding Regiment. His story was that he had loitered behind the rest of the men and had missed his path, and, not knowing the direction, had wandered about for two days and nights trying to find the road, and afraid to go far from the hill near the place where we had found him. Luckily, he had found water, but he was half starved, and had been badly frightened by the sounds of wild animals he had heard during the night. The poor chap's nerves were gone, and he was crying bitterly when I spoke to him, and could hardly be persuaded to give up his rifle, which he had carefully stuck to. We took him with us, and after three days' care he became quite the genial "Tommy" again. He attached himself to me as my assistant cook, and was very useful to the end of the journey, when I sent him on to Cape Town to rejoin his regiment. His escape was miraculous, for, as we found out, the part of Matabeleland along the Samokwe River is infested with wild animals—lions and wolves being in great numbers. Had the man known of his danger, he must have gone mad during the time he was alone in the veldt.

When we reached the river we found that it was in flood and unfordable at the drift, so we continued along the road which ran by the side of the river for the remainder of that trek without finding a drift where we could cross.

As we went on, we found that the track left the river, but we followed it, knowing that it must lead somewhere, and that it was useless to turn back. On the sixth day, finding that we were still marching due east when we should have been going south-east, I began to get anxious, and the rations were getting very low. The country through which we had been trekking was well supplied with water owing to recent rains, and was of an open nature, with large trees and small bushes, but there were no signs of natives or of cultivation. We were continually coming across the spoor of animals, and several distinct footprints of lions had been seen close to our camping grounds; but up to the present we had only seen buck of different kinds. I cautioned the men against straggling from the wagons, and made them carry their carbines whilst walking along the tracks.

The seventh day out, on our morning trek, we came to a river about a hundred yards broad, and apparently too flooded to cross with the wagons; so, outspanning the oxen, we walked down to the bank of the river, and a sergeant and corporal volunteered to try if the drift was passable. They stripped and went into the water, while some of the others sat on the bank with carbines ready to fire should a crocodile appear on the scene. For the first few yards the water only came up to their knees, then suddenly and for a few yards it rose to their chests, and then shallowed again for about forty yards, when it became deeper, and they finally had to swim a short distance until it shallowed to the opposite bank, over which they climbed and disappeared.

After waiting for quite a quarter of an hour for the two

N.C.O.'s to reappear, I began to fear that something had happened to them, and was undressing preparatory to crossing the river, when one of the men called out, "Here they come, sir," and looking across the river, I saw the two men run down the bank and jump into the river, swimming and staggering as they crossed till they arrived at our side, both out of breath and laughing hugely. The sergeant walked up to me with a distinct lurch, and said, "Beg pardon, sir; Major Giles' compliments, and will you come to dinner." I thought the man had suddenly gone mad, and seeing the corporal giggling with a crowd of men round him, I asked what he meant. He then explained that there was a convoy of twelve wagons outspanned on the opposite side of the river, and that Major Giles, an ex-Artillery and C.M.R. officer, was there; that they were loaded with liquor and stores; and finally, that Major Giles had given them a big tot of whisky, which had gone to their heads, and told them to invite me to dinner.

Several people now appeared on the opposite bank shouting and waving handkerchiefs to us. This was a proof that at least part of the story was true; so, turning to the men, I ordered, "Get your kit across, lads." Kit bags and blankets were pulled off the wagon, tied together, and put on the men's heads, and in single file we walked up the river, and, feeling our way, managed to cross without having to swim. We selected a good spot for the camp below the wagons, and deposited our kits there, and exchanged greeting with the wagon people.

I found that Mr. Redrup was the manager of a business and on his way to Buluwayo to open a store at that place, and that Major Giles was accompanying the wagons.

I told the manager to let my men have whatever they required in the shape of food and liquor, and shortly after-

wards found myself sitting under an awning stretched between
two wagons with a splendid dinner of venison and vegetables
and tinned fruits before me.   It was difficult to realise that
a short time before, our stock of provisions having finally
given out, I had been meditating shooting one of our trek
bullocks for meat for the men.

We found that since leaving the Samokwe River we had
been travelling along an old hunter's trail, and had reached a
spot about 80 miles up the Tuli River from Fort Tuli, which
was on the border of Bechuanaland.   We succeeded in crossing
our two wagons the following day, and laid in a supply of provisions sufficient to last us to Maclontsie.   On settling up with
the manager of the wagons, I was rather surprised to find that
the men had only taken advantage of the order I had given to
let them have anything they required in the shape of stores
and liquor to the extent of a bottle of Bass' beer each and
tobacco.   Having come through a long period without liquor, I
rather expected some of them to indulge rather freely, but was
agreeably disappointed.

Bidding farewell to our friends with the wagons, which,
owing to our timely meeting, had saved the situation as
regarded our commissariat department, we started off in a
more cheerful manner on our road to Fort Tuli, the country
being of a very wild nature, the trees and bushes much thicker
than before.   We had heard lions roaring in the bush whilst
encamped by the wagons.   I made the men keep more
together, and warned them not to quit their carbines or stray
from the wagons.   Whilst trekking along we came upon the
spoor of a troop of elephants; the ground being trampled
down for some distance showed that they must have been in a
large number.   They had evidently been there a few hours

previously. On nearing Tuli we saw the first signs of civilisation in a single telegraph line to some station in Mashonaland. Shortly after passing the wire, I was walking about 200 yards in front of the men and wagons, accompanied by one of my sergeants, when to our front three animals, about the size of pointer dogs, ran out of the bush across the track, and trotted away on the other side quite visible for some time. The sergeant suggested that they were wolves, but it struck me they might be lion cubs, so I pulled him towards me in the shade of the bush and told him to wait. Almost immediately a large lioness sprang to the track, sniffed the ground where the cubs had passed, and bounded away into the bush after them.

The sergeant had his carbine with him, but the action of the lioness was too quick for a shot, even if the sergeant had been in a less excited state than he was. I had only a thick walking-stick, useful for snakes but nothing else. We waited some time, expecting to see the lion; but hearing a loud report of a rifle some distance in front, we hurried on, and found an elderly man, whom I afterwards knew to be Krief, a well-known Dutch hunter, standing over the dead body of a fine lion with its head partly blown away; it had been killed by a trap-gun set by the hunter, who had been waiting for it some time. I told him that we had seen the lioness and three cubs, and he informed me that it was a lucky chance for myself that the lioness had not seen me, as she would not have hesitated to charge us on account of the cubs being near, a lioness being more dangerous than a lion if the cubs are in danger.

We watched the operation of skinning the lion, and the skilful manner in which the old hunter performed it excited our admiration. He informed me that this lion made up his total bag to fifty head, killed in various ways, mostly by spring guns. He advised me to get on to Tuli as soon as possible, as the river was showing signs of coming down —that is, rising in flood—owing to heavy rains up country. I took his advice, and soon reached the drift leading across to Fort Tuli. We crossed over dry sand, with trees growing to a considerable height in the bed of the river till within 100 yards of the opposite bank, where the river was running rather fast, with muddy water. But we crossed the wagons safely, the water coming up to the rails and to the men's shoulders as they shouted and splashed their way through, in order to scare any crocodiles that might be about. We were subsequently told that the river was full of them; but as they are easily frightened away by noise, there was really not much danger to be feared.

We outspanned below the only hotel at Fort Tuli, and I took the opportunity of looking round the place. It consisted of a fort, mostly composed of cases containing corned beef, old stores left behind by the pioneers of the Chartered Company when they passed through the place some three years previously, which were now all broken up and rotting away. There was a post-office hut and telegraph station, and half a dozen wood and iron shanties where the few white men composing the white population lived. Rain commenced very heavily, so I returned to the hotel, a wood and iron building with a bar and dining-room, and about three bedrooms, one of which I secured. The men had pitched their small patrol tents for cover, and arrangements were made with the hotel proprietors to cook dinner for the detachment that evening. So we were all fairly comfortable, notwithstanding the heavy rain.

MEN'S HUTS, MACLOUTSIE.

Whilst enjoying a rest on a bed, the proprietor came to my door, and in an excited tone of voice said, " Come and look, sir—you will never see such a sight again !' '

Jumping up, I went on to the verandah, and saw indeed a sight to be long remembered. The river was rushing by at an express rate, and far up I could see the water extending over the whole width of the river, and slowly coming down in waves about six feet high. We all ran to the bank of the river to watch the wonderful spectacle. Huge trees were being swept along, and all kinds of débris, till within an hour after the first sight of the rush of water the Shaski River was running bank to bank, the tops of the trees in the bed of the river were entirely submerged, and the river was rushing past with high waves nearly 1800 yards broad and 40 feet deep in the centre. None of the inhabitants of the place had seen the river so much in flood before. I subsequently heard that it was three weeks before the post-cart on the opposite side of the river could cross with the passengers and mails.

We left Tuli the following day, and after a couple of days' trekking in very hot weather reached Macloutsie, the head-quarters of the B.B.P. I found Major Grey there and three or four officers of the headquarters staff of the B.B.P., also the general adjutant of the column on our march to Matabele-land. To my delight, the latter, who was also returning to his regiment, the 3rd D.G., in Natal, asked permission to accompany me to Vryburg.

We spent three very pleasant days in Macloutsie, and as soon as the wagons and supplies were ready I sent them on one morning with my men, and with Captain —— remained for a farewell dinner with the B.B.P. officers of the mess. It was in the early hours of the morning before we started on horses lent to us by our B.B.P. friends for the occasion, with an orderly to bring them back to Macloutsie.

We led that orderly a dance in that lovely moonlight night, jumping the walls round the camp and taking short cuts through the gardens over the fences of the civilian residences. Discarding all roads, we rode straight through the bushy country, and after three hours' good going came into the road within half a mile of the outspan, where we found the men getting ready for the morning trek.

Leaving the horses with the orderly to be rested before they returned to Macloutsie, we trekked on with the wagons. We found all the rivers rather full, but managed to cross them by sending the oxen through the deep parts into shallow water, and fastening picquet ropes on to the wagons at one end and to the trek chain at the other and pulling them through the deep parts. The men, stripped in the water, held the sides of the wagon, generally singing, " A life on the ocean wave," or some other ditty. It was a break in the monotony of trekking through the bush, and the men seemed to enjoy it immensely.

We had no duties to perform, and had consequently plenty of time for shooting. Guinea-fowl and an occasional wart-hog (wild pig) made a welcome addition to the larder, and, in spite of the rivers and occasional rain, I am inclined to regard it as the most enjoyable trek I have ever been on, and I have been on a good many in my service.

On our arrival at Palachwi, we halted for a day for repairs to be effected on one of the wagons, and had a good opportunity of inspecting Khama's principal village. There was a large mission station in a nice situation on a hill surrounded by bush. Mr. Moffat, well known for his own work and his connection with Livingstone, who had often visited this part of Africa, was in charge. The mission natives were very much in evidence about the place, and very creditable to the missionary's influence they were. The men wore European garments, and the girls were neatly dressed. Khama the chief had, and has, a very good system of police supervision for his town. Stalwart natives walking about with knob-kerries keep order in the streets, and woe betide any native caught wandering about the village after eight o'clock in the evening; he is pounced on at once and placed in durance vile, till hauled up before Khama. Whatever the punishment was it was apparently very effective, for on the evening we passed at Palachwi, not a sign of a native, except an occasional policeman, was to be seen after that time, and we were informed by our genial host, Mr. M. Weib, who had kindly invited my brother officer and myself to take up our residence in his house during our stay—that the utmost order prevailed in the place, Kaffir beer-drinks, with the inevitable fighting, being unknown in the village.

The cattle belonging to the residents in the village, numbering some thousands, were kept some distance away near the rivers, and milk was brought daily in skins from the cattle stations to the village. The mealie lands surrounding the village yielded a sufficient quantity for food for the villagers, and a medium for payment for goods bought from the traders. We also saw a number of karosses, skins of wild animals neatly sewn together by the natives. They are a very valuable commodity, and are kept hanging up in the stores ready for sale for export purposes. The great drawback to the place was the utter lack of sanitary arrangements. To this no doubt is due the high mortality among the Bechuanas from the fever, which is their great scourge.

After leaving Palachwi we passed through Linchwe's location—a Bechuana chief credited with being hostile towards the Imperial Government, but saw no signs amongst his people of any intention to oppose the authorities. It was fortunate this was the case ; from the nature of the country, I saw that if Linchwe wanted to give trouble it would be beyond the powers of the B.B.P. to bring him to submission.

On arriving at Gaberones, where we found a troop of the B.B.P. stationed, we rested the oxen two days, during which time we played a cricket match, a team of my men v. the garrison, which we managed to pull off after a close game. There were a number of ex-C.M.R. in the troop of Police at this place, who had joined the corps on the retrenchment of the C.M.R. They gave my men a hearty reception, and a capital smoking concert was held in the men's messroom in the evenings. All the officers of the garrison were present, and we spent two most enjoyable evenings.

The hundred miles between Gaberones and Mafeking were soon covered, and we marched into the camp at the latter place, where we found our kits, which had been stored there on our march up country, all in good order. Discarding our field service uniforms, which were now considerably the worse for wear, the men donned their green full-dress kit, and, obtaining leave from camp till 11 p.m., proceeded to give the girls a treat in the town of Mafeking. We spent a most enjoyable three days in the place before proceeding on our final stage to Vryburg, during which time we played a cricket match against the town and got beaten, but had our revenge against their cracks by beating them at lawn-tennis. A large smoking concert, given at Dixon's Hotel by our civilian friends, made a very pleasant ending to our stay.

Mafeking, famous or notorious since the late war, was at that time a rather straggling town with a few fine buildings. Dixon's Hotel, quite an up-to-date building, was on one side of the Market Square, and large stores on the opposite side. Amongst the latter was Weil Brothers, who had already made a name for themselves as large contractors and owners of large depôts throughout the country, and who subsequently saved the situation with their large supplies during the siege. Of the siege of Mafeking, which to people at home seems to have been regarded as the chief event of the Boer War, I will only say that it was a much overrated performance. The town is situated on a flat, and built on almost a square forma-tion, and a bastion at either corner of the place ought to have been sufficient to keep out any number of Boers. Every one who knows the Boers is aware that attacking in the open is not one of their practices, and to talk of Mafeking ever being in danger of capture by a single Boer commando, and a not very large one at that, is simply absurd. The importance given to the siege by the outside public tends to show what can be done by the skilful wording of dispatches, whereby a confiding public are led to imagine hardships that do not exist, and to extol the qualities of the " heroic " commander.

On arriving at Vryburg, we were detained three days whilst the final settlement between the B.B.P. and ourselves took place, and I was complimented by the Chief Accountant and his staff on the manner in which the accounts of the troop had been satisfactorily wound up in such a short time.

We entrained the following day for King William's Town in a carriage attached to an ordinary passenger train, and as I wished to visit Kimberley the railway authorities kindly ac-ceded to my request and detached our carriage from the train on arrival at that place, to await the train the following day. I gave my men leave for the day, to visit the town and the diamond mines, and they received much attention at the hands of the employees of the De Beers Company, who took them underground to see the workings of the mines, and over the native compounds.

I had a good many old friends in Kimberley, and I was glad of the opportunity of seeing them once more, and of visiting the splendid club, with its magnificent collection of heads and horns of every variety of game to be found in Africa—certainly the best collection I have ever seen. My comrade of the march down had accompanied us to Kimberley, and he too was very much struck with the collection of heads at the club; we visited the mines together, and were shown the natives at work, sorting the gravel for diamonds, and also in their compounds. I was much impressed by the completeness of everything in the shape of organisation of the staff, and treatment of natives. We also visited the main offices of De Beer, and were shown the splendid reserve of diamonds, which were poured out on the counter for our inspection, and to plunge our hands into. Some of the diamonds were very fine specimens, and the value of the whole lot we saw incalculable. De Beers is the wealthiest company in South Africa, and at that time Mr. Rhodes was one of the life governors.

The following day we were attached to the train, and proceeded on our journey to King William's Town, at which place we arrived on the second morning. Although it was early, the station was crowded with civilian friends to welcome us, and a civilian band was drawn up to play us up to the barracks. I then learnt, for the first time, that the whole regiment were in Pondoland, which country had finally been annexed by the Cape Government a short time previously, and that with the exception of the non-combatant officers and their staffs, King William's Town was without C.M.R.

The whole detachment received a very hearty welcome, and were fêted to their heart's content. A dinner was given in my honour by the Mayor and leading people of the town, and I was deeply impressed by the good-fellowship extended by the great number of persons present, hitherto unknown to me, and by the kindly allusions to the regiment made by the several speakers. It was a striking proof of the friendly spirit between the C.M.R. and the civilian population of the old Colony.

CHAPTER XXI.

1894–1897.

LEAVE FOR PONDOLAND — MEET COLONEL GRANT — DISPATCHES FROM
COLONEL GOOLD-ADAMS—ARRIVE COLDSTREAM—MR. RHODES ARRIVES
IN UMTATA — COMPENSATION FOR KITS — JAMESON'S REPLY — THE
JAMESON RAID — EFFECT ON COUNTRY — POLICE WORK — NATIVE
TROUBLE IN GRIQUALAND WEST — MY SQUADRON ORDERED TO
BECHUANALAND—MEET BRYAN—A TALE OF A PEACOCK—ARRIVE
AT KURUMAN —MEETING WITH CHIEFS FROM LANGBERG.

AFTER my months of the veldt, town life was very
enjoyable; but I was not left to enjoy it long. A
telegram from the O.C. the regiment came, ordering me to
proceed to Western Pondoland as soon as possible, leaving my
detachment in King William's Town to get remounts. I
hastily packed up, and, accepting the offer of a friend, who
was visiting Umtata, to accompany him in his trap, we were
soon off to Umtata.

At Toleni, in the Transkei, I met Colonel Grant returning
to King William's Town, the troops having settled down at
their various stations in Pondoland. He explained that the
reason why I had been hurried away from King William's
Town before I had managed to replace my two horses which
had died in Matabeleland, was that one of the magistrates, who
was an old friend of mine, had been appointed Magistrate in
Western Pondoland, and had asked him, Colonel Grant, as a
favour that I might be the officer appointed to command the

HOSPITAL AT MACLOUTSIE.

C.M.R. at the same station. The colonel had agreed, and wired for me on the spot. We had a long talk together before proceeding on our ways, the colonel telling me that Government had approved of my retaining the rank of captain in the regiment, without seniority; that he had received a very flattering report from Government about the behaviour of the C.M.R. in Matabeleland; and that he was very well satisfied with myself and my men; after which we parted on our respective journeys.

The Colonial Forces Order, which was read out on parade to the whole of the squadrons in the regiment, was as follows :—

" The Governor and High Commissioner transmits herewith for the information of Ministers a dispatch which he has received from the officer commanding the B.B.P., bringing to his notice the services rendered by the detachment of the C.M.R. serving as members of the B.B.P. The Governor will be obliged if Ministers will inform Colonel Grant that he fully endorses the remarks made by Colonel Goold-Adams relative to the services rendered by the detachment of the C.M.R., who have throughout upheld the reputation of the distinguished regiment to which they belong. The Governor also wishes his appreciation of the great assistance the B.B.P. received from the services of Captain —— should be conveyed to that officer."

The following is the letter from Colonel Goold-Adams :—

" INYATI, MATABELELAND, 2nd February 1894.

" SIR,—I have already informed His Excellency by telegraph of the return of the detachment of the Royal Highlanders, West Riding Regiment, and the Cape Mounted Riflemen to

21

Maclontsie, *en route* for Mafeking, thence to Vryburg, to join their respective corps.

" I regret that I had no opportunity of personally inspecting the detachments of the regulars, but have been furnished by Major Grey, under whose immediate command they served, with a report, in which he speaks in the highest manner of their zeal, efficiency, and good conduct.

" The detachment of Cape Mounted Riflemen joined me at Buluwayo in December last, and afterwards took part in the patrols made from Inyati after the return of Major Forbes' column. I consider the detachment under Captain —— to have been the smartest and finest lot of men that I have almost ever seen. Major Grey reported that when he started on the long march up country with the men that he had got together, that the detachment of the C.M.R. were of the greatest assistance to him, he having to depend on them almost entirely to perform the most trying duties till the others got accustomed to the veldt life, and, what was new to a great number, the method of conducting a march in this country. I should be greatly obliged if His Excellency would convey to the officer commanding the Cape Mounted Riflemen my appreciation of the assistance the detachment has been to us, and of the invariable good conduct of every member of the force.—I have the honour to be, Sir, your obedient servant,

" H. GOOLD-ADAMS.

" Lieutenant-Colonel commanding the B.B. Police."

The foregoing is a correct copy of the dispatch published in C.M.R. Regimental Orders on my return to the regiment. It afforded the colonel, my brother officers, and myself, much gratification, as it showed that the work willingly performed by my men, under very trying circumstances, was appreciated by the authorities.

On my arrival at Umtata, I found my old skipper, Major ——, in command of the garrison at that place, my old squadron having been split into two troops, and stationed at two magistracies in Western Pondoland—one of which I was to command. After considerable trouble, owing to the scarcity of good horses in the district, I managed to remount myself to my satisfaction, and proceeded to Coldstream, the camp in Western Pondoland, " cold river " being the interpretation, of its Kaffir name " N'gqueleni." I found the troops under canvas in a suitable spot on the banks of the stream, the Magistrate's tents being pitched alongside of it. The Magistrate, well-known throughout the country as *Glen*, was an old friend, having been stationed at various times at Umtata and else-where at the same time as myself. He was one of a family of which all the sons, with the exception of one, a clergyman, were in the Civil Service. They were all powerfully built men, good sportsmen and athletes, the youngest one being a well-known athlete at Oxford, where he jumped second to C. B. Fry in the long jump of his year.

Coldstream was fifteen miles from Umtata, and seven miles across country from Lebode, the other magistracy and C.M.R. camp in Western Pondoland; heliograph communica-tion between the three places being obtainable, we were kept posted in the current news of the regiment. The post carried by native runners was a weekly service, and sufficient for our requirements. A plentiful supply of wood and water close at hand made the place very suitable for a camp.

We were soon hard at work building a fort, the Govern-ment having sanctioned the necessary expenditure; huts were built for the men and officers, and in the course of a few months we were very comfortable, with mess-rooms and canteen for the men, a good recreation ground cleared for cricket or football, and dismounted drill purposes—in fact, the camp soon became quite a holiday resort for visitors from Umtata. An occasional patrol to the sea-coast and on to Port St. John made a pleasant change from the ordinary camp routine, and provided good exercise for the horses and men climbing over the hilly country along the coast-line.

Umtata had by this time grown to be a fairly large town, and agreeable week-ends were often spent there, cricket or tennis matches being of weekly occurrence—or football and polo in season. As the headquarters of my squadron was in the place, it was generally the excuse for the frequent visits of my brother officer and myself. On these occasions our genial major would invariably suggest that we should remain the night and enjoy ourselves, as our camp would not run away during our absence. Having the good fortune to possess one of the best and smartest sergeant-majors in the regiment at my camp, I had no scruples in accepting the various invitations from time to time offered.

The men of the Matabele contingent, whom I had left in King William's Town, not only required remounting, but on inspection it was found that the whole of their saddlery equipment was unfit for use, owing to the severe treatment it had sustained whilst packed on the wagons, through rivers, on our homeward journey. A new issue had been given the men, and the question had now arisen who was to pay for it—the Chartered Company or the men themselves ?

Mr. Rhodes, who had resumed the office of Prime Minister

was shortly after my return touring the native territories, and on his arrival at Umtata I rode in from Coldstream to meet him. The first questions he asked were: "Had the horses and saddlery of my men been replaced and paid for by the Company?" and "Had the men received their share of the loot money?" To both questions I replied in the negative. He then took me by the arm and walked out to where his carriage was waiting for him to proceed on his journey, and told me to write him a private letter on his return to the Cape, reminding him of all the details, when he would see into the matter; he then wished me "Good-bye." That was the last occasion on which I saw Mr. Rhodes.

I wrote to him as he had requested me, reminding him that the horses had either died from horse-sickness in Matabeleland, or had been handed over to the Company's officials for use in the country, and that the saddlery had been rendered unfit for regimental work through wear and tear in the Company's service. I also referred to the conversation between us, in which Dr. Jameson had joined at Umyati, when the latter had been told by Mr. Rhodes to put the C.M.R. on the loot-list.

After a lapse of some weeks, a reply was received from Dr. Jameson, to whom Mr. Rhodes had apparently referred by letter, stating that the matter of horses and equipments had been arranged between the Chartered Company and the Cape Government, but as regards the question of share in the loot-money, Dr. Jameson had no recollection of the conversation alluded to by Captain ——; and that, in any case, it was of no use for the C.M.R. to apply, as the money had all been distributed. I acknowledged the receipt of the letter, paying a tribute at the same time to Dr. Jameson's convenient lapse of memory, and the off-handed manner in which he had disposed of the claims of men who had been instrumental in collecting some thousands of head of cattle for his benefit, and intimated that we would not press for the money. That was the last we heard of the matter, but not of Dr. Jameson.

The Colonial papers had, for some time past, been occupied with the question of the treatment of British subjects in the Transvaal. Since the discovery of the goldfields, some seven years previously, the one place brought prominently before the public of the Cape Colony was Johannesburg, the mining centre of the Transvaal, which was always being quoted as the most wonderful town in South Africa. Several people from the Transkei, who had visited the place, returned with glowing accounts of the wonderful buildings and wealth of the town, and the fortunes to be made on the share market, and not only invested their own money in shares, but persuaded others to follow their example. The consequence was that several men, hitherto comfortably well-off, were now in a position of being unable to meet their overdrafts at the banks, and had lost all they possessed—shares included. Among those who met their downfall by the craze was a popular bank manager, who speculated and lost a considerable amount of the funds of the bank he represented.

People in the Transkei had ceased to trouble their heads about the doings of Johannesburg and the Transvaal, and preferred the slower and surer method of making money by Kaffir trading, when the announcement that a body of the Chartered Company's forces had endeavoured to force their way from the Bechuanaland border to Johannesburg, and had been captured by the Boers in the attempt, caused great excitement throughout the country.

As the details of this abortive attempt to seize Johannes-burg came to light, the people of the Cape Colony saw more clearly the great blunder that had been committed. By this unwarrantable act, Dr. Jameson and his followers gave the Dutch Government the opportunity they had been waiting for. It was a revelation of the intriguing that had been going on between the British and Jews of the Transvaal for a con-siderable period, with a view to Imperial interference on their behalf in the administration of the gold laws of the country, and it gave the Dutch the opportunity of showing their "magnanimity" in not shooting down the invaders, and of being able to pose as an injured race of people whom the detested "Rooineks" were trying to oust out of their country.

The feeling between the English and the Dutch has been always of a strained nature; since the disgraceful peace after the Majuba disaster, the status of the British in the Transvaal was undoubtedly not all that could be desired, and something had to be done to put an end to the conditions under which the British lived in that country; but the solution of the problem was not to be found in the mad act perpetrated by Jameson and his fellow-filibusters. This only confirmed the suspicion of the Boers as to the intention on the part of the British community in the Transvaal to attempt to overthrow the Republic.

The ill-effects of the Raid were not confined to the Transvaal alone; it involved a great loss to Cape Colony in the retirement of Mr. Rhodes from the Premiership of the Government, who resigned owing to the outburst of public indignation amongst the people of the Cape against the Chartered Company. Mr. Rhodes must have been cognisant of the fact that the troops were on the border for some purpose best known to themselves, probably awaiting developments in Johannesburg, but that he consented to the absurd scheme of marching an armed force from the border to Johannesburg I do not believe for a moment, and I do not consider him responsible for the action of his subordinate Jameson.

The Colony could ill afford to lose such a man as Mr. Rhodes from the head of the Government; there was no other strong man of his views in the Ministry, so the country had to fall back on that repository of obsolete ideas, Sir Gordon Sprigg, as Prime Minister, and be contented with a so-called progressive Ministry, dominated by the South African Bond; it also had to watch the Imperialistic ideas of Mr. Rhodes, which had hitherto gained ground in the Colony, gradually fade away and disappear—perhaps for all time—from South Africa.

After some two years of uneventful garrison work at Coldstream, only broken by change of commanding officers in the regiment, Colonel Grant retired on a pension, much to the regret of all ranks, to whom he had endeared himself by his straightforward and gentlemanly bearing. He was succeeded by Colonel Dalgety, who had shortly before been promoted from captain to major over the heads of two other more efficient honorary majors, and was now promoted to the command of the regiment.

Rumours of native disaffection in Griqualand West began to circulate, and a movement of Cape Police was made in that direction from the farming districts in the Colony, which necessitated their being temporarily replaced by C.M.R.

My squadron was ordered to proceed to the Colony for that purpose, and to occupy stations at Komgha, Stutterheim, and

Dordrecht. We marched away from Umtata, and on our arrival at Komgha I took up my quarters in the barracks with my troop, Major W—— proceeding to Stutterheim with the headquarters, and the other troop being sent by rail to Dordrecht. The whole of us were split up into small detachments, and stationed all over the different districts, to occupy the police posts vacated by the Cape Police. Our duties consisted of patrolling round the different farms, collecting reports relating to lost or stolen stock, arresting natives found in the district without the necessary pass, and endeavouring to trace stock stolen,—a great change for men hitherto trained solely as soldiers. But the C.M.R. adapt themselves to any change very quickly; and before a month had elapsed, my troop had become quite adept at all the tricks of the police trade, and had satisfied even the farmers as to their energy in riding about the district collecting reports. It did not take me very long to notice that it was to the farms where the prettiest girls lived that the visits were most frequently made; and I was secretly much amused when, on meeting the owner of one of the selected farms, on a visit to Komgha, I asked how the men were doing, by the farmer's reply, "Splendidly; Mr. ——," mentioning one of the privates, "is a very smart policeman, and does his work well." I knew well that beyond being excellent at tennis, and having a pleasing way with the ladies, the youth in question knew as much about police work as he did about flying.

After a few months of this kind of employment, news of a startling nature came from Griqualand West. The papers gave details of the murder of two brothers, who were trading close to a mission station at Taungs, a native village situated on the railway between Kimberley and Vryburg, and told of the despatch of Police and Kimberley volunteers to the scene of the murder, and the subsequent fight between the troops and a tribe of Bechuanas under a chief of the name of Galishwe, which ended in the destruction of the village and the flight of Galishwe with some of his followers.

The escape of Galishwe appeared to have awakened the Government to a sense of danger of disaffection amongst other tribes in the event of him getting in touch with them, and to the necessity of attempting to prevent such an occurrence.

On New Year's Day, 1897, I received a telegram to this effect: "You have been specially selected, promoted to full captain. Concentrate squadron to proceed to Bechuanaland." It did not take long to collect my detachment from the district and get on the march to Stutterheim, where I found Major W——— in a state of great excitement, as he had received orders to hand over command of the squadron to me, and return to Pondoland to take command of a vacant squadron. I found everything in readiness for our move, the troop at Dordrecht having received orders to meet the train on the following day.

We were soon entrained in a special and on our way north, picking up my left troop *en route* at Stormberg Junction. I had received orders from the officer commanding Defence Department, Cape Town, to consult with the Commissioner of the Cape Police, Kimberley. The Commissioner, who was awaiting our arrival on the station platform, informed me that I was to continue the journey by rail to Vryburg, and from that place march to Kuruman, and wait further orders. He also informed me that the whereabouts of Galishwe had not been located, but that it was thought that he had not succeeded in getting away from the district up to the present, and that he had very few followers, the rest of the tribe having surrendered to the Kimberley troops.

On arriving at Vryburg we found our transport, consisting of wagons containing supplies and ammunition, awaiting us. After the necessary rest for the horses after their shaking up on the train, and an interview with the Magistrate of Vryburg on the situation, we started on the trek to Kuruman—the road to which place passed through a portion of the Kalahara Desert, a few farms not fenced in being scattered about the country, at which we found water for our requirements.

Before leaving Vryburg, the Magistrate had introduced a young Englishman named Bryan to me, and had asked me to allow him to accompany me on our march, Bryan, who was on a visit to the country, being anxious to gain what experience he could during his stay. Having no objection, and liking the look of the stranger, I invited him to join my mess, which consisted of my two subalterns, the doctor, who had joined us at Vryburg with an ambulance, and myself—and he accordingly came along with the squadron. At one of the outspans, Bryan, who had his sporting outfit with him, took his gun and went off into the veldt in the hope of shooting something for the pot, in the shape of Nanamaqua partridge, which were seen in large numbers about this part of the country, or a " koorhan," which were also plentiful. After a short while he returned dragging a fine peacock, which he produced triumphantly for our benefit. He was greeted with shouts of laughter. On being asked where he had got it, he informed us he had shot it in some bushes about a quarter of a mile away, and added that he did not know that there were wild peacocks in Africa. I told him that I shared his opinion about the peacocks, but suggested that we would probably see a wild

Dutchman before many hours had passed; and, sure enough, before we trekked on, two unkempt Dutchmen appeared. With characteristic bluster, they declared that one of my men had been seen shooting the vrow's pet peacock, and demanded compensation for same, or they would go to the Magistrate and complain. I told Bryan that it was his picnic, and the Dutchmen only wanted squaring. The Dutchmen wanted five pounds, and Bryan was about to give it when I thought it time to interfere, and producing ten shillings, told the worthy Dopper he could accept that or go to the devil. After whining and protesting that I undervalued the bird, the men accepted the money and departed. The peacock was duly dined off, and most excellent it proved to be; but poor Bryan would not look at it, and the mere mention of the bird was a very sore subject with him during his stay with the mess.

We arrived at the mission station, about one mile from Kuruman magistracy, and found refugees from the stores in the surrounding country, collected at that place. Alarming rumours had been circulated as to the threatening attitude of the natives of the district, and the Taungs engagement was much exaggerated. These people cheered us on our arrival. Selecting a good site for a camp, I had the wagons drawn up and tents pitched, and then proceeded to visit the Magistrate and endeavour to find out what was going on. Mr. B——, who was the Magistrate of the place, was pleased at our arrival, as the white population of the place had become very unsettled, owing to the wild rumours afloat; but I found that he had no information from Government as to what had taken place, and no definite orders as to what steps he was to take with regard to the natives in his district.

I reported my arrival by wire to the officer commanding

OLD MISSION, KURUMAN.

Defence Department in Cape Town, and requested orders. After some delay, I received an answer to this effect: "Take orders from Police as represented by Commissioner R—— in Kimberley." This was the kind of thing I had expected, the authorities in Cape Town absolutely ignorant of the existing state of affairs in the distant parts of the country, and the man who was head of the Defence Department only too anxious to shirk the responsibility of any decisive action that might be taken by persons placed by him in a position where decisive action was unavoidable.

Colonel ——, the officer commanding Defence Department of the Cape Colony, was a legacy left to the Colonial Government by the late General Gordon on his relinquishing the command of the Colonial forces to proceed on his ill-fated expedition to Egypt. It was rather a misfortune that he did not require the services of his military secretary in that part of the world; but, unfortunately for the Cape Colonial forces, the general had no use for him, and he remained.

What qualifications this officer ever possessed to warrant his employment in the Colonial forces, I have never succeeded in finding out; but he was appointed military secretary to King William's Town, where he was found to be like the fifth wheel of a coach—not wanted. He was then sent to Cape Town, where he became commandant of volunteers, and while occupying that position so impressed the Prime Minister of his ability to eliminate all desire for soldiering in that branch of the service—the volunteers becoming considerably reduced in numbers—that he was made chief of the Defence Department. In this position he had passed years without being called upon to justify his appointment, drawing good pay and signing circulars, etc., composed by his staff.

With a beautiful river of clear water running from a fountain above Kuruman, with trees on either side of it, planted with fruit trees of all varieties, and with vegetables of all descriptions growing in abundance, Kuruman is a real oasis in the desert.

A camp built among some rocks overlooking the magistracy, and the few stores and huts comprising the village, were occupied by a small body of Cape Police, commanded by a sub-inspector whom I recognised as the officer who had been in command at Vryburg on the occasion of my former visit *en route* for Matabeleland, and the man who had played the trick on me with the horses. He had been transferred to the Cape Police when Vryburg became attached to the Cape Colony, and had been stationed at Kuruman for some time past. We became friendly, and I found him very useful in our subsequent dealings with the natives. The mission station itself had a fine appearance— two large store - houses being the dwelling - places of the missionaries, the Reverend Messrs. Price and Brown, and we experienced much hospitality at their hands during the whole of our stay at Kuruman. On the opposite side of the river, which was divided into two streams crossed by rustic bridges, were a church and several comfortable store-houses, one of which was owned by Mr. Chapman, and occupied by himself and his wife, and another by his mother and sister. They were exceedingly picturesque buildings, covered with creepers and flowers, with fine gardens containing fruit of all descriptions. To these houses my officers and myself were made heartily welcome, and the enjoyable musical evenings and dances there are among my pleasantest memories. I applied for, and obtained, Mr. Chapman as my intelligence officer, he being a thorough linguist in Sechuana, the native language of Bechuanaland. He had lost a brother, killed in the Warren Expedition at the Langberg, some years before, and had lived in that part of the country all his life. He knew every inch of it, and was most useful to me during the expedition which followed.

Acting under instructions from the Government, the Magistrate had convened a meeting to be held at the mission, at which Toto and Lukajantje, the two chiefs from the villages situated in the Langberg mountains, were ordered to appear. On the day appointed both these chiefs arrived with a considerable following of mounted men, all dressed in European clothes of a kind. Toto was a medium-sized man of the Bechuana type; Lukajantje was smaller, with a strain of Hottentot in his appearance, with the usual vicious, cunning look peculiar to that race.

The Magistrate and I interviewed them in a large school-room at the mission, and told them that Government would hold them responsible for any rebels from Taungs who might be found in hiding at any of the villages in the Langberg, and particularly warned them against receiving Galishwe, should he seek refuge with either of them. Toto, who was the principal chief, seemed to listen with interest to what the Magistrate told them; but it was plain that he was afraid of committing himself with his followers by appearing willing to assist the Government in the matter, and repeatedly asked why he was responsible if other people invited friends to stay with them in the Langberg.

Lukajantje would not discuss the subject, and said he had

come to listen to the Magistrate. It did not require anything beyond their manner to convince me that they were in a state bordering on open rebellion; and had my wishes been consulted, I would have arrested them on the spot and risked the consequences, which could not have been more serious than they subsequently proved.

After a great deal of talking on the part of the Magistrate, Toto consented to inform him should Galishwe appear in any part of the Langberg, and the meeting ended; the chiefs departed for their homes in the mountains, driving in carts, their followers riding behind them in the usual mob fashion.

On the morning of the meeting, amongst the official letters from Vryburg was a telegram for our friend Bryan, who, on reading it, suddenly became very dejected, and in answer to our anxious inquiries said he had received bad news which would necessitate his leaving us for England as soon as possible. We managed to procure a trap and pair of horses to take him to Vryburg; and after he had disposed of a considerable portion of his field kit, which he insisted on giving away to members as a souvenir, and thanking us heartily for the good time he had enjoyed, he took his departure, much to my regret.

We did not find out till our return to Vryburg that the telegram had announced the death of his father, and his succession to a well-known baronetcy. I met him subsequently in the Boer War, where he figured as Sir Bryan ——, S.A.L.H. May he live long to enjoy it!

THE FOUNTAIN, KURUMAN.

CHAPTER XXII.

GALISHWE TAKES REFUGE IN THE LANGBERG—ORDERS TO PROCEED TO THE
LANGBERG—ARRIVE AT GAMISEP—CONTRARY ORDERS FROM DEFENCE
— REBELS FIRE ON NATIVE PICQUET — PATROL ATTACKED — LIEUT.
HOPKINS AND PRIVATE VENN KILLED — EFFECT OF MAXIM FIRE —
RETURN TO KURUMAN—ALL THE LANGBERG NATIVES REBELS.

SHORTLY after the meeting I received a telegram from
commissioner of police, Kimberley, informing me that
Galishwe had left that district, and was making his way to
the Langberg, and instructing me that I was to endeavour to
intercept him. I immediately sent out patrols in the direction
best suited for that purpose; and on the second day they
returned, bringing with them some prisoners, one of whom
proved to be Galishwe's principal fighting man, named
" Gasibikje," who, with the others, had accompanied Galishwe
in his flight. They reported that the latter had succeeded in
reaching the Langberg, as he was mounted and had gone
ahead of them.

I wired the result to Kimberley and received the following
order by telegram : " Pursue Galishwe, if necessary, into the
desert; would advise you to leave all impedimenta behind,
such as Maxim guns," etc. This order was clear enough to me.
Whether the commissioner thought that Galishwe would leave
the friendly shelter of the Langberg and take to the desert
beyond on the approach of my squadron, or that the other
chiefs would surrender him to me without opposition, is best

22

known to himself. But I knew perfectly well that he would
shelter himself behind one of the two excuses should trouble
arise, and anything of a serious nature happen to my squadron
on our arrival at the Langberg. To drive Galishwe out of the
mountains, even if opposition were not offered by the tribes
living there,—who were known to be hostile to Government,—
was a tall order for one squadron of 100 men to execute. The
Langberg range of mountains is over 40 miles in length, and of
considerable depth, consisting of ridges, hills and valleys of
bare rocks and sand; and if opposition were offered by the
natives of the place, one squadron of C.M.R. was not likely to
be able to effect what had taken Sir Charles Warren, with a
force of artillery and some 3000 men, several weeks to
accomplish some few years previously.

I repeated the telegram to the Officer Commanding Defence,
Cape Town, and stated that I was leaving Kuruman the following day with my squadron for the Langberg, taking ten days'
supplies with me. I can quite imagine the shock it must have
given the elderly gentleman, reclining in his invalid chair, when
he received it; but I suppose he consoled himself with the
thoughts that it was the Commissioner of Police's picnic and
not his, and that if any one was to be killed it would not be
him, and a few C.M.R. more or less mattered very little either
way. If the expedition was successful it would be to his credit
in the first instance; if not—well, those Police fellows always
made a mess of things, and young officers, nowadays, etc. etc.

The day after I received the order, I paraded my squadron
and left Kuruman, leaving my clerks and a guard for our
stores, and taking with me two wagons with the rations and
reserve ammunition, and also the Maxim gun, which I did not
agree with the commissioner in considering to be impedimenta;

it was well horsed, and manned by a smart C.M.R. artillery gun squad, and could accompany us anywhere possible for horses to travel. It was well that I did so, as events turned out, or in all probability this book would not have been written, and another disaster to British troops in South Africa would have been recorded.

The Magistrate who intended meeting the chiefs, Toto and Lukajantje, with the object of persuading them to give up the rebel Galishwe as a prisoner, or of forcing them to betray his hiding-place, accompanied the column, which numbered about 100 of my men, with a few Cape Police as guides. The surgeon-lieutenant with the ambulance, and Mr. Chapman as interpreter, completed the patrol. The road after leaving Kuruman was a sandy track through the veldt, and wound gradually up to the top of the nek in the Kuruman hills, a range about two miles beyond the village. From here we could see the Langberg range rising out of the sandy flats some fifty miles away, and stretching from right to left as far as the eye could see.

From the Kuruman hills to the Langberg mountains the country was of a flat description, with sandy soil and scant vegetation, except for a belt of trees, some four miles in extent, which we had to pass through before reaching Khartu. This was a village with several fine springs of water running through it; it was deserted, with the exception of one man,—I recognised him as having been at the meeting at Kuruman,— but I appeared not to recognise him, and asked him where the people were. He told me they had all gone on to the Langberg where there was to be a meeting. I could get no information whatever about Galishwe, and could see that the man was a spy on our movements. As we had nothing to conceal from him, he was told that we were going with the Magistrate to the meeting also, and that there was no occasion for the people of the village to have hidden in the bush when they saw us coming, which from his startled look I judged had been the case.

After leaving Khartu we did not continue on the road direct to the villages occupied by Toto and Lukajantje, but branched off to our left, towards the extreme right of the range, where there was a trading station owned by a Mr. Pierce, an ex-C.M.R. whom I remembered in the regiment during the Basuto campaign. On our arrival here on the second evening from Kuruman we found the Magistrate awaiting us. He informed me that he had sent a message to the chiefs to meet us at the store, and expected them the following day.

We encamped close to the store, where we found good grazing for the horses and plenty of water, a very scarce commodity in that part of the country. Mr. Pierce informed me that he got all his goods brought from Kimberley by wagon drawn by donkeys, a very slow method of travelling, taking a fortnight or more to do the single journey; also that he had a shop at "Gamisep," that being the name of Toto's own village, where he had a white man looking after the place for him. He was rather anxious about his shops, owing to the attitude of the natives, who were talking very big in their own villages about resisting should Government send a force to capture Galishwe, who was living with the chiefs, and who had held several meetings amongst them advocating rebellion. Mr. Pierce also said that the Bechuanas were well armed and fairly good shots, and that the country would be very difficult to operate in, owing to scarcity of water, which would make

ATTACK ON GALISHWE'S POSITION, GAMISEP.

C.M.R. FIRING AT NATIVES

the transport of a large column anywhere in the mountains an extremely difficult matter unless it was equipped with a sufficient number of water-carts, an article not to be found in any large numbers among the various Government stores in the country. The absence of the real article cost the Government some thousands of pounds later on, when the whole column was delayed for days whilst the carts were being built and forwarded. This was only one of the items of the bill caused by the incompetency of the legacy left to the Government by General Gordon.

The two chiefs not turning up for the meeting at Pierce's store, the Magistrate decided to go to Gamisep and interview them at their own place. On the following morning we commenced our march along the road at the foot of the mountain which led to Gamisep. Mr. Pierce accompanied the Magistrate, who drove on ahead, and followed at the usual line of march pace—as fast as our mule transport could travel in the heavy sand.

The Langberg range was composed of a chain of mountains with large kloofs or valleys, with spurs of the mountains on either side, and wide entrances from the plains narrowing up to the back of the mountain, where the villages were usually built; villages were also to be seen at the entrance of the kloof in a great many instances as we marched past them. Nearing Gamisep, we passed between high hills with rocky sides, among which huts were to be seen in large numbers, but no sign of life in any shape or form. Passing one of these huts, built with a sort of palisade made of grass mats, I rode up to it with one of my subalterns, and to my surprise saw it crowded with men, who were watching us and evidently taking notes as to our numbers. Remarking to my subaltern that it did not seem a healthy spot for us, we rode back to the men, and, taking advantage of the first opening in the hills, I directed the wagons and ambulance out on to the flat country, and followed them with the men, glad to get out of what might have proved at any moment a veritable death-trap to us all.

Keeping away as much on the flat as possible, we at last arrived opposite the village of Gamisep and Pierce's store, forming up the wagons about six hundred yards from the store. I off-saddled the men, and let the horses run on the flat in rear of us, and made the men place their saddlery in form of a square,—the Maxim gun pointing to our front on to the village.

The Magistrate met me at the place, and informed me that the meeting would be held the following morning close to the camp, and that he had received messages from Toto, who appeared to be glad of our arrival. Mr. Pierce pointed out a vlei of water up the kloof where Toto's village was situated, and I sent a message through him to the chief, telling him that I would send my horses to his vlei to get water, and to tell his people that they would not be molested by the white men in any way, provided they behaved themselves. A strong guard of mounted men took the horses up the kloof to this vlei, where they had their fill and were driven back to the ground behind the camp. I must confess that it was with a feeling of relief that I saw the horses trotting back from the kloof, as I was not at all satisfied in my own mind as to the sincerity of Toto's professions of welcome. It was evident, however, that they were playing a waiting game, and wanted us to make the first move.

I then gave orders to have the officers' tent pitched, and

told the men that they could pitch their patrol tents if they wished, which some of them did,—the others preferring to sleep in their saddles in the open. I invited the Magistrate to share my tent, but Mr. Pierce had already offered him accommodation at his shop, which he had accepted. He informed me that his spies had reported that Galishwe was in the next kloof with a few of his own followers ; that there was a very strong feeling in his favour against the Government; and that the natives resented our appearance at the Langberg. This news was more than sufficient to make me keep the men on the alert, and not allow a single native anywhere in the vicinity of the camp. I also gave orders for shelter trenches to be dug outside the men's saddles. In the event of any sudden desire to attack us on the part of the Bechuanas we could give them a warm reception.

The next morning, Toto, accompanied by about thirty or forty men, made an appearance in front of the camp ; Lukajantje did not turn up, but sent a message that he was sick and could not attend. The Magistrate and myself, with interpreter, met Toto, and demanded an explanation why he had not obeyed the Magistrate's order and gone to Pierce's store when told to do so. Toto made various excuses which showed he had been afraid to leave his village, fearing the influence of Galishwe in his absence. He denied that he had assisted Galishwe in any way, and pointed out that he was in the next kloof with six men, and that we could go and get him if we wanted him. Toto ended by saying that he would see Lukajantje, and consult with him as to whether they should drive Galishwe away from the Langberg or make him a prisoner and hand him over to us. For this purpose he asked the Magistrate to give him till the following day.

Being of opinion that Toto would act as he had promised, but believing that it was to give Galishwe time to escape from his hiding-place, I urged the necessity of testing the truth of Toto's statement at once by going to the kloof where Galishwe was stated to be in hiding. The Magistrate asked for a delay of twenty-four hours, after which, if things were not satisfactory, I could do as I wished as regards the capture of the rebel, and I was forced to be content with his decision.

That afternoon, accompanied by my two subalterns and the doctor, I rode to the kloof where Galishwe was supposed to have taken up his position, and had a good look at the surrounding country. About half-way up the kloof was a ridge of a rocky nature, stretching from one side of the kloof to the other, and by riding on to this ridge and keeping a sharp look-out, a good view of the intervening country and the back of the mountain could be obtained. It was very rocky, and sloped up to the back of the mountain, with ravines and ridges of rock all the way, capable of concealing at least a thousand men without the slightest difficulty.

Whilst sitting on our horses and endeavouring to fix on some place which would prove effective in discovering the whereabouts of Galishwe and his men, a figure of a native popped up apparently from the ground, about three hundred yards in our front, and immediately disappeared again, and although I searched the rocks with my field-glasses for some time I was unable to detect any further signs of life about the country.

As it was quite evident that we were being observed by natives unseen to us, were turned to camp. With one of the subalterns I then visited Pierce's shop, and Mr. Pierce pointed

out Lukajantje's hut in the village at the mouth of the kloof
opposite the camp. I asked him to accompany me, and we rode
to the hut, where we found twenty or thirty natives standing or
sitting about outside, who eyed us in anything but a friendly
manner. Pierce asked for Lukajantje, and that individual
appeared in the doorway. I asked him through Pierce if he
would come for a ride with me into the next kloof where
Galishwe was supposed to be hiding. He replied that he was
sick, and appeared extremely anxious to get rid of our company.
He was one of the most forbidding looking scoundrels of a native
I have ever seen, and appeared to me to be more like a Hottentot than ever. I was certain he intended mischief by the
insolent manner in which he answered Pierce, but the latter,
if he understood the language, did not deem it advisable to
interpret for my benefit, and only repeated that Luka was sick.
With this I was forced to be content, and taking my subaltern
with me, whom I found evincing a great desire to thrash a
burly brute of a native who had been scowling at us during
the conversation and making remarks to the others, we rode
off to the camp, where we offsaddled.

My attention was directed by some of the sergeants who
had remained in camp to the fact that a great number of
natives had ridden from along the road which we had travelled
the day before, and had entered the kloof next to Lukajantje's location, at the extreme end of which, under the
mountain, Toto's village was situated, and they suggested
that it was not safe for the horses to be driven to the vlei
situated in the kloof for water. There was no other place
available, and I ordered a troop of twenty-five men and an
officer to saddle up and drive the remainder of the horses, and
see that they were all well watered. After an hour they

returned, having done so, the officer reporting that there were a great number of natives in Toto's village, where apparently a big meeting was being held.

The Magistrate being still of the opinion that Toto would prove loyal and would act as he had promised, and that no action should be taken till after the meeting which had been arranged for 10 a.m. the following morning, I was forced to wait with what patience I could command for that time to arrive. That night I took the precaution of posting an out-lying picquet, and the men slept in their saddles with their belts on and arms beside them.

The following morning, just as we had finished breakfast, a dispatch rider arrived from Kuruman with a telegram for myself, which I found to be from Defence, Cape Town, con-taining the following: " As Commissioner Bell has the conduct of Galishwe affair, consult with him before taking further steps."

Here was a nice state of affairs: the man who had placed me under the orders of Commissioner Robinson, from whom I had received imperative instructions to capture Galishwe, and whose orders had placed me in a position impossible to draw back from without endangering the prestige of the Govern-ment with the natives, had taken all the time which had elapsed since he received my wire acquainting him with my orders, and my intention to endeavour to carry them out, in making up his mind how to retrieve his mistake in having, in the first instance, placed C.M.R. under the orders of a Police officer, contrary to all regulations.

I showed the Magistrate the telegram, and he agreed with my opinion that the matter had gone too far for us to withdraw without having held the meeting, so I replied to

ATTACK ON GALISHWE'S POSITION, GAMISEP: SHOWING "A COLONIAL OFFICER" ON HORSEBACK.

Drawn by C. J. STANILAND, R.A., from a Sketch by HARRY PRENDERGAST, C.M.R.

Defence, stating that I had been on the spot for two days, that the natives had been given up to that morning to conform with orders given them; that Galishwe was reported to be in the mountains, and that I would endeavour to get him before leaving.

The express rider had not saddled up his horse to return with the telegram when half a dozen shots in rapid succession were heard in the direction of the kloof in which Galishwe was supposed to have taken up his stand, and a native appeared on·horseback leading two other horses and riding as hard as he could for the camp.

He turned out to be one of the party of natives employed by. the Magistrate who had been sent up in the hills overlooking Galishwe's hiding-place to watch his movements. He informed us that Galishwe and some of his men had endeavoured to steal the horses, and had fired at him when he galloped off with them.

I ordered twenty-five men under the senior subaltern to saddle up and go and see what was going on in the kloof, where several more shots had been heard, and ordered the mules to be caught up and tied to the wagons ready for inspanning. The remainder of the horses were also caught and tied up in case of emergency. Just as the men were ready to parade, my other subaltern came up and said, "Let me go with them, skipper,—I want to see the fun." Having got my permission, he jumped on his horse's back and joined the detachment as they trotted off in the direction of the kloof, at the mouth of which I had stationed a corporal and three men in the early morning, to see that no natives came out in that direction. These men had not come in, nor sent any message; neither had I heard the report of the Martini-

Henry carbine which our men were armed with at that period.

The natives in the village were greatly excited, and could be seen climbing up the sides of the mountain, which divided the kloof where the firing had taken place from Lukajantje's place. All of them carried arms, and large numbers of them appeared coming from the direction of Toto's village, getting into the rocks at the mouths of the kloofs, and disappearing into what I now perceived to be schanzes.

Suddenly I heard heavy firing from the kloof, into which the patrol had just ridden, and knew that the.tale about Galishwe and his six men, as told by Toto, had been a fairy one, and that I had the whole of the Langberg natives in arms between us and the capture of Galishwe.

The attitude of the natives was so threatening that I ordered the Maxim gun squad to stand to their gun and prepare for action; and almost immediately afterwards a sergeant came galloping up and called out for a stretcher, as Mr. Hopkins, my junior subaltern, had been shot. He was followed by the civilian conductor of the wagons, who informed me that one of the men had been killed.

I sent the sergeant to tell the officer in command of the patrol to retire his men out of the kloof. I next ordered the Maxim gun to be limbered up, and mounting my horse, which was ready saddled—and telling the senior sergeant to keep his men ready, in the event of an attack on the wagons—I galloped off, followed by the gun, in the direction of the kloof, passing poor Hopkins on the way, as he was being carried in by some camp natives. He had just died—the bullet having struck him above the hip: he was bleeding internally.

On arriving at the mouth of the kloof, I saw the patrol

on the opposite side retiring in my direction, and the natives occupying the centre of the kloof, from which we had been observing the country the day before, and from which they now opened fire as we approached. Determined to teach some of them a lesson, I galloped up to within four or five hundred yards, and told the sergeant to come into action. The gun was swung round, and the whole ridge raked from end to end. The firing from the natives ceased at once.

I gave instructions to the sergeant to cease fire, and we joined the patrol and returned to camp, where I had the wagons inspanned and the men in readiness to march. On making inquiries as to the whereabouts of the Magistrate, I was informed that he had been seen driving away in his cart in the direction of Kuruman, shortly after the firing commenced, probably thinking his presence was no longer necessary.

Although everything was in readiness for our march, I was not going to allow the natives to think that they had driven us away. When poor Hopkins' body had been sewn up in his rug, I marched half the squadron down to the store, and in a grave dug at the back under a tree by some rocks, we buried him with military honours in the face of hundreds of the natives, who from behind rocks watched the proceedings. The patrol had been unable to recover the body of Private Venn; he had not been missed till too late, when the enemy had become too strong in numbers to attempt it without further loss of life. He was an ex-medical student—a finely built fellow, a splendid football player, and his death was a great loss to the squadron and the regiment.

Lieutenant George Hopkins had served with me in Matabeleland as sergeant, together with the other subaltern, and both received their commissions after passing the examination on our return.   Hopkins was a very great favourite throughout the regiment—a thorough athlete in every branch of sport, and a gentleman in every sense of the word; he had endeared himself very much to me during his service as subaltern in my squadron and as a friend, and his sudden loss affected me badly.   I suppose it was to be; but I never forgave myself for allowing him to accompany the patrol at his request, when there was no necessity for him to have been there.

The road by which we had marched to Gamisep ran close to the mountains, and in some places between spurs of hills, in the direction of which large numbers of natives were to be seen making their way.   I determined not to run any more risks with the men, so, waiting till Pierce and his assistants had transferred the goods from his shop to his wagons, and had departed with them, I asked one of the civilians who had been present waiting at Pierce's store if he knew of any other road back to Kuruman, by which I could keep in the open country and obtain water.   He told me that he had a trading-station some fifteen miles away in the direction of Kuruman and flat country all the way, and offered to guide us to his place.   I accepted his offer, and in the afternoon we moved off into the flat, keeping in a square formation round the wagons till we arrived out of range of the mountains, when I began to breathe more freely, and we resumed the ordinary line of march formation.

On reaching Ryan's farm we found an ample water-supply from wells for our wants, and encamped there for the night. Towards morning, some Basutos, who had been employed by the Magistrate as spies in the Langberg, arrived at Ryan's, and informed me that both Toto and Lukajantje with their followers had decided on joining Galishwe in rebellion against the Government. They also told me that it was Lukajantje's men who had fired on the patrol the day before, and that it had been decided by the chiefs that my camp was to be attacked at night in order that they might capture our arms and ammunition. The attack had fallen through, owing to the squadron leaving,—the rebels deciding not to follow us up in the open country, being afraid of the Maxim gun, which had done so much damage.

We continued our march that morning, and reached Kuruman at night without having encountered a single native on the road. I reported what had occurred by wire to the Defence Department, and to the officer commanding C.M.R. at Kuruman. I found Mr. Bell at Kuruman, where he had been sent by Government as the political officer in the case of Galishwe. We were old friends, for he had been magistrate in the Transkei for many years, and we had frequently met at his magistracy. He considered our engagement the best thing that could have happened, as it finally disposed of any theory that Government might have entertained about the loyalty of the Langberg natives. The only thing to be regretted in the matter was the casualties I had sustained, and, considering the situation we had been placed in, these were remarkably small.

CHAPTER XXIII.

1897–1898.

ORDERS TO REMAIN AT KURUMAN — ARRIVAL OF REINFORCEMENTS — OFFICIAL DOCUMENTS — DEFENCE DEPARTMENT'S SHORTCOMINGS — ADVANCE OF COLUMN—CAPTURE OF KHARTU—BADLY PLANNED ATTACK ON GAMISEP—A FAILURE—RETURN OF COLUMN TO RYAN'S FARM— COLUMN PROCEEDS TO OLIPHANT'S HOEK—NIGHT ATTACK—ADVANCE ON PUDAHUSCH—SEVERE ENGAGEMENT—C.M.R. CASUALTIES—CAPTURE OF PUDAHUSCH—COLUMN RETURNS TO RYAN'S FARM—PATROL ALONG KURUMAN RIVER—GALISHWE RETURNS TO THE LANGBERG—FINAL ATTACK ON GAMISEP—DEATH OF LUKAJANTJE—CAPTURE OF REBELS— UNDER ARREST—RETURN TO UMTATA—LEAVE THE REGIMENT—START FOR NATAL.

IN reply to my wire to Defence, I received an order to remain at Kuruman and await reinforcements. Mr. Bell sent his Basuto spies back to the Langberg, from whom we received messages from time to time informing us that the natives were busy building schanzes and strengthening their defences against our next visit.

Mr. Bell told me of important news he had received. A strong column of the C.M.R., consisting of the regular Volunteers of the Colony, was being organised at Cape Town as quickly as possible, and three hundred Burghers were being raised in the Vryburg district under their own commandants, to be sent on to Kuruman when they were ready for service. More than a month elapsed before the first contingent of the column arrived at Kuruman—a colonel in command, with Maxim battery of the C.M.R. commanded by my old chum

Tim, who had been appointed field-adjutant to the column—a lucky chance for the O.C., as we were all soon to realise. A contingent of the D.E.O.V.R. under Colonel Spence, a most popular and efficient officer; Cape Town Highlanders, under Captain Searle; Prince Alfred's Volunteer Artillery; a very smart battery under Major Inglesby; a mounted infantry company of the Duke's, commanded by Captain Johnson, who became staff-officer in name to the O.C. column, and who handed over his men to Lieutenant Mahoney, C.M.R., during the operations; the Medical Staff Corps of the Cape, under Colonel Hartley, V.C., C.M.R., Major Cox, C.M.S., and Surgeon-Lieutenant Knapp, C.M.R.; 1st City Volunteers, under Major Tamplin; Prince Alfred's Guard and Kaffrarian Rifles; and Lieutenant Wormald of the 7th Hussars, A.D.C. to the O.C., about completed the contingent. The Burghers, under Commandant Wessels, arrived shortly afterwards, making the strength of the column to approximately between two and three thousand. The force was sufficient, if properly handled, to capture the Langberg in one day, but, owing to incompetency and dissension, it took nine months to accomplish the task from the commencement of hostilities.

Attached to the column was also Lieutenant W——, who had been transferred to my squadron to replace poor Hopkins. He had served with me during the whole of his service in the regiment till he received his commission. I was delighted to have him with me, as he was a very smart and efficient young officer, with the bond between us—which always brings men together, especially abroad—of having been at the same public school. Shortly after the arrival of the column, I walked off to my own camp, and was doing the honours of my tent, when the staff-officer entered and handed me an official

23

letter, with the rather ominous remark, " Don't let it worry you," showing that he knew the contents. He backed out of the tent in an apologetic sort of manner, and left me to digest the contents, which were of the following nature :—

" Your reasons are requested for the information of the Colonial Government as to the action taken by you in—
" I. Proceeding to the Langberg without authority.
" II. Attacking Galishwe contrary to orders.
" III. Why, after the action, you did not occupy a strong position in the Langberg and await orders."

This was the secret of the silence with which I had been treated by the authorities in Cape Town since my report on the engagement. I was to be the ball in the game of ping-pong played by the noble warriors—the officer commanding Defence and the Commissioner of Police, who no doubt had repudiated their share in the action which they had forced me into, and the Defence man had taken this line of action with me.

After taking a considerable time to recover my temper from this torpedo attack, I sent the following reply :—

" I. In answer to letter No.——, I beg to state for the information of Government, that I proceeded to the Lang-berg in accordance with instructions received from Commissioner of Police, Kimberley, under whose orders I had been placed by telegrams received from O.C. Defence,—both telegrams attached.
" II. I did not attack Galishwe, my men being fired on by the rebels before the time had elapsed for the arranged meeting with the Magistrate.

"III. My position was untenable in the Langberg, being within range of rebel positions on three sides of the camp, and the absence of water made it impossible to remain in any position nearer than Ryan's Farm to the Langberg, which, had I elected to do so, the smallness of the force at my disposal precluded any idea of sending any part of it to Kuruman for supplies of food and ammunition, which were almost expended. And, finally, Kuruman, with the refugees and large quantities of stores, would have been at the mercy of the natives had the place been left unprotected."

Whether this reply, which was handed to the staff-officer, and to which I foolishly attached the original telegrams I had received from Defence and Police, was forwarded as I had handed it in, I am not in a position to state, no allusion to the correspondence having been made as far as I know. But from the reply received later on to the effect that "Captain —— was not only guilty of direct disobedience of orders in proceeding to the Langberg, and plunging the Colony into a war when not prepared for it, but of insolence to Government," I can only conclude that the Government were ignorant of the contents of the telegrams under which I acted.

I was not called upon to answer this sweeping condemnation of my conduct, an inexplicable fact in face of the graveness of the charges, my position, and the length of my service. If the Police and Defence had assumed responsibility for the telegrams under which I acted the Government had committed an act of the grossest injustice in making me the scapegoat. But I had parted with the only documents that could have proved the responsibility of Police and Defence.

As to the absurd remark about the country not being prepared for war, what had the man entrusted with the Defence Department been doing since the Basuto War of seventeen years before? Surely he was giving himself away by showing the utterly incompetent manner in which he had fulfilled his trust in not having the forces of the Government ready for any emergency at all times. Now he was attempting to make me the scapegoat of his shortcomings.

I refused to accept this reprimand and was told not to take any notice of it, that it would all come right when the facts of the case came out. The opinion of my brother officers has been that it was an effusion from the Defence without the knowledge of the Government, otherwise the proper course would have been adopted: I should have been placed under arrest and relieved from my command till a court had decided who was to blame, instead of which I remained the senior officer of the column, with the exception of the two colonels and my friend Tim, the field-adjutant.

The column was delayed some time at Kuruman, owing to the delay in the arrival of necessary stores and water-carts, which had to be manufactured for the occasion; during this period an expedition, consisting of the Duke's mounted company and the Burghers, paid a visit to the natives living along the Kuruman River, in the hope of meeting with opposition. Catching sight of some natives, they opened fire on them; the natives, who were not armed, fled; the column returned, having succeeded in driving the natives off into the Langberg and in shooting one of the Burghers in their excitement.

Eventually the column succeeded in obtaining the requisite number of water-carts, and was able to make a forward move from Kuruman. An advance party of the Duke's mounted succeeded in capturing Khartu, which they found in

the same condition as we had on two former occasions—
deserted; but the "Capture of Khartu" by the staff officer
looked well in dispatches, and settled all doubts in the intelligent minds of the would-be military critics in Cape Town
as to the suitability of the appointment of the staff officer to
the position.

The column followed in due course, and finally reached
Ryan's Farm, where two large camps were pitched, one for the
Burghers close to the ruins of Ryan's house, and the other on
the ridge opposite for the remainder of the column, and
elaborate plans were matured for the destruction of the Langberg and its inhabitants by the O.C. column and his staff
officer. It ended in the Burghers remaining at Ryan's to look
after the camp and the water supply, while the remainder of
the column, divided into two separate columns, mounted men
and infantry, the former under my command, was to march
from Ryan's in the dark about 10 p.m. and proceed to within
four miles of the position of Gamisep, when the column was
to be dismounted, the horses left in charge of guards, and the
whole proceed on foot. On arrival at the cross-roads, one
leading to Gamisep and the other along the foot of the
mountains, I was to detach half my command to proceed
along the latter route under command of the staff officer, who
took with him the Duke's mounted company and Gordonia
Volunteers. His orders were, I believe, to march to the foot
of the mountain to the left of Toto's village, and get his men
into position overlooking the village by daylight, when the
remainder of the column, under command of the officer commanding, with the guns, were to arrive at the mouth of the
kloof.

I was to take my half column, consisting of my squadron

C.M.R. and the 1st City Volunteers, to the right, which would bring me within the half-hour to the site of my former camp, and opposite Lukajantje's kraal.   Here was the inevitable result of making plans without a personal reconnaissance of the position, and without knowing or taking the trouble to ascertain the spot where resistance was sure to be encountered. On parting with the staff officer I told him as bluntly and as plainly as possible that I did not know who was responsible for the piece of strategy, but I knew that he was marching his men clean out of action, and to a position where he would not be of the slightest use.   I also added that I would be engaged before I had gone half an hour, and in the event of his hearing any firing in my direction, he was to bring his column to the spot as soon as possible and I would take the responsibility. He hurried off with his men on his mountaineering trip as I had called it, and events happened exactly as I had foreseen.

Leaving the road with my column we advanced across the veldt in the direction of Gamisep, when the Police-sergeant who was guide to the column told me that he was not certain of his position.   I knew perfectly well we were just about on our old camping-ground opposite Pierce's store, but I did not know what the ground was like between where we were and the foot of the mountain which I was to occupy. So I halted the men, and we lay down in silence till the intense darkness became a little lighter.   As soon as the outline of the mountain became visible, we marched straight for the foot of it, and encountered a donga—a large sluit at the bottom of the sloping ground we had crossed.   Some delay was caused in selecting a place to cross, as the banks were rather steep, but on finding a suitable spot we went through and up the other side.   The C.M.R. were following me in fours, the 1st City in rear, when suddenly in front of me, and about twenty yards distant, a flash lighted up the surrounding darkness, and a roar echoing amongst the rocks proclaimed the firing of a muzzle-loading gun. Before I had time to give any order a fusillade started from our right—luckily fired over our heads in the dark, and then shots from the front and left. Getting the men back under cover into the donga, I extended them along the bank and returned the fire, which apparently was strongest from a ridge of rocks about fifty yards to the right of where we had crossed and in front of which I had now extended the men.

As the early morning advanced, and the position in front of us became more clearly defined, I found that we were in the donga stretching from Pierce's store on our left round to the kloof on our right, where we had encountered Galishwe on the former occasion, and that the whole position from Luka-jantje's village to the kloof on our right was one mass of schanzes, which the heavy fire that was poured in our direction on the first alarm proved to be strongly manned, probably by the whole of Luka's men.

There were no signs of the other two columns when the day broke. The main column had evidently misjudged the distance from Ryan's, as they were to have been in position before daylight. On our left, and opposite Toto's village, the face of the hill in front of us was very steep and covered with rocks; but no sign of life was visible. The firing had ceased; so I determined to make another attempt to advance. I told the men to get ready, and on the advance sounding, to jump out of the donga and try to rush the position. Telling the officer in command of the 1st City to support, I ordered the advance to be sounded; my men immediately rushed out into the open when a tremendous fusillade opened from behind every rock on our flanks and front, and we only succeeded in reaching the foot of rocks underneath the schanzes. The 1st City remained in the donga, and a report reached me that the enemy were coming along on their left. For a few moments we were in a tight corner, when the sound of Maxims fired from the flat on our rear at the schanzes in front of us showed me that the third column had arrived, and my friend Tim had brought his guns into action.

As my men were invisible in their khaki uniform lying in the rocks and sand, I thought it very probable that we should come in for a share of the bullets from our own guns, so I told my trumpeter to sound my squadron call. The lad jumped up, and facing to the rear, sent the call echoing out, and the Maxims immediately ceased firing. Tim afterwards told me that until he heard the call, of which he immediately grasped the meaning, he had not the slightest idea where we were. Shortly afterwards a message was brought me by an officer to retire my men back on the column. We doubled back to the donga, where I gave orders to the 1st City to retire, the C.M.R. to cover this movement. Directly they moved out on to the flat the natives directed a heavy fire on them, but as they got the double fire of the maxims and my men on them, they ceased firing, and the retirement was carried out with the loss of one man of the 1st City wounded.

The main column was halted on the flat in the vicinity of my former camp, and on our arrival the Duke's were sent to occupy a position close by Pierce's store, in the donga facing the hill which separated Lukajantje's village from the kloof in which Toto lived with his followers. The natives were found to be in force in this position. Shells from the

9-pounders and the Maxim fire made no impression on the rocks behind which the Bechuanas lay in well-prepared pits or trenches. After a considerable amount of ammunition had been expended by the artillery and the infantry, with no apparent result, I was ordered down with my squadron to reinforce the infantry. Extending the men, we had proceeded about 100 yards towards the position, when on our left rear a large body of mounted men galloped out into the open from the villages to the left of Gamisep. They rode up to the main body of the column, and dismounting at about 400 yards from the wagons, commenced firing at the column and on my men, as we were marching from it. I immediately changed front and opened fire on them, when they mounted and galloped off to the village of Gamisep—or Toto's place.

The half column I had detached with the staff officer should have been on the mountain to our left, and overlooking Toto's position at daylight, but it was now midday and no sign of life was visible in that direction, so the officer commanding withdrew the Duke's from the donga, and moving the column nearer to the hill which commanded the road to Ryan's Farm, he ordered the position to be strongly held by infantry, and formed camp to await developments regarding the missing column.

The horses and men got some rest and food, much needed after the long hours of marching and firing. Several casualties had occurred amongst the infantry. Lieutenant Harris of the Duke's was badly hit in the leg by an explosive bullet, and amputation was resorted to on the spot; but the shock was too great, and he died within an hour of the operation, and was buried close to the camp. The officer commanding was by this time getting deeply concerned at the non-appearance of the other column, and had ample opportunity of studying that part of the Langberg for the first time. Doubtless he came to the conclusion that the task he had been set to perform was not quite so easy viewed at close range as it had at fifty miles' distance.

As I have before stated, the Langberg was over forty miles in extent, and was composed of mountains, kloofs, and villages, all very similar in appearance to one another, and not the best country for night expeditions to be undertaken with any degree of certainty that the particular locality on the mountain, expected to be occupied, would be successfully reached at a given time. Before parting with the staff officer, I had told him that he was leading his men clean out of action in taking the direction he did, but as he had been instrumental in drawing out the wonderful plan, it was clearly his picnic and not my business to interfere. But I did not envy the O.C. as night came on, and there was still no sign of the missing column. One thing, however, was certain—there had been no engagement in the direction taken by the staff officer, and the lack of excitement in the enemy's positions showed us that they were not anticipating any trouble with any column other than the one visible to them. So all that could be done in the matter was to take the necessary precautions to ensure the safety of our own column, and to get as much sleep as we could under the circumstances.

Nothing occurred during the night to disturb our rest. At daylight the mountains overlooking Gamisep were eagerly scanned by the members of the staff, but nothing could be seen of the absentees. The officer commanding the column sent some men who had been attached to the force for the purpose to prospect for water round the hill which had been occupied by infantry since the previous day, and the welcome intelligence was passed that water was likely to be obtained from wells at the foot of the hill.

The well-sinkers soon got to work, and before the morning had passed a decent supply of water had been obtained—sufficient for the wants of the men and a small allowance for the horses, the water-carts accompanying the column having been found inadequate for the demands made upon them.

Shortly after midday, a couple of shots were heard on the flat between the camp and the mountain to which the missing column had originally been dispatched, and two figures were seen dragging their way through the unbroken ground towards the camp. They turned out to be a lieutenant and a corporal of the Duke's mounted company, who had been sent by the staff officer to look for water, which his column was suffering very much for want of. They had wandered along the top of the mountain, when they caught sight of the camp below, and, not knowing their way back to their own people, had come down the hill to the column.

They were both done up, and were handed over to the medical staff to be attended to. Shortly afterwards some more figures appeared, and soon the whole of the men who composed the missing column came straggling into camp—all very done up, and it was a lucky thing for all concerned that the enemy did not care to leave their defensive positions and attack them as they came down the mountain, or they would have suffered from more than thirst.

They soon recovered after a good meal and plenty to drink, but all operations were at an end for a time, and, leaving the Duke's to fortify the hill they had been occupying, which was christened Spence's Kopje, after their popular colonel, who remained in command, the remainder of the column returned to Ryan's Farm, and went into quarters under canvas to await the next move. The Burghers were now sent out to patrol along the flat in front of the mountains, to destroy crops and capture what cattle they could find straying away from the villages. They returned after two or three days' absence without having been engaged at any point of the range, or succeeding in making any addition to our live stock.

On their return, preparations were made for the column to pay another visit to the Langberg, and, taking all the wagons containing stores with us, and leaving the Burghers to take charge of the wells at Ryan's, the column commenced its march. On reaching Spence's Kopje we found them all in excellent spirits, and full of amusing incidents of night "attacks" made by the enemy on their position; evidently nothing more serious than two or three natives creeping up a donga and firing a few shots at the picquets—but sufficient to make the garrison turn out behind their defences, and waste thousands of rounds of ammunition fired in the dark at an imaginary enemy.

Instead of turning to our right in the direction of Gamisep, the column kept along the wagon track which led in front of the mountains, the objective being one of the extreme ends of the range called Oliphant's Hoek. The march was a very slow one, owing to the size of our transport—an occasional skirmish at a village as we passed being the only fighting obtainable.

On arrival at Oliphant's Hoek, which was shaped like a basin with hills all round us, we formed laager and sent out patrols to the surrounding hills, burning villages and destroying crops in the shape of pumpkins and mealie lands, my men being particularly useful in this branch of the work, using their swords in cutting down crops, and slicing what they could not carry away in the wagons which accompanied the patrol. Beyond a few old women and half-starved children, found from time to time in the lands, collecting what they could find in the shape of food, we saw no sign of the enemy —the only intimation of their presence being a shot from behind some rock, fired at an individual man who had ventured too close to the mountains whilst destroying crops.

The camp at Oliphant's Hoek gave no indication of military genius in those responsible for the situation chosen. It was surrounded by hills at short range, and a donga, which could have concealed hundreds of the enemy had they chosen to avail themselves of the opportunity of rushing the camp, ran along about eighty yards in front of one of the faces of the laager.

The second night of the camp at this place, a volley was suddenly discharged at the laager from the donga. The Duke's mounted company, who were camped in front of the wagons on that face of the laager, ran back on the wagons. Some confusion occurred, but they shortly realised the position and returned the fire till the natives ceased.

My friend Tim called out to me, as captain of the week, asking if the picquets were in. I went out and visited the different corps as I passed, and found the picquets had all retired on the camp at the first alarm, with the exception of the Gordonia Volunteers' picquet, who had been posted on the rear face, with the donga on their right. I could see the position where I had placed them when they were posted. Taking a sergeant with me I walked towards it. On arriving within a short distance I was challenged, and answering the challenge, I inquired what they were doing there instead of retiring on the camp. The corporal in charge—evidently an old soldier—replied, " Thought it safer, sir, than running back into that mob of ours." On second thoughts I agreed with him, and the picquet remained where they were till the morning, the other picquets being sent back to their posts on my return to camp, as the firing had ceased and there were no signs of the enemy.

About this time two wagons, loaded up with canteen stores and goods, the property of a firm of German Jews who had been allowed to smouse with the column, were sent from Kuruman to the camp, in charge of one white man. Whilst trekking along the road between Gamisep and Oliphant's Hoek, a party of the enemy captured them, the white man escaping. The natives drove the wagons up to Toto's principal village, which was called Pudahusch, and the loads of liquor, cigars, tobacco, and goods, badly needed by the column, were distributed amongst the tribe, who must have had a royal time whilst the liquor lasted.

A patrol was sent out on the arrival of the white man at the camp; but by the time they arrived on the scene the wagons had been driven safely into the village at the top end of the kloof—to which place it was not deemed advisable to follow them up. The patrol returned to camp, leaving the spoils in the hands of the enemy.

The column then began the return march, this time in two parties, one of which, consisting of the Duke's mounted company and Gordonias with medical staff, under the staff officer, climbed up the end of the mountain opposite Oliphant's Hoek; and, keeping along the top, marched parallel with the remainder of the column, which, with the wagons, kept along the road at the foot of the mountain, in the direction of Pudahusch.

We arrived with the wagons opposite the mouth of the kloof in which was situated the principal village of the Langberg, and where the Chief Toto was reported to have taken up his residence, leaving Gamisep to the care of Luka-jantje. The kloof at Pudahusch was in the shape of a triangle—the base being a flat occupied by us, the two sides being parts of the mountain joining at the apex, beneath which was built the village. The column that marched along the summits of the range had not arrived at the spot overlooking the village, but were expected to be in position the following morning, when, on receiving a heliograph or other signal from them, an attacking party was to be formed from our column to advance up the kloof and attack the village, the column from the summit to co-operate in the attack.

The following morning orders were given for the attacking party of our column to muster on the flat below the camp, and there to await the signal to advance from the column on the summit of the mountain, when they had arrived at their position. Our column consisted of my squadron C.M.R. and the Cape Town Highlanders in the attacking line, supported by the Duke's, with Maxim guns. Colonel Spence of the Duke's commanded the column. We took up our positions in extended order as mentioned, my men forming the left of the line, in touch with the Highlanders on our right, the Duke's some 300 yards in our rear. The whole lot sat down on the veldt and waited for the signal.

It was not till ten o'clock that the flash of the heliograph was seen from the top of the mountain about half-way up

the kloof, on the western or left side of the position.   The
message sent by the staff officer told that he was in position
that there were no enemy on the western side of the kloof
but all on the eastern.   For this piece of news he should subsequently have been tried by court-martial for imparting false
information.   If he had signalled, "As far as he could judge
there were no enemy on the western side," it would have
been a less serious matter, as it was not to be expected that he
could see along the sides and base of the mountain he was on
with any degree of certainty; but the message he sent misled
the officer commanding the column on the flat into really
thinking that the staff officer must have verified the truth of
the message before sending it to camp.

The order was given to advance, and we proceeded on our
way up the kloof, which was about 600 yards wide at the
mouth.   After advancing for about 300 yards the kloof
gradually narrowed till my left-hand man was about fifty
yards from the foot of the mountain.   The latter appeared
to me to have more than the usual amount of abandoned
schanzes in various parts of it.   I pulled out my field-glasses
to have a good look at what I thought a suspicious-looking
low wall under some large rocks, and distinctly saw a man's
head peep over the top and vanish again.   I continued to
look to make sure if it appeared again, and I saw a man come
from behind a rock and disappear below the wall.

This was enough.   I stopped and looked back to where
Colonel Spence was riding between us and the supports.   See-
ing me stop, he rode up and asked what was the matter.   I
replied, pointing to the schanzes, "That place is manned, sir."
He asked why I thought so, and I told him what I had seen.
He then said—

" But —— " (meaning the staff officer) " has signalled saying there are no enemy on this side."

" Excuse me, sir," I said, " but —— be damned."

" I quite agree with you, my boy," he answered. " If you really think the place is manned, will you change front with your C.M.R. ? "

I saluted and ran back to where I had been walking in the centre of the squadron; and, blowing my whistle, signalled, " Change front to the left on the centre."

The men immediately swung round facing the mountain, bringing the squadron to about 200 yards from the foot of it, and I had just glanced along the line to see if they had completed the change of direction, before giving the word " Forward," when a terrific rifle fire was opened on us all along the line.

The men immediately fell flat on the ground in the sand. It was impossible to see who had been hit, the dust rising in small clouds where the bullets had struck all about us. I had never been in such a warm corner before ; bullets were striking the dust up close to my body. I looked round to see what the rest of the column were doing, and saw a mass of men running back on the supports, a regular panic having set in.

My men soon collected what they could in the way of stones to make temporary cover, and we commenced firing at the schanzes in our front. I guessed that one or more of my men had been hit, but how many it was impossible to say. Any movement on our part before the Maxim opened fire over us meant a hail of bullets, and I have no doubt that the enemy had flattered themselves with the idea that they had shot all the men who remained on the ground. They had seen the others disappear so hurriedly, they could not understand my

24

men remaining, and they must have got a shock when, the Maxim being too hot for them, some of them tried to get fresh cover, and my men, spotting the move, poured in a hot fire on them as they ran.

We lay in this uncomfortable position for over an hour, the Maxim gun saving the situation as far as we were concerned and checking any desire on the part of the enemy to show himself in order to get a shot at us, by the rapid fire it kept on the schanzes in our vicinity whenever we were threatened. We were lying in the sand with practically no cover, our blue putties affording a good mark of our positions ; and the wonder was that half the men were not hit, as the Bechuanas are by no means bad shots. The greater number of them are hunters, and, being used to accompany Dutch people on their shooting expeditions, are good judges of distance.

Colonel Spence saw that the only chance of getting the enemy out of the schanzes without incurring the heavy loss that would result from a frontal attack, was to take them in the flank and rear ; so he sent a company of the Duke's back to the mouth of the kloof, and occupying the side of the hill, they advanced on the flank of the schanzes situated to our front. Now was our chance. No sooner did the enemy catch sight of the Duke's coming on their rear and side, than they broke out of their cover and bolted up the hill in all directions. We poured in a heavy fire, the Maxim raked the hill as they ran, and very few of the enemy who had held that position lived to boast of having made the white man run. The Cape Town Highlanders fixed bayonets and charged up the kloof, joined by the mountaineering party under the staff officer. They burnt the whole village without any

BURNING OF PUDAHUSCH.

resistance from the natives, who retired over the mountains to the next kloof.

My men were congratulated by their comrades of the columns for the manner in which they had stood the trying time, and my hand was nearly wrung off by Colonel Spence and my pal Tim. When we returned to the main body I found that I had lost three of my men. They were all shot at the first discharge—one of them named Milne receiving seven bullet wounds—the other two, Bayly and Price, receiving two and three wounds. The two latter were killed instantly, but young Milne lived till we reached camp; nothing could be done for him, however, as he was riddled with bullets. All three were buried in one grave that evening, but the natives afterwards dug them up—probably to see how many the grave contained. Subsequently we buried them in the graveyard at Spence's Kopje, where a very handsome stone has been erected by Bayly's mother to the memory of her son and his comrades of the C.M.R. who were killed in the Langberg.

The officer commanding the column was particularly sympathetic with me on the serious loss of his and my men, and never even demurred when I told him in no measured language my opinion of his staff officer, and what I considered he deserved for his share of the trap we were nearly all caught in. For had I not by chance caught sight of the natives in passing, and had we gone on up the kloof, we would have been caught in a regular trap, and must have suffered much more heavily. As it was, we had escaped with the loss of my three men.

After having successfully burnt out Toto, the column returned to Ryan's Farm, to await reinforcements which were on the road up—Kaffrarian Rifles, reliefs of Prince Alfred's Guard, and a native contingent drawn from Butterworth in the Transkei, composed mostly of Fingoes. On the arrival of this force it was purposed to attack Gamisep and kill or capture the rebel chiefs, who were all together in that part of the Langberg.

Reports reached the officer commanding that Galishwe was endeavouring to escape from the Langberg, and that he and a large party of men had been seen along the Kuruman River some sixty miles distant, and that an engagement had taken place between the rebels and a party of Cape Police who had occupied that part of the country. I was immediately sent off to the spot where the rebels were said to be located, taking with me my squadron of C.M.R. and the Duke's mounted company, together with the necessary transport.

We marched over Khartu to Kuruman, and from there proceeded along the river valley for about thirty miles, when we came across the camp of the Cape Police. Here I was informed that Galishwe had returned to the Langberg some days before, the Police having followed him up for a considerable distance in that direction. I formed camp alongside the Police, and remained for two days, resting men and animals, before we began our return march to Ryan's.

The country was very fine in the valley, with vegetation all along the river, affording a pleasing rest for the eye after the eternal sand of the Langberg district with the dust storms. We passed several dwelling-houses and stores with fine fruit gardens on the banks of Kuruman River. They were all deserted, but had remained untouched by the natives, and locked up just as the occupants had left them in their hurried flight to Kuruman; also several native villages were seen and visited by us, but not a sign of a native was visible on the whole of the march from Ryan's to the Cape Police camp, or on the return journey. So it was apparent that the natives in the Langberg at that time were more numerous than the Government had anticipated, the whole of the natives from the lower district having evidently thrown in their lot with the rebels, probably the result of the action of the patrol which was sent out shortly after the arrival of the column at Kuruman.

We returned to Ryan's camp, and found that several patrols had been sent out during our absence to various parts of the Langberg. This had resulted in the rebels leaving the outlying parts of the range, and concentrating at Gamisep, where it was clear the final blow would have to be struck. Reinforcements of Kaffrarian Rifles had reached Khartu, and were encamped at that place awaiting the arrival of the native contingent, who were to be used as beaters amongst the rocks in the forthcoming attack.

The Burghers, who—with the exception of a few officers, Dutchmen—were mostly from Vryburg district, had been kept quite apart from the remainder of the column. They lived in a separate camp, and only received orders through their own officers, and had not accompanied the column on any of their expeditions. But on the return of the column to Ryan's Farm they were invariably sent out by themselves, foraging and destroying villages, etc. On one of these expeditions they had killed some natives who were supposed to be friendly and under the protection of the missions, and trouble had ensued. It ended in the Burghers being disbanded and several of them tried for breach of discipline. Eventually it fizzled out, and nothing more was heard of it, but these same Burghers became very prominent some two years later, when they took possession of Vryburg from the British, and made themselves particularly troublesome to the Mafeking garrison.

All reinforcements having arrived at Ryan's, the whole column moved on to Gamisep, which was attacked by the infantry, the native contingent being let loose with their assegais amongst the rocks. The enemy, after making a short stand, broke from their defences, and were shot down or taken prisoners in all directions. Lukajantje was shot dead in the schanze, which he held to the last. His head was taken possession of by a well-known Volunteer officer, who packed the skull in his belongings and took it to Cape Town, but the affair was brought to light in the newspapers and there was a big outcry, which ended in the officer leaving the Colonial forces. Toto was taken prisoner with his leading men, and they were sentenced to long terms of imprisonment. Galishwe made his escape into the desert, but was shortly afterwards captured at some wells. He was tried for murder, but got off with imprisonment, and has since been released and given land to live on. All the natives were taken away from the Langberg, the villages destroyed, and the country confiscated and made a Government reserve. At present it is uninhabited.

The column returned to Kuruman, and preparations were made for the return of the troops to the Colony, the different corps moving independently owing to scarcity of water along the route. The Cape Police took charge of all the rebels who were kept at Kuruman Magistracy whilst the preliminary examination was being held. I had to attend the court to identify and give evidence against Toto and others, which detained me for several days at the Magistracy.

Having completed this duty at the Magistracy, I returned to my men at the camp by the mission station, and made preparations for our departure. The officer commanding the column and his staff were also at the mission station, and were to precede my squadron in returning to Umtata, when on the day before their departure my friend Tim, the field adjutant, came to my tent, and cursing his luck at having to perform the duty, asked me for my sword, and told me I was to consider myself under open arrest, and proceed to Umtata and report myself there. I could either accompany the squadron or travel by myself. When I asked for an explanation he told me that he knew no more than I did, but supposed that it would be all right when we got back to Umtata.

None of my friends among the Volunteers would believe that I was under arrest, and chaffed me on the subject, telling me that I would probably be surcharged by the Government for the cost of the war, but when they realised that it was really a serious matter they became very indignant, and the expressions of disgust and contempt which were let fall would not have delighted the ears of an important personage had they reached them.

Leaving my squadron to return to the Colony under command of the senior subaltern, I started off with my servant to ride to Vryburg, where I awaited the arrival of the men and accompanied them by train to Kei Road. Leaving my baggage here to follow me, I took the post-cart to Umtata as soon as possible. I reported myself to the adjutant of the regiment, who repeated to me the orders he had received concerning my arrival. I was to remain in open arrest, and live in the officers' quarters; my freedom was to be in no way interfered with; I could walk anywhere I wished, or indulge in any sport; in fact, I was like an officer on leave in barracks, no duties to attend to.

The colonel and his staff duly arrived in Umtata, my squadron having been stopped at Indutywa for duty for an indefinite period. I passed my days playing golf or tennis with my brother officers and civilian friends, but all my queries as to what charge I was under arrest for received the same answer—"Don't know, old chap; don't worry yourself."

After about two months' detention at Indutywa, my squadron marched into Umtata, but it was not the same squadron that had marched away little more than a year previously. The men were utterly disgusted with their treatment—the subaltern who had taken command of them was one of the worst soldiers in the regiment, and did not know how to command men, and there was great dissatisfaction in the ranks, mostly caused, I was informed, by the manner in which I had been treated by the authorities.

About a month after the arrival of my men, during which time I got heartily sick of the suspense of waiting day after day for something definite to happen, the adjutant came to my quarters one morning, and, calling me by my Christian name, said, "The colonel wants you, old chap," and whilst I was dressing, he stamped about the room with suppressed feelings, but failed to keep in an occasional "Oh, damn!"

On arrival at the orderly-room, I found the colonel sitting there alone; picking up a letter, he read that my services in the Colonial Government were no longer required. I demanded to know what I had been charged with, and he tried to look me in the face while he told me that he did not know, and stammered something about Government. I walked back to my quarters, packed a bag, and took the first post-cart to Kei Road, and from there I proceeded to Cape Town, and went straight to the Defence officer. I found him in his office, and demanded to know what charge had been made against me. Beyond being told, in a very sympathetic voice, that it was Government, I could get nothing more from him.

The editor of the *Cape Times* wanted to take my case up, but I declined, determined to get to the bottom of the mystery by other means; so, after two or three vain appeals for an interview with the Prime Minister, I returned to Umtata. I put my case into the hands of a well-known barrister and M.L.A., who promised to bring it before the next Parliament. In the meantime nothing could be done, as by the laws of the Colony the Governor has the power of dispensing with the services of any officer without inquiry—a law, when applied to a military officer, without parallel in the British Empire. An officer, with twenty years of record service, to be dismissed without even being told what he had been guilty of, was one of the most unfair and iniquitous acts ever perpetrated by the Cape Government.

My friends, both civil and military, were very much concerned for my welfare, and the conclusion arrived at by all of them was that I had been made a scapegoat to cover the blunders of some more responsible persons, who had impressed on the civilian members of the Government the enormity of my offences against them. The appointment of a new Governor at the Cape, in the person of Sir Alfred Milner, greatly aided their schemes, as he had not been sufficiently long in the country to assess his ministers at their proper value, but would accept them at their own valuation. That this valuation was out of all proportion, the Governor found out in course of time.

The general behaviour of both the colonel and the staff officer while at the Langberg led me to the conclusion that this was the reply to my exposure of the rotten state of the Defence department, which had been unable to meet the sudden demand made upon it by the outbreak of the natives. The only thing to be done was to await the opening of Parliament the following year, and lay the whole matter before Government, as an appeal to the Home Government would probably have been referred back to the Governor and things would have been in a state of as-you-were.

I received many invitations from friends to stop with them pending Parliament reassembling, but it was too long a period to remain inactive, and the continual meetings with men of my late squadron, who never missed an opportunity of expressing their regret at what had occurred, and the knowledge that nearly half the squadron had purchased their discharges and left the regiment in disgust on my account, made my stay in Umtata unbearable. So I decided to move, and after a few bitter partings from my old chums and comrades, I left Umtata to try to forget my dismal feelings in another Colony, and to wait my time when the truth would out—as it eventually, to a certain extent, did. "Good luck!" was shouted by everybody as the post-cart taking me to St. John's passed through the streets of Umtata, for I was known from the oldest to the youngest member of the town; I had the good wishes of all, and I am convinced that with the exception of two men—the colonel and the subaltern, his tool and spy—I had not an enemy in the whole of the territories.

At St. John's, a beautiful little village, I spent a week with an old friend, the officer in command of C.M.R. there, who was greatly upset at my departure after a friendship of close on twenty years, and then I stepped on the little tug which was to carry me round to Durban in Natal.

CHAPTER XXIV.

1899.

MY start was a bad one. The weather, which was fairly boisterous at the beginning, developed into a gale, and the small coaster I was on, the *Umzimvubu,* named after the river at St. John's—having up to this time treated me to a series of buck-jumping and rolling, which made it impossible to move from the one position I had taken up when I boarded the vessel—could no longer make headway. The skipper decided to turn about, and we were swept past St. John's and finally succeeded in reaching East London, in the opposite direction intended at the start.

The tug, which had been badly knocked about during the passage, required some refitting before proceeding to Natal, so exchanging on to the *Dohne's Castle,* which was on its passage from Cape Town, I reached Durban the following day in a more comfortable manner than would have been possible on the small coaster.

I found Durban very much altered since my former visit by sea, nearly twenty years previously—the large steamer easily crossing the bar and entering the harbour, delightfully situated under the bluff on which the lighthouse stands. A small battery, armed with guns manned by the Natal Naval Volunteers in case of emergency, commands the entrance to the harbour and town. Durban is the cleanest and best regulated town in South Africa—its wide streets are beautifully kept, and the strings of rickshaws pulled by Zulus in their fantastic attire, and the weird gestures made by them as they caper about plying for hire, are quite novel sights to the new-comer. The electric tramcar service is by far the best existing in South Africa, and a trip from the Town Hall round the Berea, in which the whole of the town and harbour with its shipping comes into full view, is one of the most interesting a visitor can indulge in, especially on a fine moonlight night, with the electric lights shining in all directions.

A fine embankment had been built stretching from the wharves to the foot of the Berea, and large hotels, clubs, and boat-houses erected on ground that had been under water on my former visit. In the centre of the town was the fine Town Hall opposite some very well-laid-out gardens, close to the railway station, the buildings of which would do credit to any large town in England.

Taking the mail train which leaves Durban in the evening, I continued my journey on to the Transvaal, wishing to see for myself the state of things which were supposed to be existing in Johannesburg since the Jameson fiasco. The Natal Railway is simply a triumph of engineering art, conducted on a single line. The manner in which the numerous curves are negotiated whilst winding in and out of the innumerable mountains and valleys, is marvellous if not very reassuring to the passenger, who, until he gets used to it, momentarily expects to be toppled down the side of a precipice or shot over one of the narrow bridges which span the mountain streams.

The journey through the northern part of Natal is very interesting, the scene incessantly changing; the majority of the farm-houses are of the most substantial kind, and prettily situated amongst trees at the foot of the hills. My old friends the Drakensberg Mountains stood up against the sky-line as a boundary between this British country and the two very much the reverse Republics.

On arriving near Newcastle, that ill-omened mountain Majuba is plainly discernible, and it was interesting to watch the different shapes it assumes as the train winds in and out of the hills which have to be traversed before Laing's Nek tunnel is reached, Majuba appearing first on one and then on the other side of the train, as we approach it.

Passing the graveyard where the ill-fated General Colley and the men who fell with him are buried, the train shortly afterwards runs through the tunnel under Laing's Nek which connects Majuba with a similar mountain, and down the slope on the other side, till it reaches Charlestown, the border town of Natal. At this place the engine and staff of the train were changed for the Transvaal officials, and the passengers were treated to a sudden transition from Scotland to Holland. The Natal railways are run almost without exception by Scotchmen, and my introduction to the Transvaal was when my ticket was demanded by a Hollander. After examining it carefully, he appeared to consider it a favour that he handed it back and allowed me to proceed. A short distance from Charlestown

and in sight of it is the Dutch border town of Volksrust.
Dutchwomen in their kappjes, as the large old-fashioned poke
bonnets made of linen are called, and men in their slouch hats
and " crackers " or leather trousers, were to be seen wandering aimlessly about the station and street. The journey
from Volksrust to Standerton is uninteresting, the railroad
passing along large flats of veldt without a break in the
scenery or a tree to be seen till Standerton is reached. The
town itself is a typical Dutch Dorp, a square in the centre
with churches and houses built round it on the side of a hill.
From Standerton to Elandsfontein, the junction of the Cape
and Natal lines, the country is more hilly, especially in the
vicinity of Greylingstaadt, where there is a small range of
mountains running east and west of the line for a considerable
distance. From Elandsfontein Junction, afterwards, during
the war, changed to Germiston, the distance is very short to
Park Station, Johannesburg, the line passing through the
several groups of mines between the two places.

On getting out of the train at Park Station, we were
greeted with familiar calls of touts shouting out the names
of various hotels. Selecting one not far from the station, I
was transported there with my luggage, in the hotel bus, and
found everything much on the same lines as in a good colonial
hotel at Cape Town. I was shown a good room by the
proprietor, who had been a steward on a liner, and who
paid every attention to the comfort of the travellers in the
hotel, which, judged by the number of names on the visitors'
board, must have been a popular one.

The next morning I started to look round the town, and
was much struck with the size of the place, the largeness of
the buildings, the busy thoroughfares, and the crowds of people

on the Market Square and Exchange Buildings. It seemed hardly credible that the town had only been in existence ten years. Every language under the sun was to be heard in the streets—Dutch, English, French, Kaffir, down to the lowest of all languages—Yiddish, which was to be heard at almost every corner, where the Jews seemed to congregate. The Zarps, as the Dutch police are called, were composed of all nationalities except English ; and they swaggered about in their semi-German uniform, with side-arms, as if it was by their consent other people were allowed to be alive in the country.

I met two or three old friends in Commissioner Street, the hub of the town, who impressed upon me the down-trodden condition of everything British in the Transvaal, since the collapse of the Reform Committee ; and who told me that most of the British who had no large interests in the country were clearing out of it, and that nothing good could be derived from the gold mines till the question of British or Dutch supremacy had been settled finally.

That a grievance existed in the minds of the British population against the Dutch Government, was beyond a doubt—but of what the grievance consisted, it was hard for the visitor to obtain any definite understanding, beyond this, that the Colonial or British prospector had found the gold, that British enterprise had worked the mines, and extracted the gold from the country ; and that the Dutch Government, or foreign advisers of the President, had placed prohibitive taxes on the necessaries for the mining industry, such as machinery and dynamite, and on the gold itself. Also, that no mine-owners or directors had any say with the Government as to the administration of the Gold Laws, the franchise not being in existence. No Britisher was allowed to vote towards electing competent members to sit in the Dutch Volksraad, or Parliament, which was practically run by the President and his Hollander Secretary, Leyds. On the other hand, the Dutch took the view that the Raid was nothing more or less than an attempt of the Britishers to get possession of the gold area by force of a rush, a view shared by a good many other people besides the Dutch. They were determined to keep the control of the country in their own hands, and were suspicious of all overtures made by the Randites on any subject connected with the Transvaal, any intervention by the Home Government on behalf of the Uitlanders being deeply resented by the Boers.

My experience of Dutchmen up to my present visit had been limited to the Colonial and some Free State Dutch, but it soon became apparent that the Transvaal Boers in no way differed from those I had been accustomed to in their intense hatred of the British. They had been brought up for generations with the idea that their worst enemy was the British, a feeling that has been not lessened but accentuated to the highest degree since the last war. All the concessions that have been made to them by the Home Government, before and since that campaign, have been accepted by them only as a sign of weakness on the part of the Government, and have strengthened their determination to claim more and more indulgences till they finally get their desire—an independent South Africa, free from the British Crown.

On my return journey to Natal I had to wait a considerable time at Elandsfontein Junction for the Natal train, and amused myself by walking about this mining village. Passing the hotel close to the station, I noticed a group of men who had ridden up to the hotel and, dismounted, were having

25

a heated argument over the decision of a judge at the race meeting they had evidently just returned from. One of them, a typical young Colonial by his appearance, was venting his displeasure in somewhat violent terms, cursing in English and Dutch alternately. Just as I passed, and probably meaning it for my hearing, he shouted as if in answer to some question, "Yes, the swine, English. There is too much of that language spoken in this country. Damn the lot of them." They entered the hotel. I asked one of the hotel attendants, a Jew, who the man was who was so pronounced in his opinions about the English, whose language he appeared to speak so fluently. I was told that he was a Zarp, and that they had been to the races, and lost money over the decision of the judge in a particular race in which some pulling had been indulged in—hence their displeasure. I was not sorry when the train arrived and I was able to get away from such inhospitable regions back to Natal, where one did hear the Queen's English spoken, and people removed their hats when " God save the Queen " was played.

I had made up my mind to remain in Natal until I received communications from my barrister friend in the Cape Colony as to the result of my application to Parliament for an inquiry into my case, and I lost no time in endeavouring to procure a billet in one of the Volunteer corps for which Natal was famous. I interviewed the officer commanding Volunteers and the staff officer, and was fortunate enough to find myself well known to most of them by name, and personally to others, through having served with them in Basutoland. I soon found an opening in the cadet branch, and was given three schools to look after. This kept me going for the time, and after a month or two I found that I had almost every college

and school in Maritzburg on my list; I had to obtain two
assistants, and was fortunate in finding them in an ex-C.M.R.
N.C.O. and an ex-Imperial officer, both of whom worked
right loyally for me up to the time that war broke out,
when they became officers in the Natal Staff and did
well.

The system of cadets at that time in Natal was, to
the best of my belief, unique in the Empire. Every able-
bodied schoolboy in the Colony was compelled to be a cadet,
and it was a pleasure to watch the keen interest these
youngsters took in their work. The efficiency obtained by
them compared very favourably with their older brothers in
the Natal Volunteers, both in their drilling and musketry
attainments.

I have seen between two and three thousand of these boys,
ranging in ages from ten to seventeen, at the camps held
yearly at Durban, going through the physical drill exercise in
their own time to the music of their own bands, from start
to finish without a single mistake and in perfect time, and
the manual and firing exercises before the inspecting officer
would have done credit to any regiment of trained men. The
marching past of the different school corps was equally good.
To see company after company of these well-set-up youngsters
marching past the saluting-post in their uniform of blue
jerseys, with school badge on the left breast, blue knicker-
bockers and stockings, and smart field-service cap of yellow
and black with badges, carbines held steadily at the shoulder,
the different bands taking up the different march tunes as
each school followed in succession, keeping perfect dressing,
amid the cheering of their friends and relations, who crowd
along the line behind the inspecting officer, and are as proud

of their boys as the occasion warrants them to be, is a sight well worth seeing.

I find myself asking if this is not the solution of the problem which is troubling the mother country ? If the Natal method of every able-bodied boy becoming a cadet till his education is completed, then on to the senior cadet corps till he reaches the age of eighteen, then compulsory service in the Militia, and from thence to the Reserves with yearly training, were adopted throughout the British Empire, think of the possibilities of such a movement in the course of a few years! England would possess a civilian population trained from boyhood, and able to hold their own against any combination they would ever be called upon to face in the protection of their native country.

Coming events were already beginning to cast their shadows over Natal. A general feeling of uncertainty as to what was about to happen, became manifest among the people, and it was soon apparent that the military authorities had received some sort of intimation that the men might be required for more serious work than garrison duty.

Maritzburg at that time had three Imperial regiments stationed in the town — the 5th Royal Irish Lancers, the Dublin Fusiliers, and the 3rd Battalion King's Royal Rifles; also the 10th Mountain Battery R.F.A.; while at Ladysmith were the 18th Hussars, and the Gloucester and Leicester Regiments, also Artillery. The Maritzburg garrison were exercised daily in long marches into the country and back, and the marked improvement in the appearance of the men soon became clear, even to outsiders. The first week or so stragglers could be seen from both regiments as they entered Maritzburg on their return to the camp at Fort Napier; but, after a month of hard work, it was a pleasure to watch these regiments—especially the Dublin Fusiliers, or "Dubs," as they were familiarly called by everybody, as they swung up the street to their band, as fresh-looking on their return from a thirty-mile outing as when they started.

The High Commissioner had met Mr. Kruger in Bloemfontein for the purpose of discussing the treatment of the Uitlanders in the Transvaal, but it had ended in Sir Alfred Milner declining to discuss matters any further with the President, owing to the characteristic evasion of the question by the latter. The situation had gone from bad to worse. Hundreds of refugees were arriving in Natal daily from the Transvaal, bringing all kinds of reports as to the threatening attitude of the Boers; later on we heard that the Boers were massing at Sands Spruit, close to the border of Natal.

General Penn Symons, who was commanding the troops in Natal, left for the northern part of Natal, and the Maritzburg garrison followed him. It was a fine sight to see the Dublin Fusiliers marching out of Maritzburg — a splendid battalion of men, mustering 1200 strong, in splendid training and all as keen as mustard at the prospect of a brush with the enemy. The subsequent gallant behaviour of this splendid regiment is now a matter of history in the British army, and was one of the principal reasons of the distinction and honour that have been paid to all Irish regiments by Royalty, in the creation of the Irish Guards.

The movement of the Imperial troops, and the threatening attitude of the Boers on the border, caused the mobilisation of the Natal Volunteers. The Natal Carabineers were among the first to leave for Ladysmith, and the Border Mounted Rifles and Natal Royal Rifles also left for up country.

Just about this time, and not a moment too soon, General Sir George White, with about ten thousand troops, arrived at Durban from India, and practically saved the situation for the time in Natal. They went forward, without stopping, to Ladysmith.

An irregular corps was also raised at Maritzburg, and called the Imperial Light Horse. It was composed of men who had lived in the Transvaal and been compelled to leave their billets owing to the attitude of the Boers, and they were all very anxious to "get their own back." The command of the regiment was given to Colonel Scott Chisholm, who had recently completed his term of service as Colonel of the 5th Lancers, and had remained in Natal anticipating the war that was shortly to take place. He was a fine officer, and very popular with the Lancers. As soon as they were complete, the Imperial Light Horse left for Ladysmith, where General White had concentrated his forces; General Penn Symons having occupied Dundee, a town farther north, with his column, of which the Dublin Fusiliers and the K.R.R. formed part.

Maritzburg was in a great state of excitement when the news arrived that the Boers had anticipated their Declaration of War by advancing into Natal and capturing Charlestown, and were making their way south. A Home Guard was raised, consisting of all the able-bodied civilians of Maritzburg, and leaders elected from amongst the prominent citizens. The Commandant of Volunteers and the whole of his staff had gone forward to Ladysmith on the first movement of the Volunteers, and amongst them my two Assistants; in consequence, I had my hands full with the Cadets and the Home Guard, and wishing to get to the front I was not very contented with my lot.

The news of the battle of Talana Hill, and the death of

General Penn Symons and the subsequent advance of the Boers on to Ladysmith, added to the already panicky state of affairs in Maritzburg. I was very much pleased when the Colonial Secretary sent for me, and told me it had been decided by the Natal Government to raise a Mounted Corps of men, mounted and equipped at the expense of Natal, and to offer their services to the Imperial Government, and asked me to assist them in the matter—the corps to be called the Colonial Scouts.

Notices were sent out calling for volunteers for the Corps, and the show-ground where the headquarters had been placed was soon inundated with applicants to join. Major H——, of the Natal Civil Service was the chief organiser, and I took over the duties as his chief adjutant and adviser. The first squadron of one hundred men was soon raised, and qualified men elected as officers. They were mounted and equipped and sent off to the front, and another squadron taken in hand, which, when completed, was sent off after the first. In this manner the whole five squadrons were raised and ready for the field within eight days, as the squadrons had been sent off independently under their own squadron commanders.

Major H—— did not go up, and as there was no work for an adjutant, I was asked to take command of the last-formed squadron; this I did, and marched away from Maritzburg en route for Mooi River, where a column under General Barton had been concentrated.

The boys of the Cadet bands played my squadron through the Maritzburg streets as far as the bridge on the Swaart Kop road, when they cheered us till we were out of sight. We off-saddled for the night, and I felt exceedingly grateful at getting my first night's sleep for about ten days. The next morning at daylight we resumed our march.   I had been very careful in the selection of the men who composed the Colonial Scouts, the men enlisted being mostly Natal men, who had all had training as Cadets, and could ride well; the balance were men from Cape Colony and Transvaal refugees.   I had also a good many ex-C.M.R. time-expired men, and the whole five hundred were as fine a body of men as any of the corps who had already taken the field.   There were five officers to each squadron, one captain and four lieutenants—each subaltern having a troop of twenty-five men to look after.   I had four excellent subalterns to my squadron, the sergeant-major being an ex-C.M.R. and the rest of the N.C.O.'s carefully selected for their qualifications, and before we reached Mooi River the squadron was almost everything in the shape of efficiency I could wish for, and gave me no trouble whatever, a very rare experience with newly-formed troops.

In the meantime the Boers had advanced on to Ladysmith; the battle of Elandslaagte had been fought, and the Boers were beaten at all points—at the cost of a good many lives to the British, amongst them Colonel Scott Chisholm, the Commanding Officer of the Imperial Light Horse, and Captain Knapp of the same corps.   The latter was an ex-member of the C.M.R. and one of the staff mess I had joined at Butterworth in my early days in the regiment.   The Gordon Highlanders lost heavily, only three of the officers escaping untouched, but they had the satisfaction of killing the German filibuster Colonel Schiel, and a few more adventurers of the same class, who had made themselves particularly obnoxious to the British in the Transvaal on the eve of the war.

It did not take the Boers long to recover from their defeat at Elandslaagte.   Joubert's column advancing from Dundee restored their confidence, and they again moved on towards Ladysmith. General White went out with a strong column to meet them, and to divert the Dutch attack from the British retreating column under General Yule, which had evacuated Dundee and was retiring on Ladysmith. An unsatisfactory action was fought—the British losing about one hundred men in casualties; but General Yule was enabled to reach Ladysmith with his column unmolested, which was the object of General White's movement.

The Free State had decided to join the Transvaal in the war against Britain, and their commanders and the Transvaal troops now joined hands in the vicinity of Ladysmith. General White decided to attack them in force, and endeavour to inflict a severe defeat which would make the Boers give up their invading tactics. The effect of this engagement was disastrous, and resulted in the first reverse our troops sustained.

Colonel Carleton with the 10th Mountain Battery R.F.A., the Royal Irish Fusiliers, and half the Gloucester Regiment, with some of the Hussars, started from Ladysmith at midnight for Nicholson's Nek, for the purpose of taking up a position at that place which would enable him to cover the left flank of the main attack under General White. The main attack was divided into two columns—General White taking the centre, and General Hunter the right, with Carleton's column on the left. Heavy fighting with infantry and artillery took place with the centre and right columns, and a great deal of damage was inflicted on the Boers, but the column eventually had to retire on Ladysmith, when it was discovered that the left column under Colonel Carleton had been surrounded and forced to surrender to the Boers.

This came as a great shock to Natal. It was reported that the mules of the Mountain Battery had bolted with the ammunition, which had caused confusion amongst the column, and the Boers, taking advantage of the mishap, had surrounded them. Whatever the cause may have been, there is no doubt that it had a most damaging effect on the British troops, and, being the first instance of wholesale surrender of a column, without being fired on to any extent, it must have given the Boers a very bad and erroneous impression of the quality of the British Army.

This disaster put a stop to General White's offensive tactics. The garrison were now practically besieged; the last train had passed the Tugela River, and communication with the other column was cut off. Our nearest position south of Ladysmith was Estcourt, with Major-General Hildyard, who had recently arrived with reinforcements, in command. The garrison only consisted of three or four battalions of infantry, one of which was the Durban Light Infantry, two squadrons of Colonial Scouts, and some batteries of Artillery; also the 2nd Battalion Dublin Fusiliers, who had been sent back from Ladysmith after the retreat from Dundee to recuperate after their losses at Talana Hill, where they greatly distinguished themselves by taking the position at the point of the bayonet.

The Boers had by this time completely surrounded Ladysmith, and a large number of them had crossed the Tugela River, occupying Colenso, from which they were sending out looting parties to the surrounding farms. It was expected that they would push on towards Maritzburg. General Barton was in command at Mooi River, and troops were daily arriving for Estcourt or Mooi River. The next bad piece of news that we received was of the Armoured Train disaster, by which a party of Dublin Fusiliers and Durban Light Infantry under Captain Haldane, whilst reconnoitring from Estcourt in the direction of the enemy, had been held up at Chieveley, a number of the men killed, wounded, and taken prisoners, only a few escaping on the engine and tender, amongst the captured being Captain Haldane and Winston Churchill. The latter accompanied the train as war correspondent, and behaved extremely well in the trying time which ensued when the trucks became derailed and the Boers poured in a steady fire at close range.

Rumours of all kinds were floating about Mooi River, that the Boers were marching on to Maritzburg, and that Estcourt would shortly be besieged, and Mooi River in turn would be cut off. The period of inaction we were subjected to at that time was inexplicable to myself and other men who knew the Dutch. There were at least 8000 British troops in Estcourt, and 6000 at Mooi River, and we were allowing ourselves to be turned out at all hours of the day and night in anticipation of a Boer attack. The merest glimpse of a smasher hat on the skyline in any direction was sufficient for a patrol to saddle up and cautiously ride in the direction of the supposed enemy. The whole thing was very depressing.

Knowing, as a good many of us with Colonial experience did know, that the only way to fight the Boer is to play him at his own game, meeting him with mounted men on all his foraging expeditions, or cutting him off from his main body, it was very galling to see the numbers of infantry that were being massed before any forward move was made. The infantry did well. No troops in the world could have done better, if they could have done as well on all occasions, as the British infantryman, but it was heartbreaking work for them—trudging out from camp six or seven miles, owing to a false report of the enemy being in a position, and then back to their camps at night. It would have disgusted most men, but Tommy was as cheerful as possible, and took it all in a day's-work style that could only be admired.

I maintain, and always will, that if the country had been flooded with mounted infantry and Colonial troops well mounted, with infantry simply used for lines of communication, the Boer War would not have lasted six months:· fighting them in their own ways — rushing their positions mounted—with a chance of cutting them off—and not paying too much attention to white flags. The Dutchmen will not stand when the odds are not in their favour. Once get them on the run, they will not stop as long as there is any chance of a pursuit till they reach their homes, bury their rifles, produce their family Bibles, and swear that they have never left their homesteads. I know the breed, and any man who does, bears me out in this sidelight of the Boer character.

We heard the guns of the fight at Willow Grange and reports that our people were not getting the best of it, but no move was made from Mooi River—and it seemed to us that the name of General "Stand-back," which had been given by the troops to the commanding officer of the garrison, was not inappropriate. The rubbing-in part came when the Boers, numbering some two or three hundred with two guns, actually came on the ridge between Highlands Station and Mooi River and commenced shelling the bridge which spans the river.

No attempt was made on our part to spoil their target

practice, but when they finished their fun at our expense, and returned whence they came, Thorneycroft's Mounted Infantry were sent after them to see the direction they went in. They returned to camp, having lost one man killed and two or three men wounded, after seeing the Boers rejoin their main body. This was evidently as far south as the Boers cared to venture, for in the next few days they had entirely disappeared from the vicinity of Estcourt, and communications with that place were again open.

It was most welcome news when we heard that General Buller had arrived in Maritzburg and was shortly to come to the front. The spirits of the whole garrison began to revive after the heartbreaking inaction of the last month. Orders were received for General Barton to proceed to Estcourt with our brigade, which was done, the infantry marching with the mounted men by the road; the distance of twenty odd miles' hard going was covered in the day, the splendid infantry not turning a hair. On arrival at Estcourt we found that General Hildyard's force were all ready to move forward to Frere, for which place they started the following morning, Barton's brigade remaining at Estcourt.

It was a fine sight to see the Naval Brigade arriving at Estcourt the day after us, bringing with them powerful 12-inch guns firing lyddite shells, which we all fondly hoped would pulverise the Boers. They also brought some 4·7-guns with them, and the sailors looked in such splendid condition and so fit for anything that they were quite refreshing to look at. Estcourt was now full of generals, and troops were arriving daily till there must have been at least 20,000 men of all arms at Frere and Estcourt.

CHAPTER XXV.

1889–1901.

GENERAL BULLER went through to Frere the first week
in December. It was not long before we got orders to
proceed there also, and we went into camp not far from the
station.

Lord Dundonald was in command of the Cavalry Brigade,
and constant patrolling and reconnaissance parties were the
order of the day. During one of these patrols three of
my scouts rode into some Boers, mistaking them for our
own men. One of them managed to escape, but the other
two were wounded and captured. These Boers were close on
to Chieveley at the time they were seen, and it was rather a
surprise, as they were not supposed to be anywhere south of
Colenso. They soon made off when they found they had been
discovered, but I lost my two men.

It was now apparent from the preparations that a

forward move of the whole army was about to take place, and
orders were issued to the different brigades as to the positions
they were to take up. The Cavalry Brigade formed the
seventh, and were to take up position on the right flank of
the general advance. On the morning of the 15th December
the advance began.

It was a magnificent spectacle—as far as the eye could see,
regiment on regiment of infantry moving in perfect order
over the long slope of veldt, which runs from Chieveley down
to Colenso and the river Tugela. I was greatly surprised at
the absence of any attempt to screen the front of the advancing troops by cavalry, and at no scouts being utilised in
any way to safeguard the infantry advance. The cavalry being
right away on the right flank, and advancing in the direction
of Hlangwani Hill, could not very well see what was taking
place in the centre and on the left flanks of the army, and
when about half-past six in the morning a most terrific crash
of musketry broke out on our left front, it was plain to every
body that our troops had fallen into one of the various traps
the wily Boer usually lays for the unprepared enemy.

No excuse can be made for the blunder which had been
committed. The infantry and artillery had been sent to
occupy positions the approaches to which had not been scouted
—a blunder which would have been considered unpardonable
if a captain had taken a squadron of men to the position.

I am afraid that too much confidence was placed by our
generals in the various statements made by the natives or
irresponsible Natal farmers, who were always ready to
volunteer statements as to the actual position of the Boers,
and too little confidence in the intelligence of the Colonial
volunteer in his capacity as a scout. As a result, troops were

often sent on wild-goose chases about the country on the strength of reports that were without foundation—episodes of this kind lessening the confidence of the men in their officers and very considerably demoralising the troops. Of one thing I am certain—that had any one of the mounted corps been sent in advance of the army, the whole of the Boer position south of the river would have been exposed without a tenth of the casualties being incurred by our troops.

The Boers had at length shown the cards which they had been holding up their sleeves for years past, and they were a revelation even to men who had spent their lives amongst them. How they managed to procure such splendid artillery and up-to-date rifles without the knowledge of the British War Office, is a mystery. The shell-fire that greeted the British at Colenso was a terrific one, and it was wonderful how little attention the men paid to it, considering it was the first time, I suppose, that any man in the army had been under shell-fire, this being the first occasion the British Army had met a white race in warfare in the present generation.

The roar of the big guns and rattle of musketry was kept up, with various slight lulls, all the morning, except in the brigades on the right, who failed to back up the mounted troops in their attack on Hlangwani Hill. The position which General Buller subsequently found was the key to Ladysmith, and which was actually in our possession for a time, had to be abandoned, for a misunderstanding evidently existed between Lord Dundonald and General Barton, and the latter did not back up the attack. A number of infantry who had reached the banks of the river below the Hlangwani Hill were cut off in the retirement which followed, and were taken prisoners by the Boers. There were a great many casualties among the mounted troops, but not nearly so many as was to be expected from the heavy fire directed on us.

The general retirement was now made back to Chieveley— the troops returning as if they were coming home after a field day; and it was not till we returned to camp that we knew the extent of the damage that had been inflicted on our force, and learnt the details from the Natal papers the following day. The abandonment of two batteries of guns was a very sore subject for weeks; nothing would persuade any member of the force that the guns could not have been recovered if the general had wished, and the feeling was general that the Boers could not take any credit for their share in the matter.

The mounted men were moved back to Frere owing to the scarcity of water at Chieveley, and the Scouts moved back two squadrons to Mooi River and one to Nottingham Road, where the Durban Light Infantry had been stationed since Willow Grange. My squadron was stationed at Mooi River, from which place we were constantly patrolling with the 19th Hussars in the direction of the Drakensberg Mountains.

General Buller was evidently intending to await further reinforcements before making another forward move; and there being nothing to interfere with sports, etc., Christmas was kept up in great style at all the camps from Chieveley to Nottingham Road—cricket matches and foot sports being largely indulged in, whilst the cases of special luxuries in the shape of provisions which arrived for all the troops testified to the liberality of the good citizens of Natal.

General Sir Charles Warren arrived with a brigade about the New Year. The army must by this time have numbered close on 30,000 men, and everybody was wondering

26

at the delay in moving forward to make another attempt to relieve Ladysmith. The Boers were apparently tired of inaction and of waiting for the army to advance, so they caused a diversion by attacking Ladysmith on 6th January. We were all very much relieved when the news came through by heliograph that the garrison had held their own in the face of a determined attempt on the part of the Boers to carry the place by assault.

We anxiously awaited the list of casualties; when we did receive it, it was rather a formidable one. Amongst the number, I regret to say, was one of my younger brothers, two of whom were at the front, who had been severely wounded. He died subsequently from the effects. This news made me more anxious if possible to get to grips with the Boers without further delay.

Troops were now moved forward again. An advance was made in the direction of Springfield, and the Tugela River was crossed by a division of the army under Sir Charles Warren, the mounted men being utilised mostly in protecting the flanks of the infantry.

After six days' incessant fighting, in which small progress was made, Spion Kiop was occupied by our troops under General Woodgate. Severe fighting took place on the top of this position. Through some blunder, our troops, when they arrived on the summit, did not occupy the whole of the position, which was strongly held at that time by the Boers, but allowed the enemy to remain in position at the end of the plateau, where they were quickly reinforced by men and guns and poured a heavy fire into our troops, who were unnecessarily crowded into a small space. General Woodgate was mortally wounded, and the command was given to

Colonel Thorneycroft, who, with his corps of Mounted Rifles, formed part of the attacking force. The troops more than held their own till night came on, when for some reason unknown Colonel Thorneycroft ordered a retirement, and Spion Kop was abandoned. The Boers had also had enough, and retired, so the kop was unoccupied for some time with the exception of killed and wounded. The Boers, as usual, were the first to discover the mistake that had been made, and returned to the summit and re-occupied the place; they allowed our medical staff and burial parties to proceed with their work of burying the dead and carrying away the wounded.

General Buller must have received a shock when he heard that Spion Kop had been abandoned and General Warren was re-crossing the Tugela. He hurried down from his headquarters, and watched the troops re-crossing the river on their return to Springfield. The second attempt to get to Ladysmith failed as the first one did, through a blunder.

Bethune's Mounted Infantry and S.A.L. Horse were sent away to the east of Chieveley towards Weenan County to endeavour to draw part of the Boers in that direction, and the Colonial Scouts were ordered to proceed to Zululand to worry the Boers who were occupying Helpmakaar at the end of the range of Biggarsburg Mountains. Leaving a troop to remain as bodyguard to the general, we entrained and proceeded to Durban, where we took the coast line to Zululand and marched to Eshowe, the principal town in Zululand, which we found garrisoned by the Natal Volunteers, some regulars, and Naval Brigade with 4·7-inch guns. The independent squadrons having been now merged into a regiment, with a colonel and an adjutant, had been sent to us. The colonel had served in the Natal Volunteers for many years, and was in command of the Border Mounted Rifles at the time when the Natal Government appointed him to command the Scouts. He brought his adjutant with him from the B.M.R. The colonel was supposed to have a thorough knowledge of the Zulu language and country—hence the appointment. We left Eshowe for the north of Zululand the day after our arrival, leaving all our wagons and stores at that place, and taking only what we could carry on our horses; the idea being to live on the country for food, and to enable us to get about more freely in the mountainous district we were proceeding to. After a couple of days' marching we got into very rough country; heavy rains set in accompanied by mist, which made it impossible to see a hundred yards in any direction. It was a very trying time both for men and horses. We were soaked through; we had no food; the rain formed pools of water where we were standing, and it was impossible to lie down, as there was no shelter of any description where we had halted. Colonel A—— managed to get some natives to sell us mealies, and we subsisted during the deluge on these alone, sharing with our horses. I don't think anybody knew what part of the country we were in, and the fact of the natives having taken us for Boers, and not being surprised at our appearance, was proof enough that we had arrived on the Boers' hunting-ground for supplies.

The natives were astonished when they were offered payment for the mealies, and still more so when Colonel A—— informed them that we were British. We were told that a commando of Boers had passed the native kraals two days before, collecting sheep and goats, and had not returned, and that we were on a mountain overlooking Isandlwana of ill-fame on one side and Helpmakaar in front of us, where the Boers were in possession with some artillery. There was nothing to be done except remain where we were till the weather cleared, and console ourselves with the knowledge that if we were getting soaked through and no sleep, our friends the Boers were in a similar condition, and it was no use grumbling.

As soon as the weather moderated, we made the best of our way down the side of the mountain on to the flat, where to our delight we discovered a store kept by a Scotchman with his wife and two daughters. They immediately set to work, and in a very short time hundreds of loaves of fresh bread made their appearance. These and a plentiful supply of tinned meats, washed down by coffee, made the last three days of misery fade from our memories. As our clothes got dry they completely vanished.

We found that we were on the battlefield of Isandlwana, where the 24th Regiment had been massacred during the Zulu War of 1879. The graves were still visible. We were told that the Boers had returned in the direction of Rorke's Drift to Helpmakaar, and that they had not interfered with the store in any way. Colonel A—— seemed anxious to get out of the neighbourhood, for some reason, and the regiment marched on to N'qutu, a small magistracy on the borders of Zululand and Natal, where we found a small detachment of Natal Police, with the Magistrate and two stores, in one of which I recognised the owner as an old Umtata man whom I had known well a few years before. He was very pleased to see me and took me to his house, where I was entertained at dinner, and spent a pleasant hour chatting over old times. The Magistrate did not seem to welcome the visit of Colonel A—— and his men in the spirit he should have done, and complained that the Boers, who had hitherto left them alone, might now come and attack the place. He asked Colonel A—— to withdraw, and the regiment was marched to a camping-ground about two miles distant from the magistracy, where we remained while patrols were sent out, and information as to the Boer movements was being collected from natives, with whom Colonel A—— seemed to have perfect understanding.

One afternoon, shortly after the arrival of one of these native spies in the camp, Colonel A—— became very much excited, and shouted for the horses to be brought in and the men to saddle up. He mounted, and taking with him the men who were ready, rode off, telling me to follow as soon as possible with the remainder. We started off along the Eshowe road, and, having my suspicions about the cause of this sudden departure, I questioned some natives as to what news they had brought; they told me that the Boers were coming to N'qutu, bringing their big guns with them, but how far off they were they did not know.

The Maxim gun which had been attached to the Scouts on the expedition, and which was manned by a sergeant and privates of the Natal Police, was trotting after the others, when I stopped it and told the sergeant the state of affairs, and ordered him to remain with my squadron till the others had saddled up and followed the colonel. On making in-quiries, I found that the other squadrons had gone off, leaving the men who had been posted as videttes still out on the veldt, and in ignorance of the move which had been made; I sent men out to call them in, and by the time they were all collected it was dark and commencing to rain. I then marched off with my squadron and the Maxim gun along the road the rest of the regiment had taken.

I sent on a sergeant with a message to the colonel, telling him that I had been delayed getting in the videttes, that the Maxim gun horses were getting somewhat knocked up, and that I could not go much farther; I asked for instructions, and halted my squadron on the banks of a small stream to await the reply. The sergeant returned about midnight, and confirmed my suspicions that we were simply bolting from the Boers. He informed me that the rest of the regiment were halted on the road leading down from the high plateau we were on to the low country in the direction of Eshowe—that the men were stretched all along the road, sitting down in the rain, holding their horses, which remained saddled, and, having guessed what was the matter, were grumbling and swearing at the manner in which they were being treated. They were about five miles distant, and the colonel had given orders for me to come on as soon as possible.

At daybreak, as soon as the surrounding country became visible, I moved on with the men and Maxim. We could see for miles around us in the direction of N'qutu, and not a living thing was visible. We were all wet through and very miserable, and matters were not much improved when we arrived where the rest of the regiment had bivouacked the night before and found the place deserted. The colonel with the rest of the men had continued their retiring move to the N'kandhla forest, where we finally overtook them.

No explanations were given except that the wagons with provisions and grain were on the way from Eshowe to meet us. Later in the day a Natal Policeman with a civilian rode up to where we were encamped, and informed the colonel that N'qutu had been captured by the Boers early that morning—the Magistrate with his staff and Natal Policemen, together with the civilian inhabitants, taken prisoners, and sent off to Dundee.

Our informants had ridden off when they heard the Magistrate give the order that there was to be no resistance to the Boers' occupation, an order which confirmed the suspicions that had already been aroused as to the Magistrate's being a pro-Boer. One of our Scouts who had been sent to gaol at N'qutu by the colonel for picking some mealies from the native lands, had also been made a prisoner with the others and sent away.

The wagons shortly afterwards arrived. Tents were pitched, and a camp formed on a nek between two hills at the side of N'kandhla bush. The Boers only numbered a few hundreds with four field guns, and after looting N'qutu, they followed our tracks along the ridges, till, finding that we had left the high country, and were not likely to give them any trouble, they turned their attention to the magistracy at N'kandhla. At this place they were forestalled by the Magistrate, who after blowing up the magazine rode off with the few remaining white men to Melmoth, where some K.R. Rifles and two squadrons of Colonial Scouts were stationed. These squadrons had been raised in Maritzburg after the departure of our five squadrons for the front, and had been sent round to Zululand as soon as they were completed. We had not come into touch with them up to the present, and the colonel did not seem anxious to make any effort to do so. We heard the explosion of the magazine at N'kandhla, and received information from native spies that the Boers had occupied the place. But for a considerable time no attempts were made on our part to find out what strength they were in, or what they were doing so far away from their base at Helpmakaar.

After a long time had been wasted in waiting to see whether the Boers intended making any further move in the direction of Eshowe, we made a move in the direction of N'kandhla magistracy. The road was a footpath through the forest and could only be traversed in single file, and my squadron was to form the advance guard. I took with me half the squadron, dismounted, and, leaving our horses to be led with the remainder of the column, we commenced our march through the forest just after sundown, with native constables of the Native Police as guides. The footpath wound in and out, up and down in the forest, sometimes through dense bush, and then across an open glade, which had to be crossed in the moonlight, and from which we could see the overhanging rocks on the top of the forest on the high country away in our front. After marching about three hours in single file, we reached the foot of the ascent leading up to the top of the forest, and on to the bare country surrounding N'kandhla magistracy. I halted to give my men a rest, and to await the arrival of the remainder, who were delayed owing to the difficulty experienced in leading the horses along the slippery footpaths.

The colonel and the rest of the squadrons having arrived, a further rest was given, and we then pushed forward up the hill. It was terrible going—the footpath seemed to be almost perpendicular in places, and the thick overhanging trees made it impossible to tell what progress we were making. I was walking behind the native guide, with my sergeant-major and the remainder of the troop in file following me. The strictest silence was observed, as we expected to find a Boer picquet on the top of the mountain where the footpath emerged into the open country. The plan had been given out that the column was to reach the magistracy by daylight, and the grey dawn was appearing before we at last reached the summit of the forest and stepped into the open.

Not a sign of a Boer was to be seen. We went forward till we struck the main road from Eshowe to N'kandhla, which encircled the forest. I extended my men right and left of the road, and we went along as fast as we could walk and got over the ground very well considering the fatiguing time we had experienced during the night.

We came across several small stretches of water swollen from the recent rain, but they did not stop us. Catching hold of one another's rifles, the men waded through the water, which in some instances reached as high as their chests. The cool water acted as a stimulant to our over-heated bodies, and the thin khaki clothes we wore dried on us as we marched. We were now nearing N'kandhla, and the remainder of the column had not put in an appearance, but I knew that they would probably trot on after us, when they got through the bush, and expected them to arrive any moment.

At last we topped the ridge and saw N'kandhla lying on the nek between two hills in front of us, about four hundred yards from where we were. Some figures could be seen in the dim morning light, close to a building on which a flag was flying, but the light was too bad to distinguish whether it was the Union Jack or the Vierkleur (the Dutch flag).

Looking back I could see our mounted men some four hundred yards off, coming on at a trot, the colonel in front. So, waving my hat to him, we doubled down an incline towards a building which stood enclosed in a garden surrounded with sod walls, through which a stream ran below the magistracy on the ridge.

We had almost reached the walls before we were seen by the people we had observed on the ridge, and it is doubtful whether they saw my party first or the mounted men who were following, as the shots which announced our discovery were not aimed at my party. My men opened fire, and we ran past the building, through the stream, and up towards the magistracy; as we reached the level, a hundred yards from the nearest house, we saw twenty or thirty mounted Boers galloping out of the place, and disappearing off the ridge at the back.

We were the first up to the buildings, and I felt much pleasure in hauling down the flag, which was found to be a small Vierkleur. I stuck to it, and it is in my possession to this day. The mounted men pursued in the direction the Boers had taken, but could not get within range of them, as they rode in amongst some hills where it was not thought advisable to follow them without reconnoitring.

We took up our quarters at N'kandhla, my squadron occupying the deserted store we had passed on our way to the magistracy — the colonel and the other squadrons taking up their position on the ridge by the magistracy and post office. We found everything had been wantonly destroyed by the Boers; articles they had not required were broken up or burnt. Some of my men were completely knocked up by our unaccustomed foot-march; as for myself, I simply could not have moved if the Boers had returned any time during two days after our arrival.

Shortly afterwards we came into touch with the garrison at Melmoth, and patrols were kept up by both parties till the

Boers withdrew from Zululand, the reverses to their forces round Ladysmith requiring their presence in that part of the country. We got into heliographic communication with the B.M.I., and heard the latest news from the Column—that Buller had met with a third repulse in attempting to force his way to Ladysmith, and that the troops were now about to attempt another advance. We also got orders to return to Eshowe, as the Boers had finally evacuated Zululand. We returned to Eshowe in time to take part in some sports that had been organised by the Natal Royal Rifles. They were a great success, much amusement being afforded by the Naval Brigade in their attempted feats at horsemanship in the mounted wrestling combats.

Two days after our return to Eshowe, I received orders for my squadron to act as escort to two naval guns and their crews, who were returning to H.M.S. *Terrible* at Durban, the ship having received orders to proceed to China.

I was to see them safely across the Tugela and entrained for Durban before returning to Eshowe. We had a most enjoyable trip; the sailors and my men became great friends, and it was a very usual thing to see ten or twenty of my men on the drag-ropes of the heavy 4·7-guns, and the Bluejackets riding on their horses very much pleased with themselves. A lieutenant and a midshipman were the two officers with the guns; both were disgusted at not having had a shot at the Boers, having been at Eshowe since they landed at the commencement of the war. We crossed the guns safely over the Tugela, swinging them across on the wire hawser. Leaving my squadron to rest the horses, I accompanied the sailors to Durban, where they embarked on their ship. I parted from them at the station, and received as they proceeded three cheers for the " 'Orse Soldier Officer " such as only sailors can give.

The news had arrived at Durban that Buller's last attempt to get through the Boer position had been successful, and that the Boers were in full retreat; also that Ladysmith was practically relieved. I returned to the Tugela by the first train, and hurried back to Eshowe with my men as soon as possible, where I found everybody celebrating the Relief of Ladysmith. Colonel A—— received orders to return to Maritzburg, and the Scouts were disbanded, the Natal troops having completed their share of the campaign with the relief of Ladysmith. A great many of the disbanded Natal corps joined the Imperial Light Horse and other irregular corps, and did very good service. After superintending the handing in of equipments and horses for the whole Scouts, I reported myself at Ladysmith, and was attached to the Staff pending a vacancy in an irregular corps.

Ladysmith was a scene of wild disorder. Train-loads of stores were arriving constantly; the railway had been repaired, and the inhabitants looked particularly well and happy after the trying time they had experienced during the siege. The troops were all moved out from Ladysmith, and a large camp was formed on the Modder River; the Boers still occupied the Biggarsburg Range, and daily skirmishes took place between our irregular cavalry and small parties of the enemy. On 10th April the Boers hauled a big gun to the top of a high hill and treated the whole camp to a shell fire, and it was not till the troops moved forward to attack the position that they vanished as quickly as they had appeared.

When the troops had had a good rest, General Buller

began his forward advance to Northern Natal and the Transvaal, the Boers retiring before the advance, and offering slight opposition. General Hildyard had command of the left of the army, which was extended to make the flanking movement over the Drakensberg Mountains. This made the defence of Majuba Hill and Lang's Nek impossible by the enemy, against the advance of the main army under General Buller. The squadron of Light Horse to which I had been posted was attached to General Hildyard's Brigade, and we were used mostly for scouting purposes. On the Queen's Birthday, while approaching Danahauser Station, a party of Boers fired into us from a hill at the back of the little village, and managed to hit seven of us—myself included—four of the seven being killed.

This was the finish of my Natal Campaign. I was sent to Mooi River Hospital, where I remained in company with other unfortunates who had been wounded from time to time during the relief operations, and were not sufficiently re- covered to be sent on to other hospitals in Maritzburg—till a new hospital was erected at Howick, a suitable spot for invalids, to which a great many wounded were forwarded.

I remained there several months before it was decided to send me to England. On the voyage between Durban and Cape Town, my wound, which was in the groin, gave trouble, and I was landed at Cape Town and sent to Wynberg Hospital, where after a month's gradual improvement I was ordered home to Netley, there to recover or pass in my checks as the case might be. There were some sixteen hundred of us officers, N.C.O.'s, and men on the ship *Aurania*, which had been converted for the purpose of transporting invalids, and took us from Cape Town to Southampton.

CHAPTER XXVI.

1901–1902.

THE voyage and the good treatment at Netley soon pulled me round, and three months after admission I walked out with the aid of one stick quite comfortably, with three months' leave to enjoy myself amongst my relations, whom I now met for the first time since leaving home twenty-one years before.

It was at Netley that the reverse side of war was brought home to any thinking person. Hundreds of young soldiers of all branches were there walking about with cork legs, or minus arms, or otherwise permanently damaged. They were all quite cheerful, contented to remain cripples for life in the knowledge that they had done credit to their Queen and regiment. I remember one young private of the 5th Lancers who had lost both his legs by a shell at Ladysmith. He had been provided with a pair of cork ones as a substitute, and used to afford any amount of amusement to the onlooker in the grounds at Netley, by his endeavours to walk without the aid of his crutches. He used to come some awful-looking croppers, but he always got up laughing and had another shot, till some hospital attendant would assist him round.   A remark this young fellow made to me one morning showed the hold General Buller had on the hearts of the army in Natal.   He had recognised me as having seen me in Natal, and invariably squared himself up on his cork legs, with his back to a tree, and treated me to a salute as I passed to my accustomed seat in the grounds, accompanied by my sister, who spent every day at the hospital with me.   I expressed my sympathy with him in having been so badly knocked about, but the youngster replied with a smile, "Yes, it is a bit rough; but never mind, sir, we would do the same again for Buller, wouldn't we?"

I was not permitted to enjoy my full three months' holiday with my relations.   In a little more than two months from leaving Netley I received a letter from the War Office informing me that I was to sail by the *Avoca*, sailing a week from date of notice, and report myself fit for service at the Cape.

On reaching Cape Town, and proceeding to the castle to report myself, I was informed that Colonel Steinaecker had offered me the position of adjutant in his regiment, and in the event of my accepting the billet, I was to proceed to Maritzburg in Natal, where the depôt of the regiment was stationed.   Some months previously, while at Howick Hospital, I had met Colonel Steinaecker, who was an inmate of the place, recovering from an attack of malarial fever.   He had known me in Cape Colony during my service in the C.M.R., and he asked me if ever I was fit enough to take the field again whether I would go to his regiment of Irregulars which was serving in the low country of the Eastern Transvaal.   I promised him I would, and was very pleased to find on my arrival at Cape Town that the colonel had not forgotten our conversation.

I accepted the offer and continued my journey on the *Avoca* to Durban, at which place I landed, and wired to Maritzburg, informing the officer commanding the depôt of Steinaecker's Horse of my arrival, and that I was leaving for Maritzburg that evening. I was extremely gratified on the arrival of the train to find Colonel Steinaecker himself on the platform waiting to greet me. He carried me off to the Imperial Hotel, where he was staying, and had also taken a room for myself, and before we retired for the night I was well posted in the doings of his corps, and the events that had happened in the Transvaal during my absence from the country.

The following morning I accompanied Colonel Steinaecker to the Show Ground, where some fifty or sixty men of Steinaecker's Horse were being prepared to join the regiment up country. They appeared a likely enough lot, all of them having served six months or more in one of the corps at the front. The rate of pay given to Steinaecker's Horse was higher than, that given to any other corps at that time serving in the field, owing to the fever-stricken district in which the regiment was called upon to serve, the Transvaal-Portuguese Border. There was thus no difficulty in obtaining good men for the corps, notwithstanding the fact that the mortality in the regiment was far in excess of that of any other in the Transvaal.

I found the subaltern in command at the depôt a very smart young fellow, who had been seconded from the Lanca-shire Fusiliers to Steinaecker's Horse, and was now enjoying

27

the delights of Maritzburg after a year spent in the low
country.   He had suffered from several attacks of malarial
fever, but seemed to have quite shaken them off by the change
of climate.   He spoke enthusiastically of the corps and the
work they had been doing in the Bush country, and told
me that the men were very rough material, but only "wanted
handling."   I was shortly to discover that they needed it
badly.   Discipline was not one of the strong features of the
regiment up to the time of my joining the corps.

Colonel Steinaecker, who was about to pay a visit to
Newcastle in Natal before rejoining at Komati Poort, gave
me orders to proceed the following day with as many men
as were ready to join the headquarters of the regiment at
Komati Poort.   We entrained in the evening, and began our
long railway journey through Natal on to the Transvaal.

On crossing the border at Charlestown, the train travelled
at a slower rate of speed than in Natal, and at dusk we were
shunted into a siding at the town we happened to reach,
where we remained till the following morning, when we
proceeded as usual.   This, I was told, was due to train
wrecking tactics of the enemy, who had been particularly
busy at this special time in doing as much damage to the
railway and to travellers as they could, by placing charges of
dynamite under the railway lines at spots most advantageous
for themselves, to enable them to do the necessary looting
without fear of reprisals.

In course of time we reached Pretoria without mishap,
and changed trains on to the Eastern line or Delagoa Bay
Railway.   About a hundred men of the Liverpool Regiment
joined the train at Pretoria on their way to rejoin their
regiment at Waterfall.   The same precautions were observed

as before, but on this occasion they did not avail us. On the afternoon of the second day, when about two miles from Belfast Station, an explosion was heard, and we were all violently jerked off our seats in the carriages. It did not take long to realise what had happened, for the pit-pot of the Mauser and the crash of a pom-pom showed that we were held up.

Jumping out of the carriage as quickly as I could, I found the men tumbling out of their carriages into the ditch that lined the railroad—Steinaecker's Horse and Liverpools mixed up. We found that the engine had been blown off the rails, and one truck full of goods was lying on its side; the Boers, who were on a hill about three hundred yards away, were firing into us for all they were worth with their Mausers and a pom-pom which they had with them. They got a surprise packet on this occasion for which they had not reckoned. We got the men well under cover, and ran alongside the line to the front of the engine and poured in a heavy fire on the attacking party, who found that instead of the train-load of provisions they had expected to obtain, they had nearly two hundred men all prepared for the emergency, and just as keen on the fight as they were. After a quarter of an hour had passed in exchanging a good many rounds of ammunition, the Boers suddenly ceased firing and disappeared from the position they had occupied — their movements no doubt hastened by the appearance of some mounted men from Belfast. We found that only three casualties had occurred on our side—two of the Liverpools and one of my men being hit, but not dangerously.

We marched on to Belfast Station, where we remained for the night, while a gang of men repaired the damaged line and brought the train on, with the exception of the engine and the one truck.   The next morning we resumed our journey, and eventually arrived at Komati Poort without further alarming incidents.   Komati Poort is the last station in the Transvaal before crossing the Crocodile River into Portuguese territory, and is the hottest place in South Africa. At the time of my arrival it was garrisoned by the Duke of Cornwall's Light Infantry, a battery of Artillery, and the headquarters of Steinaecker's Horse.   It was also the terminus of the Imperial Military Railway, and there was a large staff of the I.M.R. in the place.

A wood-and-iron building twenty yards from the railway station was the only hotel in the village, and in spite of the rigour of martial law it was evidently doing a good business in the thirst-quenching line—judging by the crowd of people who were hanging over the verandah surrounding the building, watching our arrival.

The direction of the camp was pointed out to me by one of the Station Military Police, and, leaving our baggage at the station till called for, I proceeded with the men in that direction, followed by ten or twelve disreputable-looking men in riding breeches and shirt sleeves, wearing dilapidated-looking smashers with the badge S.H. on one side, showing me that they were members of the corps.   They were all more or less in a state of semi-intoxication, and inclined to be friendly in a patronising manner.   I deferred telling them what I thought of their manner till a more suitable occasion.

After walking about eight hundred yards through sandy country with bushes and trees dotted about, which put me very much in mind of parts of Matabeleland, we came to a large wood-and-iron double-storeyed building built on

a ridge of rock, which I was informed were the headquarters.

I was met by an elderly man in shirt-sleeves—I had not
met any one with the slightest suspicion of a coat on, up to
date—who informed me that he was the quartermaster, and
the sole representative of the officers of the regiment; that
the squadrons were all away on the border, and would not
return to Komati Poort till the following week; and that the
few stragglers who had accompanied us from the Station Hotel
were the rank and file of the regiment who had been left
behind for various reasons when the regiment left, some
months previously, on an expedition to Swaziland. The
quartermaster added pathetically that he could do nothing
with them.

Below the ridge of rocks was a sandy flat on which had
been built very fine stables, capable of holding three hundred
horses; a few tents were dotted about the vicinity, this was
without any regard to regularity; the site, I was informed,
where the camp was fixed when the troops happened to be in
Komati Poort, which I judged was a rare occurrence.

A wagon was sent off to the station to bring our baggage
to camp, and a sufficient number of marquee tents having
been drawn from the regimental store and erected, I soon
had my detachment under canvas—in the shape of a properly
pitched camp.

The guard tent, which was pitched at the entrance of the
camp, and was taken possession of by the guard, with a
sentry mounted in front of it, was the subject of much
adverse criticism on the part of a few who, while the camp
was being pitched, had contented themselves with •looking
on whilst my men were working, and had not offered to do a

stroke. I found that the messing arrangements were of a very primitive order. There was no officers' mess; the quartermaster messed by himself, but invited me to partake of his hospitality till I could make arrangements for myself. On inquiring the reason of some of the men being in the disreputable state I had found them in the village, I was told that the hotel was kept by a Greek, and that although the selling of liquor was strictly forbidden except by a written permit, the men of Steinaecker's Horse had no difficulty whatever in getting as much as they wished. The regulars who were camped on the other side of the Crocodile River, on the Lebombo Hills, with the exception of one company stationed in the village, were not allowed near the hotel, but no notice being taken by the Military Police when any members of Steinaecker's Horse visited the hotel, the habit had grown till it had reached rather serious dimensions. The men drank more than was good for them in the tropical climate, and they had been dying in rather alarming proportions from fever.

I determined that a fresh start should be made with the advent of the fifty men I had brought with me, and issued orders that no man was allowed to enter the village except on duty. I also wrote to the commandant, requesting him to give orders to the Military Police to arrest any man found in the village unless on duty. This had a good effect. The old hands muttered rebellion, but as they were in a minority they sulkily accepted the order, and waited the return of the squadron to see how long it would hold good.

I found that the corps had latterly received two hard knocks. One had taken place at an out-station called M'pisane's, where the whole detachment of thirty-five men had been killed or taken prisoners by a Dutch commander under Ben Viljoen. Captain Francis, who was well known throughout the country as one of the finest hunters in South Africa, was killed with fifteen men, the remainder had been taken prisoners, and were not yet released. The other reverse had taken place at Bremersdorp in Swaziland, where three squadrons under command of Captain G ——, seconded from Gordon Highlanders—had been surprised and driven out of the place, losing a subaltern and thirty men taken prisoners, and several killed and wounded. They had retired to the Portuguese border, and had not yet returned to Komati. From accounts we heard from various sources, the latter disaster would not have happened if the men had been kept better in hand. Lack of discipline was put down as the principal cause,—the ordinary precautionary duties not having been performed, the Boers swooped down on them and caught them unprepared.

About this time a troop of horses arrived from Middleburg for remounts to the regiment. They were nearly all salted animals,—horses that have recovered from horse sickness, or become acclimatised to the low country, where the disease is very prevalent. The animal suddenly gives a cough, staggers a few yards, and then collapses, and in a very short time is dead; the froth oozing from its nostrils and mouth showing that the animal is dead from horse sickness;—leaving the unfortunate rider to carry his saddle and bridle to the nearest Kaffir kraal—if he can find one—or to the next camp.

These salted horses are very valuable, and cost as much as treble the ordinary price. When the risk run by men riding on unsalted horses through the Bush country, infested with wild animals, is taken into consideration, the price cannot be regarded as excessive.

My detachment were soon mounted; and I found myself in possession of two splendid animals, who carried me without a fault during the year and a half the corps was in existence, from the time I became associated with it.

Colonel Steinaecker now returned to Komati Poort; and the arrival of three squadrons of the corps from Swaziland gave us a busy time. No time was lost in refitting the men, and making up the deficiences in their equipment caused by their hurried evacuation of Bremersdorp. Information had been received from our Native Scouts that the Boers had crossed the Usutu River in Swaziland and were moving in the direction of Pigg's Peak, a mining concession in Swaziland. Colonel Steinaecker decided to intercept them.

Leaving the headquarter staff at Komati Poort, the remainder of the regiment, with the exception of a detachment stationed at the end of the Selah Railway at Sabie Bridge, marched off for Pigg's Peak. It was a very trying march. Owing to the intense heat during the day, and the attacks of the mosquitoes at night, the men got no rest, and on our arrival at Jeppe's concession we were glad of a twenty-four hours' halt beside a fine stream of water. All of us had discarded our coats on leaving Komati Poort. They were strapped on the front of our saddles, and we rode in our shirt-sleeves—the only uniform suitable to the low country.

After the halt we pushed on and arrived at Pigg's Peak, where we found the mine manager and his assistants had fortified the manager's house and the building round the mouth of the mine, in anticipation of a visit from the

Boers. The mine had been partially worked during the war, and the gold stored at the place, as there was no means of sending it through to Delagoa Bay, and it was conjectured that the Boers were aware of this fact.

At the back of the manager's house, which was built close to the mine on the side of a hill, the country rose up in the shape of a conical mountain, overlooking and dwarfing the surrounding hills, hence the name of Pigg's Peak—Pigg being the concessionaire. Twenty-five men on the top of this peak were perfectly safe from attack, and we now occupied it with a troop of men and one Maxim gun; the remainder of the men were encamped along the base of the hill, ready to occupy various positions allotted to them which had been made shell-proof.

Colonel Steinaecker, I, and several of the officers, took up our quarters in the mine manager's house, from which place a splendid view was obtainable of the country in Swaziland, on the border of which Pigg's Peak was. Patrols and scouts were sent out daily, till the Boers were finally discovered at a drift on the Usutu River. Leaving a troop to occupy the position on the top of the Peak, the remainder of the regiment marched out at dusk in the direction of the enemy.

Guided by Native Scouts attached to the corps, we timed the march splendidly, and appeared on the front and both flanks of the Boers at daylight. They were encamped on the bank of the river, with wagons and carts. We fired a volley from three sides and then closed in on the wagons. Some of the Boers made a rush for the drift, but we had managed to work round and intercept them, on seeing which they surrendered without any further resistance. We found several old men, women, and children, who fortunately had not been injured by our firing. We destroyed most of the carts and wagons, leaving enough for the old men and women with which to return to their own people. We marched all the prisoners back with us to Pigg's Peak, and from this place they were taken on to Barberton.

Feeling was very bitter at that time between the men of Steinaecker's Horse and the Boers; and the prisoners would have been roughly handled if the officers had not kept a strict hand on the men. Some of our men had been made prisoners at Bremersdorp, and shamefully treated by their captors, who at first refused to accept the statement of the officer that Steinaecker's Horse was an enrolled British troop, and on more than one occasion threatened to shoot the men. The Boers took their boots from the men and made them walk barefooted, and it was only on receipt of a communication from Lord Kitchener stating that the prisoners were British troops that the Boers released them and made them walk to Standerton, from which place they were returned to Komati Poort.

Some of this same commando were now our prisoners, and were recognised as having been amongst the worst of the offenders in the harsh treatment our men had received. I was very glad when the last of them left the camp at Pigg's Peak without anything of an unpleasant nature having occurred. It was simply for the credit of the regiment that the men held their hand, and not out of sympathy for the prisoners, who to my mind deserved the usual treatment meted out to other uncivilized men during war-time.

One squadron now returned to re-occupy the stations along the Portuguese border, the other two remained at

Pigg's Peak. My duties required my presence at Komati Poort, and I left for that place. Starting in the afternoon, I intended to reach Jeppe's concession that night, but darkness overtook me before I reached the house. When I arrived where the tracks branched off, I rode a few yards off the road and off-saddled under a tree, tying my horse to another one a few yards from me, and lighting my pipe, I lay down in my saddle to pass the time away till morning, eventually going to sleep. I was awakened by my horse snorting and pulling back from the place where he was made fast. I jumped up and went to the animal and found him trembling violently, and evidently very frightened, but knowing me and hearing my voice, the animal gradually became quiet and stood still.

I thought that a snake had probably caused the alarm, so I loosened the animal from the tree and led him to the saddle and put the bridle on, and sat holding him till daylight, when, resuming my journey, I found the right track by the wagon spoor, and five minutes afterwards came to the house. I knocked up the owner of the place, who was also in charge of the mine, which was not being worked, and proceeded to offsaddle. Mr. S ——, who recognised me, was astonished to see me, and said, "Where on earth have you come from, Captain? Where are the men?"

I told him I was alone, and also how I had passed the night. "Good Lord!" he said; "why, the country is full of lions and all sorts of animals—it must have been a lion or wolves after the horse"; and he proceeded to regale me with the stories of the doings of these ferocious animals in that part of the world. I thought of the old adage, "Where ignorance is bliss," etc., but said nothing, and made a mental note about sleeping in the veldt in future whilst in the low country.

After a good breakfast and a feed for my horse, I continued my journey—feeling, I must admit, rather thankful when I saw Komati Poort appearing through the bush, and determined in future to carry a carbine when on similar journeys.

My time was now fully occupied in getting headquarters into the state of order to which I had been accustomed. I was obliged to make one or two necessary examples, discharging the so-called regimental sergeant-major, and reducing sergeants whose only inclination seemed to be for gambling. I promoted men who subsequently justified their selection, and a change for the better all through was soon apparent. When Colonel Steinaecker arrived with a squadron from Pigg's Peak a similar process had to be gone through; on this occasion the weeding out included a couple of officers who objected to soldiering, and a marked improvement took place in the general quality of the regiment, which received official intimation of the fact from the general officer commanding the district on his visit of inspection.

There being about twelve officers at Komati Poort, an officers' mess was initiated. It was a great factor in the regenerating scheme, and a canteen was erected in the camp, in which only beer was allowed to be sold, in specified canteen hours. The hotel was placed out of bounds—much to the discomfiture of the Greek proprietor, who found a difficulty in disposing of his vile Portuguese rum and other spirits, which had so greatly added to the number of the inhabitants of the graveyard. The heat was so excessive that all drills and parades were conducted before 7 a.m., and the men kept out of the sun as much as possible during the day till evening, when cricket was indulged in, with other sports, to keep them healthy. The decrease in the sick reports and deaths from fever resulting from this régime was very marked.

The next move was made in a northerly direction. The Boers had threatened several of the stations of regulars on the lines of communication—the railway being protected by the blockhouse system all the route from Pretoria. Mr. Viljoen's commando was still roaming about the low country after their success at M'pisane's, and we went out in company with some mounted infantry to try to intercept the commando on their return from a feeble attempt on the Buffs at Nels Spruit.

After marching mostly at night through the Bush, guided by natives, we arrived in the vicinity of Sand River, where we had been informed the Boers were encamped. The Mounted Infantry had somehow or other lost touch with us, and were missing; but it did not seem to affect our colonel, whom I have always suspected of being the only person likely to know how it occurred. We proceeded cautiously, and shortly located the enemy in a stretch of sand formed by the dry bed of the river. Our appearance caused great surprise to them, and in their confusion to get to their horses, we had and took our chance. Firing into them along the line, we galloped through them, using revolvers. They scattered in all directions; those that reached their horses got away in the Bush; in a great many instances those that failed to do so remained, where they were overtaken by the men. After a warm half-hour, not a trace of the commando was to be seen. To our regret, Viljoen escaped, but I had his rifle in my possession for months, till I gave it away to a friend who was trophy-hunting.

When our regiment was rallied, we found that our casualties were two men wounded, but the Boer losses were considerably over a hundred killed at the bed of the river. There were no prisoners on this occasion, the Boers contenting themselves with firing and endeavouring to escape, and Steinaecker's Horse had got their own back with interest for M'pisane's and Bremersdorp. This was the last ever heard of a Boer commando in the low country, or in the part occupied by Steinaecker's Horse.

We returned to Komati Poort by easy stages. On nearing Crocodile Poort, the column halted for the night, when, as usual, large fires were lighted to protect the horses and sleeping men from the wild animals, which were very numerous along the Sabie. About midnight, when all the men were sleeping except the mounted sentries, who were standing inside the fires, which they replenished as required, a lion suddenly jumped over a fire, seized one of the sentries, and jumped back again into the bush with the unhappy man in his jaws. The alarm was raised, and the men seized their rifles and went in pursuit; some men fired, and the animal dropped his prey and disappeared. The unfortunate man was carried back to the camp, where he was found to be almost disembowelled. He died a few hours later in great agony, and we buried him at Crocodile Poort bridge. This horrible and unexpected death cast a gloom over the corps which many deaths in action would not have occasioned.

The regiment was greatly complimented over the Sand River affair; information was received that the corps was to be a permanent one for service on the border, and orders were issued to recruit up to full strength. Except for constant patrolling to intercept dispatch-riders from Portuguese territory to the Transvaal—carrying dispatches from ex-President Kruger to the Boer commandoes in the field — our duties were now confined to garrison work at Komati Poort, Pigg's Peak, and Sabie River.

CHAPTER XXVII.

1902–1904.

RUMOURS were now in circulation that the Boers were
making overtures towards peace, and that a meeting had
been arranged between Louis Botha, who was in command of
the Boer forces remaining in the field, and General Officer
commanding at Pretoria, but nothing definite appeared to
have been settled up to that time.

One day the colonel received a communication from the
British Consul at Delagoa Bay, stating that some foreigners
had landed, and were supposed to have documents in their possession from Mr. Kruger to the Boer commandant. We were
ordered to redouble our vigilance on the border, as it was
supposed that an attempt would be made to enter the Transvaal at some point between the railway and Ressano Garcia,
across the river, and opposite Komati Poort, at the end
of the Portuguese territory, which extended some sixty miles
along the Lebomba range of hills. We doubled our picquets
till we had a cordon of stations no farther than a mile distant
from one another along the whole border, and maintained

constant patrolling day and night between the stations. The country was dense bush, in which it was not very easy to find a person who was desirous of avoiding capture, but the number of wild animals prowling about precluded the idea of the attempt being made by a single man on foot, especially a man not conversant with the country. We kept up unceasing patrolling for a week, when our trouble was at last rewarded. A Native Scout came to where I was offsaddled and reported that three white men were riding from across the border, about half a mile from the place where we lay.

We saddled up, the party consisting of a corporal and three men, and went along a footpath in the direction indicated by the guide. After travelling over the rough ground, in and out of bushes, for about three hundred yards, we heard the sound of horses approaching over the rocky ground. We rode in the direction in extended order, and while I was negotiating a large patch of bush in front of me, two shots rang out, and a voice shouted, "Hands up!" On getting round the bush, I saw two men on horseback with their arms held up, their rifles dropped on the ground.

The corporal and the other men appeared, and an explanation was given. The corporal, who had been on my right, had ridden into an open piece of ground, and seen three men in file in front of him; the leading man was in the act of firing at one of our men on the right of the corporal, when the latter raised his carbine in one hand and fired. Both shots went off together, the corporal's bullet striking the man clean between the eyes. He fell from his horse. The stranger's bullet whistled past one of the men's heads and missed him. The corporal had shouted "Hands up!" which order the others had immediately obeyed.

28

I made the prisoners dismount, and searched them; one of them informing me in broken English that the man who had been killed was the leader and had the papers. I searched the fallen man, who was quite dead, and found a packet of papers addressed to General Louis Botha, and also other letters which indicated that the dead man was Count von Wass, an Austrian, as his companion informed me. The other two men were young Hollanders, and had not been in South Africa before. Taking all the dead man's property with us, I left the two men and the native to take the body to the nearest station and to bury it. I took the two prisoners on with me to the station, where I collected four men from the picquet as escort, and made our way back to Komati Poort, reaching that place in the night. I handed the prisoners, who were very disheartened at the death of their comrade, over to the guard, and took the dispatches and the personal effects of the dead man to the colonel. He was delighted with my news, which was immediately telegraphed off to Pretoria, with the addition that I was bringing the dispatches on to Pretoria the following morning by train. The effects of the dead man were sent to his relations in Europe; about a year afterwards they had a stone erected to his memory where he was buried.

The two Hollanders were kept prisoners in the guard tent, till on instructions from Pretoria they were taken by an escort and handed over to the Portuguese authorities, by whom they were sent out of the country.

I left Komati Poort by the train at 10 a.m. for Pretoria, carrying with me the intercepted dispatches, which I duly handed over to Major Maxwell at Lord Kitchener's house in

Pretoria the following morning. Later in the day I received congratulations for having obtained such valuable documents, and an official letter was sent to the officer commanding thanking Steinaecker's Horse for the great service the regiment had rendered the State in preventing the documents from having reached their intended destination.

I remained two days in Pretoria before I returned to Komati Poort, and enjoyed the short change very much. I found that negotiations were taking place between Lord Kitchener and General Botha, and the opinion seemed general that the outcome would be a cessation of hostilities and declaration of peace.

On my return to Komati Poort, I found that Colonel Steinaecker had been suffering for a considerable period from attacks of malarial fever, and had been obliged to go on the sick list. Shortly after my return he was sent to the hospital ship then lying in Delagoa Bay, where he remained for a month, when he was invalided to Europe for a change of climate. He had pluckily fought against the fever for two years before finally giving in, and then gave in only on our representing that probably there would be no more fighting, and it was imperative that he should regain his health to enable him to retain command of his regiment.

At length the Order was published that peace had been proclaimed and Steinaecker's Horse were to remain at Komati Poort—the men to act as a border guard to prevent un-authorised persons entering the country, and that we were to be made up to full strength to enable us to carry out this extensive work. A subaltern and fifteen men were also sent to England to represent the regiment at the Coronation; a subaltern who belonged to the Indian Staff Corps was sent in command who had received the D.S.O. for good work on the border some months before I joined the corps.

As there were numerous applications from men who had served throughout the war in irregular troops which on the declaration of peace were disbanded, to enlist in Steinaecker's Horse, and as there were about sixty vacancies, I went to Johannesburg to select the men, and easily managed to recruit the required number of the stamp I wanted. The regiment was now complete, and I set to work to try to make them what I considered efficient before the return of the colonel from Europe. After six months he came back quite recovered in health, and very pleased with his experiences at the King's Coronation.

Our friends the Duke of Cornwall's Light Infantry, which had dwindled down to barely a hundred men, owing to the men invalided through fever, left shortly after the end of the war for Pretoria, where the men were rejoining the regiment from hospital. The Buffs had left Nels Spruit, and with the exception of the Lincoln Regiment at Barberton, Steinaecker's Horse was the only regiment left in the low country. The fever season came on again, but the men were in better quarters—they had more exercise and no spirituous liquors— and in consequence the fever had little or no effect on the regiment. Only a few deaths from black-water fever occurred amongst the older soldiers, but among the victims was the corporal who had shot the Austrian Count von Wass.

We had been inspected on several occasions by the general commanding the district, and had been complimented on the efficiency and good conduct of the regiment, and the men were now a pleasure for me to handle on my various drill parades. Suddenly a bomb was exploded which upset all our calculations and plans for the future. A communication was received from General Lyttleton, who was commanding the troops in Africa, stating that the Imperial Government could not afford to keep up a regiment for the protection of the border, and that it would have to be done by the South African Constabulary, a corps which had been raised for the policing of the Transvaal. The general requested the presence of the officer commanding Steinaecker's Horse and his adjutant at Pretoria, to talk over the matter.

This caused great consternation amongst the members of the corps. It had been definitely stated by Lord Kitchener that Steinaecker's Horse was to be a permanent force for the low country, and men had enlisted for three years' service not more than six months previously. However, it was no use arguing the point amongst ourselves; so to Pretoria the colonel and I went to interview the general.

After a week, in which the pros and cons were argued, it was decided by the general that Steinaecker's Horse were to be disbanded; that any men who were eligible and who wished to join the South African Constabulary, could do so; and that the remainder would be discharged, receiving full pay up to the end of the following October, which would bring the corps up to the term of service of three years from the date on which it had first been formed—October 1900; the officers who did not join the South African Constabulary, or were ineligible, to receive three months' pay by way of compensation; the disbandment to be carried out by the end of February, which gave us just a month to collect the out-stations, and to hand over the horses and equipments to the Imperial authorities sent for that purpose.

Colonel Steinaecker and I returned to Komati conscious

that we had done our best for all ranks, and the disbanding
was commenced. Sixty men and two subalterns elected to join
the South African Constabulary, and were sent to occupy the
border with horses and equipments. The remainder of the
men were paid up for the following seven months, and had
free passages to any part of the world their homes lay in.
Their horses were valued, and sent off to Middleburg to be
sold; and by the end of the month the staff, consisting of
myself, quartermaster, and paymaster, left for Pretoria to
hand in the final accounts of the regiment. Colonel Steinaecker left in the middle of the uncongenial process of
disbanding, saying that he was off to 'Maritzburg, where he
would be found if wanted, as he was heartily sick of the whole
service. He went without saying good-bye to me, telling the
others that he could not do so without breaking down. He
left a letter on my desk the morning he left, which speaks for
itself, and which I append as written:—

"KOMATI POORT, *Feb. 9th*, 1903.

"MY DEAR ——, I cannot leave the old regiment without
thanking you sincerely for the good work done by you in it.
The exquisite tact with which you handled the men and
officers in your adjutant's duties saved many a one from
strong measures and helped me considerably. The splendid
discipline, the drill, etc., are mainly due to you, and I hope
that you may have further opportunities to exercise those
soldierly qualities which you possess so largely. Wishing you
all success,—I remain, ever yours,

"F. STEINAECKER,
"*Lt.-Col. late O.C. S.H.*"

I have not seen Colonel Steinaecker since Komati Poort, but have heard that he returned to the low country, where he received two farms from the Government for his services, on which he is now farming and, I sincerely trust, prospering. He was a good soldier and warm friend, and nothing better can be said of any man.

I applied for an appointment as adjutant to one of the Volunteer Regiments which were in the course of formation in the Transvaal, but was told that the scheme was not definitely settled. In the meantime I was to be employed on the Military Compensation Board, a part of the repatriation instituted by the Imperial Government for the purpose of assessing the amount of damage which had been sustained by the Boers in the loss of their homes and stock during the war.

The head offices of the central Judicial Commission were in Pretoria, from which place, after I had been made acquainted with the duties that I had to perform, I received instructions to proceed to the Standerton district, and take over the Bethal farmers' claims in conjunction with the Magistrate. A military officer was attached to each magistracy in the Transvaal for the disposal of the claims of protected Burghers who had surrendered under the proclamation of Lord Roberts; all other claims were assessed by the Magistrate.

I found Colonel Lambert Browne claims officer at Standerton. He was a retired Indian Army officer, and had served with my brother in India, with whom he had been great friends; and I spent a pleasant week in his company while waiting for my travelling wagon and cart to arrive from the Repatriation Department. I found that Bethal was a sub-district of Standerton about forty miles distant.

My outfit when I arrived consisted of a travelling wagon with ten mules, with driver and leader, and a smart Cape cart with four good mules and a driver, for personal convenience in making short visits to farms near my base. I arrived at Bethal and found the only habitable house in the place was a temporary building of wood and iron used as a hotel. All the other buildings had been destroyed by the column under General French some two years previously. The farms in the district had also been destroyed. The Boer families who had returned from exile and concentration camps were domiciled in temporary structures of wood and iron, the materials of which had been supplied by the Repatriation Department.

The Magistrate's Court was held in a marquee tent, and we of the staff lived in bell tents, one of which was placed at my disposal to live in, and an office given to me in the repatriation buildings, in which I could take the evidence of the various claims. A riding horse was also kept for my benefit at the camp, to enable me to visit places unsuitable for a cart to travel.

For the first six months my time was occupied in hearing claims and taking evidence of farmers whose dwellings were situated within a radius of ten miles from the village. It was rather amusing to hear a farmer claim £10,000 as the value of a building that had been destroyed, and on visiting the ruins to find that the house consisted of a sod and green brick building, containing four small rooms, with an iron roof, costing £50 at the very utmost. The amount of stock he was supposed to be in possession of before the war, and the amount he possessed at the time of his surrender, as shown by the receipts given him by the officer to whom he surrendered, would never tally, but on the discrepancy being

pointed out, the claimant would reply, " Yes, that was so
but the other cattle had died or been used for meat by the
commandoes before he surrendered," for the Boer is an in-
veterate liar. They really took it for granted that the
British Government were not only going to pay them what
they thought it would cost to build a larger house than they
had previously owned, but would pay them in full for every
head of cattle that they and their friends had consumed
during the war before they thought fit to surrender. Another
trick they had was to conceal the manner in which the former
owner of a farm had met his death, when a claim would be
made by the relatives of the deceased on his behalf. They
would say that the man died in Natal, and on being asked
when and how, would profess ignorance, till on being told that
the claim would not hold good, they would admit that the
former owner had been killed in action in Natal. During my
investigations in the Bethal district I proved that there were
more men killed in action in that district alone than the
Boers ever admitted having lost during the whole war.

Now and again a farmer would put forth a claim in a
reasonable manner, only claiming what he knew he had paid
for the building of his house and a fair price for the stock,
and such men had no cause to grumble at the award given
them; for when, on being investigated, the claim was found
to be less than the actual loss the farmer had sustained, the
claim was often recommended to be paid in full, instead of a
half or third, as was usually the case.

The last six months of the Commission were spent by me
in travelling from farm to farm—encamping on one farm
and visiting others in the vicinity. Dances were often got
up for our benefit; but the conversation generally worked

round to compensation, even by way of a mild flirtation. They are of a very practical turn of mind our Boer brothers and sisters. The lot of the Military Claims Compensation Officer was not an enviable one, and I was rather thankful than otherwise when the last farm had been visited and the last damage assessed, and I had returned to Pretoria. My mission ended to the satisfaction of the Commission, as the following communication seems to indicate :—

> " CENTRAL JUDICIAL COMMISSION,
> PRETORIA, 25*th April* 1904.

" This is to certify that Captain —— has been employed under this Commission from 1st April 1903 to 31st March 1904 as member of the Bethal Claims Compensation Commission.

" I have much pleasure in stating that Captain —— has discharged his duties to the entire satisfaction of this Commission, and with marked ability.

> " J. HUNEBERG, Major, *Secretary*."

Thus ended my military service in South Africa after a period of twenty-five years, during which time I have visited, as the reader will see for himself, every part of South Africa from the coast to Shangani River, 80 miles south of the Zambesi, and taken my share of the work that fell to my hand at the moment, I trust with credit to the regiment I had the honour to be associated with. There only remains for me to add a brief chapter of retrospect and prospect in South Africa.

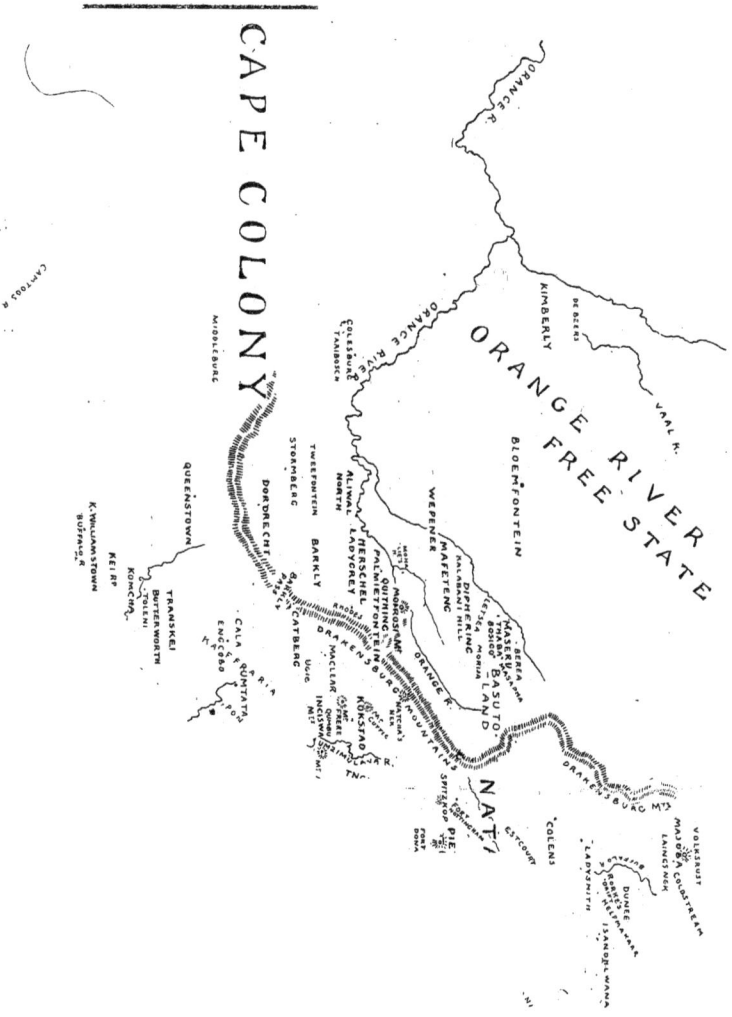

CAPE COLONY

ORANGE RIVER FREE STATE

BASUTOLAND

NATAL

CHAPTER XXVIII.

RETROSPECT AND PROSPECT IN SOUTH AFRICA—CONCLUSION.

IT is twenty-eight years since I landed in South Africa, and twenty-five years of that time have been spent in the country.

This period has practically seen the rise of modern South Africa — the acquisition of Rhodesia and the discovery of the gold fields having taken place during that time.

It has seen the great struggle between Briton and Boer which for twenty years many of us in the Colony knew was inevitable—the Boer War of 1899–1902, which undoubtedly makes a new era in South Africa between the two races that have so long contended there.

It is only natural that, in concluding this personal narrative of my life in South Africa, I should contrast the conditions as I leave it with those that existed when I first went to the Colony twenty-eight years ago. The reader will have observed, I am not a man of affairs. In South Africa I gave very little attention to political matters, and was concerned mainly with a soldier's duty of obeying the instructions of those above him. The friend who inspired this book says I have the "simple view of the soldier." Whether this is a compliment or a reflection on my capacity I am not sure, but to my mind the changes which have taken place in South

Africa do not promise well for the development of that country as a British possession.

Twenty years ago the prevailing sentiment in South Africa was loyalty to Great Britain, not amongst the home-born only, but Colonial-born also. The feeling centred round the figure of Queen Victoria, the mention of whose name was the signal for hats off. Apart from this there was a deep-seated feeling of affection for the old country, and of pride in being a part of the Empire. The Union Jack was our proud symbol in South Africa as much as in any part of the Empire.

I am bound to say my observation and my experience give me good grounds for believing that those feelings have passed away, as it seems to me, for ever. Loyalty is a word that brings a contemptuous sneer on the face of British colonists in the Colony, and bitter words from the lips of British women who have suffered with their menkind.

The Union Jack evokes no enthusiasm; the name of the King is honoured in the conventional way, but without any emotion; the National Anthem might be a Salvation hymn for all the notice taken of it; and the word Imperialism is utterly discredited. The cause of the change is not difficult to find. When the war broke out all Englishmen felt that the time had arrived when the Boers would learn once and for all time that Britain was the only power that could rule in South Africa, and that the British Government had at last become awakened to the fact that her prestige was in danger, and that it behoved all men in the Colony who still had love for the old country to join the British forces and assist in bringing the Boers to their senses. The manner in which the Colonial forces upheld their end of the stick was duly appreciated by the British Commander-in-Chief at the end of the campaign; but on the cessation of hostilities the Colonials were hardly prepared for the amazing generosity of the Government to the rebels, and the shameful neglect of the Colonials, who had by the sacrifice of home, time, and money dreamed of a far different treatment than that which was meted out to them. All appointments of a military nature in the Transvaal, such as adjutants to the Volunteer forces, instead of being given to men of Colonial experience and specially qualified for those positions, were given to inexperienced Imperial officers, in some cases subalterns of infantry regiments who had not a single qualification in handling Colonial mounted men. Also, Civil Service appointments were filled up by young men imported from England for the purpose, whilst hundreds of experienced Colonial Civil Servants' claims were ignored; in fact, any man who had served in any capacity against our newly made friends, the Boers, need not apply for any appointment under Government.

I know dozens of capable men with exceptional service who were kept hanging about for months in the hope of obtaining employment. They saw novices pitchforked into billet after billet, till, sick and tired of everything, they have cursed the day they ever took up arms for the Home Government, and left South Africa for other colonies, where the fact of being a Britisher by birth and inclination would not prevent a man earning a living at the profession he had been brought up to be proud of, and convinced that South Africa was an impossible place for any Briton who had any respect for himself.

The truth must be faced that the quarrel between Briton and Boer is not accidental and temporary. It was indeed embittered by Majuba Hill and by the Jameson Raid, but the hostility is really racial and permanent. Although the Dutch may inherit many of the qualities which have given England backbone, the Boers in South Africa have these qualities counteracted by others of a less admirable kind. The words truth, honour, and morality, while known to them, convey meanings which to the Englishman rob them of the quality which he understands; courage they may have of a sort, but it is of the skulking kind. The pluck to pot at an enemy from behind a safe shelter has no relation to the traditional courage of the British soldier. Their manners, their religion, their aspirations, admirable as they may be for themselves, are not admirable to the British eye and instinct, and the Boer knows it, and hates the British for that reason. On the other hand, up till the last Boer War at least, his contempt for the British army was immense.

Because of these things there can be no true and permanent union of the two races in South Africa. As I write these closing lines the papers report fervent speeches of General Botha on the one hand and Dr. Jameson on the other, talking of happy days in store for the Colony, and in England this beautiful state of affairs is regarded as a triumph for the Liberal Government, who are responsible for the condition of the country. I deliberately state my conviction that neither General Botha nor any of the Boer leaders believe in or desire a union of the two races, nor do I believe that they have any intention of making equal rights as between Dutch and British anything but a mere political cry, convenient for furthering their ulterior design. At present it is of course their interest to talk about burying the hatchet, and shaking hands over the graves of those who fell in the war. There may be much shaking of hands as in friendship, and protestations of loyalty to the British Empire, but I believe that when the Dutch find the time ripe, they will throw off even the semblance of a British connection, and at the same time throw overboard those whom they are now claiming as brothers, united by the blood shed in the late war.

Printed by
MORRISON & GIBB LIMITED
Edinburgh

Lightning Source UK Ltd.
Milton Keynes UK
UKHW022159271218
334533UK00008B/1245/P

9 780282 683801